Conflict Resolution for the Helping Professions

ALLAN EDWARD BARSKY
University of Calgary

Brooks/Cole
Thomson Learning™

Australia • Canada • Mexico • Singapore • Spain • United Kingdom • United States

Social Work Editor: Lisa Gebo
Assistant Editor: Julie Martinez
Editorial Assistant: Susan Wilson
Marketing Manager: Caroline Concilla
Signing Representative: Laura Foran
Project Editor: Jennie Redwitz
Print Buyer: Mary Noel
Permissions Editor: Susan Walters
Production Service Coordinator: Donna King, Progressive Publishing Alternatives
Copy Editor: Progressive Publishing Alternatives

Illustrator: Progressive Information Technologies
Cartoons: Donato Damiano
Compositor: Progressive Information Technologies
Cover Designer: Bill Stanton
Cover Image: "The Challenge," by Doris Cyrette
Cover Printer: Webcom Limited
Printer/Binder: Webcom Limited

Library of Congress Cataloging-in-Publication Data
Barsky, Allan Edward.
    Conflict resolution for the helping professions/Allan Edward Barsky.
       p. cm.
    Includes bibliographical references and index.
    ISBN 0-534-35923-x
    1. Conflict management. 2. Mediation. 3. Human services—Vocational guidance. I. Title.

HM1126 .B37 1999
303.6'9—dc21   99-046673

For more information, contact Wadsworth/Thomson Learning
10 Davis Drive
Belmont, CA 94002-3098
USA
http:\\www.wadsworth.com

International Headquarters
Thomson Learning
290 Harbor Drive, 2nd Floor
Stamford, CT 06902-7477
USA

UK/Europe/Middle East
Thomson Learning
Berkshire House
168-173 High Holborn
London WC1V 7AA
United Kingdom

Asia
Thomson Learning
60 Albert Street #15-01
Albert Complex
Singapore 189969

Canada
Nelson/Thomson Learning
1120 Birchmount Road
Scarborough, Ontario M1K 5G4
Canada

*Dedicated to the beloved memory of my
father, Shlomo ben Moshe,
whose name means Peace*

Contents

Chapter 3

Negotiation   60

Chapter 4

Mediation   116

Chapter 5

Mediation with Groups   184

Chapter 6

Advocacy   219

Chapter 7

Conclusion   *256*

Preface

Helping professionals deal with conflict in virtually all aspects of their work—with supervisors, co-workers, clients, families, social systems, and other community members. In order to deal effectively with conflict, helping professionals need to understand the nature of conflict and a range of approaches for dealing with conflict. This text and its companion Instructor's Manual provide educational materials designed to help adult learners integrate the theories, values, skills, and practice of conflict resolution.

In terms of theory, this text offers a range of perspectives on conflict resolution—from rights and power-based, to interest-based and transformative conflict resolution. This text encourages learners to deconstruct various models of conflict resolution in terms of their underlying values and assumptions. Learners are also encouraged to relate each model to various theories and models of intervention from their identified helping disciplines: what do I know from my professional education and experience; how does this compare and contrast with what I am learning about conflict resolution; what types of conflict resolution roles can or should I assume in my practice; what types of conflict resolution roles are inconsistent with my ordinary practice?

Given the value-driven nature of conflict resolution, discussion questions and exercises in this text provide opportunities for students to explore their own values. In particular, students need to examine their attitudes and beliefs towards anger, power, autonomy, privacy, paternalism, and social justice. Although most helping professionals would say they value collaboration and peaceful means of dealing with conflict, these values are often difficult to implement in practice.

In order to help learners translate conflict resolution theories into practice, this text provides realistic case examples to demonstrate the use of common conflict resolution strategies and processess. Skills inventories provide learners with checklists of behaviors and activities that can be used in conflict interventions. Learners can experiment and practice skills through the use of role plays. Learners can also reflect upon their experience of dealing with conflict with family, friends, and clients: how have they dealt with conflict in the past; how has the material in this text affected how they might respond differently in the future? Most learners find that conflict resolution education has very practical and immediate applications, both in their personal and professional lives.

Although this text takes a broad look at conflict resolution, it focuses on three conflict resolution roles: negotiation, mediation, and advocacy. These roles have been selected because they are the most common ones used by helping professionals. Some instructors will design courses that focus on just one of these roles. Research assignments and exercises can be used to explore other roles that are of interest to class members.

Helping professionals are faced with an array of difficult conflict situations—angry clients, power struggles within the agency, cross-cultural misunderstandings, fights over limited resources, and so on. This book does not try to provide all the answers; however, it does provide a place to start.

ACKNOWLEDGMENTS

This book originated from courses and materials I developed for Ryerson Polytechnic University in Toronto and for the University of Calgary. When I began teaching conflict resolution in 1992, there were few educational materials designed specifically for helping professionals. Although many helping professionals contributed to this field through research, training, and practice, most of their writings were restricted to particular areas of practice; for example, family mediation or victim-offender reconciliation programs. As I began to build a set of learning materials based upon more comprehensive approach to conflict resolution, I was fortunate to work with many talented and insightful students. I thank these students for experimenting along with me and providing constructive feedback as we learned together.

I extend my gratitude to Lisa Gebo, Susan Wilson, and others at Wadsworth Publishing, first, for their willingness to take on this project, and second, for their ongoing assistance in seeing it through to fruition. Modeling the principles of conflict resolution, we were able to deal effectively with our differences and build a very positive working relationship. Wadsworth also arranged for the following reviewers, who provided many suggestions that helped to strengthen this text:

Lucille R. Cormier

Burt Galaway
University of Manitoba

Bart Grossman
University of California, Berkeley

Patricia Kerstner
University of Phoenix

Rob Lawson
Western Washington University

Michelle Le Baron
George Mason University

Mary Finn Maples
University of Nevada

Susan Rice
California State University, Long Beach

Katherine Shank
Northwestern University School of Law

Robert J. Wellman
Fitchburg State College

One of my graduate students, Kathy Lyons, also provided valuable feedback.

I worked on much of this text while on Sabbatical in Israel. Dean Rueben Schindler and the Bar Ilan University School of Social Work must be thanked for providing me with a home base for work. I am also indebted to Dvora Levin of Mossad Neaman, as well as Lee Li-on and Peretz Segal of the National Center for Mediation and Conflict Resolution for introducing me to various conflict resolution initiatives in Israel. The nature and intensity of conflict in Israel provided a potent environment for me to reflect upon my work. This experience forced me to re-evaluate many values and beliefs around conflict resolution, coming away with even stronger convictions about the important roles helping professionals can play in this area.

Finally, I must thank those closest to me. My partner, Greg Moore, has followed me across the globe to be my unpaid research assistant, an affable diversion, and a true confidante. My brothers, sisters-in-law, and nephews have been an unwavering source of moral support. My mother has been my best publicist, expressing her pride in whatever I've done and selling this book to friends and strangers alike, even before it was written. Love you for always . . .

Allan Barsky

About the Author

Allan Edward Barsky, LL.B., M.S.W., Ph.D., is Associate Professor with The University of Calgary Faculty of Social Work. He has a combined background in social work, law, and conflict resolution, with particular experience in the areas of divorce, child welfare, and community mediation. Dr. Barsky is the author of *Counsellors as Witnesses,* as well as numerous articles in the *Mediation Quarterly,* the *Negotiation Journal,* the *Canadian Social Work Review,* and the *Family and Conciliation Courts Review.* He has also contributed a monograph on power and neutrality in child protection mediation to the National Institute on Dispute Resolution in Washington, DC. Dr. Barsky is a regular lecturer on mediation and cultural diversity issues at professional conferences. He is a Past President of the Ontario Association for Family Mediation, founding Chair of The University of Calgary Conflict Research, Resolution and Education Group, and a National Director of *Network: Interaction for Conflict Resolution.* Dr. Barsky has also acted as consultant with Israel's National Center for Mediation and Conflict Resolution.

About the Cover

The drawing on the front cover is entitled "The Challenge." Artist Doris Cyrette depicts a conflict between parent and child, though it could be between any two individuals with differing power and positions. In Canadian Ojibway art, the divided circle is symbolic of one Great Spirit and the struggle of good and evil. For other people, this symbol may hold different meanings: the need for yin and yang to work in harmony, a positive energy that mediates between disputing individuals, or a special time and space where people can come together to resolve their differences.

CHAPTER 1

INTRODUCTION

1

A 14-year-old girl named Pawn has just been convicted for theft of a car. The judge requests a psychosocial assessment to help decide an appropriate sentence—perhaps probation with some type of voluntary counseling. Pawn is subjected to a battery of tests and interviews by a range of helping professionals. The professionals meet for a case conference.

A Freudian[1] psychiatrist concludes, "Pawn's antisocial behavior derives from deep-rooted conflict between an overactive id and a defective ego; Pawn requires at least two years of psychoanalysis."

A cognitive therapist counters, "Pawn has distorted thought patterns which tell her that she can only expect positive attention when she acts out; Pawn requires six months of therapy based upon cognitive restructuring."

A systems counselor chuckles and suggests, "The real issue lies in the scape-goat role that Pawn plays in her family in order to deflect attention away from her alcoholic father; Pawn and her parents must attend three weeks of structured family therapy."

The conflict resolution professional finally responds, "Great! Then we all agree . . . There is a problem . . . and we have identified several possible solutions."

One client. Many points of view. Difference of opinion is just one of many types of conflict that helping professionals encounter in their everyday practice. The vignette highlights the polarization of professionals based on divergent theoretical perspectives. But is it only the conflict resolution expert who can see the common threads and work towards joint problem solving? In fact, all helping professionals are conflict resolution practitioners. Some of us just don't know it yet.

This text provides a comprehensive set of educational materials, designed for helping professionals interested in the theory and practice of conflict resolution. While you may be studying conflict resolution from the perspective of a particular profession—nursing, psychology, social work, education, community development, pastoral counseling, corrections, or child

---

[1]Freud (1963).

1

and youth work—the essential aspects of conflict resolution extend across professions. The advantage of an interdisciplinary text is that you will be challenged to look at conflict situations from diverse points of view. Ideally, the composition of your class will include people from a broad range of backgrounds and perspectives. Expressing your different values, attitudes, and opinions will stimulate conflict and enrich your learning experience.

In this Chapter, I begin with a definitional framework for key terms in the field of conflict resolution. The next section provides an overview of conflict resolution theory, including its roots in specific disciplines. Given this basis, I explain the structure of this text and suggestions on how to use it most effectively. The final sections provide a set of discussion questions and class exercises, as well as a detailed case study ("Conflictia") that forms the basis for certain exercises used throughout the text.

CR ROLES AND DEFINITIONS

Deliberate choice of language is crucial to effective conflict resolution. Many conflicts arise because of miscommunication. Perhaps the speaker was unclear or the listener made an error in processing the message. Alternatively, neither is to blame. Rather than look for responsibility, the conflict may be resolved by rectifying the parties' understandings of one another and moving on. Better yet, consider whether the conflict could have been pre-empted.[2]

I have already used a number of terms having technical meanings and usage. To clarify these and to pre-empt any further misunderstandings, I want to ensure that we have common interpretations of these terms, as well as others that will be used throughout the course of this text.

Conflict resolution (or CR) refers to the various ways in which people or institutions deal with social conflict. **Social conflict** exists when two or more parties express differences in beliefs, values, or interests, whether the divergence is real or perceived (Levinger & Rubin, 1994; Wilmot & Hocker, 1998).[3] Conflict in and of itself is neither good nor bad. Rather, the manner in which we deal with conflict determines whether it is constructive or destructive. In a school situation, for example, teachers and counselors have different points of view on how to allocate resources in the school's budget. If these differences escalate into hostile relations, the result will be destructive. If

---

[2] Pre-empting and other "professional jargon" used throughout this text are defined in the glossary. Pre-empting is also described further in Chapter 4.

[3] When some helping professionals hear the term "conflict resolution," they wonder if it is related to "intra-psychic" or "subconscious" conflicts. While psychodynamic theory may help CR practitioners understand how individuals behave, conflict resolution is directed towards social conflict (conflict between people) rather than conflict within one person's psyche.

these differences spur both types of helping professionals to work together for a creative solution, the result will be positive. Conflict can be viewed as an opportunity and motivation for change. The ability to express conflicting values and beliefs advances two values held by most helping professionals: freedom of expression and respect for diversity among individuals and groups.

People can respond to conflict in a variety of manners, ranging from avoidance and withdrawal to collaboration and problem-solving to litigation and fighting. This book focuses on ways that helping professionals can respond constructively to conflict in three specific roles: negotiator, mediator, and advocate. Chetkow-Yanoov (1997) suggests that there are at least seven other CR roles: facilitator, healer, expert/consultant, arbitrator, administrator, buffer, and penalizer.[4] At this point, I will just highlight some of the distinctions and overlaps between roles.

To simplify the discussion, consider a two-party conflict: A husband and wife are in the middle of a divorce and one of the issues concerns how to divide their family property. The term **party,** adopted in CR from legal jargon, refers to any individual, group, or corporate entity (e.g., a social agency, a government, or a business enterprise). An **interested party** is a party who has a direct interest in how a conflict is resolved. In the example, the husband and wife are the interested parties. Each has a direct stake in how their property is divided. Husband suggests, "I've worked hard to earn a living and pay for this house. You're not entitled to 20%, never mind half." In defense, wife responds, "You're the one who ran off with another woman. As far as I'm concerned, that means the house is mine." If we designate the husband and wife as Party 1 (P1) and Party 2 (P2) respectively, we can represent the conflict as in Figure 1.1.

FIGURE 1.1

Conflict

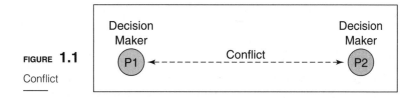

Broadly speaking, **negotiation** refers to any manner in which two or more parties interact with each other in order to deal with a conflict situation. Husband and wife could sit down at the kitchen table and calmly discuss how to divide their property. They could become embroiled in a heated argument.

---

[4]Other conflict resolution roles include ombuds, investigator and hybrids of other roles (e.g., mediation-arbitration). See the glossary for definitions of these.

They could try to manipulate one another by threatening to destroy property, changing locks on the door, or lying about the true value of their retirement investments. Each of these are means of negotiation. In a simple negotiation, the conflict and the communication both flow directly between the parties to the conflict, as illustrated in Figure 1.2.

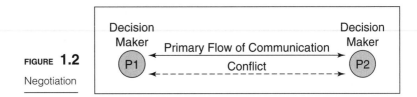

FIGURE **1.2**

Negotiation

Negotiation occurs not only between clients, but between co-professionals, as demonstrated in the case conference scenario described at the beginning of this chapter.

"Negotiation" and "bargaining" are often used interchangeably. Some writers refer to negotiation to describe interest-based CR, in order to distinguish it from the notion of positional bargaining (positional and interest-based negotiation are described in Chapter 3). I avoid use of the term bargaining, because of its questionable connotations in common parlance (i.e., trying to get something cheap; trying to gain something at another party's expense). Instead, I refer to several different models of negotiation.

An **advocate** is a person who acts in support of an interested party during a negotiation. In the divorce situation, one or both spouses may have their own advocates. Wife hires a lawyer to help her win possession of the matrimonial home. She asks the lawyer to take her lecherous husband to court. The lawyer encourages her to consider negotiation, where the lawyer will meet with husband's lawyer to try to work out a reasonable settlement. Assuming each spouse has an advocate (AD1 and AD2), the situation appears as in Figure 1.3.

Note that the arrow with the solid triangle head represents the direction of the conflict, directly between P1 and P2. The primary flow of communication is between the two advocates. The advocates have direct communication with their own client, however, in this pure advocacy model no direct communication takes place between P1 and P2.

In legal situations, such as divorce, we often think of lawyers as advocates. However, a vast range of helping professionals can and do assume advocacy roles. A professor can advocate for a mature student to be accepted into a university program in spite of low grades. A discharge planner in a hospital can advocate for a patient who wants to remain in the hospital until

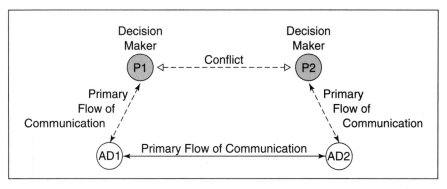

1.3

Advocacy

home support systems are in place. A feminist counselor can advocate for subsidized child care for single parent families. A probation officer can advocate for vocational upgrading support for a client on probation.

An advocate affects the balance of power between parties by providing one party with information, conflict resolution skills, or other resources. Advocates are particularly useful, even necessary, when one party is at a power disadvantage in relation to the other party (Ellis & Stuckless, 1996). When one party hires an advocate, the other often responds by hiring its own advocate.

Some literature refers to "advocating for oneself." Given the definitions described above, this is negotiation rather than advocacy. Advocates and the other CR helping roles described below can be referred to as "third parties." **Third parties** play a role in the CR process, but they do not have a direct interest in the specific resolution of the conflict. AD1 is a partisan who desires a positive result for the husband, but AD1 will not have to live with the ultimate division of property in the same way as the divorced spouses will.

An **expert/consultant** is a professional who provides information, expertise or advice to one or both interested parties to help them resolve a conflict. The expert/consultant does not facilitate communication or direct the process of conflict resolution between the parties. Consultation is a form of education. For example, husband or wife may agree to go to a psycho-educational group to learn about the process and stages of dealing with separation. The group counselor plays the role of expert when she provides information and suggestions about how to deal with one's former spouse. If they have children, they will learn how to deal with their mutual anger and distrust, so that their children do not get caught in the crossfire. In this scenario (Figure 1.4), the wife's expert (P2) is providing suggestions to her, but the husband and wife still communicate directly with each other in order to resolve their differences.

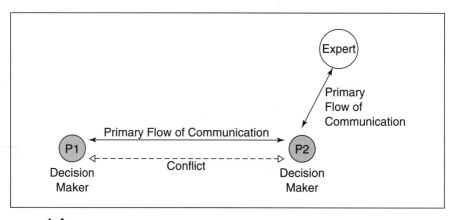

FIGURE **1.4**

Expert/Consultant

Other examples of expert/consultants include supervisors and pastoral counselors. Human service professionals, for instance, may go to their supervisors in order to obtain advice about how to deal with a conflict between them. Pastoral counselors may provide spiritual or moral guidance to clients who are struggling with interpersonal conflicts.

An **assessor** is another expert role that helping professionals frequently assume. If wife and husband agree to submit to a custody evaluation, the clinician will assess both parents' abilities to parent their children. The clinician will make recommendations about the best interests of the children: where the children should reside; how they should spend time with both parents; what parenting responsibilities should fall upon which parent (Chisholm & McNaughton, 1990). The older child has been wetting her bed since her parents separated; accordingly, the assessor recommends that both parents follow a certain bedtime regimen in order to support the daughter through this difficult time. The parties are not necessarily bound by the recommendations; however, they will tend to heed the recommendations because they are coming from an independent third party with expertise in child custody. If husband and wife were in court, the judge may ask them to go for a custody evaluation. The assessor will make recommendations to the judge, but the judge will have ultimate authority to decide which parent will have custody and how visitation with the children will be arranged. The situation with a judge (J) and expert assessor (AS) would present as in Figure 1.5.

Both parties provide information to the assessor, who provides a recommendation to the judge. The judge imposes a decision on the parties. This CR model does not provide for any direct communication between the husband and wife.

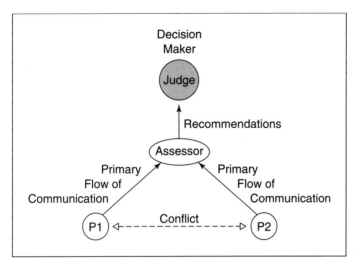

FIGURE 1.5

Assessor

A **facilitator** is a professional who assists with communication between parties to a conflict.[5] Facilitation functions include bringing the parties together, providing a space for discussion, clarifying misunderstandings, encouraging joint problem solving, and assisting each party to hear the others (Barsky & Trocmé, 1998; Chasin et al., 1996; Kaner, 1996). A facilitator could work directly with the interested parties or with their advocates. A teacher notices that a student's school-work has been deteriorating since his parents' separation. The teacher decides to take on the role of facilitator and calls both parents for a meeting. The teacher helps them talk about how their son is falling behind in class. In order to deal with this problem, the parents decide to spend more time helping their son with his homework. Assuming that P1 and P2 do not have advocates, the situation presents as in Figure 1.6.

The communication flows back and forth between all three individuals.

A **mediator** is a third party who assists interested parties in negotiating a conflict. A mediator controls the mediation process, but does not have authority to decide the outcome for the parties. In other words, a mediator is a type of facilitator who follows a particular model of intervention, using specific skills and strategies. The mediator coaches the parties on how to deal with conflict constructively, and conversely, moves parties away from dysfunc-

---

[5] "Parties to a conflict" is legalese for "interested parties" or individuals who are directly involved in the conflict. Some CR literature refers to "parties" as "conflictants" or "disputants," but these terms reinforce adversarial feelings between the parties.

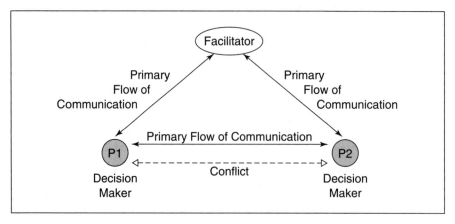

FIGURE **1.6**

Facilitator

---

tional patterns of interaction. More detailed definitions, including whether a mediator must be neutral or impartial, are analyzed in Chapter 4. Figure 1.7 shows that the mediator (M) facilitates communication between the wife and husband, but the wife and husband have ultimate decision-making power over how to divide their property.

Advocates or other helping professionals can also participate in mediation (Noble, Dizgun & Emond, 1998).

Some people use the terms mediation and conciliation interchangeably. Others distinguish conciliation as a process which is outcome-oriented (to fa-

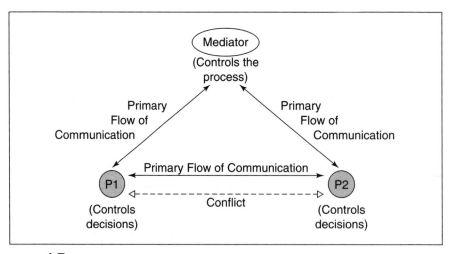

FIGURE **1.7**

Mediator

cilitate settlement), whereas mediation is more process-oriented (to facilitate better relationships and deal with underlying psychosocial issues). According to this dichotomy, conciliation tends to require only one or two sessions, whereas mediation may take four to eight sessions. Conciliators tend to be more interventionist than mediators, offering suggestions and directing the parties towards specific options for settlement. In the 1970s and 1980s, the term conciliation was used most frequently to refer to services that were attached to courts, tribunals, or other mandated government agencies (Noone, 1996).

In this text, I talk about various models of mediation, but avoid use of the term conciliation. People tend to confuse conciliation with reconciliation. Reconciliation suggests the aim of the CR process is to return the parties to a previous form of relationship; e.g., to work out an arrangement for separated spouses to move back together, as an intact family. Although the parties in some mediations choose to reconcile, this may not be their goal. Divorce mediation is designed to help former spouses redefine their roles so that they can live peacefully, separately, and apart. If separated spouses want to reconcile, then family counseling might be more appropriate to help them with this transition. This topic is raised again when we get into the debate on the difference between mediation and therapy.

A **healer** is a facilitator who helps parties work through the underlying causes of a conflict. Psychotherapists, clergy (Brossart, 1980), and elders within certain cultures often assume the role of healer. Whereas the mediation field is still debating the extent to which mediation involves therapeutic processes (if at all), healers specifically focus on underlying psychosocial issues. Techniques for healing include helping parties listen sensitively to one another; explore taboo ideas; overcome historical hatreds; depart from traditional customs; discontinue behavior which victimizes other groups; improve self-understanding; accept responsibility; provide apologies; and reconcile previous relationships (Montville, 1993; Chetkow-Yanoov, 1997). Many models of psychological intervention clearly place the therapist in a healing role: for example, Rogerian-humanistic therapy, psychoanalysis, narrative therapy, and cognitive restructuring (Corey, 1996). Traditional healing processes also exist within many ethnic communities: *ho'opononopono* among native Hawaiians, family group conferencing among New Zealand's Maori people, *fa'amanata'anga* among the Kwar'ae of the Solomon Islands, and healing circles among Native North Americans, to name a few (Hudson, Morris, Maxwell, & Galaway, 1996; Tannen, 1998; Umbreit, 1997a). In our diagrams, the role of a healer appears very similar to that of a mediator or facilitator.

Figure 1.8 could represent a couples counselor, clergy person, or elder who is helping both the husband and wife reconcile their marriage (Picard & Melchin, 1988). Unlike a mediator, a healer could work with just one of the parties; for instance, helping the wife come to terms with her husband's running off with a younger woman.

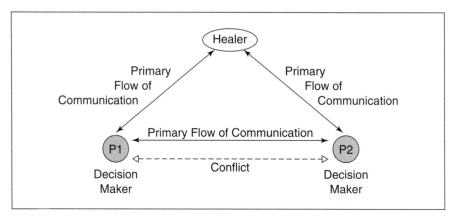

FIGURE **1.8**

Healer

An **arbitrator** (Figure 1.9) is an independent third party who hears evidence from the conflicting parties and decides upon an appropriate resolution for them. A judge is a type of arbitrator, imposed on parties who are involved in court proceedings. Labor laws and other forms of legislation sometimes impose specialized arbitrators on conflicting parties (Barsky, 1997a; Goldberg, Green, & Sander, 1989). In other situations, parties choose arbitration on a voluntary basis. When arbitration is legislatively mandated, the rules of the arbitration process are predetermined for the parties. If arbitration is voluntary, the parties can select their own arbitrator and establish the rules of arbitration by agreement. Note that there is little or no communication between the parties during arbitration.

If the parties are represented by advocates, then the advocates communicate with the arbitrator. In our divorce situation, the spouses direct their

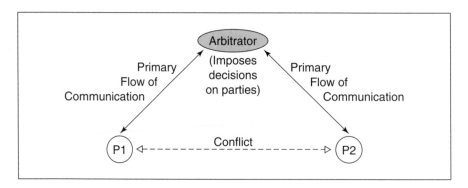

FIGURE **1.9**

Arbitrator

lawyers about how to represent them, but the judge and lawyers control the process and communication once in court. If the spouses came to you in your capacity as a helping professional to arbitrate a dispute, would you accept this role? Consider whether arbitration is consistent with the ethics of client self-determination (Rave & Larson, 1995).

For most helping professionals, an administrator is someone who manages the employees and resources of an organization. In a conflict resolution context, an administrator is a professional who assists with implementation of the resolution of a conflict (Figure 1.10). In our divorce mediation, for example, the former spouses agree that the husband will pay monthly child support. An administrator could be involved as a monitoring agent, to ensure the husband pays support as agreed (e.g., at an agency that enforces child and spousal support agreements). In addition to a monitoring role, administrators operationalize agreements by encouraging compliance, facilitating ongoing communication between the parties, providing interpretation of disputed clauses, and identifying potential trouble spots early on (Chetkow-Yanoov, 1997). The role of an administrator looks similar to that of a mediator or facilitator, but the administrator generally comes in after another third party has facilitated the basic agreement.

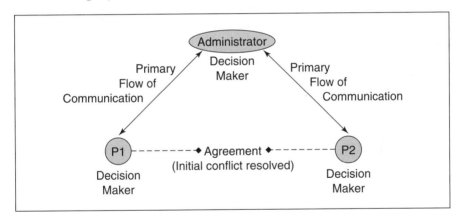

FIGURE 1.10

Administrator

A **buffer** (Figure 1.11) is an individual or agency that separates conflicting parties during an intense, destructive phase of conflict. The role of United Nations peacekeepers is a prime example of the buffer role (Chetkow-Yanoov, 1997). Peacekeepers provide a physical barrier between two warring factions, in order to stabilize a situation. The buffer role is temporary. It is designed to allow time for other conflict resolution processes to work out a more permanent solution (Rikhye, 1984). Peacekeeping is a bit of a misnomer. Peace*keeping* may ensure an absence of war, but absence of war is not the same as peace. Peace*making*, a term adopted by some mediators, goes

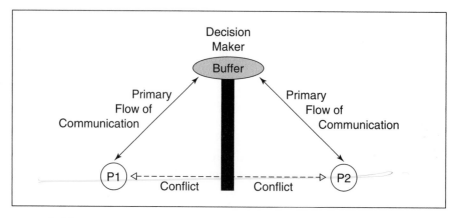

FIGURE **1.11**

Buffer

beyond peacekeeping. True peace requires mutual understanding and re-spect, ongoing constructive communication, and a relationship that can deal well with differences (Fisher & Brown, 1989). A truce enforced by buffers hopefully provides an opportunity for peacemakers to help the parties bring about a full and lasting peace.

Supervised access is an example of the buffer role in our divorce situa-tion. If our wife and husband are hostile towards one another, a buffer may be necessary to safeguard the spouses and the child. Some social agencies offer supervised access, where the custodial spouse brings the child to the agency and the non-custodial spouse meets the child at the agency. The agency may simply supervise the transfer of the child from one parent to the other, or may supervise the entire visitation. In families with a history of vio-lence, the agency can make arrangements so that no contact exists between the former spouses. In contrast to a facilitator, a buffer blocks direct commu-nication between the parties and communication is primarily top-down from the buffer to each party.

A **penalizer** (Figure 1.12) is an individual or agency with the power to impose sanctions on parties for misconduct. Criminal law courts impose sanc-tions such as fines and incarceration. Some clergy teach that a divine power will punish those who act in an evil manner. Teachers sanction certain types of student behavior through grading, granting privileges, and withdrawing them. Social workers, psychologists, and other mental health professionals may frown upon the use of sanctions as means of social control. Still, there are many examples where such helping professionals do make use of sanc-tions. A divorce counselor, for example, may discontinue services to a spouse who becomes abusive. Some helping professionals justify the use of sanctions

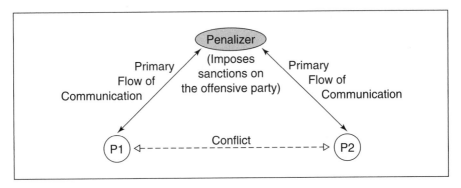

FIGURE **1.12**

Penalizer

to promote constructive conflict resolution behavior. In jurisdictions with "mandatory mediation," conflicting parties are required to try mediation before they can have access to the public court system. Police sometimes drop charges when parties agree to go to a community dispute resolution center. Parole officers advise parolees that they will be returned to jail if they breach conditions of parole. Are these examples of undue coercion or creative use of authority? Ethically, one must consider whether the ends justify the means (Loewenberg & Dolgoff, 1996; Murray et al., 1996). Whereas most helping professionals feel comfortable in facilitative roles, they are likely to experience an internal values conflict if they are pressed into the role of penalizer. The penalizer's decisions are top-down and the parties are not encouraged to communicate with one another.

While there are legitimate roles for penalizers, this book focuses on non-coercive conflict resolution.

Interventions that employ the ten roles described above are sometimes called conflict management, dispute resolution, or alternative dispute resolution (ADR). These terms are related, but entail conceptual differences. Conflicts range from mild differences, to disagreements, to campaigns, to litigation and fighting (Wilmot & Hocker, 1998). Disputes fall within the latter, more intense part of this range. **Dispute resolution** refers to formal institutions that provide conflict resolution services, particularly within law-related systems. The "alternative" in ADR refers to alternatives to court processes (Mustill, 1996). First popularized in the 1970s, ADR was seen as a way to divert cases from an expensive, formal, and adversarial court system, to cheaper and more informal ADR programs (Bush & Folger, 1994). ADR could mean any alternative to court, including negotiation, arbitration, healing, and assessments (Hart, 1987; Roth, Wulff, & Cooper, 1993). Some practitioners use ADR to refer specifically to mediation, given that court-affiliated mediation programs are the most popular type of ADR program. The term ADR seems to suggest that court is the pre-eminent form of conflict resolution. In order to avoid the notion that mediation and other forms of CR are simply alternatives to court, some CR professionals have reframed ADR to mean "Appropriate Dispute Resolution."

CR professionals often reframe "dispute" to "conflict" in order to focus their clients on the positive aspects of conflict. The presence of conflict means there is energy that can be utilized to produce change. Permission to express differences is vital to the operation of a free and democratic society. For many people, even the term conflict feels uncomfortable. Their experience suggests that conflict is fighting, wars, violence, exploitation, rivalry, or humiliation (Chetkow-Yanoov, 1997). Perceptions of conflict are culture bound. Some cultures place high value on harmony and cooperation; others place high value on competition and individuality (Irving & Benjamin, 1995; Barsky, Este, & Collins, 1996; LeBaron, 1994). CR professionals need to respect people's experience and culture, but must also help people explore new ways of viewing and dealing with conflict.

On its face, the term conflict resolution implies that the purpose of intervention is to resolve or end the conflict. Some professionals prefer the term "conflict management" because it suggests that conflict is an ongoing phenomenon to be dealt with in a strategic manner. For others, conflict management suggests that conflict is dealt with in a top-down manner, by people who have the power to control or suppress conflict. In contrast, the term conflict transformation has been used to describe processes that focus people on more constructive ways of dealing with conflict in their relationships. This book adopts the term conflict resolution with the understanding that the purpose of intervention is to resolve the parties' *underlying* concerns, whether that means ending the conflict, improving their relationship, or learning how to deal with conflict in more constructive ways.

THEORETICAL CONTEXT

In order to trace the roots of conflict resolution, we need to consider whether we are talking about CR as a theory, discipline, or technique of practice. The formalized study of CR in the field of collective bargaining and labor relations began in the early 1900s (National Institute for Dispute Resolution, 1987). In the helping professions, mediation and other collaborative forms of CR began to emerge as distinct models of practice in the 1970s; however, the use of CR techniques and strategies in the helping professions extends back much earlier (Deutch, 1973; Zastrow, 1999). This text covers both "emergent" and "contractual" CR. Contractual CR refers to models of practice where the professional is specifically hired as a CR practitioner; for example, a separating couple that agrees to hire a family mediator. The spouses sign an agreement to mediate, which establishes the role of the mediator and makes the terms of the mediation process explicit. In contrast, emergent CR occurs when a helping professional uses skills and strategies of CR, but is not specifically hired as a CR specialist. The CR role emerges out of another form of relationship; for instance, a teacher who mediates an argument between students, a nurse who facilitates a tumultuous case conference, a probation officer who negotiates a contract for work with a client, or a clergy who arbitrates a dispute between parishioners. Because these practitioners do not have an explicit agreement with the conflicting parties to assume a CR role, their functions are likely to differ from a contractual CR professional. In some situations, a practitioner's prior role allows her to move into a CR role; in other situations, the prior role inhibits such a transition. CR theory and literature extend across both contractual and emergent CR (Pruitt & Carnevale, 1993).[6]

CR draws from a broad range of disciplines including psychology, business administration, law, education, social work, political science, strategic studies, and radicalism. Ironically, turf wars are not uncommon among CR professionals from different disciplines. What type of theory drives CR? What are the values and ethical bases that underlie CR? What professional background do you need to be certified as a CR professional? Can just anyone hang up a shingle and practice? Some arguments about restricting CR practice to certain professions are raised under the guise of ensuring competence and accountability. CR does not fall under the natural domain of any single discipline, though there may be different disciplines that fit best with certain types of conflict situations.[7] Diversity among CR professionals should be encouraged, rather than stifled. Many disciplines have made significant contributions to CR.

1. Psychology

Psychology has provided us with many theories on the etiology of conflict. Communications theory, for example, teaches us about functional and dysfunctional ways in which people impart and receive messages (Barsky, 1983; Nicoterra, 1995; Putnam & Sandak, 1991). Consider a simple question from

---

[6]People who take courses in mediation or other models of CR often do so with the intention of developing a practice in contractual CR. Although good opportunities exist in this growing field, there are still far more uses of CR on an emergent basis, as part of one's other professional roles. Another wonderful facet of emergent CR is that many CR strategies and techniques can be used in your personal life as well as in your professional life.

[7]For example, medical practitioners for situations where medical expertise is required, or teachers where educational expertise is required. Some CR roles do not depend upon substantive knowledge of the dispute. Mediators, for example, are experts in process. Advocates with substantive expertise, on the other hand, may be required to assist a party with weak knowledge in a particular area.

Sally to Gil, "Do you want to go to the movies?" Simple? Perhaps not. When the process of communication is broken down into components, we see ample room for misunderstandings. Before asking the question, Sally formulates her thoughts, "I want to go to a movie with Gil." She then puts these thoughts into words or codes. Wanting to avoid sounding too direct, Sally chooses not to make a statement, but rather *ask* Gil if he wants to go. Gil hears the question and must interpret it. Assuming there are no problems with his hearing, proficiency in English, or cognitive abilities, Gil still has a number of choices for interpretation. He concludes that this is an open question, not thinking that Sally really does want to go to a movie. He was not thinking about going to a movie, so he says, "Not really."

One role for CR professionals is to facilitate more effective communication. If we know how communication is coded, transferred, and uncoded, we can teach, model, and facilitate more effective communication. Microskills training and interviewing courses are based on communication theory (Evans, Hearn, Uhlemann, & Ivey, 1997; Ivey & Ivey, 1999; Wood, Sept, & Duncan, 1998). Basic listening skills such as paraphrasing, reflection of feelings, and summarization are crucial to conflict resolution. Reflective listening allows the listener to check back with the speaker to ensure that the message intended was the message received. Further, use of reflective skills helps build a trusting relationship, since the listener demonstrates empathy with the speaker. Consider the last verbal argument you witnessed. Both parties were talking, perhaps even talking loudly. Was anybody really listening?

Decision-making theory combines research and knowledge from economics, psychology, strategic studies,[8] game theory,[9] and even mathematics (Edelman & Crain, 1993; Nicoterra, 1995; Yilmaz, 1997; Young, 1961; Zey, 1992). In order to help two or more people make joint decisions, CR professionals need to develop an understanding of how individuals make decisions (Pruitt & Carnevale, 1993). If you were thinking about asking your boss for a raise, what factors would influence your decision? Would your decision be based on a rational cost-benefit analysis, taking into account the risk that your boss might fire you? Would emotions such as pride, frustration, or hope affect your decision? Would past experiences shape your choice? Would your choice be a conscious decision or would subconscious processes affect your behavior?

CR also draws upon systems theories (Shulman, 1992). Systems theories teach us that a relationship between individuals or groups is not simply the sum of the parts. Interactions are dynamic processes. Components of a

---

[8] Studies for military strategy and national defense.

[9] Game theory is an approach to determining how parties will act and respond to one another under specific circumstances, using mathematical models. Many of the models assume that participants will act rationally, meaning that they will try to minimize risks and maximize gains to themselves.

system are interdependent. The way one individual in a system acts affects how others will respond. CR specialists can help clients understand that they can really only control their own behavior; however, they can try to behave in ways that are more likely to bring about positive responses in the other. Systems tend to work towards a certain homeostasis or equilibrium, making it hard for people to move away from engrained patterns of interaction (Corey, 1996; Chetkow-Yanoov, 1992). Your boss always puts on a tough face, making it difficult to approach him; as a result, you usually avoid confronting him. How can you change your pattern of interaction, not knowing whether your boss will respond in kind?

Some models of CR are based on very specific systems theories. For example, family mediation models have been developed based on strategic and structural family therapy (Aponte, 1991; Irving & Benjamin, 1995), Bowenian family therapy (Maida, 1986), and Milanese family therapy (Gadlin & Ouellette, 1986). Other models are less specific about their theoretical premises, allowing the CR professionals to do their own interpretations (Marlow, 1997). The risk of using CR strategies without a theoretical or empirical foundation is that we have no premise to say what will be effective and what will not be effective.

Many CR models build upon a generic problem-solving approach, common to most helping professions. The typical problem-solving approach is a staged model, which directs the professional to proceed through a prescribed sequence of steps. For example, 1) Identify the problem or issues; 2) Identify the underlying concerns, needs and interests of the parties; 3) Generate options; 4) Build agreement; and 5) Implement and monitor the decision (Fisher, Ury, & Patton, 1997; Kruk, 1997). During implementation and monitoring, other problems may be identified, sending the parties back to step one. Anthropologists note that while linear models fit well with western cultures, other cultures are more comfortable with circular models (LeBaron, 1994). Rather than move through steps sequentially, circularity suggests that there is no fixed beginning or end, with iterations back and forth through various stages. How the problem is seen, for instance, depends on what is happening at other points of the process. One might have to revisit problem definition while working on agreement building or implementation. None of the stages are fixed at just one point in time. Because this is an introductory text to CR, I cannot hope to cover the full breadth of CR models in any detail. We will explore how some of the basic models can be tailored to meet the needs of different cultural groups (Lederach, 1986).

Much theory that informs CR practice is dependent upon the context of the conflict. Developmental theories, such as Erikson's (1950) psychosocial stages of human development, are useful for family-based conflict. Parent-youth conflict, for instance, may be explained by the transitions that a family experiences when a youth moves from childhood to adulthood. As youths strive for autonomy and identity development, their parents may have difficulty with challenges to their authority. Knowledge of developmental stages allows the CR practitioner to help both parents and youths view conflict as part of the family life cycle and redefine their roles in relationship to one another.

Another branch of developmental theory that has specific interest to CR professionals is the process of dealing with loss. Kübler-Ross (1997) identifies five stages which people go through when they face their own mortality: denial, anger, depression, bargaining, and acceptance. These stages apply well to various sorts of loss issues. Conflict often occurs around loss: loss of a relationship (such as a job or marriage); loss of physical abilities (perhaps from a car accident); loss of property (resulting from theft or other crime); or loss of independence (from illness, aging, etc). When people are in early stages of dealing with loss, they have difficulty acting in "rationale" manners. Denial may mean that they refuse to acknowledge that conflict exists. Anger may cause them to desire retaliation rather than constructive resolution. Depression may sap their motivation and energy to deal with conflict. If a CR practitioner can identify the stages affecting a particular individual, they can help that person move on. They can also help the other parties empathize with the grieving individual.

2. Business Administration

Business administration has contributed to conflict resolution in a number of ways. First, compared with other disciplines, business has a long history of using mediation and arbitration (Douglas, 1962; Kauffman, 1991). Both forms of CR are built into management-labor relations, including the process of collective bargaining and grievance procedures for employees. Second, the role of management is basically one of conflict resolution: how to manage people and how to manage other resources of the enterprise (Elangovan, 1995). Organizational behavior theory helps us understand the operations of power and politics in business settings, as well as in not-for profit agencies (Robbins, 1998). Perhaps surprising to some helping professionals, management has been a leader in analysis of cross-cultural conflict; with globalization of business, management has explored differences in management styles and negotiation styles between people from different countries (Rahim & Blum, 1994). Finally, business schools have been leaders in development of negotiation theory (Lewicki, Litterer, Minton, & Saunders, 1998). While one might assume that negotiation theory from business is all about how to win in a competitive, capitalist environment, business and workplace literature since the 1980s contains numerous examples of CR models that focus on process, relationships, and collaboration (Dana, 1996; Lax & Sebenius, 1987; Lewicki, 1997).

3. Law

Traditionally, the Anglo-American legal system was based on an adversarial model of conflict resolution (Bossy, 1983), with justice based upon an analysis of the rights of individuals (Rawls, 1971; Dworkin, 1977). Under this model, conflicting parties could bring their conflicts to court for a determination of rights and resolution prescribed by a judge (Barsky, 1997a). The adversarial system provides a fixed procedure designed to give conflicting parties equal opportunity to present their arguments before an impartial judge or panel of judges. The adversarial process may provide "just solutions," but often at the expense of the relationship between the conflicting parties (Conley & Barr, 1990). Although many of us still think of courts as the forum for legal disputes, only a small percentage of lawyers do courtroom work. Most lawyers help clients by negotiating contracts or other legal agreements in order to prevent potential conflicts or to resolve disputes once they have arisen. Even among cases that get filed in court, fewer than 10% are actually resolved by a full trial of the issues. Most cases are resolved by negotiations, between the parties or between their lawyers. Trials are like the tip of the iceberg, the most visible part. The bulk of the iceberg sits below the water's surface, highlighting the fact that we are not even aware of most disputes, since they are resolved informally and in private.

Until the 1980s, few law schools provided skills or training in CR processes other than trial advocacy. Since then, negotiation, mediation, and other forms of CR have become much more popular. Indeed, some helping professionals have complained that lawyers have become too dominant in the field of CR. Research has identified different approaches to CR between lawyers and therapists who become CR professionals (State Justice Institute, 1998). Lawyers tend to focus more on rights and settlement of overt legal issues; therapists and other helping professionals tend to focus on process and establishing a positive relationship between parties (Marlow, 1987). However, these trends are just generalizations. Many legal theorists have challenged traditional legal approaches to CR, encouraging lawyers and other CR professionals to focus more on process, underlying interests, and relationships between the parties (Auerbach, 1983; Fisher, Ury, & Patton, 1997; Marlow, 1997; Menkel-Meadow, 1984; Mnookin & Kornhauser, 1979).

4. Education

Education does not have a definitive theory of CR, though it has been a leader in development of educational materials and models of peer mediation[10] (Bodine, Crawford, & Schrumpf, 1994; Deutch, 1973; Girard &

---

[10]Peer mediation in schools generally refers to mediation between students, with a student mediator. Teachers and school counselors provide training and support for the student mediators.

Koch, 1996; Pastorino, 1997). Many components from CR theory can be traced to constructs in education. Since the 1940s, various models of education have been designed to instill cooperation and conflict management skills in children (Maryama, 1992). One of the unique contributions that education has brought to CR concerns translating abstract theory and complicated processes into terms that can be easily understood by children as young as three or four (Kraybill, 1985). In fact, you might say CR experts could have learned all they needed to know from their kindergarten teachers: Be nice to others; clean up after yourself; don't fight; if you make a mistake, say you are sorry; if you want something, ask nicely; and when someone else is speaking, be quiet (Fulghum, 1988). Although these teachings are often presented as universal rules of etiquette, they are steeped in cultural assumptions that do not apply across all groups. What is considered a polite request among one group might be considered rude or inappropriate in another.

I have had students complain that some conflict resolution readings I provide are too elementary for university students to be studying.[11] In fact, some of the most practical CR materials do sound basic.[12] The challenge comes when you have to put them into practice, at the moment of heated conflict. Think back to the last time you were involved in an argument; how many of the golden rules did you break? Working with some of the brightest and most skilled helping professionals, I have often had to remind them of the basic tenets for constructive interaction. Well-adjusted adults sometimes lapse into making faces and hurling insults when they feel angry or hurt. "If you catch me doing this, please let me know."

There is also a growing literature on conflict in educational institutions (Holton, 1998; Rogers et al., 1998). Ironically, many of the same institutions that study and teach conflict resolution are fraught with conflict problems themselves. Universities and similar institutions are supposed to promote excellence, independent thought, and academic freedom, while constrained by limited resources, departmental politics, and convoluted bureaucracies: a perfect combination if you want to foster conflict. Consider your experiences in your place of learning: what types of conflict occur and how are they handled?

5. Social Work and Related Sciences

Social work is similar to education in that it plays an important role in CR, but borrows from many other disciplines (Kruk, 1997). Some of the primary contributions of social work come from the field of community

---

[11]In Israel, kindergarten teachers respond to disruptive students by saying, "Don't act like Members of the Knesset (Parliament)."

[12]Even the Bible suggests that you treat others as you would like them to treat you.

development. Social workers have been at the forefront of coalition building, interdisciplinary cooperation, and strategic alliances to advance the causes of disadvantaged groups in society (Bratton, 1997; Zastrow, 1999). Social psychologists have also contributed to community approaches to conflict resolution. Kurt Lewin's 1940's theories of majority-minority relations, for example, have been used to develop workshops and exercises to build better relationships between ethnic groups with deep-rooted histories of conflict (Bargal & Bar, 1992b). Volunteers and other lay people provide some of the most crucial community work in CR. Unfortunately, their work often goes unnoticed, due to inadequate documentation in research or other professional literature.[13]

6. Political Science and Strategic Studies

Political science and strategic studies analyze how governments, nations, social movements, and other political institutions respond to conflict. Helping professionals who work with individuals, families, and small groups may wonder about the relevance of conflict resolution at international and other macro levels.[14] However, the Harvard Program on Negotiation and many other CR institutes often draw parallels between conflicts at these different levels (Fisher & Brown, 1994; *Negotiation Journal*). International conflicts in the Middle East, Bosnia, Northern Ireland, and so on have surprising similarities with conflicts occurring in families, schools, neighborhoods, and workplaces. Conflicts at both levels often entail strong emotions (anger, mistrust, fear), blocked communication, and unmet needs or wishes. Strategies which work at one level can often be transferred to the other.

Tension often exists between "strategic studies" and "peace and conflict studies." Both are legitimate areas of conflict resolution. However, as with the lawyer-therapist dichotomy, the orientations of these studies vary significantly. Strategic studies look at how to prevent war, how to win war, and how to encourage states to resolve problems through political processes (negotiation) rather than through force.[15] Peace and conflict studies focus upon nonviolent, collaborative means of conflict resolution. Although both branches prefer not to use force, strategic studies are generally more willing to look at

---

[13]Bargal and Bar (1992) suggest the use of Participatory Action Research as a way to wed research and provision of services. Nonprofessionals are more inclined to participate in this form of research, since they can use the research information during the process of intervention.

[14]A macro level of professional practice refers to community development, public policy development or other interventions with systems larger than individuals, families, and small groups (i.e., micropractice).

[15]In the *Journal of Strategic Studies*, Miller (1997) defines peacemaking as, "A strategy pursued by an external power, based mainly on diplomatic, although possibly on economic and military measures, designed to promote conflict resolution" (p. 106).

the use of force and the threat of force as valid alternatives. As a helping professional, you will have to gauge for yourself whether you are willing to use force or power. You likely place high values on peace and client self-determination. When, if ever, is the use of force justified? To defend a client from physical harm? To defend a client from emotional harm? To defend a client from social harm?[16] Does it depend on the type of force—physical, psychological, economic, political?

7. *Radical Perspectives*

Radical helping professionals may be familiar with a "Conflict Model" of practice (Gould, 1987; Rossides, 1998). According to this model, the practitioner's role is to agitate conflict in order to stimulate social change. Marxist, structuralist, and other radical practitioners view oppression in society as a dominant factor in their work (Burstow, 1992; Carniol, 1995; Ellis & Stuckless, 1996; Fook, 1993; Freire, 1970; Girdner, 1989; Marx, 1964; Sandole & Van der Merwe, 1993). Acting on behalf of certain minorities—for example, women, people of color, gays and lesbians, or people with disabilities—these practitioners use strategies such as protests, strikes, boycotts, and civil disobedience to fight for social improvement. Rather than work on a consensual basis with existing social institutions, the Conflict Model confronts them, using short-term social disorder to transform society. The premises behind the Conflict Model are significantly different from those behind most conflict resolution models. The term "conflict resolution" is broad enough to include all means of dealing with conflict, but most professionals in the conflict resolution movement strive towards collaborative problem solving. Some radical professionals question or even reject mainstream conflict resolution, suggesting that it ignores the power differentials between privileged and oppressed groups in society. According to this view, models which promote peace and harmony suppress conflict and permit continued oppression of disadvantaged groups (Nader, 1992). How can oppressed groups in society expect to be dealt with fairly if they rely solely on collaborative processes and the goodwill of their oppressors? This type of question needs to be taken seriously, regardless of whether you see yourself as a radical professional.

My own bias is that both collaborative and radical conflict processes have legitimate roles. In fact, they are not mutually exclusive. One may need to use them in combination. A client may need to initiate conflict with a welfare worker in order to upset the *status quo*. Following this confrontation, negotiation may be useful in coming to a new understanding. This book focuses on collaborative processes, but the limitations of collaborative

---

[16]Examples of social harm include unemployment, poverty, discrimination, and inadequate education.

processes and alternative conflict responses will be raised for discussion throughout the text. For radical professionals, collaborative conflict resolution may not fit with certain aspects of your work—challenging societal institutions and people in power; upsetting the *status quo*. However, you may find collaborative CR applicable for work within a particular group; for example, building coalitions and alliances, working with colleagues within an agency, and helping clients handle conflict with others who have similar power or status in society.

8. Eclectic and Integrative Approaches

For all CR professionals, as you read on and work through the exercises, consider whether collaborative CR can work fairly if there is a significant power differential between the parties. What is your role, if any, with regard to redistributing power. If collaborative CR is not appropriate for a particular situation, then is there a better alternative? CR is about selecting the best means of conflict resolution. Unfortunately, some mediators and other CR professionals fall into the trap of becoming so enamored with one mode of CR that they promote it to the exclusion of all other modes. Two possible directions are to take an eclectic or an integrative approach. By using an eclectic approach, the practitioner assesses the situation and selects theories or models of CR that best fit the situation. By using an integrative approach, the practitioner looks for ways to integrate or combine the best features of various approaches (Corey, 1996). For learning purposes, you may want to focus upon one approach at a time. As you become familiar and comfortable with various approaches, consider how you can match approaches with various situations or combine aspects of various approaches.

Constructive Feedback

A positive environment for adult learners requires a safe atmosphere for taking risks, opportunities to individualize learning activities, and room for the learners to take responsibility for their own learning. Although the style of the instructor contributes or detracts from these factors, everyone in the class plays a key role. After all, there are far more learners than instructors in the class.

In order to foster a safe atmosphere in the classroom, offer your colleagues unconditional respect[17] and constructive feedback. Giving

---

[17]Chapter 3 describes how to "separate the person from the problem." A person might vehemently disagree with another individual's beliefs or values, but still demonstrate respect for the individual.

and receiving feedback are skills that are useful CR practice, as well as in learning situations. Giving feedback means sharing our thoughts about another person's behavior, enabling the other person to reflect upon whether the information is helpful and whether to try to make changes based on the feedback. In order to provide constructive non-threatening feedback, consider the following guidelines:[18]

1. Focus on *behavior* rather than on *person*.

   "The pace of questioning was very fast," rather than "You were very fast."

2. Focus on direct *observations* rather than on *inferences*.

   "Your voice was raised," rather than "You sounded angry."

3. Focus on *description* rather than *judgment*.

   "Your reframing allowed the client to see things from your perspective," rather than "Your use of reframing was good."

4. Focus on *here and now* or in *future*, rather than on *there and then*.

   "The next time a client confronts you like that, you could try an empathy statement," rather than "You missed a good opportunity to use an empathy statement."

5. Focus on *behavior* in terms of *more or less*.

   "To make your point more dramatically, you could use larger hand gestures."

6. Focus on *sharing ideas* rather than *giving advice*.

   "One alternative would be to terminate the meeting," rather than, "You should have terminated the meeting."

7. Focus on the *value* it has to the receiver.

   "Your arguments were direct and assertive, two skills that you said you wanted to improve."

8. Give feedback in *small amounts*.

   Select one or two good points, rather than flood the person with feedback.

---

[18] These tips on feedback are derived from a flyer entitled "Constructive Feedback." Unfortunately, I do not have any further information about the author or source.

9. Focus on what the person can *use*.

Avoid making suggestions about things the recipient cannot change (e.g., "The problem is you are too tall").

10. Be aware of appropriate *time and place* for giving it.

Sometimes feedback about sensitive issues should be left for a private exchange, rather than in front of others

11. Use *clear and concrete* examples.

"The mood in the room lightened up when you told the Sherpa anecdote," rather than "Your story thing was nice."

12. Use "I" statements rather than "you" or "we".

"I try to be quite assertive," rather than "You need to be more assertive."

The recipient of feedback also plays an active role in the exchange of feedback. Strategies for receiving feedback include:

- Hear & understand what has been said to you—reflect back what you have heard, clarify, and ask for more information to ensure that you have understood the message intended
- Check out feedback with others
- Give yourself time to reflect on feedback
- Decide what you will do with the feedback. You may decide to validate what the other person said and try to incorporate the feedback in future. Alternatively, after deliberation, you may decide for yourself that no change is necessary at this time. Offer thanks for feedback in order to acknowledge the other person's honest attempts to offer constructive feedback.

Ideally, feedback for learning purposes is separated from sanctions, such as grades or remuneration. Some CR courses are offered on a pass-fail basis in order to reduce student anxiety about grades. Some CR professors allow students to negotiate their grades. I avoid giving grades for role plays, to encourage students to take risks and feel less inhibited about showing themselves making "mistakes" (how else can we learn). Instead, I ask students to provide process recordings[19] or detailed analyses of their role plays. Grades are based on the students' analysis of the process, rather than the performance itself.

---

[19]An example of a process recording is provided in Appendix 2.

USING THIS TEXT FOR EFFECTIVE LEARNING

I would like to say that this text is prepared in a way that allows you to select chapters of interest and read them in any order. Unfortunately, I cannot. The topics presented build upon one another in the sequence presented. Chapter 2 describes the nature of a reflective practitioner in CR practice, including issues related to professional awareness and conscious use of self. If you are familiar with these concepts in relation to your previous clinical education, this section may serve as a refresher. However, some of the materials are specific to the field of CR. Chapters 3 to 6 deal with three models of CR: negotiation, mediation, and advocacy. The theories and strategies presented in the negotiation chapter are crucial for mediation and advocacy, both of which are forms of assisted negotiation. Chapter 7 provides concluding suggestions about CR for helping professionals and makes a valiant attempt to say something really profound and insightful. If you happen to skip a section and come across a strange term, you may find easy access to a definition in Appendix 1, the Glossary. Appendix 2 includes a list of resources for further information and research, including books, articles, videotapes, WEB sites, associations, a sample process recording, and sample codes of ethics. Appendix 3 describes various roles helping professionals can play in support of the mediation movement. Appendix 4 describes decision trees. The bibliography includes all of the resources cited throughout the text.

I have attempted to structure this text based on the tenets of andragogy; i.e., adult learning (Knowles, Holton, & Swanson, 1998). Adults come into the class with significant life experience and knowledge that can be used to enrich the class. Adults have the capacity for self-directed learning, based on internal motivations. The role of the educator is to provide a safe environment for learning and to offer support (MacKearcher, 1997). The materials provided are not intended to be prescriptive. I present a range of models of CR for you to explore and experiment with. Ultimately, you will have to decide which ones to integrate into your practice. Often, the most successful exercises and assignments are those initiated by students themselves—be imaginative and creative.

Different people learn best in different ways—through reading, discussing, observing others, or doing it themselves (Kolb, 1974; Lewicki, 1997). Accordingly, each chapter contains theoretical abstractions, discussion questions, and class exercises that you can observe or experience firsthand. Professors often ask students to prepare for classes by reading the material ahead of time; this makes sense, for professors, since most of them are abstract conceptualizers. While this ordering works for some students, others learn best by doing first and then going back to the theory. Throughout the text, I emphasize the value of preparing for any CR intervention. If you decide to "wing it" for class exercises, you may find yourself at a disadvantage compared to others who read the materials and prepare in advance. However, as long as you reflect back on the experiential exercises and go back to the theory, you can effectively integrate theory and practice. Am I condoning procrastination and cramming at the end of the course? You can certainly choose the best way for you to learn without me telling you.

Throughout the text, I provide self-inventories to help you reflect upon your progress and focus your learning. Some inventories are designed to assess your value orientations and preferred styles of conflict resolution. Others help you identify your CR strengths and learning needs. I have included more exercises than you could possibly complete in one course, so pick and choose exercises that best meet your professional development goals. Some jurisdictions have moved towards competency-based accreditation for CR professionals: that is, in order to obtain a license or certification to practice CR, you will be required to demonstrate specific skills and knowledge. The inventories in this text can help you prepare for these requirements. If you intend to apply for some type of accreditation, contact your local CR associations in order to determine their specific requirements (see Resources in Appendix 2 for more information).

The exercises at the end of each chapter include conflict situations from a broad spectrum of contexts: family counseling, child welfare, mental and physical health, education, professional ethics, gerontology, social assistance, criminal justice, interdisciplinary practice, anti-oppression, human services, and religious counseling. Feel free to alter some of the case facts to bring the exercise closer to your own preferred area of practice. However, students often find it exciting to play roles that are new or unfamiliar.

KEY POINTS

- Social conflict exists when two or more parties express differences in beliefs, values, or interests, whether the divergence is real or perceived.

- Conflict resolution refers to any means of dealing with conflict, including negotiation, mediation, and advocacy.

- Alternative forms of CR can be differentiated by: who has decision-making power; what is the role of the third party intervenor (if any); whether communication flows between conflicting parties directly or indirectly; and whether the process is adversarial or collaborative.

- Helping professionals can use elements of CR within their traditional helping roles (emergent CR). Alternatively, helping professionals can undertake explicit CR roles (contractual CR).

- CR draws upon a range of theoretical perspectives in order to analyze conflict and develop models of intervention.

DISCUSSION QUESTIONS AND EXERCISES

1. WARM UP EXERCISE: "How Long is this Class, Anyway?"—Before the class gets started, we need to decide how long the class is and how we are going to spend this time: lecture, theoretical discussion, practice role plays, videotapes, etc. Let's make this a class decision. Your mission, should you choose to accept it, is to discuss these issues and present your instructor with the decisions. You have 15 minutes.

   Debriefing Questions
   A. What strikes you most about how people dealt with this conflict?
   B. What roles did various people in the class play?
   C. What skills techniques did different people use?
   D. What made dealing with this conflict more difficult than you might have originally thought?
   E. What did you learn about how you deal with this type of conflict?

2. MEANING OF CONFLICT: This is an exercise in "free association." When you hear the word "conflict" what are the first images that come to mind? Write down three or four words that came to mind, to be shared with the class.

   Debriefing Questions
   A. Which of the words have positive connotations? Negative connotations?
   B. How do you personally feel about dealing with these different types of conflict?
   C. What is the relationship between diversity and conflict?

3. ROLES AND NEUTRALITY: Identify your role as a helping professional (e.g., teacher, therapist, vocational counselor). In the course of your work, does neutrality play a role? If so, what is this role? Does neutrality depend upon your model of practice (e.g., solution-focused, behavioral, ecosystems)? Your professional values? What does your profession's code of ethics say about neutrality?

4. MAPPING CR: During a Parent-Teacher Association meeting, two parents, Ms. Jones and Mr. Singh, complain that a boy named Kyle Bragin is bullying their children. Kyle's parents become defensive and say that lit-

tle Bonnie Jones and Rajib Singh must be lying to their parents; Kyle is a good son. As the arguments escalate, Kyle's teacher tries to separate everyone. Once tempers cool down, the school guidance counselor, Mrs. Finch, asks to meet all four parents in her office to see if there is some way they can work out this problem together. Describe the role that each person in this scenario is playing. Draw a diagram, indicating the directions of the conflicts and flows of communication between all of the parties.

5. CAT AND DOG, PART I: How do you stop a cat and a dog from fighting?
6. CAT AND DOG, PART II: In a cat and dog fight, which animal has more power? Why? Will the one with more power win the fight?

Cartoon drawn by Donato Damiano, Montreal artist

7. MANDATORY MEDIATION: Is it ethically appropriate to force people to go to mediation to resolve their conflicts?
8. UNDERLYING THEORY: Identify a theoretical perspective you are familiar with from your previous education or practice. List the key elements of this theory, including its assumptions, descriptors, and predictions about human behavior. How does this theory help you understand the nature of social conflict and how you could intervene in a constructive manner?
9. ETHICS OF VIOLENCE: When, if ever, can a helping professional justify use of violence to resolve conflict? Consider the code of ethics of your own profession and various models of practice within it. Try to come

up with an ethical rule that is based on your values. Give examples to illustrate the limits of your rule (that is, when violence is justified, and
when it is not justified).

10. PERSONAL CONFLICT RESPONSES: Assume that one of your co-
    workers, Zoey, is lazy and unreliable. When Zoey misses work or falls
    behind, Zoey's work falls into your lap. Your supervisor, Jamna, knows
    what is going on, but has done nothing about it.[20]
    Your natural reaction would be to:
    a. Do Zoey's work and avoid getting into any conflicts.
    b. Confront Zoey and Jamna in an assertive manner.
    c. Get angry and blow off steam.
    d. Bring Zoey and Jamna together to problem solve with you.
    e. Make a deal with Zoey that if she does half her work, you'll pick up
       the other half.
    f. Other (specify) _____

- What are the positive aspects of your natural response?
- What are the potential risks or problems with your natural response?
- Which of the other responses would you like to learn to do more effectively?
- If you approached Zoey to negotiate a solution, would you see Zoey as
  _____ a friend?   _____ an adversary?   _____ a professional colleague?
  _____ the cause of the problem
  _____ other? (specify) _____
- Is your primary goal
  _____ not doing Zoey's work?   _____ getting Zoey to do her fair share?
  _____ reaching agreement?   _____ reducing your anger?
  _____ developing a better relationship with Zoey?
  _____ Other?
- If you meet with Zoey, how do you begin?
  _____ Tell her you will not do her work?
  _____ Suggest a fair solution?
  _____ Tell her what you'll do if she doesn't agree?
  _____ Tell her you will go to your supervisor if she does not agree?
  _____ Take the most comfortable chair?
  _____ Therapize or counsel her?_____
  _____ Other? (specify) _____
- What is your basic strategy?
- What do you find to be the most persuasive way of influencing people
  like Zoey?

---

[20]Some of the questions below are derived from Ertel (1991).

Conflictia

The following case study provides a context for selected exercises throughout the text. The details in this case are meant to enrich the exercises and provide a real-life flavor. If you prefer to set the role-plays in your own community, develop a background information sheet that can be shared with the other students you are working with.

Conflictia is a city-state, established in the year 2001 by the League of Collaborative Nations as a pilot site for a new society in which various helping professionals have been provided with special training and expertise in conflict resolution. Conflictia is neither a Garden of Eden nor a Paradise Island. The city is populated with people who have real problems, diverse needs, and limited resources.

Approximately 600,000 people live in Conflictia. The demographics of Conflictia's population include the following:

Economic Level	Ethnic Background	Religion	Educational Level of Adults	Employment Status
8% Wealthy	33% Asian-Pacific	25% Islam	10% Less than high school (grade 12)	8% Unemployed, looking for work
15% Upper-middle economic class	10% South American	20% Buddhism	55% High school graduate	22% Unpaid, work in home
42% Middle economic class	20% North American	15% Roman Catholic	30% University degree or college diploma	16% Employed in financial and service industries
25% Marginal income and wealth	25% European	10% Protestant	5% More than one university degree	9% Employed in agriculture
10% Live below poverty line	12% African	15% Hindu		16% Employed in high technology
		2% Judaism	**Age Distribution**	12% Self-employed (business)
		1% Wicca	23% Under 18	
		12% Other	27% From 18 to 30	15% Employed in manufacturing
			40% From 31 to 65	12% Employed in helping professions
			10% Over 65	

Politically, Conflictia operates under a parliamentary democracy with a single Council of Representatives. Three parties currently hold seats in the government: 1) the Right of Center "ROC Party;" 2) the Left of Center "LOC party;" and 3) the Somewhere in the Middle "SIM Party." ROC's leader, Conne Servativ, is Head of State, by virtue of her party's majority vote in the last election. Amber Valenz is party leader for the SIMs. Sasha Lizte leads the LOCs.

Diversity Plus is the largest mental health and social service agency in Conflictia. This agency provides services to adults, children, families, and groups with problems ranging from mental illness to conflict with the law, immigration, domestic violence, drug abuse, and family planning. Diversity Plus hires a broad range of helping professionals, including psychologists, social workers, family therapists, nurses, pastoral counselors, human service workers, and youth care providers. Some services are publicly funded, based on a means test.[21] Others are fee for service.

The largest hospital in Conflictia, Conflictia Hope, has 280 beds. Conflictia Hope is a general hospital, but has special units for people with cancer, AIDS, and heart disease. Conflictia Hope employs medical doctors, nurses, psychologists, and social workers.

Two schools in the city's downtown core are Conflictia High School (grades 9 to 12) and Conflictia Elementary School (Kindergarten to Grade 8). Both schools employ teachers and guidance counselors. Conflictia Elementary offers special programs for children with emotional problems, learning disabilities, and cognitive impairments.

Conflictia Justice Center includes a variety of services for people who have breached the criminal laws of Conflictia. It employs judges, lawyers, probation officers, and other counselors. The Justice Center is mandated to promote "restorative justice," meaning that it encourages offenders to rectify damages they have caused and repair relationships with those they have hurt.

ROLE PLAY 1.1: "IN THE BUFFER"

There is trouble in Conflictia Hope Hospital. Two patients in a shared room are fighting over whether to turn the television on or off. Plato is bored and

---

[21]To be eligible for publicly funded services, family income must fall below the poverty line established by the government on an annual basis.

wants to turn the television on in order to watch a soap opera. Phineas has a headache and hates soap operas. He wants the television off. Nyron[22] is a nurse who hears them arguing and comes into the room.

To Prepare for this Role Play:

PLATO and PHINEAS: Before getting started, think about the role you are playing and how you will portray it. Write down a few notes to focus your thoughts. What is the reason for being in the hospital? What are your possible arguments for how to deal with the conflict over the television? Why has this conflict escalated into a fight? How will you respond to the nurse if the nurse acts authoritatively, meekly, etc.?

NYRON: You are going to take on two CR roles, buffer and arbitrator. Refresh your memory about these roles, if need be, by re-reading the sections on buffers and arbitrators. Write down some of your strategies and sample sentences that you might use. Do not try to memorize them. Do not bring your notes when you go into role. The notes are just a tool for preparation and reflection.

OBSERVERS: As you watch the role play, try to identify at least three strategies that Nyron uses in handling this conflict. How did the parties respond to each strategy?

Debriefing Questions:
- What did Nyron do that contributed positively to the process?
- What did Plato and Phineas appreciate about the way Nyron handled the conflict?
- What other CR approaches could a nurse use in a similar conflict situation?
- If the conflict escalated into a fight how would (or should) a police officer respond?

---

[22]Role play names can be changed to match the genders of the people playing various roles. Often, I use names beginning with the same initial as the role, in order to help you remember who is playing which role (e.g., Nyron–Nurse).

THE REFLECTIVE CR PRACTITIONER

The key distinction between helping professionals and lay helpers is that professionals make deliberate choices about how to intervene, based upon their discipline's knowledge and value bases (Schön, 1990). This applies equally for conflict resolution. Since conflict is pervasive in human interaction, everyone is constantly involved in conflict resolution. Some people have a natural aptitude for CR; others learn their CR skills through normal socialization processes (e.g., following family and cultural norms; learning how to behave within the school system). Since CR professionals are not unique in their use of CR, their advantage (if any)[1] lies in their ability to use themselves consciously, drawing from CR theory, skills, and values.

In this chapter, I focus on the process of reflection used by professionals to link theory, skills, and values with practice (Figure 2.1) (Kolb, 1974; Lewicki, 1997).

The first section, "Personal and Professional Awareness," explores ways in which you can become more conscious about how you respond to conflict situations. "Value Base" highlights the common values among CR professionals and identifies areas of disagreement among CR professionals. "Conflict Styles" provides a framework for analyzing your predominant orientation towards dealing with conflict. "Basic Skills" provides definitions of communication skills that are fundamental to all modes of CR: listening, questioning, and making statements. While these skills are common to all helping professions, the examples provided are specific to conflict situations. Your challenge is to integrate these values and skills with the theory presented throughout this text. As you read on and participate in the exercises, leave yourself time to

---

[1]Be careful about assuming that a professional is the best one to intervene in a conflict situation. In many circumstances, the parties do not trust professionals as much as others in their social systems (friends, family members, neighbors, etc.). Although this text focuses on roles of professional helpers, community developers and educators may be interested in how to instill conflict resolution skills and principles within a community context (Chetkow-Yanoov, 1997; Roderick, 1987–88).

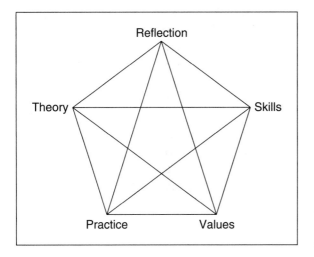

FIGURE **2.1**

Reflection Diagram

reflect back on what you have learned and to relate it to your outside experiences.

PERSONAL AND PROFESSIONAL AWARENESS

Reflection in professional practice is like looking in a mirror, except that the reflection goes beyond one's physical appearance. When practitioners reflect on themselves, they strive to become aware of how they present themselves (physically), what thoughts are going on in their mind, and what feelings are being evoked. Ideally, practitioners have a high level of self-awareness during their interventions (reflection in action). Since we are all in the process of developing greater self-awareness in the moment, we can all benefit from deliberating before an intervention and reflecting back afterwards (Pratt, 1989; Wallerstein, 1990). This process may be as simple as taking a few moments before and after an intervention to mull over thoughts and feelings in your head. Writing journals or brief descriptions of your reflections can be used to heighten your awareness, while providing a record that will enable you to review your progress over time. The exercises and inventories at the end of this chapter will also help you become aware of how you tend to respond to conflict. Finally, peer consultation or clinical supervision can support your reflective efforts. Consultants or supervisors help you identify underlying thoughts and feelings. They ask questions to raise insights and encourage you to explore areas that you might have missed. In other words, they assist with reflection by holding up the mirror so you can look more closely at yourself (Kadushin, 1992; Rich, 1993).

When conflict arises, emotions are apt to mount: anger, fear, frustration, excitement, despair, vengeance. Different people respond differently. CR professionals need to be aware of their emotions—not to squelch them, but to ensure that these feelings do not impair their ability to deal with conflict effectively. Reflection helps practitioners identify their natural emotional responses to various types of conflict, particularly what "pushes their buttons." Once awareness is raised, practitioners can strategize how to deal with difficult situations (Brinkman & Kirchner, 1994; Noonan, 1998), rather than simply lay blame. Reflection is also part of self-care for a professional. By attending to your own feelings, you can ensure that you do not become overstressed, disillusioned, or consumed by the conflicts you are working with (Grellert, 1991).

1. Emotions

In order to help others respond effectively to conflict, professionals must begin with themselves (Hunt, 1987). We use ourselves as a guide—if a situation makes you mildly angry and your client furious, you can begin to question what has caused the difference in your responses: Are you acting on different information; are your perceptions different; are you affected by the same conflict in a different manner? Given these differences, an intervention that works for you may not work for the client.

Anger is one of the most pervasive emotions in conflict situations. Depending on how we use anger, it can energize us towards either constructive or destructive responses. If we try to hold anger in, it will tend to build inside and come out in ways that we have no control over: for example, headaches or other somatic responses, passive-aggressive behavior, or conflict avoidance. Conversely, if we ventilate or dump our anger on another person, then we are likely to exacerbate the conflict. If we can learn to channel our anger towards dealing with the rudimental problems, then it acts as a positive force.

If you are angry about something, consider the underlying source of the anger. Anger is a secondary emotion (Picard, 1998). For example, your anger at a client may be rooted in frustration with the client's lack of progress in therapy. Your anger at a supervisor may be derived from fear that the supervisor will chastise you for making a mistake. Your anger at colleagues who are leaving your agency may be caused by feeling hurt or abandoned. Once you identify the underlying emotion, you can begin to process it. This could mean letting the client know you feel frustrated by the lack of progress made in therapy, asking your supervisor for support rather than censure, or letting your colleagues know that you will miss them. This allows you to take responsibility for your own anger, while communicating your underlying feelings in a non-threatening manner.

Display of emotions varies depending on the model of intervention. A psychoanalyst presents with little emotion, allowing clients to open up and transfer their feelings onto an empathic, nonjudgmental listener. A motivational educator, in contrast, presents with excitement and dramatic techniques in order to sell the message. Similarly, different models of CR work best with different types of emotional expression. Mediators who want to demonstrate impartiality avoid displaying pleasure or displeasure with one party or the other. Advocates who want to persuade decision-makers might use emotional displays to win sympathy. Negotiators who prefer not to tip their hand (e.g., disclose their bottom line) mute their expressions of emotion. Certainly, different situations call for differential use of self. As you develop your own style of CR, remember to build on your strengths. Some negotiators are more effective when they approach conflict calmly and rationally. Others are more effective when they express their exuberance, umbrage, or fear. How you display emotions should also take the other person's cultural norms into account.

2. Cultural Awareness

Because culture affects the way people understand and respond to conflict, CR professionals must become aware of their cultural predilections. Rather than prescribing a singular approach to CR, this text presents an array of approaches. This allows practitioners to select CR approaches that are consonant with their own cultural attitudes and norms. Cultural awareness also helps practitioners select CR approaches that are culturally appropriate for the people they are dealing with.

As a Canadian, I know that my country of origin values "peace, order, and good government." These terms are written into the Constitution and form the basis for Canada's justice system. When working with CR practitioners in Israel, I became keenly aware of how my "Canadianness" set me apart from most Israelis. On the surface, Israeli responses to conflict seemed argumentative, confrontational, and chaotic. Conversely, many Israelis saw me as nice and even-tempered, but too naïve and indirect. I had to learn how to interpret Israeli interactions from their cultural perspectives and how to adapt CR approaches to fit with the cultural common sense in Israel. As an Israeli colleague noted after one of my workshops:

> When I hear you talk about conflict resolution, it all seems to make so much sense. But when I try to translate it in my head from English to Hebrew, it doesn't seem to work. I can't just translate it word for word.

I also had to learn not to take on any airs of cultural superiority. It is not that Israelis have disdain for peace, order, or good government; however, they tend to have different patterns of interacting and implementing these constructs. By reflecting on my experiences, I was able to identify areas of similarity, as well as areas of difference. In the process of learning about other cultures, I became more conscious of my own.

3. Conscious and Artistic Use of Self

Many models of CR, including some presented in this text, provide practitioners with explicit stages, strategies, and techniques for intervention. While these guidelines provide a secure framework and manageable steps for developing professionals, CR is not simply a technical intervention. Professionals need artistry to implement CR in creative and flexible manners (Birkhoff & Warfield, 1997). While some writers argue that artistic ability is an innate talent, I believe that artistry can be developed through reflective processes. Through self-reflection, CR practitioners learn to intervene in conflict consciously and deliberately. The magic of CR occurs when practitioners go beyond techniques and discover elegant interventions befitting the unique conflict situation.

VALUE BASE

Values are priorities. They indicate our preferences about what is good or important to us. As CR professionals, values guide both our goals and the means to those goals. Who you are on the inside determines much of how you will implement skills and intervene in conflict. If you value peace, then the model of practice you select will be directed to meet this goal. Ideally, the model uses peaceful means to bring about peace. If not, can you justify using nonpeaceful means, fighting, to bring about peace (Corey, Corey, & Callahan, 1993; Loewenberg & Dolgoff, 1996)? CR theory and practice must be predicated on values, and not simply what research proves to be effective.

1. In Search of Common Values

Given the breadth of CR models and the range of backgrounds among CR professionals, it would be misleading to say there is a common value base of CR. A common value base does exist among practitioners who favor collaborative, non-violent conflict resolution. These professionals are guided by the values of peace, respect for diversity, consensus building, and community (MacFarlane, 1996). Some people find professionals of this ilk to be optimistic, perhaps even naïvely so. However, a good part of CR is selling the process to conflicting parties. When conveyed in a genuine manner, the confidence and idealism of CR professionals inspires clients to strive for similar ideals.

An elderly man is mugged by a young thug. The man feels violated, humiliated, dismayed and vengeful. The last thing on his mind is to have a chance to meet face-to-face with the thug and talk things out. What can a CR practitioner offer the man?

> People are basically good. Right now you are wondering how I could possibly say this about the youth who mugged you. Perhaps you are right. But what do you really know about him? What does he know about you? Would you like the opportunity to tell him who you are and how you feel about what he has done? Do you think he would have mugged you if he knew who you were?

It would be hypocritical for CR practitioners to say that all CR professionals must have the same values—if we respect diversity, then this includes diversity within the field. In fact, there are significant debates within CR about a number of values, including privacy, satisfaction, social justice, empowerment, and recognition. Most helping professionals ascribe to the ethic of confidentiality; that is, a professional who learns personal information from a client will keep that information private, unless the client consents to release such information. Many CR professionals argue that one of the advantages of mediation and negotiation is that they are confidential processes. This allows parties to work out their differences in a safe environment, without having to worry about how others will respond. Some CR professionals, however, raise concerns that conflicts should remain in the public domain. Court, for example, is open to the public in order to ensure open accountability. In addition, decisions made in one case can be used as precedents to support decisions in similar cases in the future. Under this concept of justice, fairness is achieved when like cases are decided alike. When negotiations, mediation, or other CR processes are closed to the public, accountability is more difficult to gauge and precedent cases are not made known to society (Freshman, 1997). When you are deciding whether your CR process should be open or closed to the public, the extent to which you value client privacy must be factored in.

2. Satisfaction, Social Justice, and Transformation

Bush and Folger (1994) suggest that there are three different value orientations for mediation: satisfaction, social justice, and transformation.[2] The Satisfaction Story is predicated on the belief that mediation satisfies people's needs and interests. Through mediation people are able to resolve their differences informally, amicably, and in a manner which produces mutually

---

[2]Bush and Folger also identify a fourth orientation, oppression, which suggests that mediation is not a valid means of CR. The oppression perspective is described in Chapter 1 in relation to radical practitioners.

agreeable solutions. The Social Justice Story is based on the notion that mediation organizes individuals around common issues and promotes stronger social ties. This provides the community with an opportunity to organize disadvantaged groups in order to challenge the power brokers and promote social justice. The Transformation Story suggests that the promise of mediation is its capacity to transform conflicting parties and society as a whole. Bush and Folger identify two components of transformation: empowerment and recognition. Empowerment refers to the ability of mediation to promote client self-determination, choice and autonomy. Recognition refers to the ability of mediation to enhance interpersonal communication and empathic understanding among conflicting parties. Depending upon which orientation you accept, your choice of models of CR will vary significantly. When you approach a conflict, what do you value? What is your ultimate goal for the process? Any resolution of the conflict? A fair solution? An efficient solution? Social harmony? An enduring solution? In case you have not noticed, I have avoided presenting a definitive answer. As you work through the readings and exercises, you will develop your own value base for CR.

3. Attitude toward Power

Although most helping professions believe in a client's right to self-determination, various professionals have different attitudes towards the use of power in their work. At one extreme, some professionals see themselves as impartial facilitators; that is, professionals who support clients to fulfill their goals in a nondirective manner. In contrast, other professionals believe that they are justified and perhaps, required to use their power to influence the way clients and others make decisions.

A professional's attitude towards the use of power may depend upon the situation. For example, a child protection worker will remove a child from a family if there is immediate risk to the child's welfare. If, however, the child's immediate safety is assured, the worker will try to work with the family on a voluntary basis.

Reflect upon your own attitudes towards the use of power in your type of work. When are you more likely to exert your influence? When are you less likely to do so? Understanding your attitudes towards power will help you decide upon the types of CR roles and models of intervention that you will use. For example, a liberal-minded family therapist is more likely to encourage family members to come up with their own solutions to family conflicts. A radical feminist therapist is more likely to influence decisions by altering the power balance in the family to give the women more power. An administrator with an egalitarian style is likely to share power with others in the organization. An authoritarian administrator will use decision-making power without inviting input from others. As you explore various approaches to CR, consider the role of power and how it fits with your own attitude towards power.

4. Professional Ethics

Professional values are often expressed in professional codes of ethics. The same is true in many areas of CR. There is not one code for all CR, or even for any branch of CR such as negotiation or mediation. If you are practicing CR as part of your other professional identification (e.g., youth worker, psychologist, teacher), you are bound by the code of ethics of that profession, if any. Some professions, including social work, have articulated specific policies for members who practice CR (NASW, 1991). In certain realms of CR practice such as family mediation, CR associations have developed their own codes of ethics (Academy of Family Mediators, 1998; Family Mediation Canada, 1996). In most jurisdictions, membership in a CR association and adherence to its code of ethics is voluntary. This means that CR professionals who wish to operate on a different set of standards and values do not have to belong to any association. No wonder that you will find CR professionals with very different values. Sample codes of ethics are provided in Appendix 2. Note the differences and similarities between them. Note further, how many values questions are open for interpretation.

CONFLICT STYLES

"Conflict style" refers to one's preferred response or natural inclination when faced with conflict. Certainly, people respond differently to different types of conflict situations; however, people do have general tendencies to respond to conflict in particular manners. The Thomas-Killman Conflict Mode Instrument (1974)[3] helps CR professionals determine their own preferences, as well as those of others they are working with. By assessing your own conflict style, you can develop greater control over how you respond to particular conflict situations. By assessing others' conflict styles, you can determine appropriate interventions (e.g., how to persuade them; how to encourage them to use different approaches to conflict).

---

[3]The Thomas-Killmann Instrument is one of the more popular frameworks among CR professionals for analyzing conflict styles, but it is certainly not the only one. The Myers Briggs Scale (M
1987), for example, is an interpersonal styles inventory commonly used in business setting
Taxonomies of management styles also provide frameworks to analyze interactions with pe
have different preferred modes of operating: Introverts—Extroverts, Sensors—Intuitive:
Thinkers—Feelers, and Judging—Perceiving (Nicoterra, 1995). See Appendix 2 (Resour
addresses to order copies of either of these instruments.

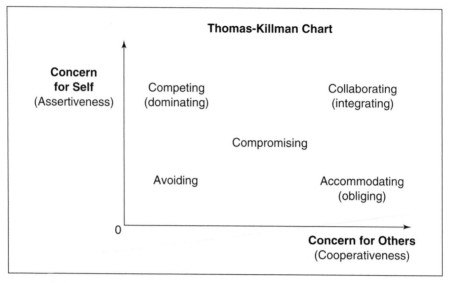

FIGURE **2.2**

Thomas-Killman Chart

The Thomas-Killman Instrument begins with the proposition that there are two primary orientations towards conflict resolution, assertiveness and cooperativeness. Figure 2.2 describes these dimensions as concern for self (assertiveness) and concern for others (cooperativeness).

1. Avoiders

The bottom-left quadrant of the diagram describes avoiders, people who are low on concern for self and low on concern for others. Avoiders may deny that conflict exists, consciously or non-consciously. Alternatively, they acknowledge that conflict exists, but do what they can to avert or withdraw from conflict. By avoiding conflict, they tend to satisfy neither their own needs nor the needs of others. I forgot to write a letter of reference for a student. When the student calls, I do not answer and do not call back. I avoid having any conflict with the student (at least for now), but I really do not satisfy either of our needs.

2. Accommodators

The bottom-right quadrant, accommodators, denotes people who have low concern for their own needs and high concern for the needs of others. Accommodators value positive relationships with others. They go out of their way to please others, even at the expense of their own needs. My boss asks me to stay late to complete a work plan and budget for a project. I am tired, but agree to stay late tonight and even offer to work through the weekend. My boss will be happy, but I'll be exhausted.

3. Competitors

The top-left quadrant, competitors, characterizes people who are low on concern for the needs of others, but high on concern for their own needs. Competitors are out to win. They exert power to influence others or impose their will. Personal success is important. Amicable relationships with others are not. A professional colleague disagrees with my assessment of a client. I respond by pointing out all of the errors in my colleague's thinking. Even if I am right, at what cost to my colleague and to our relationship?

4. Compromisers

The middle section of the diagram, compromisers, demonstrates people who pay some attention to the needs of others and some attention to their own needs. They opt for solutions that are partial wins, for themselves and for others. Unfortunately, compromises are also partial losses for themselves and for the others. The solutions may be fair, but nobody is completely satisfied. I want government to provide full public funding for mediation services. Government balks. I suggest a compromise that government subsidize up to half of the cost for people whose income is below the poverty line. If government accepts, at least I have achieved part of what I set out to accomplish. Compromise tends to foster better relationships than competition, but not as good as collaboration.

5. Collaborators

The final quadrant, collaborators, illustrates people who have high concern for their own needs, as well as for the needs for others. They seek out solutions that are "win-win" (i.e., mutually beneficial). Collaborators encourage joint problem-solving. A client claims I have breached my obligation to keep information confidential. I invite the client in to discuss these concerns and to see if there is a way to work things out in an amicable fashion.

6. Selective Use of Styles

Given the structure of this model, you might conclude that we should all be striving towards collaboration. However, different conflict styles are useful for different purposes. Avoidance, for instance, seems to satisfy nobody's needs. Yet many of us use, and could use, avoidance strategies in certain situations. A member of a therapy group is whispering to a neighbor. The whispering is disruptive, but you may decide to ignore it because it is not important enough to confront at this time. Pick your fights, as well as your efforts at collaboration. Collaboration has its costs: time, energy, mental fatigue. Sometimes, avoidance is just easier than dealing with the conflict.

Accommodation is useful when the relationship is more important than the particular dispute. An involuntary client[4] comes in for the first time and demands a break for a cigarette. You are very busy, but you accommodate the client. Confronting the client now may be counterproductive until you have built some rapport. Accommodation can be used as a strategy—if you accommodate someone now, that person may feel more obliged to accommodate you later. Of course, accommodation can lead the other person to continue to expect accommodations. Accommodation is particularly useful when the issue is much more important to the other person than it is to you.

Competition may be required to protect oneself from immediate dangers (self-defense) and to respond to others who are competitive. A landowner is planning to demolish a building, leaving your clients homeless. You have offered to meet with the landlord and clients to work things out, but the landlord does not respond. You refer the clients to a lawyer to help them with a court action to stop the demolition. Unfortunately, people often give in to competition without giving the other alternatives a sufficient chance to work. As you will see in later chapters, there are many strategies to move people from competitive styles to more collaborative ones. If competitors can see that they lose nothing through collaboration, then they may be persuaded to try it.

Exercise 4 (below) provides other conflict situations and asks you to identify which type of conflict style is most appropriate.

To some extent, conflict styles are culturally determined. For example, Americans tend to have a higher degree of competing style; Chinese individuals tend to have a higher degree of avoiding and obliging styles (Rahim & Blum, 1994). Whereas western cultures place high value on individual rights and freedoms, Chinese culture places high value on harmony and community. Within western cultures, women tend to be more accommodating than men. This results from socialization processes, where women are encouraged to care for their families and men are encouraged to be successful in a competitive work environments. CR practitioners need to be able to recognize these types of cultural and gender differences, as well as within-group variations. Consider, for instance, when people who tend toward accommodation are placed in a conflict with people who are competitive. Do you encourage

---

[4]An involuntary client is a client who is required to attend counseling or other helping services; for example, someone convicted of a criminal offense or suspected of child abuse who must go for counseling services. The client would not have sought services unless there were legal consequences or other sanctions.

people to use their traditional styles? If not, are you showing disrespect for their traditional norms and values?

Some theorists question whether conflict styles are fixed personality types or predispositions that vary depending upon the situation (Nicoterra, 1995). Most CR models of intervention assume that conflict styles are not fixed: CR professionals can use different styles depending on the needs of the situation; they can also encourage others to move from one conflict style to another.

BASIC SKILLS

Skills are the doing part of CR: how you behave, how you communicate, how you interact with others in the conflict. Skills translate your theoretical knowledge and value base into what you do in practice. All conflict interventions are based on how you present yourself, verbally and physically. In this section, I introduce communication skills that are basic to virtually all forms of CR.[5] In the chapters on negotiation, mediation, and advocacy, I describe how to use these skills with particular CR models and identify other skills that are specific to each model. The fundamental communication skills are listening, questioning, and making statements. I also touch upon some special issues for written communication in CR.

1. Listening

Active listening refers to the intentional use of self in order to demonstrate to a speaker that you have heard and understood what the speaker has said. If you listen passively, you may have heard and understood the speaker, but the speaker has no way of knowing this. Empathic listening can be demonstrated through the use of attending, paraphrasing, reflecting feelings, and summarizing (Ivey & Ivey, 1999).

Attending skills comprise behavioral, non-verbal responses to indicate listening and understanding: leaning forward, maintaining regular eye contact, nodding one's head, constructive use of silence, etc. Facial expressions should be consonant with the messages that are being conveyed (for example, smiling at good news). Utterances, such as "uh-huh" and "mm-hmm" are attending skills, but these can be distracting. Accordingly, utterances should be used sparingly, if at all. Vocal qualities, such as the pitch, pace, and fluidity, can also be used to demonstrate interest and understanding in what is being said.

---

[5]For more detailed explanations of communication skills, see Ivey & Ivey, 1999; Nichols, 1995; or Barone & Switzer, 1995.

Some people find intentional use of silence to be the most difficult skill, particularly in a conflict situation. To novice practitioners, silence feels like a non-response. However, silence is a very powerful tool. Silence breaks up the flow of communication. In the heat of the moment, people may need time for feelings to de-escalate. Silence demonstrates to others that you are taking time to think. It also gives the other person time to think about what they have said. Cooler heads may prevail. Within some cultures, silence also demonstrates respect.

Attending behaviors are particularly important in CR, because people often mirror the expressions and behaviors of those around them. "Smile and the whole world smiles with you," goes the cliché. Though this is far from an absolute truth, you can either escalate or de-escalate conflict through the use of particular attending behaviors. If someone starts to yell, rather than raise your voice, try speaking softly. Besides catching the other person off guard, you are modeling the type of behavior you hope the other will adopt. If people are flailing their arms in anger, try to restrain your gestures.

Although attending skills are important, nonverbal cues are often difficult to interpret. Verbal listening skills provide the speaker with explicit feedback about how you are receiving their messages. Paraphrasing refers to restating what the speaker has said. A paraphrase can be constructed with words that are similar to those used by the speaker or with words that are quite different, but still conveying the same message. The following exchange between an addictions counselor (Agnes) and her client (Clara) demonstrates how Agnes can use both types of paraphrasing.

> CLARA: *Don't tell me that I have to stop drinking.*
> AGNES: *You don't want me to tell you that you have to stop drinking.*
> CLARA: *Darn right! You think it's easy just to get up one morning and never pick up a bottle again.*
> AGNES: *I guess you're telling me that I do not know how hard giving up alcohol would be for you.*

Paraphrasing shows people that you understand what they think and believe. Reflection of feeling is similar to paraphrasing, but indicates that you understand the person's affect or emotions. You can reflect back feelings that are explicit in the person's statement, or ones which can be implied from the way the person presents the message.

> CLARA: *When I come to see you, I just get more depressed.*
> AGNES: *You feel discouraged when you come here.*
> CLARA: [sobbing]: *I don't know what else you want from me.*
> AGNES: *I can see how sad you feel right now.*

Whereas paraphrasing restates what someone has just completed saying, the skill of summarizing refers to restating what the person has said over a longer time frame. To summarize, highlight the key messages presented by the person throughout that period.

> AGNES: *Let me see if I understand what you've been telling me, Clara. You don't think that I should be telling you to stop drinking, because I do not know how hard that would really be. I haven't been very helpful. In fact, you feel more depressed since you've been coming to see me. Anything else you want to add?*

Summarizing, reflecting, and paraphrasing lets people know how accurately, or inaccurately, you have understood them. The tone and wording of your questions should invite the person to give you feedback and correct any inaccuracies. You are not telling the person what they think or feel. You are asking (implicitly) whether you understand how they think or feel. This clarifies communication, pre-empting further conflict.

Effective listening requires accurate observation and interpretation skills. Remember that a simple message goes through a series of stages before you can respond to it. When you hear someone speak, you need to determine what the speaker means. Pay attention to verbal, as well as non-verbal cues. A client may call you a wonderful helping professional. Depending on the client's tone of voice and facial expressions, you may take this as a complement (the client is being genuine) or as an insult (the client is being sarcastic). In order to become more deliberate about this decoding process, try to separate out your direct observations (the client is smiling) and possible interpretations (the client is happy, nervous, or hiding something).

Effective listening is absolutely crucial to CR. When faced with conflict, people often become defensive. They feel the need to refute the message they received and tell their own story. This exacerbates the problem, because the other side now feels defensive and responds in kind, perhaps even more forcefully. Consider the following sequence between two children playing in a sandbox.

> CHUCKIE: *Hey, you threw sand in my face!*
> CHELSEA: *No, I didn't.*
> CHUCKIE: *Yes, you did!*
> CHELSEA: *No, I didn't!!!*
> CHUCKIE: *Yes, you did!!!!*

What better than a strong argument to win a debate? Ironically, one of the most persuasive techniques for persuading others is to listen to them. Active listening demonstrates to others that you have really heard them. People who feel they have been heard are more apt to listen to you. When faced with a conflict, show the others that you understand "(a) that they feel strongly, (b) what they feel strongly about, and (c) why they feel strongly about it"

(Gould & Gould, 1988).[6] Note what happens if Chelsea listens rather than fights back.

CHELSEA: *Hold on a minute. You're very angry.*
CHUCKIE: *Yes, you're mean.*
CHELSEA: *You're very angry at me.*
CHUCKIE: *Of course, I'm angry.*
CHELSEA: *You're angry because you think I threw sand at you on purpose.*
CHUCKIE: *Well, didn't you?*

You may think this example is too contrived; however, a little active listening can move conflict a long way toward peaceful resolution.

Remember the cultural components to communication. Words, vocal qualities, gestures, and facial expressions have different meanings among different cultures. Familiarity with the other person's culture will help you interpret their language and nonverbal behavior so that you can convey messages in culturally appropriate manners (LeBaron Duryea, 1994). For example, active listening may be inappropriate in certain cultural contexts. If status and hierarchy are the norm within a particular culture, a subordinate may offend a supervisor by using paraphrase and reflection of feeling. Rather, the subordinate can demonstrate interest and respect by listening silently and using appropriate nonverbal responses (e.g., head nods, restrained eye contact). Once again, the point of this discussion is not to prescribe a particular type of interaction, but to make practitioners aware of the choice of skills and how they can influence dealing with conflict.

2. Questioning

Questions are useful for finding out other's thoughts and inviting people's participation in a dialogue ("What do you think?"). If you are gathering information for an assessment or evaluation, remember to cover the five "w's": who, what, where, when and why. However, questions are intrusive. Think how you feel if someone peppers you with a series of questions. Novice interviewers tend to overuse questions, rather than engage people in a more natural conversation. You can encourage people to open up and be frank through active listening skills much more readily than through a succession of questions.

Questions can be either open or closed. Open questions encourage respondents to answer in their own words, without limiting their choices. Closed questions give respondents a limited choice of answers, for example, "yes" or "no." Compare the following examples.

---

[6]The power of effective listening is beautifully demonstrated by in a videotape, Gould & Gould's (1988) *From No to Yes*. This film is part of an entertaining series of management education videotapes by John Cleese. Although the context is business, the lessons are directly relevant to the helping professionals.

1. Closed: Do you support the Pro-Choice stance on abortion?
   Open: What are your views about the Pro-Choice stance on abortion?
2. Closed: Which value is more important, individual freedom or safety?
   Open: How do you prioritize values such as freedom and safety?

Closed questions are useful when you want to know specific information or when you want to encourage the respondent to provide a brief answer. Open questions are useful when you want to encourage the respondent to open up and when you do not want to limit the range of possible answers. In number 1 above, the closed question suggests that there are only two possible positions: supporting Pro-Choice and opposing Pro-Choice. In fact, the respondent may have an alternate position (e.g., conditional support; or support for a stance which neither opposes nor accepts the Pro-Choice position). The open form of the question does not box the respondent into an artificial choice. Dichotomies tend to reinforce argument and lock people into sides. Inviting discussion about many points of view tends to open up dialogue.

In CR, the clarity of questions is vital. People with opposing views often misinterpret one another, imputing false motivations on one another. If a patient advocate asks a nurse, "When can the patient return home?" the nurse could interpret this in two ways: what needs to happen before the patient is discharged; or on what day and at what time will the patient be discharged. If the nurse assumes the advocate is asking for a specific date and he does not know the date, then he may think the request is unreasonable. If the advocate wanted to know, "What needs to happen before discharge," then a more specific request would ease communication.

Questions should be worded in a nonjudgmental manner so that clients do not feel they are being challenged or blamed. If you ask a new client, "Why were you late for your appointment?" the client may interpret this as a personal affront. To avoid putting the client on the defensive, you could try, "Did you have any trouble finding our office?"

Finally, statements should not be disguised as questions. If I ask a student if she would like to present her assignment to the class, this suggests that I am giving her an option to say yes or no. If I want her to present her assignment, I should say so directly. People who are conflict avoiders or accommodators tend to use questions rather than state opinions or make direct requests. In order to be more assertive, they need to let the other person know what they really think or want. Being assertive does not mean being aggressive or nasty.

3. *Making Statements*

Statements are used to provide facts or opinions. Facts connote objective truth, whereas opinions connote an individual's subjective reality. Without getting into a philosophical debate about truth and reality, people often state personal opinions as if they were universally accepted facts. In CR, separating facts and opinions can be used to deconstruct conflicts. If I say, "This student has a severe learning disability," I am presenting it as fact. If you have a contrary assessment, I have just insulted you because I have suggested that you don't know simple truth. If I state my assessment as an opinion, I can acknowledge that your opinion is different, but not necessarily wrong. Once we acknowledge that there is a legitimate difference of professional opinions, we can work together in a more collegial fashion (Fisher & Brown, 1988).

As with questions, statements should be clear and nonjudgmental. If you want the other person to accept the truth in what you are saying, say it in terms that are easy for the other person to understand and accept. Assume Lionel is a liberal psychiatrist speaking with Cassie, a conservative community worker. If Lionel speaks in the language of a liberal psychiatrist, his message may be doomed to failure. Consider the following example.

> LIONEL: *We need to establish affirmative action programs for people with major disorders on the first DSM axis in order to provide them with equal access to job opportunities.*

First, the community worker may not be familiar with the term "major disorders on the first DSM axis." Cassie is more likely to understand "mental illness." As someone who identifies as a conservative, Cassie is also likely to reject anything related to "affirmative action." To Cassie, this sounds like reverse discrimination. If Lionel uses terminology that is familiar to Cassie, the probability of her hearing and accepting his message increases. Lionel can refer back to points that Cassie has made, showing that he has heard her and is building on her perspectives (Gould & Gould, 1988), as follows:

> LIONEL: *You seem to be concerned about the fairness of requiring businesses to hire people with mental illness. On the other hand, I don't think you're saying that these people should not be working. I'm wondering if we can figure out ways to improve access to jobs for people with mental illness, without imposing unfair restrictions on businesses.*

The trick is to learn how to speak persuasively and assertively, without coming across as combative or presumptuous. Use "I" statements to explain your thoughts and feelings: "I feel incensed about . . ." or "I believe the problem resulted from . . ." These types of statements let people know where you are coming from, without imposing your thoughts or feelings on others. When you offer ideas or opinions, explain the facts upon which they were based. If there is disagreement, you do not have to back down. You can make your points firmly, but stay respectful and amicable (Gould & Gould, 1988). Avoid blatant rejections of the other person's ideas. Rather than, "That's ludicrous," try "I look at the problem from a different perspective . . ."

Remember to use active listening and questioning, even for the purposes of persuasion. Active listening encourages the speaker to trust you and open up to your ideas. Questions can be used to facilitate insights. Rather than tell a client to leave an abusive relationship, ask the client questions about the patterns of abuse and whether the client thinks the abuse will stop. Even though you are encouraging the client to leave, you are respecting the client's right to decide whether and when to leave.

When in doubt about what to say next during a conflict situation, use listening skills (including silence). Asking questions and making statements are more risky.

4. Written Communication

Although general writing skills are important in CR, they really go beyond the scope of this book. For classic texts on effective writing, consider Strunk and White (1995), Williams (1996), and the publication manual of the American Psychological Association. In this section, I highlight concerns related to CR strategies. In later chapters, I describe writing skills that are required for certain models of CR; for example, using neutral language as a mediator; using persuasive language as an advocate (Kaminski & Walmsley, 1995).

Some people are more comfortable with oral communication, others with written. Oral communication is generally more informal, flexible, and timely. Written communication provides the writer with more time to think about what to say and how to say it; the reader also has more time to read and interpret it.[7] In CR situations, your choice of written, oral, or combined forms of communication should be made with strategic purposes in mind.

With written communication, the writer has the benefit of more time to ensure that the messages are conveyed clearly, concisely, and nonjudgmentally. The reader can deliberate over the message before responding. Written communication also makes it easier for both parties to use advocates or consultants to help them interpret and respond to messages.

Because the reader retains a record of the communication, writing can have a powerful effect on the reader. This can be a plus or a minus. If you make a mistake while talking, the mistake may be passed by or easily forgotten. If you make a mistake in writing, the problem takes on a higher level of significance. Documentation provides a fixed record of communication that can be used as (a) a framework for implementation of agreements or (b) evidence in procedures to resolve future conflicts.

Technological advancements—including fax, e-mail, and the Internet—have meant that people can communicate through writing instantaneously, cheaply, and to broad audiences. These advancements can enhance CR in

---

[7]Levels of formality and pacing do vary. In some cases—such as court trials—oral communication is very formal. With e-mail and other technologies, written communication is often informal and instantaneous.

terms of providing new channels for sharing ideas, exchanging information, and promoting causes. Unfortunately, many conflicts have been exacerbated by miscommunications made through these technologies; for example, confidential e-mail messages being sent to people by mistake, hurtful messages sent in the heat of anger, and messages that are easily misinterpreted because the sender was more concerned about sending the message quickly than accurately. Using communication technology tends to be more impersonal than face-to-face exchanges. People often convey insulting messages through technology that they would never dream of conveying in person. In addition, written communication does not convey emotions in the same manner as oral communication (Tannen, 1998). Consider a counselor who has just had a difficult interview and e-mails her supervisor, "This client is crazy and should be locked up." If this message were conveyed in person, the supervisor might realize that the counselor is joking and blowing off steam. Although the statement may come across as judgmental, the statement looks even worse when it is transmitted via e-mail. E-mail does not convey the worker's sense of frustration or intention to be funny. Because of the potential for miscommunication, be particularly cautious with humor in written communication.

All communication skills require deliberate choices about how to present yourself, orally, behaviorally, and in writing. Although professionals try to minimize miscommunications, errors are apt to happen and further conflict may result. Remember that communication is not just a one-time event; it is ongoing. If miscommunication occurs, bring the parties together to clarify everyone's understandings. As noted earlier, blaming one side or another for miscommunication does little to resolve it. The focuses need to be on how to fix the problem and how to prevent it from re-occurring.

KEY POINTS

- Reflective conflict resolution professionals are defined by their ability to link CR theory, values, and skills.
- Reflection refers to the process of becoming aware of one's use of self, including thoughts, feelings, and behaviors presented during an intervention.
- Reflection includes developing awareness of one's own culture, enabling the practitioner to recognize differences with clients or others, so that responses to conflict can be adapted for diverse cultural contexts.
- Choice of models of CR depends upon one's value base, the goals one aspires to as a professional.
- A practitioner's attitude towards power will determine how facilitative or how directive that practitioner will be when intervening in conflict situations.

- Although CR does not have a value base common to all practitioners, collaborative, non-violent CR is based on the values of peace, respect for diversity, consensus building, and community.
- Individuals tend to favor one of five conflict styles: avoiding, accommodating, competing, compromising, or collaborating.
- Different situations require CR professionals to adopt different conflict styles.
- Effective communication skills are integral to all CR processes.
- Listening skills are particularly important in CR to demonstrate understanding to other parties and to clarify any misunderstandings.
- Clear, concise, and nonjudgmental language pre-empts conflict and fosters effective communication.

DISCUSSION QUESTIONS AND EXERCISES

1. WATCH AND SEE: Observe a segment of a movie or television program in which there is a conflict. Ensure that you watch the process leading up to the conflict, as well as what follows the conflict. Identify the sequence of non-verbal communication between the parties. (a) What are your direct observations? (b) How do you interpret them? (c) What are some other possible interpretations for the observations that you made? (d) How did the other party interpret this communication?

   Use the following example for your format.

   a) OBSERVATION 1: A vein pulsing on Kelly's left temple.
   b) INTERPRETATION: Kelly was angry at Maude.
   c) ALTERNATE INTERPRETATION: Kelly was hyped up from having just run upstairs.
   d) OTHER PARTY: Did not seem to notice.

2. PERSONAL VALUES INVENTORY: Consider the following list of values.

   - Peace
   - Harmony
   - Respect for other people
   - Personal privacy
   - Personal security
   - Life
   - Mental health
   - Physical health
   - Wisdom
   - Mutual understanding
   - Family

- Work
- Financial success
- Winning
- Amicable relationships
- Personal privacy
- Upholding laws
- Community welfare
- Other (specify) _____

Divide these values into three groups: Value Highly, Value Moderately, Value Little. Within each group, rank order each value, with 1 being the highest value, 2 the next highest, etc.

   After you have completed this exercise individually, try to come up with a rank ordering that represents the class's highest five values. First, divide the class into small groups (3 to 5 per group), and have each group come up with its own list. When each group has come to a consensus, have one representative from each group get together and work out a list of values that represents the whole class. At each stage, try to work on a consensus basis (i.e., try to build agreement among all participants). If after 15 minutes, agreement does not look possible, use majority votes to settle differences.

   DEBRIEFING QUESTIONS: What were the most difficult parts of this exercise? Did any of your personal rankings change as you moved into group decision making? If so, what led to these changes?

   DIARIZE: Mark two dates in your calendar, one near the middle of this course and one near the end. On each of these dates, reflect back to your values list. Consider whether any of your values have changed and keep track of these changes in writing.

3. CULTURAL AWARENESS: Identify three cultural groups to which you belong (e.g., by nationality, ethnic background, race, religion, sex, sexual orientation, or political viewpoint). Analyze how each of these three groups deals with various issues raised in this chapter: anger, display of emotions, power, and use of various communication skills. How do you think your culture affects the way you deal with conflict? If you are not sure about your culture's attitudes towards some of these issues, interview relatives or others from your cultural groups. For further information, conduct a literature search particular your cultural groups (Irving & Benjamin, 1995; LeBaron, 1997).

4. CONFLICT STYLES IDENTIFICATION: This exercise is designed to help you identify your predominant style(s) of handling conflict. Identify three situations where you have been faced with a conflict: one with a family member, one with a co-worker or classmate, and one with a client. Before reading on, write down a brief description of what happened in each situation.

In each of the three situations, identify the manner in which you dealt with the conflict: avoidance, accommodation, competition, compromise, or collaboration.

Are there any patterns in the way that you deal with conflict? Does it depend on the situation? Which conflict styles give you the greatest difficulty? Refer back to your answers to exercise 10 in Chapter 1—are the conflict styles identified in that exercise consistent with the ones you have identified in this exercise? If there are differences, how do you explain them?

5. CONFLICT STYLES SCENARIOS: For each of the following scenarios, select the most appropriate conflict style and provide reasons for selecting that type of response.

   a) You are the administrator of a social agency and you need to decide how much money should be spent on paper clips.
   b) A client threatens to commit suicide.
   c) A colleague wants to go to a family member's wedding and asks you to take his shift. You want to go to a movie that night.
   d) You support a client's right to choose euthanasia. A colleague says she opposes euthanasia.
   e) You are working with a student who you believe dresses inappropriately.
   f) Your professional association says that a client has raised a complaint against you for malpractice.
   g) You tell a client who is concerned about HIV that HIV testing is done on an anonymous basis. You find out that the test is not truly anonymous and wonder whether to tell the client.
   h) The agency which funds your services tells you it is cutting your budget by 5%.
   i) You are facilitating a therapy group. One group member is constantly late and another says the late person should be thrown out of the group.

6. WORLD'S WORST CR: This is your opportunity to show how bad a CR professional you can be. Write down five things that you think run counter to everything you know so far about good conflict resolution skills. Designate one person to play a helping professional, working with a couple of newlyweds. The couple is arguing about whether to keep the toilet seat up, or down, after use. The helping professional will intervene using the list of five rotten CR skills as much as possible. Observers should take note of what strategies and techniques the helping professional uses. Have fun with the role-play. [about 5 minutes of role-playing]

   DEBRIEFING: Refer back to the section on Feedback in Chapter 1 to refresh your memory about giving and receiving feedback. (a) Helping professional, what horrible techniques did you try to use; how did the couple respond to them? (b) Couple, how did you feel when the helping professional . . . (c) Observers, in spite of your colleague's best attempts at being horrible, what effective CR skills did your colleague demonstrate? [repeat exercise with a new person taking on the helping role]

7. LISTENING: For each of the following client statements, provide an example of reflection of feeling or paraphrase:

   a) The police just barged into my apartment and started going through all of my personal stuff. I was so scared, I couldn't say anything.
   b) My son tells me that you're always picking on him in class. He never had problems with any of his other teachers.
   c) The doctor said my tumor is malignant. Now, you're telling me that I shouldn't worry!
   d) I've been waiting to see you for over an hour. Don't you think I've got better things to do than waste my time hanging around your waiting room.
   e) When I received your bill, I could not believe how much you are charging. There's no way I'm going to pay such an outrageous fee.

8. MIRRORING: In order to develop greater control over non-verbal skills, you need to be able to see yourself in action. Practice in front of a mirror or on videotape. Try to convey a range of messages: satisfied, agree, disagree, concern, interest, hope, surprise. How do you use your hands and facial expressions to convey different messages. Ask a colleague to give you feedback, to see if the colleague interprets your messages as you intended to convey them.

9 "I" STATEMENTS: For each of the following statements, identify the underlying message and reframe it into an "I" statement:

a) You are making me nervous.
b) You need to be more careful.
c) The problem with your idea is that you aren't looking into the future.
d) If you cannot be reasonable, then there's no use talking to you.
e) The best solution is to divide it in half.

10 COMPLIMENTARY CIRCLE: Giving and receiving positive feedback are underused skills in CR. It is easy to take people for granted and embarrassing for a humble helping professional to receive compliments. This exercise provides an opportunity to show your colleagues how much you appreciate them. Everyone in the room gets into a circle. In turn, give the person to your right a piece of positive feedback. Use the sentence stem, "What I appreciate about ____ [insert name] is ____ [insert compliment]." Recipients of compliments respond by thanking the previous speaker. The instructor goes first.

Communication Skills Inventory

The following inventory lists the key skills identified in this chapter. You can use this inventory to monitor your progress and to focus your professional development. For each skill, circle the letter that signifies the level where you believe you are today. Place a check mark (√) where you plan to be at the end of the course. This will help you prioritize your learning. Mark your diary to remind yourself to come back to this inventory, halfway through the course and at the end of the course. Underline where your progress is at the midway point of the course. Put an asterisk where you are at the end of the course.

You can also use these inventories for feedback from others. When you are participating in a role-play or assignment, provide a blank copy of the inventory to a colleague and ask for specific feedback on the criteria that you are trying to improve upon. Focus on no more than four skills at a time.

Coding: a—Needs Improvement; b—Competent; c—Very Good; d—Outstanding

ORAL SKILLS

Attending	a - b - c - d
Constructive use of silence	a - b - c - d
Paraphrasing	a - b - c - d

Reflection of feeling	a - b - c - d
Summarization	a - b - c - d
Open question	a - b - c - d
Closed question	a - b - c - d
Appropriate pacing	a - b - c - d
Questions and statements are nonjudgmental	a - b - c - d
Clear questions and statements	a - b - c - d
Concise questions and statements	a - b - c - d
Statements are assertive, but not aggressive	a - b - c - d
Culturally appropriate language	a - b - c - d
Other: _____	a - b - c - d

WRITING

Nonjudgmental	a - b - c - d
Clear	a - b - c - d
Concise	a - b - c - d
Assertive, but not aggressive	a - b - c - d
Culturally appropriate language	a - b - c - d
Other: _____	a - b - c - d

ROLE-PLAY 2.1: "LISTENING TO ANGER"

There is trouble in Conflictia. People from Asia are very angry that they have been left out of the power structures in Conflictia. Asians are underrepresented in government, education, and professional roles.

The two role-players for this exercise are Amal (a person of Asian descent with a degree in education) and Verna (a vocational counselor with Diversity Plus). Amal has come to Diversity Plus to help him find a job. Amal is very frustrated, believing that he has been discriminated against by prospective employers. During this role-play, Amal will direct his anger at Verna. Verna will use listening skills to demonstrate empathy. In order to prepare for the role-play, Amal can list examples of bigotry he has experienced and how he can convey his anger (through facial expressions, voice, and choice of words). Verna can prepare by reviewing the section on listening skills. Observers should keep track of the skills used by Verna, using the Communications Skills Inventory.

Debriefing Questions
What emotions did Amal display? How were these emotions displayed? Give examples of listening skills used effectively by Verna. How did Amal respond to each of these skills? What skills did Verna use that had the effect of diffusing conflict?

ROLE-PLAY 2.2: "POLICIES FOR DIVERSITY PLUS"

Being a new agency, Diversity Plus needs to develop its policies and standards of practice. An interdisciplinary team has been appointed to identify the key values to which Diversity Plus aspires. All future policies will be based on this list.

The interdisciplinary team consists of Sarit (a social worker), Yota (a youth counselor), Penelope (a pastoral counselor), and Nicolai (a nurse). Before going into role, all role-players should prepare a list of values based on their ascribed roles. Think about what your profession stands for. Also, consider your vision for the agency. What ideals would make Diversity Plus an inspired place for you to work? (If the specified roles are not familiar to you, you can change the professions to ones that are more familiar to you).

Yota will take the lead in facilitating the discussion. Begin by creating a comprehensive list of values on a chalkboard or flipchart. Let everyone have an open discussion about the values (15 minutes). To close the discussion, ask everyone to mark asterisks (**) next to the items they value most. Each person is entitled to put up seven asterisks, and can distribute these asterisks in any combination (e.g., one asterisk for one value, six for another). When each person has had a chance to mark seven asterisks, count the asterisks for each value. The values with the most asterisks will represent the values with the highest priorities. Save the results of this exercise to refer back to for exercises later in the course.

Debriefing Questions:
What was the source of the values which you identified during the role-play? Family? A specific culture? Broader society? Your profession? What types of conflict resolution are most consistent with the list of values generated by your list of values? What types of conflict resolution would not fit? How did you decide to distribute your asterisks? What were advantages of using the asterisk process for decision making in this case? What was problematic about it?

CHAPTER 3

NEGOTIATION

Recall from Chapter 1 that negotiation refers to interactions between two or more parties involved in a conflict. Negotiation includes formal negotiation, where the conflicting parties get together explicitly for the purposes of bargaining or resolving a specific dispute. However, it also includes emergent negotiation, where conflicting parties have not expressly declared their intentions to negotiate (Fisher & Brown, 1988). Because of the pervasiveness of conflict in social interaction, virtually all interactions between individuals or groups could be viewed from the perspective of negotiation.

In this chapter, I focus on negotiation between parties who are directly involved in a conflict; for instance, negotiations between helping professionals and clients, between co-professionals, or between client systems (Shulman, 1992). Chapters 4 and 5 explore mediation, where an independent third party helps both interested parties negotiate. Chapter 6 analyzes advocacy, where an individual allied with one party helps that party negotiate. Accordingly, Chapters 4, 5, and 6 build upon the theory and interventions described in this chapter.

The following section describes clinical and legal issues pertaining to negotiations and contracting. I devote the largest part of the chapter to a comparison of four approaches to negotiation: power, rights, interests, and transformation. These approaches are integrated in a Negotiation Preparation Tool that provides a strategic approach to analyzing conflict situations in order to prepare for negotiation.

CONTRACTING

Most helping professionals are familiar with negotiating, though they generally use different terminology. For instance, helping professionals "contract" with clients in the early stages of a problem-solving process (Zastrow, 1999). In the process of contracting, they try to come to an agreement about what is the problem for work; what are the professional's roles and obligations; what are the client's roles and obligations? Although helping professionals ascribe to the principle of client self-determination, they often unwittingly impose terms on their clients. To illustrate, consider the following explanation of client confidentiality, its extents and limitations.

> Professional to client: Everything we discuss in our sessions remains confidential. In other words, I will respect your right to privacy. I will not tell anyone about what you say, unless I have your express written permission. There are a few exceptions. For instance, if anything raises concerns that a child or other person may be put at risk of harm, I have a professional obligation to take steps to help that person avoid the harm . . .

Here, the professional is telling the client what confidentiality means, rather than negotiating it. The professional may ask the client to agree, but even then, the terms of the contract for confidentiality are all or nothing. Genuine negotiation with the client would allow the client and professional to discuss all the terms of the contract and develop individualized terms that meet the needs of this client. Consider a client who does not want confidentiality. This client might negotiate an agreement where the professional is not bound to keep anything confidential—the client may even ask the professional to broadcast information about the client. In other words, free and informed negotiation enhances a client's right to self-determination.[1]

Literature on work with involuntary clients, in particular, views clients and clinicians as having conflicting interests (Palmer, 1983). In child protection cases, for example, social workers are mandated to investigate allegations of child abuse and neglect. Parents suspected of abuse are interested in privacy and autonomy. The workers are interested in ensuring the safety of the child. In order to engage parents on a voluntary basis, the worker tries to negotiate terms of a working arrangement that satisfy the interests of the parents and the worker. Ideally, the parents and worker turn an involuntary relationship into a purely voluntary one, where both the parents and worker agree to a certain working relationship. If the worker is unable to secure the child's welfare needs through voluntary interventions, the worker can impose the authority of the child protection system (e.g., by initiating court proceedings). In between these extremes, the worker can use various levels of bargaining and persuasion in order to fulfill the child protection mandate (Murdach, 1980; Tjaden, 1994).

---

[1]In legal literature, contracting between individuals is called "private ordering." This term suggests that the parties to the contract are free to negotiate or arrange their affairs as they see fit, without state intervention or limits. Capitalism and free markets are based on the principle of private ordering. Socialism puts constraints on private ordering. The rights of the community, in certain circumstances, will supersede the rights of individuals to private ordering.

When negotiations lead to an agreement, the agreement might be a legally binding contract. Contracts are essentially promises that each party makes to the other. Contracts can be enforceable even if they are not drafted by lawyers or signed and witnessed. Legally drafted agreements are easier to prove in court. However, oral and implied contracts are also enforceable. An oral contract is a verbal agreement. An implied contract exists where the parties do not explicitly say they are entering an agreement; however, an agreement can be inferred from the pattern of behaviors that existed between the parties. For instance, even if you do not verbally promise confidentiality to a client, you may imply such a promise indirectly: you meet with the client in a private office; the certificate on your wall says you are a licensed professional; and you encourage the client to trust you and share personal information. Although verbal and implied contracts are enforceable, written contracts have a number of advantages.

- Both parties are clear about whether or not they have entered into a contract.
- The terms can be spelled out specifically, to ensure that both parties have the same understandings.
- Written contracts tend to solidify the commitment of both parties.
- Before the contract is signed, lawyers, supervisors, or others can review it in order to provide legal or other professional advice.
- If there are future disputes then the document can serve as evidence of the parties' agreement.
- Terms of the written agreement can be modified with subsequent written agreements, providing a paper trail of the sequence of events.

Oral agreements tend to be less formal and take less time to produce. People often use oral agreements when they assume there will be no problem with enforcement. Implied contracts are problematic because neither party can be sure if they have entered a contract and if so, what the precise terms of the contract are. As a helping professional, preferred practice suggests you be deliberate about entering contracts and explicit about their terms, whether the contract is oral or written.

Written contracts are particularly important when the subject of the conflict has serious legal ramifications (e.g., criminal behavior, child abuse or neglect, physical injuries, monetary losses). Many agreements do not have legal ramifications and may not even be intended to be legally enforceable. In family therapy, a counselor may help family members negotiate a "family contract." The contract may specify the roles, privileges, and obligations of each parent and child in the family. The contract encourages each party to fulfill a certain set of obligations. However, the family members do not intend it to be a legally enforceable contract. In other words, if one family member does not live up to the terms of the agreement, the others cannot go to court to make that person comply.

In most jurisdictions, drafting formal documents is a function restricted to licensed lawyers. If a non-lawyer drafts a formal contract, that person may be subject to criminal charges for "unauthorized practice of law." The role of a helping professional in writing informal agreements with clients is to help them articulate their wishes and expectations for one another. This role does not include giving clients legal advice or ensuring that a contract is written in a legally enforceable manner. Non-lawyers should also ensure that their "informal agreements" avoid the trappings of a legally binding contract.

- Use a title for the document such as "Memorandum of Understanding," "Unofficial Peace Treaty," or "Non-binding Family Agreement," rather than "Contract" or "Agreement."
- Do not have the clients or witnesses sign the document.
- Use plain language, rather than technical, legal language.
- Include a sentence that states the document is not intended to be a legally binding agreement.

These points will make it clear to clients that the agreement is, in fact, an informal one. In some situations, a helping professional will help clients come to a general understanding and then ask the clients' lawyers to draft the general understanding into a legally binding agreement. This ensures that the clients have an opportunity to get independent legal advice[2] before they sign the agreement and make it enforceable. If you are concerned about the legal ramifications of negotiations and contracting, ensure that you obtain legal advice. You may also have an ethical obligation to ensure that clients have an opportunity to consult with a lawyer to ensure they are apprised of their legal rights.

APPROACHES TO NEGOTIATION

Negotiation theory can be categorized in a number of different manners: contractual versus emergent (Pruitt & Carnevale, 1993); positional versus principled (Fisher, Ury, & Patton, 1997); exchange of discourse versus exchange of resources (Rifkin, Millen, & Cobb, 1991; Slaikeu, Pearson, Luckett, & Myers, 1985). Although I cannot describe all theories of negotiation in one chapter, I try to capture the breadth of theories by focusing on

---

[2]Independent legal advice refers to separate legal advice for each party. One lawyer cannot advise all of the parties to an agreement because there may be a conflict of interest between the parties.

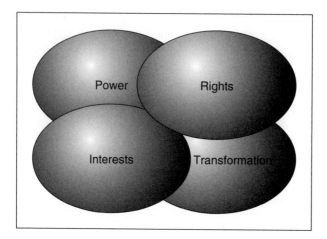

FIGURE **3.1**

Four Approaches to Negotiation

four approaches to negotiation: power, rights, interests, and transformation.[3] Each approach can be applied separately, as well as in combination (Fig. 3.1).

The power approach to negotiation views parties as competitors. Each party uses its power to try to influence the other and gain advantage. Conflicts are resolved by who is strongest, e.g., the party with the greatest physical strength, the best weapons, the most political clout, the highest intelligence, or the largest financial resources. In the purest form of power-based negotiations, there are no rules of fair play. Parties can lie, cheat, bludgeon, or commit other savage acts on one another. Winning is the highest value.

The rights approach was intended to be an "enlightened response" to the barbarism of the power approach by imposing rules of fair play. Rather than presume that "might is right," the rights approach suggests that "right is right." Under this approach, the legal system creates a set of procedures and rules designed to treat people fairly, regardless of their position of power or powerlessness (Bossy, 1983). The rule of law suggests that laws rather than force govern people. Laws dictate who is entitled to what, and under what circumstances. If the parties are uncertain about who is right or what is right, they can go to court for a determination by an impartial judge. To the extent that the law is clear, parties need not go to court. They can negotiate based on their rights. While the rights perspective encourages greater civility, legal battles are still "civil wars" (i.e., the process is adversarial).

---

[3]Van Es (1996) uses four categories, attributing each to a particular era: (a) the "warrior" concept, dating back to the Byzantine Empire; (b) the "mercantile" concept, dating to the Renaissance; (c) the "civil" concept, attributed to the Enlightenment; and (d) the constructive concept, attributed to the 20th Century.

The interests approach,[4] popularized in the 1980s by the Harvard Negotiation Project (Fisher, Ury, & Patton, 1997), shifts the focus of negotiation from adversarial conflict resolution to joint problem solving. Interests are the parties' underlying concerns, what they really want to achieve. Parties try to resolve conflicts by identifying mutual interests and ways of satisfying one another's interests, regardless of their rights or power. Interest-based negotiation asks parties to focus on negotiating what is truly important to them, rather than trying to win by achieving a solution that fits with their original positions. When the interest approach is implemented effectively, collaboration replaces competition. The quality of the ongoing relationship between the parties is more important than determination of their legal rights.

The transformative approach suggests that the primary purpose of negotiation and other forms of CR is to change the way that people view and deal with conflict. According to Bush and Folger (1994), transformation occurs through the processes of empowerment and recognition. *"Empowerment* means the restoration to individuals of a sense of their own value and strength and their own capacity to handle life's problems. *Recognition* means the evocation in individuals of acknowledgment and empathy for the situation and problem of others"* (Bush & Folger, 1994, p. 2). While the other approaches focus on how to resolve conflict, transformation focuses on the moral and personal growth of the parties. The actual conflict need not be resolved. Accordingly, transformative negotiation is oriented towards individual and relational processes, rather than producing specific outcomes. The exchange of communication between parties is more important than how resources are distributed between them.

The following sections provide more detailed descriptions of these models. First, however, I want to illustrate how these contrasting CR approaches relate to practice. Consider a conflict involving sex discrimination: women in the community earn only 70% of what men do for work of equal value. You are working with a group that wants to rectify the problem. You can approach this case from any of the four approaches.

From a power perspective, the cause of this conflict is based on the imbalance of power between men and women; for example, men hold the greatest number of managerial positions, where salary decisions are made. In order to address this imbalance, your strategy may depend on placing more women in management (positions of power). Men will become relatively less powerful.

In contrast, a rights approach starts with the premise that men and women have equal rights. This includes the rights of women to equal pay for work of equal value. The fact that women are earning 30% less than men

---

[4]The interests paradigm is the cornerstone of Fisher, Ury, and Patton's (1997) model of "principled negotiation."

means that these rights have been violated. Your strategy may begin with informing employers about equality rights and negotiating ways to implement them. If employers do not agree to abide by these rights, you may decide to go to court or a human rights tribunal for a judicial determination and enforcement.

Using an interest-based approach, you need to assess the underlying interests of the parties. Women want equal pay for work of equal value. Their underlying concerns include fairness and respect. Businesses and managers want to minimize their expenses in order to maximize profits. However, they can also agree that workers should be treated with fairness and respect. Your approach would be to engage the parties in a joint problem-solving process, so that each of their interests can be satisfied. Ultimately, this will result in better working relationships and mutual benefits.

The transformative approach suggests that the conflicting parties need to gain (a) a better understanding on one another's situation, and (b) a stronger sense of control over their own destinies. For businesses, this means learning about the impact of discrimination on women and acknowledging the validity of women's feelings. For women, this means learning and acknowledging the pressures on businesses and managers. Neither party has to agree with the other. However, your intervention ought to help each party take greater control over their roles in the conflict. Both parties can be transformed, regardless of whether the specific conflict about equal pay is resolved to both parties' satisfaction. Even if the women do not obtain full parity in salaries, their participation in a constructive CR process provides them with a greater sense of pride and purpose.

Although the issues have been simplified, this scenario highlights some of the key differences in applying different models. As you work through the various approaches to negotiation in more detail, consider the assumptions of each and how each approach views success.

POWER-BASED NEGOTIATION

This section begins with a definition of interpersonal power, followed by a description of a power-based approach to negotiations.

Interpersonal power refers to the capacity of individuals or groups to influence one another (Pinderhughes, 1983). Power is a dynamic process since it occurs in interactions between people. One person may have more power or influence over another in some situations, but less power over the other in different situations. Consider, for instance, a clinical supervisor's power in relation to a clinician. The supervisor has the authority of the agency to direct the clinician about how to intervene with particular clients. The clinician is likely to heed the supervisor's advice even if the clinician disagrees, provided that the advice is about professional matters, within the agency's mandate. The clinician is less likely to heed the supervisor's directives about matters that the clinician believes are personal or beyond the agency's mandate. Further, the clinician is more likely to rebel if the supervisor uses power to dictate on repeated occasions. Accordingly, after a person exercises power over another, that person will have less power to influence the other in the future.

Power-based negotiations are essentially competitive interactions. Because the primary goal of the interaction is to maximize personal gain, parties using this perspective will adopt whatever strategies they can to influence the other side (Druckman, 1993). These strategies include positional negotiating, intransigence, secretiveness, bluffing, threats, and use of force, as described below.

In positional negotiating, each party takes a stance and argues in favor of that stance. Rather than start with problem definition, each party starts by offering a solution.

> PHYSICIAN: *This client needs to go on a diet to lose weight.*
> FEMINIST THERAPIST: *This client needs an opportunity to explore her body image and the unrealistic expectations society places on women.*

Once a party offers a solution, backing down becomes difficult. Neither party wants to look weak or lose face. Since both parties are reluctant to move from their original positions, deadlocks are not uncommon. The question becomes, "who is right, the physician or the feminist therapist?" In power negotiations, might is right. If the physician has greater status in the agency, the position of the physician will prevail. Alternatively, the therapist might find allies in the agency to support her stance and win the debate.[5] Regardless, positional negotiations set up at least one party to be the "loser."

When positional negotiations are headed towards an impasse, parties generally agree to compromise. In other words, both parties give in, at least partially. Each saves face, knowing that the other side is also reducing its demands. Still, both parties are generally reluctant to make concessions, since one party's loss is the other's gain (i.e., the parties are playing a zero-sum game). The need to appear tough leads to further intransigence on both sides.

Positional negotiations encourage parties to use the following strategies:

- Make as extreme an offer as is tenable: If both parties know they will need to compromise, their initial positions will not reflect what they really want or what they view as a reasonable solution. By inflating initial offers to settle, there is "room to negotiate." Neither party wants to make too extreme an offer, to ensure that they do not put off the other. The first offer must be sufficiently reasonable to demonstrate seriousness

---

[5]Debating and alternatives to debating are described in greater detail in Chapter 5.

about the negotiations. The parties will go through a series of offers and counter-offers, eventually communicating more realistic goals and expectations (Ellis & Stuckless, 1996).[6]

- Let the other side make the first offer: The first party to make an offer is placed at a strategic disadvantage. Not knowing how the second party will respond, you do not know how extreme an offer to make. If your offer is close to your bottom line and the counter-offer is extreme, you leave little room to maneuver in negotiations. If your offer is too extreme, the other party will refuse to negotiate with you.

- Be secretive: Because the object is to win, information becomes a valued commodity. Parties do not want to share information—particularly their bottom lines. Unfortunately, neither party can make an informed decision if the other party is holding back relevant information.

- Bluff: Bluffing is a form of deceit, though the term bluffing tends to carry fewer negative connotations. Bluffing is related to secretiveness, but goes further. Rather than simply withhold information, you intentionally provide misinformation. An example of bluffing in poker is to pretend that you have a better hand than you actually have. The appearance of strength influences others, even if you do not have the actual strength (cards) to back up the appearances. Bluffing has three downsides: the ethics of bluffing are questionable,[7] the other side might call your bluff, and people may not want to deal with you if they know you are a bluffer.

- Be patient in negotiations: If you look anxious to settle quickly, you weaken your bargaining position. The other side knows that you are more likely to make compromises. Accordingly, the incentive in positional bargaining is to draw things out, to show that you can withstand conflict over a long duration. Delay tactics may also be a sign that the other party has no real interest in resolving the conflict. If the *status quo* gives one party an advantageous position, that party has no incentive to bargain in good faith (Pruitt & Carnevale, 1993).

- If you make compromises, make small concessions: Neither party wants to give up more than they have to, so any concessions tend to be small.

- Tit-for-tat: This strategy suggests that you should respond to an opposing party in the same manner that the party treats you. If the other party is cooperative, you will be cooperative. If the other party becomes competitive, you will become competitive (Rapoport, 1974). Ideally, this encourages both parties to cooperate. Unfortunately, tit-for-tat often turns into a game of chicken. One party makes a threat and the other

---

[6]Ellis and Stuckless refer to this process as a "convergence-concession" approach.

[7]Helping professionals generally agree that intentional deceit is unethical; however, some might argue that the ends justify the means. In other words, if a person needs to bluff in order to achieve something of higher moral value, then deceit is justified.

party responds in kind. The threats escalate and it becomes difficult for either party to back down.

- Threaten: Threats are commitments to punish the other side if it does not accept your position. Threats are more likely to persuade the other side if the proposed sanctions are large and the threats are credible. Credibility depends upon whether it seems reasonable that the threats can and will be carried out. Threats and similar exercise of force may produce compliance in the short-term. However, they may also generate resentment, resistance, and withdrawal. Under certain circumstances, threats may be viewed as legitimate. For example, the criminal justice system is essentially a system of threats: laws are established; if people break the law, they can expect to be punished. This type of threat has legitimacy because it has the general support of society and because the nature of the punishment fits the crime.
- Harass: Harassment refers to punishing the other side until it gives in to your demands. As with threats, punishment may produce compliance, but harms the relationship between the parties. When people are harassed unjustly, they will eventually rebel (Pruitt & Carnevale, 1993).

If both sides use these types of strategies, then negotiations become protracted and adversarial. Agreement becomes difficult. Even when agreement is reached, parties are often dissatisfied. The solution is a compromise and the relationship between the parties is antagonistic.

As these examples suggest, positional negotiations present many problems, particularly for helping professionals. Still, it is important to understand the nature of positional negotiations in order to learn how to respond to others who approach negotiation from this perspective. You can either play the game with them or encourage them to play a different type of game, based on one of the other approaches to CR.

In extreme cases, the only rule in power negotiations is that the party with the greater power wins. In most interactions, however, the parties have a tacit understanding about the rules of the game: you can use conventional weapons, but not nuclear weapons; you can punch the head, but not below the belt; you can use harsh words, but you can't use any physical violence. Although these rules of the game put certain limits on the types of power that can be used, the ultimate goal is still personal victory.

Power does exist in relationships, so, at the very least, it must be acknowledged. Certainly, there are times when use of power is justifiable, even necessary. The most common example cited is self-defense, when the person is being attacked. This appears to be a zero-sum game: either the attacker suffers or the person attacked suffers. Too often, however, people assume use of power is required when there are other alternatives. If you are being attacked, use of force may incite the other to use even greater force. In aikido and other martial arts; for instance, you learn to move with force rather than against it. If someone charges at you and you ready yourself by planting your feet, force will meet force. Both of you will suffer from the impact. Alternatively, you could use the momentum of your charging opponent to your advantage; that is, move with the force rather than against it (Edelman & Crain, 1993). The interest-based approach, described below, demonstrates how helping professionals can apply this strategy in various social conflicts.

Helping professionals frequently work on behalf of disadvantaged individuals or groups. The "disadvantage" often relates to negotiation power. Helping professionals can help disadvantaged people gain negotiation power through advocacy techniques, described in Chapter 6. Power, however, may not be a critical problem if the helping professional can engage the parties in one of the non-power approaches of negotiation. Rather than having one party try to use its power over the other party, for instance, parties can join forces to work towards mutually acceptable goals (Wilmot & Hocker, 1998). Using power *with* another person, rather than *over* another person fits with the interest-based and transformative approaches to negotiation, described below.

RIGHTS-BASED NEGOTIATION

Rights-based negotiation is premised on what the relevant laws prescribe. Negotiators argue their positions based upon their respective rights or entitlements. Whereas power-based negotiators try to influence the other side by exerting various forms of influence, rights-based negotiation comes down to which party has the better legal arguments.

If you are negligent in your professional practice and a client suffers as a result, your client could sue you for compensation. If you know the client would win in court, there is no need to actually proceed through a trial. You could negotiate compensation based on your projection of what a court would award, "bargaining in the shadow of the law" (Menkel-Meadow, 1984; Mnookin & Kornhauser, 1979). A client who is denied welfare could initiate a case with the welfare appeals tribunal. However, the welfare worker could negotiate with the client based on what they believe the tribunal would decide. In both cases, the parties save the costs and aggravation of going through adversarial hearings.

Clear laws make it easier for parties to negotiate their rights. If the law is hazy or uncertain, the parties do not know which way a judge might decide. In conflict situations, parties have a tendency to view conflicts from their own perspectives, often reckoning that a judge would decide in their favor. "I'm right, so you must be wrong." If neither party is willing to budge from this position, they need to go to a judge or other arbitrator to decide which one really is right. Even when laws are clear, they may be open to different interpretations and judicial comment. Because parties have little control over how rights are established or interpreted, rights-based negotiations can be frustrating.

The rights approach is most easily recognized in terms of public laws and legal disputes. However, this approach also applies with regard to rules in communities, social agencies, and other organizations. Community norms and ethics, for example, prescribe appropriate types of behaviors. Your sense of right and wrong may tell you that divorce is a valid option for couples with irreconcilable differences. A colleague may believe that marriages are inviolable. Your sense of right comes from certain cultural values, namely autonomy and freedom. Your colleague's beliefs come from a particular religious perspective. Negotiation based on rights is problematic because there is no universal agreement on what actually is right. Neither side has room for compromise unless someone gives up a fundamental belief.

Agency policies create rules for clients and helping professionals. Some agencies, for example, restrict services to clients who are national citizens or legal immigrants. How would you respond to an illegal immigrant in need of your services? If you resort to a rights perspective, you must refuse the client. The client and you cannot negotiate away the rules of the agency. If you agree to provide services, you are contravening policy and putting yourself in conflict with the agency. If you believe that serving illegal immigrants is morally right, you could advocate within your agency to change the rules (i.e., recognize a different set of rights).

Communities and organizations establish rules to create a sense of order. At its best, a rights approach prevents conflict since everyone knows their respective rights. Little time and energy is spent negotiating. For the most part, people comply with the laws tacitly. Accordingly, clear and fair laws promote efficient transactions between people. Rights also temper illegitimate use of power. Laws prohibit certain types of violence, coercion, and exploitation. Laws also encourage games of fair play: negotiating in good faith, arbitration, court trial, due process, etc.

On the downside, a rights orientation favors rules over relationships (Conley & O'Barr, 1990). Although the rights approach places limits on the illegitimate use of power, the process to resolve disputes is adversarial: my rights versus yours. One side wins; the other loses. The system does not encourage parties to look for creative solutions for their mutual benefit. If a case has to be decided by a judge or arbitrator, the emotional and financial costs are highly taxing on the parties. Parties also lose the ability make decisions for themselves.

One of the primary concerns about the rights perspective is determining who establishes rights in the first place. In democratic societies, elected governments are given the primary responsibility for making laws and initiating law reform. Elections and political processes tend to be adversarial.

are winners and losers. Minority views and people without
on lose out. Those with political power ultimately determine how
llocated in society. Similarly, rights in communities and organiza-
etermined by those with power. Minority rights may be protected by
constitutions or other laws; however, laws can also be used for social control.

Given the limitations of the rights approach, what are the alternatives?
How can we have justice without law (Auerbach, 1983)? What is the basis for
negotiation if we do not rely on a base of rules (Conley & O'Barr, 1990)?

INTEREST-BASED NEGOTIATION

Interest-based negotiation refers to joint problem solving, where parties focus
on resolving their mutual interests rather than advancing their individual
rights or positions. Some authors call this principled negotiation[8] (Fisher, Ury,
& Patton, 1997) or an integrative approach[9] (Ellis & Stuckless, 1996).
In terms of conflict styles, interest-based negotiation favors collaboration.
Interest-based negotiation (IBN) draws theoretical support from game theory: positional and rights orientations view conflict as zero-sum games—if
one party gets more, then the other party will get proportionally less. In contrast, IBN encourages parties to play cooperative games and seek out win-win
solutions. In many cases, fighting over resources leads to losses by both parties (e.g., the cost of hiring lawyers, time and energy devoted to fighting, and
destruction of one another's resources). If people problem-solve cooperatively and find common ground, they can actually create and share new resources (Alberta Agriculture, Food, and Rural Development, 1997). Accordingly, IBN encourages trust and amicable relationships between the parties.
If the parties can truly collaborate for their mutual interests, the relative balance of power between them becomes a non-issue.

The Harvard Negotiation Project suggests a seven-part framework for
negotiation.

1. Focus on Interests, Not Positions.
2. Invent Options for Mutual Gain.
3. Apply Objective Criteria.
4. Improve Communication.

---

[8]The principles provide a framework for the parties to follow in order for negotiation to be
constructive for both parties.

[9]The approach is integrative by focusing on the interests of both parties, rather than one party's
interests versus the other's. Further, integrative negotiation encourages the parties to satisfy their
interests in terms of both process and outcome (e.g., to develop a fair process as well as a fair
outcome).

5. Build a Positive Negotiating Relationship.

6. Consider Alternatives. Obtain Commitments (Fisher, Ury, & Patton, 1997).

These components do not represent a sequence of steps, but rather strategies to be used in various combinations. When problems arise in negotiation, these points can be used as a diagnostic checklist to determine the nature of the difficulties and strategies to employ to move negotiation forward. The relative importance of a particular component depends upon the particular situation.

1. Focus on Interests, Not Positions

So what exactly are interests, and how do they differ from rights or positions? Positions are strategic stances or demands of the parties. Interests refer to their underlying needs, values, concerns, or desires. In order to identify interests, ask the parties why they are pursuing certain positions or demands. What is truly important to them, at a fundamental level. Consider the following scenario.

> Ferdinand has a 12-year-old daughter, Demi. A child protection worker, Whoopi, has been asked to investigate Ferdinand for possible child abuse. Upon meeting with family members, Whoopi is concerned for Demi's safety and decides to place Demi in temporary foster care. Ferdinand contests this decision. He has used corporal punishment with Demi, but does not believe this constitutes abuse.

Whoopi's position is that Demi must be removed from her family home. Ferdinand's position is that Demi should remain with him. If they pursue a power or rights perspective, both will become entrenched in their positions. They will tend to restrict their vision of possible solutions to Whoopi's position or Ferdinand's position.

In contrast, if they pursue an interests perspective, they will try to understand one another's interests and look for creative solutions that are satisfactory to both of them. If you asked Whoopi why she wanted to place Demi into foster care, Whoopi would say that she is interested in Demi's safety, ensuring that she is not abused and that her psychosocial concerns are being met. If you were to ask Ferdinand about his underlying interests, he would say that he loves Demi and is interested in her welfare. Both Whoopi and Ferdinand could agree that they were interested in Demi's welfare. They have different understandings about what this means or requires. However, they have a common goal and can engage in a joint problem-solving process to resolve their differences (Barsky, 1997b). Their selection of possible solutions opens up.

- Arrange for an independent helping professional from the community to conduct a family assessment and suggest services, if needed.

- Have a relative move into the family home to assist with parenting.
- Develop an agreement about what types of punishment are appropriate and what types are inappropriate.
- Ensure that Demi has a counselor or support person to confide with.
- Refer Ferdinand to parenting skills training.
- Provide Ferdinand with liberal access while Demi is in foster care.

Ferdinand does not want Whoopi making life difficult for him. Whoopi does not want to make life difficult for him either. They could agree to work out a plan to resolve their differences as quickly and amicably as possible, so Ferdinand's family can get on with life without interference from Whoopi.

In order to prepare for negotiation, identify the other parties' interests, as well as your own. The natural tendency is to see conflict from one's own perspective. Try to put yourself in the others' shoes. Why are they advocating a particular position? What underlying concerns are important to them? Consider the use of role reversal to help you understand the viewpoints of other parties. Role reversal is a type of role-play where you assume another party's role and have a colleague assume your role. By taking on the other party's role you gain an experiential understanding of that party's interests.

If conflicting parties have similar interests, they can easily agree upon a common goal. If the parties' interests conflict, they may be able to identify common goals by exploring deeper levels of underlying interests (Pruitt & Carnevale, 1993). The hierarchy of interests includes desires, values, and basic needs (Warfield, 1993). I will use a brief case to illustrate.

> Dorothy, aged 52, lives with her 82-year-old mother, Miranda. Miranda's health has been deteriorating. After Miranda fell in the bathtub, Dorothy decided that Miranda should move into a specialized nursing home. Miranda wants to stay at home. Their counselor wants to help them identify common interests in order to engage them in joint problem solving.

- **Desires or wants are based upon cognitive decision-making processes.** Miranda says she wants to live at home because that is where she has lived all her life. She has never lived in an institution and would not know how to adapt to all of the changes. Dorothy wants Miranda to go to a nursing home because a nursing home can provide better care for Miranda. Each person has a valid argument, base on their own reasoning. Unfortunately, their desires conflict.
- **Values are non-reasoned choices that define a person's core convictions about what is important.** Underneath Miranda's desire to remain at home lies her value for independence. Moving into a nursing home would mean giving up her independence. In contrast, Dorothy's original position is based on her value for health. Miranda and Dorothy might agree to negotiate based on two principles: independence and

health. This would provide a basis for joint problem solving. However, if they do not agree on these principles, the counselor can ask them what underlies their stated values.

- **Needs are more basic requirements than values.** Physical requirements include food, water, sleep, shelter, and safety from bodily harm. Psychosocial needs include security, identity, recognition, respect, status, and self-actualization (Maslow, 1987; Chetkow-Yanoov, 1997). Miranda's value for independence may be based on her need for survival. She does not believe that she can survive without independence. Similarly, Dorothy's value for health may also lie in her need for Miranda's survival. Accordingly, both can agree to work towards a common goal. The focus of the problem is what it will take to ensure Dorothy's survival. If they cannot agree on a common goal at this level, the counselor can help them explore even deeper levels of interests.

As the parties move from positions to desires, values, and needs, they tend to move from the specific to the general. If parties cannot agree upon specific goals, they may find it easier to agree upon more general principles. Once general principles are in place, the parties can work out more of the specifics.

2. *Invent Options for Mutual Gain*

Options are possible solutions. When people become entrenched in conflict, their initially perceived choice set tends to be narrow. Remind yourself and the parties you are negotiating with that it is important to keep an open mind, to be creative.

Once both parties have agreed upon general principles, they can work together to invent possible solutions. In order to become creative, parties need to suspend judgments. For example, brainstorm as many ideas as you can. Do not worry if they are reasonable or viable. Do not have concern about whether the ideas are better for one party or another. Just raise as many ideas as possible. As you brainstorm, list all the ideas on a flipchart or chalkboard. Even ridiculous ideas can spawn constructive options. If you are not sure about what options are available, you can gather information about resources in the community.

In Dorothy and Miranda's situation, they might brainstorm the following options. Let Miranda stay home and put Dorothy in the nursing home; hire a home aid to help with Miranda's care; put off the decision until the next crisis; have Miranda spend time with different family members in order to give Dorothy respite; don't allow Miranda to take baths, look for a supportive housing arrangement that provides more independence than the nursing home; turn Dorothy's house into a nursing home and take in more patients.

Avoid making decisions about whether options are worth considering until all of your ideas are exhausted. If one person throws up an idea, it is very easy for the others to reject it. If each successive idea is rejected, then no options will be left. If you list all of the options, then the choice is not "yes" or "no," but which of the options is best (or least harmful). Parents can use this strategy with children. If a parent asks, "Would you like a tuna sandwich for lunch," the child can reject this, hoping the parent will come up with a better offer. If the parent says, "Would you prefer tuna or peanut butter," the child cannot simply say no. If the child knows there are only two choices, the child will choose between them.

People tend to be more creative under certain conditions: when they are at ease, when stress levels are low, and when they are motivated by positive goals (Pruitt & Carnevale, 1983). Accordingly, try to establish an environment that is conducive to these conditions. Use humor to lighten the mood. Develop a positive working relationship and goals for work before moving into option generation and problem solving. Choose a convenient time and tranquil place for negotiating. In positional negotiations, parties often use time as a pressure tactic: for instance, serious negotiations are left until the eleventh hour, just before a crisis point (e.g., the strike deadline, the court date, the straw that breaks the camel's back). Another positional strategy is to start negotiations late in the day, just before the weekend. Parties do not want to give up their Friday evening or weekend, so they pressure themselves into settling as soon as possible. In IBN, parties need ample time to work through problems and try to come up with creative solutions. The parties may establish time lines for decisions, but these should be based on identified interests rather than pressure tactics.

Ideally, the parties invent an "elegant option," a win-win solution that resolves the conflict to everyone's satisfaction. It is creative, ingenious, and often quite simple, at least in hindsight. When parties are not able to identify an elegant solution, they may have to select between less than perfect solutions.

3. Apply Objective Criteria

Once an exhaustive list of options has been created, the parties need a way to choose between them. Make the choice of criteria a joint decision rather than have each party come up with its own criteria. Search for objective criteria: what standards would a neutral third person suggest; what principles would experts in the field suggest; what precedents have been used in similar situations? When suggesting criteria, consider ones that will appeal to the other party. If your suggestions appear self-serving, the other party will reject them.

Dorothy and Miranda might defer to the expertise of a gerontologist: how do other families make decisions about the care of elder parents; if a choice has to be made between independence and physical health care, what criteria should be used to make the decision? They might explore literature to see what has been written about the issues. The gerontologist or the literature does not make the decision for Dorothy and Miranda. They just use these resources for ideas. Ultimately, they have to decide upon the criteria and apply them (Parsons & Cox, 1997).

4. Improve Communication

In Chapter 2, I described the importance of communication skills in conflict resolution. Active listening skills are particularly important for building positive relationships between parties. To be effective, you must not only listen, but ensure that the other parties know that you are listening and understanding them. Demonstrate that you are a reasonable person, open to persuasion. Admit areas of ignorance and use questions to become more informed. Ensure that your statements are clear, nonthreatening, and assertive.

Determine whether there are particular problems in communication: for example, lack of opportunities for communication, misinformation, or mistrust. Where these problems exist, how can you rectify them?

Many conflicts are aggravated because the parties never make opportunities to communicate. If one party is a conflict avoider, demonstrate that communication is in both parties' best interests. Find out what they fear (Adler, Rosen, & Silverstein, 1998): if they fear rejection, yelling, or physical violence, establish ground rules to make the interaction safe. In Dorothy's case, she may have been scared to talk to her mother about the nursing home because of feelings of guilt. By putting off the discussion until a crisis occurred, neither side has had an opportunity to process their ideas and feelings with one another.

Ideally, establish face-to-face communication in an amicable environment. Distance technologies may be more convenient, even necessary in some situations. However, in-person communication tends to be more humanizing. You can see one another's expressions and interact spontaneously. If you need to use distance technologies, video-conferencing, and telephone conference calls are the most humanizing. Fax, e-mail, and regular mail tend to be more formalized and disengaged. They also require a lapse of time as communications are transferred back and forth. In some circumstances, formalizing and drawing out communication can be advantageous (e.g., to allow heads to cool).

If conflict is aggravated by misinformation, provide opportunities for full and frank disclosure. If parties are positional, they tend to guard their own information and treat the other person's information with mistrust. By moving into joint problem solving, exchange of information becomes reciprocal.

When areas of mistrust persist, construct alternatives that are not dependent upon trusting one another. Discussing sexually transmitted diseases with a new partner, for example, is very difficult. If you ask your partner about past sexual and drug use behavior, the partner may question your love and trust. You want to trust your partner, but with fatal diseases like AIDS, trust is difficult. In order to remove the area of mistrust, the partners can agree to be tested for sexually transmitted diseases together. They depend upon an independent source of information—the health practitioner who tests them.

5. *Build a Positive Negotiating Relationship*

One of the key differences between interest-based and positional or rights-oriented negotiation is the emphasis that IBN places on relationships. Parties negotiate to improve interactions, not simply to solve a particular problem.

Game theory illustrates that parties are more likely to cooperate when an ongoing relationship exists between the parties (Rapoport, 1974). If two strangers are involved in a one-time conflict knowing that they will never see each other again, they have no incentive to make amicable relations one of their goals. Family members, co-workers, neighbors, and so on are in ongoing relationships. If negotiations are adversarial, one party might win the immediate battle but lose out in the bigger picture. An employer, for example, may have greater bargaining power than employees. However, if the employer simply coerces employees into submission, the employees will become angered and resistant. Both sides will eventually lose out. In order to encourage conflicting parties to build a positive negotiating relationship with you, help them understand your interdependence and the prospects for conflict over the long run.

One of the key principles suggested by Fisher, Ury, and Patton (1997) is to "separate the people from the problem" (p. 17). In other words, the focus of negotiations should be to resolve the problem. Express strong views about a problem, asserting your position passionately, without attacking the person. You are more likely to persuade a person who you have treated with respect than one who you have offended.

You do not need to like a person in order to negotiate effectively with that person. Helping professionals often work with "repugnant clients;" that is, clients with attributes that the professional finds offensive. Clients may express racist views, smell from stale cigarettes, spit when they talk, or speak in condescending tones. Still, helping professionals abide by the ethic that everyone deserves respect. They must find ways to work with the client, in spite of these concerns. Treat the person with respect. Deal directly with the problem. If the problem is related to the relationship, raise that as an issue. If someone is "pushing your buttons," take time out to reflect on why this is happening. Ask a supervisor or peer to help you debrief.

IBN encourages parties to consult with one another rather than make unilateral decisions. If Dorothy tells Miranda that she has found a nursing

home for her, Dorothy has left Miranda out of the decisio⹁.
Instead of presenting Miranda with a *fait accomplit*, Dorothy s.
the concerns and try to come up with a joint decision.

Fisher and Brown (1988) suggest that a positive negotiating relatiⷀ.
is one that can deal effectively with differences. Parties need not agre
with one another in order to have a good relationship. I have had some of my
most heated and contentious discussions with people I love dearly. Disagreeing does not mean rejection. People can have positive rapport even if
they have different values, attitudes, and beliefs. They must simply respect
diversity.

For certain people and within certain cultures, however, disagreement
does have negative connotations. Consider, for instance, individuals with poor
self-image or weak interpersonal boundaries. Disagreement comes across as
personal rejection. When negotiating with someone with low self-esteem, be
particularly careful to separate the person from the problem. Give the person
ample positive feedback. Reaffirm that you are not attacking them when you
are disagreeing. Build on positives.

In Chinese and other eastern cultures, harmony is highly valued
(LeBaron Duryea & Grundison, 1992; Irving & Benjamin, 1995). The
concept of a relationship that deals well with differences fits better with an
individualistic society. Within communitarian cultures, more emphasis needs
to be placed on peace and congenial relations. If possible, work towards
common goals rather than trying to satisfy each party's separate ones.

Fisher and Brown (1988) identify six unconditionally constructive strategies for building positive negotiation relationships.

- **Rationality**—even if they are acting emotionally, balance emotions with
  reason.[10]
- **Understanding**—even if they misunderstand us, try to understand
  them.
- **Communication**—even if they are not listening, consult them before
  making decisions on matters that affect them.
- **Reliability**—even if they are trying to deceive us, neither trust them
  nor deceive them; be reliable.
- **Noncoercive modes of influence**—even if they are trying to coerce
  us, neither yield to that coercion nor try to coerce them; be open to
  persuasion and try to persuade them.
- **Acceptance**—even if they reject us and our concerns as unworthy of
  their consideration, accept them as worthy of our consideration, care
  about them, and be open to learning from them. (p. 38)

---

[10]Adler, Rosen, and Silverstein (1998) provide a useful framework for how to manage feelings such as
fear and anger in negotiations.

These principles encourage negotiators to act in ways that promote a positive relationship, regardless of whether the other party reciprocates. Negotiating morally is valued in and of itself (Van Es, 1996). The six principles apply to formal negotiations as well as informal or emergent ones.

Many people question the wisdom of Fisher and Brown's guidelines. "Sounds great from an ideological perspective, but won't they allow people to walk all over you?" Actually, it is great ideologically. The six guidelines correspond with professional ethics such as unconditional positive regard, respect for all people, client self-determination, and being nonjudgmental. As for the pragmatic concern, these principles do not suggest that you go soft and allow people to take advantage of you. They support the notion of being respectful of others while being assertive with your interests. If you are being attacked, confront the problem rather than the person. Identify ways to confront that do not put the other person on the defensive. Remain open to working together for an amicable solution. If you are unable to arrive at a reasonable solution, you do not need to come to any agreement.

Radical professionals may still see this approach as being soft: If individuals or groups are being oppressed, they have the right to fight back. Does oppression justify the use of deception or coercive modes of influence? Must people offer respect or acceptance to those who oppress them? As you go through the experiential exercises, try different approaches. Consider what methods are most effective in dealing with oppressive parties. Return to the values you identified in Chapter 2 in order to see if these are consistent with your experiential understandings.

6. Consider Alternatives

Whereas options are possible solutions (ends), alternatives are possible CR processes. Negotiation is one method of CR, but there are many others: avoiding, fighting, mediating, litigating, flipping a coin, and so on. When a party decides to engage in a CR process, the result is not certain. In order to map out various alternatives and their likely outcomes, one could draw a decision tree (see Appendix D; Elangovan, 1995; Walls & Fullmer, 1995). Given a particular conflict situation, consider what attributes you are looking for in a CR process: cost-effectiveness, timeliness, fairness, affability, mutual satisfaction, etc. Once you have identified your goals, select a process that is most likely to satisfy these goals.

The term "BATNA" refers to a party's best alternative to negotiated agreement (Fisher, Ury, & Patton, 1997). By considering one's own BATNA, a party can decide whether it is better to negotiate or to select another alternative. In Dorothy and Miranda's conflict, Dorothy's alternatives include taking some sort of unilateral action: e.g., refuse to care for Miranda or go to court to have her mother declared mentally incompetent. Neither of these is very appealing to Dorothy. She loves her mother. Working things out on an amicable basis is important to her. If Dorothy and Miranda cannot negotiate a resolution on their own, Dorothy's BATNA is to try to resolve the conflict with the aid of their counselor. Since Miranda also wants an amicable settlement, she may be persuaded to try this alternative.

To some extent, the use of BATNAs falls into the power approach to negotiation rather than interest-based. The stronger your BATNA, the stronger your bargaining power. If your agency fires you for breaching client confidentiality, your alternatives include negotiating, walking away, looking for another job, and suing for damages. If you have a strong case based on your legal rights, your BATNA is going to court. Because your BATNA is strong, the agency will be willing to negotiate a favorable severance package. The agency will want to avoid court. Although you are the more powerful party, you do not have to use your power coercively. You can choose to negotiate using the interest-based approach.

In contrast, consider a situation where you are in a less powerful position: The government decides to deregulate your profession, believing that money can be saved by hiring non-professionals and by closing down your regulatory body. Assume that government has support of the general electorate. What are your alternatives to negotiation with government? Your profession could initiate a strike, but public support would not be with you. You could go to court, but there is no basis in law to reinstate your professional status if the government decides to deregulate. You could mediate, but government has shown no willingness to cooperate. Since your BATNA is weak, the government can take unilateral action, with little concern for your interests.

Using a power approach, you could take steps to strengthen your BATNA. For example, create a public awareness campaign to educate the electorate about the advantages of licensing in your profession. With public support, the potential effectiveness of a strike improves. By gaining relative power, you may be able to bring the government to an interest-based negotiating table. Alternatively, you could take steps to weaken the government's BATNA. The government's BATNA is taking unilateral action to deregulate the profession. Governments obtain their legitimacy through democratic processes. Although the government was elected and has the legislative authority to pass such laws, changing laws without consultation puts their legitimacy into question. By questioning the morality of the government's process, you weaken its BATNA and encourage it to engage in public consultation (a form of negotiation). Chapter 6 provides a more detailed description of how to use various sources of power. At this point, I want to focus on IBN.

Rather than negotiate specific outcomes, you could negotiate a process. Processes can be designed to be expedient, fair, or just. Some situations call for quick resolution. You and a colleague are deciding about where to go for lunch. If you take the time to go through the steps of IBN, your lunch hour may be over before you have a decision. Consider a quick alternative: each person gives one suggestion and you flip a coin to decide which of the two suggestions to follow. If there are more than two people, put all of the suggestions in a hat and draw one. The process is fair and you still have time for lunch.

If parties have tried IBN but reach stalemate, they could decide to negotiate a process giving an impartial third party the responsibility for making the decision. Divorcing parents who are contesting where a child should live, for instance, could agree to have an independent family assessment (Chisholm & McNaughton, 1990). The assessor[11] would conduct home visits with both parents and observe the child in each home. The parents would agree to abide by the recommendations of the assessor. The assessor would make the decision based on a professional assessment of the best interests of the child.

Impasse during IBN often occurs when there is a zero-sum game; that is, when a fixed pool of resources has to be divided. For distributive decisions, there are many techniques for creating a fair process.

- Taking turns — If there are a number of objects to be divided, each person can take a turn selecting an object. To reduce the advantage of going first, you can adjust the order of selections. Person A selects first. Person B gets the next two selections. Person A gets the next two selections, and so on.
- Separate who makes the division and who chooses — Person A divides the resources into two pools. Person B selects which pool to take. Person A will have an incentive to make the pools equally attractive.
- Buy-sell agreements[12] — Person A sets a price for the entire property in dispute. Person B can buy out Person A according to the price provided. If Person B chooses not to buy at that price, then Person A buys out Person B at the same price.

These examples demonstrate how IBN is not a mutually exclusive process. Through IBN, parties can agree to participate in other processes in order to determine all or some of their outstanding conflicts. Different processes have different advantages and disadvantages. By matching the appropriate process with the goals of the parties in a particular situation, parties are able to satisfy their mutual interests.

---

[11]An assessor is a professional with expertise in making certain types of assessment. The recommendations of the assessor can be binding or nonbinding, depending upon the prior agreement of the parties. If the recommendations are nonbinding, one or both parties may disregard them. If the assessor is a trusted expert and conducts the assessment fairly, the parties are more likely to follow the recommendations.

[12]Also called "shot-gun agreements," although this term has obvious connotations of violence.

7. *Obtain Commitments*

Parties who reach their own decisions about how to resolve a conflict are more likely to follow through on their decisions than decisions imposed by a third party (such as a judge in court or a supervisor in an agency). Parties tend to be more committed to their negotiated solutions because they have agreed to the terms. In contrast, imposed decisions may be disappointing to one or both parties. Dissatisfied parties frequently try to thwart implementation.

That said, negotiators must ensure that they have true commitments from one another. Some parties give the appearance of acquiescence without really giving a commitment to follow through. Others do not like confrontation, so they say they are agreeing, without having any intention of implementing the decisions.

In order to ensure that commitments are genuine, check out how the other parties plan to implement the decisions. Are the plans realistic? Do you detect any hesitance? Have you allowed the other parties to say they really are not satisfied with the agreement? Let them know that you do not want just any agreement, but one that both sides can live with and one that both sides will be able to follow. Railroading people into agreements does not work if you are depending on each other to implement the decisions.

In Dorothy and Miranda's situation, Miranda may be worried that Dorothy will reject her if they do not come to an agreement. Accordingly, Miranda might agree to a plan that she is not really happy with, just to appease Dorothy. In the excitement of coming to an agreement, Dorothy may not be aware of Miranda's concerns. If these concerns are not raised, Miranda will have trouble following through. To encourage Miranda to raise her concerns, Dorothy might say, "Before we say this is a done deal, let's review the plan. What do you like about it? What concerns do you still have?" This allows Miranda to raise her concerns without feeling defensive.

Help the other party make commitments. Implementation may require assistance from other people. "Great, we've come to an agreement between us. But how do I explain this to my family and to my neighbors?" The conflict does not end when parties reach an agreement. Accordingly, both parties have an interest in helping one another with implementation.

Consider a conflict between supervisors and counselors about the agency's overtime policy. The supervisor and counselors might agree that counselors can take time off on Fridays in lieu of overtime pay. This may suit their interests, but how does the supervisor sell this plan to the program director or other agency powers? The counselors do not want to give the supervisor a problem, because the problem is their problem, too. How can the counselors help their supervisor explain their solution to the program director? If the supervisor cannot follow through on the agreement, how can you alter the agreement to make it more feasible? IBN is about working together, giving each other workable solutions.

8. Limitations of Interest-based Negotiation

Since the 1980s, IBN has become one of the most popular models of negotiation among CR professionals. Proponents of IBN maintain that the model promotes joint decision making, so that both parties are satisfied with the resolution. The model works particularly well when: (a) the parties are flexible, (b) they are able to suspend their individual ambitions, (c) they have faith in their own abilities to negotiate, and (d) they have had prior success in resolving some issues (Pruitt & Carnevale, 1993).

In spite of the advantages of IBN, it does have limitations. One or more parties may be reluctant to engage in IBN because of lack of trust, anger, or other strong emotions. As game theory demonstrates, mistrust and anger promote competition rather than collaboration (Rapoport, 1974). Non-consensual CR processes, such as court, can be imposed on reluctant or unwilling parties. In contrast, IBN requires parties to submit voluntarily. If the parties cannot be sold on the advantages of IBN, then other processes may be necessary.

IBN is difficult when the conflict comes down to a difference between strong principles. If a conflict is based on a difference of positions, the parties can look underneath the positions to see if they have common underlying interests. If, on the other hand, the conflict is based on a fundamental difference between the parties' core values, there may be no middle ground and no opportunity for reaching a mutually satisfying agreement.

IBN may also be inappropriate when an expedient, authoritative decision is needed. If there are many parties and a decision is needed quickly, IBN may take too much time. Further, if the decision is relatively unimportant, investing an inordinate amount of time in the decision-making process is counterproductive (Pruitt & Carnevale, 1993).

IBN entails a number of cultural biases, including rationality and individuality, as described above. This approach also fits best with cultures where disclosure and confronting conflict directly are valued. IBN may be less appropriate within cultures where face-saving and conflict avoidance are valued over disclosure and confrontation. As you work through the materials and exercises, consider whether and how IBN could be reconstructed in order to deal more effectively with such cultural differences.

Finally, IBN may be inappropriate if your goal is not to reach a mutually satisfying agreement. If you are being exploited by a more powerful party, using the power approach may be necessary. If your objective is to obtain a just solution, the rights approach may be more appropriate. If your aim is more visionary, to construct a higher order of relations between individuals and groups, consider the transformative approach.

TRANSFORMATIVE NEGOTIATION

As noted above, Bush and Folger (1994) adopted the term transfc
mediation to connote an approach to mediation designed to promote empowerment and recognition between the parties. In this section, I provide a brief
overview of how transformation can be applied in a negotiation context, without the aid of a third party. Chapter 4 provides a more detailed analysis of this
approach in the context of mediation.

To illustrate the transformative approach, consider the following scenario.

> Humphrey is a human service professional working in a government-mandated
> workfare program. Humphrey's client, Camilla, is 23 years old, unemployed, and
> educated to a grade 10 equivalence. She has few job skills and sparse job experi-
> ence. Humphrey offers her a workfare position, doing physical work in the city's
> parks at minimum wage. Camilla refuses this position. She wants to go to college
> to learn computer skills, so she can work her way to a better paying career.
> Humphrey has seen her vocational test results and they indicate that she has
> poor aptitude for this type of work. She insists that she wants to learn computer
> skills. Humphrey cannot force her to work, but if she does not agree to a plan
> with Humphrey, she will lose all social assistance benefits.

If you view this situation from a problem-solving approach, you could employ
the IBN framework and try to work out a mutually agreeable solution with
the client. On the other hand, the transformative approach suggests that the
object of your efforts is to work towards empowerment and recognition.

1. Empowerment

Empowerment refers to any process where individuals or groups gain greater
control over matters that affect them (Barsky, 1996). At a psychological level,
empowerment is marked by enhancement of one's self-esteem, confidence,
and perception of self-efficacy. At a social level, empowerment involves gaining power through education, politicization, and collective action (Freire,
1970; Torré, 1986). Bush and Folger (1994) suggest that parties are empowered when:

- They realize more clearly what their *goals and interests* are and why they
  are important;
- They become more aware of the *options* available to them (what choices
  are available and that they have control over them);
- They improve their conflict resolution *skills*, including their ability to
  listen, communicate, organize and analyze issues, present arguments,
  brainstorm, and evaluate alternative solutions;
- They gain awareness of *resources* already in their possession or available
  to them to achieve their goals and objectives; and

- They reflect, deliberate, and make conscious *decisions* for themselves about what they want, and are able to analyze the strengths and weaknesses of various choices before making decisions. (pp. 85–87)

Humphrey can empower Camilla by applying these principles in his interaction with her. First, Humphrey can help Camilla identify her goals and interests. Initially, she says that she wants a career in computer programming. Humphrey probes deeper, "Why do you want to be a computer programmer?" Camilla acknowledges that she has to find a job that meets her basic needs (food and housing), but that she is also interested in a career that she makes her feel proud.

In terms of options, Humphrey has access to information that Camilla does not know. His agency has lists of job opportunities. He can also help Camilla locate alternate sources of funding if she wants to return to school rather than join the workfare program.

Camilla's communication and problem-solving skills are limited. If Humphrey negotiates without empowering Camilla, she will have trouble articulating her concerns and coming up with reasonable options. Instead, Humphrey asks Camilla if she would be willing to learn some basic conflict resolution skills. She agrees. They set aside a session where he teaches her about basic listening skills and assertiveness skills (similar to those described in Chapter 2). They role-play some situations, so that Camilla can practice the skills. She can use these skills to negotiate with Humphrey and she can take these skills away to use in other aspects of her life.

Camilla has had difficult experiences in school and work. Most of the feedback from her teachers and employers has been negative. Accordingly, Camilla has little self-confidence when it comes to working. Humphrey can help Camilla build her self-confidence by asking her to identify her strengths. Although she initially reported having no job skills, Humphrey helps her identify that she is reliable, friendly, and honest. She also helped raise two younger siblings while her parents were away at work. From this experience, she has learned time management skills, cooking, and conflict resolution.

One of Camilla's best friends got a job in computer programming and really likes it. Camilla thought it would be a good job for her, but she really has not thought about it very much. Humphrey helps Camilla reflect on her life goals, including what she wants from a career. He asks her to complete a three-question homework assignment. What type of job would you like to see yourself in five years from now? Which of your personal strengths will help you achieve this type of goal? What are three or four of the greatest challenges that you think you will face? They agree to discuss the answers at their next session.

Camilla and Humphrey may or may not come to an agreement about a job or work placement. However, Camilla will be empowered whether or not they resolve the conflict to their mutual satisfaction.

Helping professionals usually see themselves as the ones who facilitate the empowerment of clients; however, helping professionals can also use the Bush and Folger framework to empower themselves. Humphrey, for example, can reflect on his own goals and interests. Although his initial position is that Camilla should go on workfare, his underlying interests are to foster Camilla's self-determination and to fulfill his agency's mandate. If these interests conflict, he will have to choose between them. However, working through the other steps, he may be able to come up with options that he did not originally identify. Helping professionals are in an ongoing process of professional development. By reflecting on their conflict resolution skills and experiences, they can improve their practice and empower themselves. In turn, empowered professionals are better able to empower and recognize their clients (Pinderhughes, 1983).

2. Recognition

Recognition is comparable to the Rogerian therapy concept of demonstrating empathy; that is, demonstrating you understand another person's world from that person's frame of reference. Rogers (1957) identifies empathy as one of the core conditions[13] for developing a positive counseling relationship. Counselors can demonstrate empathy through the listening skills described in Chapter 2: attending, paraphrasing, reflecting feelings, and summarizing. According to Ivey and Ivey (1999), demonstrating empathy is most effective when the counselor's feedback is concrete, immediate, nonjudgmental, respectful, and authentic. However, a counselor must also ensure that empathy is conveyed in a manner that is culturally appropriate. Within some groups, for instance, listening in silence is more appropriate than using paraphrasing and reflecting back. Although recognition and empathy share some similarities, recognition entails techniques designed specifically for dealing with conflict.

In conflict situations, people (including helping professionals) often become angry or defensive. This creates a tendency to become wrapped up in one's own interests and problems, to the neglect of the other party's. Bush and Folger (1994) use the term recognition to remind conflicting parties to avoid becoming self-absorbed, but rather recognize the other party's situation: Recognition occurs when parties "voluntarily choose to become more open, attentive, sympathetic, and responsive to the situation of the other party" (p. 89).

---

[13] The other core conditions are genuineness and unconditional positive regard. Other literature refers to these as conditions for "therapeutic alliance."

A party can provide recognition to others through thoughts, words, and actions:

- By reflecting on the others' situation out of a general concern for their predicament;
- By consciously letting go of one's own viewpoint in order to open up to seeing the others in a different, more positive light;
- By trying to understand how, what seemed to be a hurtful or irrational act by the others might be the product of the other parties' reasonable response to stresses they have been enduring;
- By openly acknowledging one's changed understanding of the others;
- By apologizing for having "thought the worst" about the other party or for past "retaliatory conduct;" and
- By changing one's behavior to accommodate the other's interests, in light of the new understanding. (Folger & Bush, 1994, pp. 89–91)

The experience of recognition means *giving* recognition, rather than *receiving* recognition. However, there is an interactive effect between recognition and empowerment. When a party receives recognition, the validation is empowering. Conversely, an empowered party is more confident and self-assured, making it easier for that person to offer recognition to the other.

In Camilla's case, Humphrey can offer recognition by trying to gain a better understanding of where she is coming from. It would be easy for him to get wrapped up in his own job: he has made an assessment, offered Camilla a suitable position, and wants to wrap up this case so he can get on to his next client. Work is piling up. If Camilla will not be reasonable, then he is wasting time with her. To recognize Camilla, Humphrey begins by reflecting on his role as a workfare counselor. He sees himself not only as an agent of the workfare program, but as a human service professional who has a genuine interest in helping clients help themselves. He must start where the client is. He realizes that he has not been seeing things from Camilla's perspective and decides to try to suspend his initial assessments and judgments. He thinks, "If I were in Camilla's shoes . . ." He begins to see Camilla in a different light—not as a resistant client, but as a client who is advancing her own interests. She has probably had negative experiences with other bureaucracies, so her anger is not aimed at him personally. She has said that she wants to be a computer programmer: from her perspective, maybe that is reasonable. Humphrey shares his understandings with Camilla and asks her if he is understanding her more accurately. She corrects him on a few points and he remains supportive. He apologizes for sounding as if he knew what was best for her. He offers to work together with her to develop a career plan that meets her needs.

Offering recognition often leads the other party to offer recognition in return. Camilla says that she understands that Humphrey was trying to help her and that he was just trying to do his job. Humphrey is caught off guard by her level of insight and recognition. As a helping professional, his focus is to help his client, but Camilla's words do make him feel appreciated.

Transformation can be viewed as a means to move the parties towards interest-based negotiation. If the parties are empowered and recognize one another, they are better able to work together and resolve differences to their mutual satisfaction. Bush and Folger, however, purport that transformation is an end in and of itself. Successful negotiation results from empowerment and recognition, regardless of whether the parties come to an interest-based agreement. Through transformation, people have a greater understanding and appreciation of one another. They also have a more positive sense of themselves and their capabilities. Agreement is not necessarily the ultimate goal. People can come away from a conflict, disagreeing with one another, but still having grown from the experience.

Given the transformative approach, you may be wondering what is the difference between transformative conflict resolution and therapy. How would Humphrey's intervention differ if he decided to intervene based on systems theory? Feminist theory? Psychodynamic theory? Humanistic theory? I leave these questions for you to consider as you work through the exercises. Similar questions are raised in Chapter 4, this time in relation to transformative mediation.

3. *Limitations of Transformation*

In one sense, asking about the limitations of transformation is the wrong question. Transformation is about changing people, cultures, and the world. It is a movement based on high ideals and visions. How can one speak of limitations when the movement is based on high ideals and visions for humanity? Success or failure is not based on a single conflict or interaction, but fundamental changes in society.

Because research into the effectiveness of transformative CR is only beginning to emerge, strengths and limitations of the approach are difficult to gauge. Proponents have strong convictions in its effectiveness (Lang, 1996). Questions for further study include: when does transformative negotiation work; what factors contribute to its effectiveness; and under how well does this model work when there is a significant power imbalance between the parties?

On its own terms, the goal of transformation is neither winning, settlement, fairness, nor justice. Parties seeking these goals are likely to opt for other processes. For instance, parties embroiled in conflict are often angry with one another. They want to fight it out, take revenge, or give the other side its just desserts. If they are not motivated to engage in transformative negotiation, they will tend to resist the process.

Although transformative negotiation is arguably most effective when both parties are motivated towards transformation, the approach can be employed by a single party whether or not the other party follows suit. One party can offer empowerment and recognition to the other, regardless of whether the other returns the same. In fact, the approach is based on the premise of offering empowerment and recognition because they are inherently good, not because you expect reciprocity. "I will act morally, regardless of the actions of the other parties." When evaluating negotiation for success, the important question is, "How well did *I* follow the principles of transformation?"

CULTURAL ISSUES

Culture refers to shared beliefs, values, language, and behavioral norms that occur among groups with common experiences. Such groups can be defined by ethnic background, nationality, religion, gender, sexual orientation, socio-economic status, education, and disability (LeBaron, 1997). Cultural issues are pervasive in negotiation. For helping professionals, cultural issues arise in a number of realms.

- Various professions are reaching out to diverse communities in order to provide better services. Existing models of practice and system requirements may not meet their needs.
- As recent immigrants work their way through employment services, health services, welfare programs, schools, and other bureaucracies, they often come into conflict with helping professionals who are the gatekeepers and service providers in these systems.
- Disadvantaged groups are becoming more organized, so that they are better prepared to negotiate for social justice and confront systems where helping professionals work.
- As diverse groups move into helping professions (including conflict resolution), older professional values and cultural norms are being challenged.
- In many jurisdictions, courts and legislatures are recognizing freedom from discrimination for people from diverse backgrounds; helping professionals are often responsible for implementing these rights (e.g., access to employment, school, or social services).
- Conflicts also arise within cultures. Although some cultures prefer to resolve intracultural conflict on their own, others welcome the assistance of helping professionals from outside of the community (Duryea LeBaron & Grundison, 1992).

Cross-cultural conflicts arise at various levels: misunderstandings due to differences in language or cultural interpretations, disputes over allocation of resources between majority and minority groups, conflicting values, and mistrust from previous experiences of oppression or exploitation. Although it is important to recognize cultural components to disputes, be careful about stereotyping or blaming a particular culture for causing conflict. If this is a two-party conflict, both cultures play a role in the development of the conflict and its resolution.

Each negotiation approach has different implications for conflict and culture issues. Consider a conflict between a client (Clarence) from a disadvantaged group and a therapist (Thelma) from an advantaged group in the community. During a session, Clarence yells,

> *You pretend like you care about me, Thelma, but that's only for an hour. Then you go home to your nice house in your nice neighborhood with your nice family.*

From a power perspective, Clarence perceives that Thelma comes from a position of greater power and influence. He is a client from a background of poverty, low education, and social discrimination. Thelma has a good job, educational background, and home. Clarence also sees her as a person with authority. As a helping professional, Thelma does not want to exploit Clarence with her power. If she wanted to use her power with good intentions, she might employ her authority and expertise to give Clarence advice on how to behave.

> *You are getting angry. Why don't we try to calm down and talk to each other like civil adults.*

The reason Clarence verbally attacked Thelma may be seen as a way for him to exert power. By asking him to calm down, she may be trying to take away his power. Clarence may respond by becoming even angrier. Conflict will escalate unless Thelma can find a way to diffuse it.

If Thelma uses a transformative approach, she will demonstrate empathy with his frustration. She will also try to understand his cultural background. Rather than becoming defensive, she will try to offer him support. Rather than quell his power, she will try to empower him.

> *You don't think I really care about you. This seems to be affecting our working relationship. Please tell me more about how you would like to see my role.*

In addition, Thelma might explore Clarence's cultural background by speaking with other helping professionals from his culture (Barsky, Este, & Collins, 1996). She may learn, for instance, that her sense of professional boundaries is perceived as a lack of caring within Clarence's culture.

From an interest-based perspective, Thelma would encourage Clarence to engage in joint problem solving with her. Her strategies could include "separating the person from the problem" and "balancing reason with emotions." Within certain cultures, these presumably positive suggestions could be detrimental. Separating the person from the problem could be seen as insensitive. For some groups, a positive relationship with the person is inseparable from being able to work together on problems (LeBaron, 1997). Clarence has already indicated that Thelma is emotionally detached from him. He is more accustomed to sharing details of his private life with a person he knows more personally.

In terms of balancing reason with emotions, Thelma might run into trouble once again. Emotions are expressed differently among different cultures. The fact that Clarence raised his voice may be an expression of anger. However, his culture may have a different sense of what type of voice levels are appropriate in a given context. For Thelma to respond in a calm, rational tone, Clarence might interpret this as further evidence that Thelma does not care about him. Accordingly, emotional expression must be construed within a cultural context. Vivid display of emotions does not necessarily mean a lack of rationality. On the other hand, some people demonstrate little emotion even though, underneath, their feelings are affecting their ability to make reasoned decisions.

These examples just touch the surface of issues related to culture and conflict. Consider literature and research on specific cultures and conflict when you are working with people from a particular culture (Brett, Adair, Lempereux, Okumura, Shikhirev, Tinsley, & Lytle, 1998; LeBaron Duryea, 1994; Irving & Benjamin, 1995; LeBaron, 1997). More cultural issues are discussed in Chapters 4 and 5.

NEGOTIATION PREPARATION TOOL

Given the four approaches to negotiation, you may decide that one is most consonant with your own personal and professional values. If so, that approach may become your predominant framework for negotiating. Otherwise, you may decide that different approaches are required for different types of circumstances. In any event, preparing yourself is vital for effective negotiation. The following preparation tool is designed to help you assess a conflict situation and devise an appropriate plan for negotiation, regardless of your chosen approach.

The framework is not a fixed recipe to be followed step-by-step. Apply it loosely; that is, feel free to use various parts of the tool without following all of its suggestions. Different conflict scenarios will call for emphasizing different parts of the tool.[14] Return to the tool at various stages of negotiation to re-evaluate your strategies. Initially, for example, you may decide to use rights-based strategies, and later decide to move from contention to interest-based cooperation. The tool is divided into four sections: analysis, strategies, skills, and evaluation.

---

[14] This tool draws from Lewicki (1997), Druckman (1993), Fisher and Urtel (1995), and Bush and Folger (1994).

Negotiation Preparation Tool

1. Analysis
   (a) Define the issue under dispute. On the surface, what is the conflict about? (cf., Lewicki, 1997)
   (b) What is the nature of the difference underlying the conflict?
   - Difference of interests?
     A difference of interests often comes down to the problem of how to distribute limited resources. Distribution can be based upon the parties' relative power, rights, or joint interests. Can the pool of resources be expanded before distribution is made?
   - Difference of understandings?
     A difference in understandings can be based upon differences in the parties' thought processes, perceptions, memories, beliefs, and interpretations, or differences in the information they are relying upon. To resolve differences in understandings, see communication strategies, below.
   - Differences of ideologies or beliefs?
       Beliefs, ideologies, values, and attitudes form during childhood and generally remain stable throughout adulthood. When a conflict is based on a difference in ideologies or beliefs, trying to change the other party's ideologies or beliefs is difficult, if not impossible.[15] Rather than try to change someone's ideologies or beliefs, negotiation could focus on exploring differences and validating one another's perspectives (see transformative approach). Another alternative is to de-link ideologies from interests: Agree to disagree on ideologies and then negotiate other issues based on one of the other approaches. (Druckman, 1993)
       Conflicts are often multidimensional. If the conflict is based on more than one type of difference, identify each of these and assess which aspect is the primary cause of the conflict.
   (c) What additional theories of psychology or social systems help you to understand the conflict between the parties (e.g., game theory, conflict styles, systems analysis, developmental theory, feminist analysis, sociocultural theories)? How do your chosen theories help you interpret the situation?
   (d) What is your overall goal for negotiation?

(continued)

---

[15]Chapter 5 presents certain models of intervention for changing attitudes and ideologies; however, these are aimed at community development rather than negotiating specific disputes.

Negotiation Preparation Tool (Continued)

(e) Based on your goal, what are your specific objectives? How will you know you are successful? (Consider process objectives as well as outcome objectives.)

(f) What approach(es) are most likely to help you achieve your overall goal?

2. Strategies

Use the information from your analysis to help you select strategies, below. Focus on the section related to the approach you identified in 1(f). The four approaches are power, rights, interests, and transformation. Communication is separated out as its own category, since it overlaps with various approaches.

(a) Power-based Strategies

    i. What is your original position? Have you already disclosed this? If not, how will you disclose it?

    ii. What is the other party's original position?

    iii. What concessions are you willing to make? Under what circumstances will you compromise?

    iv. What is your bottom line for negotiation?

    v. What is your best estimate about the other party's bottom line?

    vi. What information will you share with the other party?

    vii. What information will you not share?

    viii. What information do you hope to obtain from the other party?

    ix. What strategies will you use in negotiations (e.g., debate, play tit-for-tat, being intransigent, bluff, threaten, use force; make extreme first offer, make small concessions)? For each strategy that you intend to use, identify the reasons for using it and the risks involved (consider clinical and ethical issues).

    x. How can you improve your relative power (see Chapter 6 for sources of power and additional strategies to improve them)? (Also, consider use of BATNA as described in (c) below.)

(b) Rights-based Strategies

    i. What laws, policies, or other rules are relevant to the present conflict?

    ii. What do these laws, policies, or rules say about your rights?

    iii. What do these laws, policies, or rules say about the other's rights?

    iv. Are the rights of any third parties relevant (e.g., the community's rights, a child's rights)?

    v. What arguments support your rights?

     vi. What arguments support the other's rights?

    vii. How can you counter the other party's arguments?

   viii. If the laws, policies, or rules do not favor your rights, how can you change them (e.g., law reform, advocate changes in agency policy, develop community support to change rules)?

    ix. What is the most effective way to communicate your rights to the other party (e.g., informal dialogue, formal face-to-face negotiations, exchange of letters)? What are the advantages and risks of this form of communication?

    x. If you and the other party cannot agree upon whose rights prevail, how can you obtain a determination of rights (e.g., court, administrative appeal, arbitration)? (Consider mapping out your choices using a "decision tree" to analyze alternatives (Appendix D; Elangovan, 1995; Walls & Fullmer, 1995).)

    xi. Would legal advice or legal representation assist your case?

(c) Interest-based Strategies

The following questions and strategies are based on Fisher, Ury, and Patton's (1997) seven-point framework:

    i. Focus on Interests, Not Positions: What are your interests? What are the other's interests? Which interests do you have in common? Which interests conflict? Are these conflicting interests based on any deeper interests that you do share (e.g., underlying desires, values, or needs)?

    ii. Invent Options for Mutual Gain: Identify all possible options for solution. Is it better to brainstorm individually or together? What other sources of information can you access to help you invent options? Do not evaluate the options until you have finished identifying them.

   iii. Apply Objective Criteria: What standards can be used to assess the options? What sources can you explore that might help you identify objective criteria (e.g., experts in the field, literature, precedent cases)?

   iv. Improve Communication: See (d) below.

    v. Build a Positive Negotiating Relationship: Consider use of unconditionally constructive strategies: rationality, understanding, consultation, reliability, noncoercive modes of influence, and acceptance. What makes employing these strategies difficult in the present conflict? How can you try overcome these challenges? How can you encourage collaboration?

(continued)

Negotiation Preparation Tool (Continued)

vi. Consider Alternatives: What are your alternatives to a negotiated agreement? Which of these is your BATNA? What are the
other party's alternatives? Which one is the other's BATNA?
(Consider using decision trees (Appendix D) to identify
alternatives and BATNAs from each party's perspective.) How
will you know when it is best to terminate negotiation and move
to another alternative? What are the advantages and risks of
your BATNA? If the other party has a strong BATNA, what incentives can you use to encourage that party to negotiate?
Rather than negotiate for a specific solution, would it be useful
to negotiate a process designed to produce a fair result? How
can you improve your BATNA? How can you worsen the other's
BATNA? (Note that these last two strategies are power-based
rather than interest-based strategies.)

vii. Obtain Commitments: What commitments do you need in
order to make an agreement work? What commitments are you
prepared to make? What commitments is the other party prepared to make? Are these commitments feasible? How can you
solidify the commitments? How can you help the other party
make commitments? What strategies can you use to ensure
that commitments are followed by all parties?

(d) Communication Strategies

i. What past problems, if any, stem from miscommunication?
How can you rectify these problems? (e.g., If the conflict is
caused by the parties' relying on different information, then
sharing information is important; if the parties have different
interpretations of the information, then they can explain these
differences to one another; if parties cannot understand one
another, consider the use of an interpreter.[16])

ii. What communication problems do you foresee in upcoming
negotiations? How can you pre-empt these?

iii. What is your purpose for communication? (e.g., to demonstrate
that you hear and understand the other party, to persuade, to
build trust, to share information, to reach an agreement)

iv. Given your purpose for communication, what is the best forum
for negotiation? (e.g., face-to-face, electronic mail, telephone)

---

[16]An interpreter is not only someone who can translate from one language to another, but one who
can explain different constructions of language that arise from different cultural experiences.

  v. How can you tailor the forum for negotiation so that it promotes constructive communication? (e.g., sufficient time,
good working space, low stress, few distractions)

  vi. If direct communication is problematic, what type of
facilitator(s) might help the process? (e.g., representatives for
each party, mediator, supervisor)

(e) Transformation-based Strategies

The transformative approach is based on two types of strategies,
empowerment and recognition (Bush & Folger, 1994):

  i. Empowerment Strategies: How can you empower yourself?
How can you empower the other party? What are the potential barriers to empowering yourself or the other party? How
can you resolve these barriers?

  ii. Recognition: What reflective processes will help you think
about and understand the other's situation (e.g., journaling,
speaking with a supervisor, reading literature, role reversal,
active listening with the other party)? How can you offer
recognition through words? How can you offer recognition
through your actions? What will make offering recognition
difficult? How can you address these challenges?

3. Skills

Once you have identified your primary strategies, consider which
of the following skills are required in order to implement these
strategies.

(a) Uses basic communication skills (for example, listens effectively
to the other side, asks questions to gain information and assure
better understanding, and makes statements assertively without
becoming aggressive. Refer to Chapter 2 for more details.)

(b) Demonstrates Roger's core conditions:
- Difference of interests? Empathic understanding
- Unconditional positive regard
- Genuineness

(c) Demonstrates rationality—balances emotions with reason

(d) Demonstrates reliability (honest, open, credible)

(e) Demonstrates openness to persuasion and creative ideas

(f) Separates the person from the problem

(g) Focuses on problem solving

(h) Demonstrates acceptance—even if the other party rejects you or
your concerns

(continued)

Negotiation Preparation Tool (Continued)

(i) Obtains agreement to follow an agenda (organizing issues to be negotiated)

(j) Establishes constructive rules for interaction (e.g., information will be shared; neither party will threaten force; time lines for negotiations)

(k) Acknowledges power issues

(l) Uses persuading skills:
  i. Demonstrates having heard the other side, before actively trying to persuade
  ii. Articulates own position, rights, interests, or beliefs (depending on the approach used)
  iii. Uses "I" statements to express personal feelings, values, or ideologies
  iv. Builds on the other's ideas, values, or interests
  v. Uses language that the other party can accept
  vi. Asserts positions or interests without becoming harassing, threatening, or manipulative (unless these are consciously selected strategies)
  vii. Backs up opinions with objective facts or information
  viii. Uses appropriate emotional displays to support statements, without detracting from them (e.g., expressing strong convictions, hope, sadness)
  ix. Deals directly with arguments from the other party rather than ignoring, discounting, or side-stepping around them

(m) Paces communication effectively (balances processing of information with moving the negotiation process ahead)

(n) Analyzes the total pool of shared information so as to understand areas of agreement and disagreement

(o) Creatively brainstorms and invents options so as to understand areas of agreement and disagreement

(p) Uses flipcharts or other form of notes to maintain records and provide visual cues for negotiators

(q) Builds on the positives (e.g., constructive moves of the other party; areas of commonality)

(r) Respects other party's freedom to agree or not agree

(s) Articulates and records terms of agreement, if any

(t) Refers back to negotiation preparation tools for assessment, strategies and skills

(u) Provides authentic apology

(v) Accepts apology graciously
4. Implementation and Evaluation

Planning, implementation, and evaluation of negotiation are iterative processes. Although this tool is presented in sequential form, you can move back and forth through various sections as you negotiate. In order to move from planning to implementing, jot down a few notes to remind you of your primary assessments, key strategies, and skills. Keep these as a checklist to help you focus and troubleshoot while you are in negotiation. During the process, remain open to new understandings of the dynamics and the need to alter your strategies accordingly.

(a) What was my original understanding of the nature of the conflict? Is this understanding still valid?

(b) Do the strategies seem to be working? Are we moving towards my stated goals and objectives? If not, why? Consider process objectives, relationship objectives, and outcome objectives.

(c) What are the strengths and limitations of the strategies I have been using? What other strategies would be useful at this point?

(d) What are the strategies of the other party? What are the strengths and limitations of these strategies? How can I best respond to these strategies?

(e) If difficulties exist, would it be useful to bring in help (e.g., a consultant, an advocate, a mediator, a buffer, an arbitrator)?

(f) What ethical dilemmas or values issues need to be considered?

Videotaping or audiotaping sessions provides an excellent means of reviewing your use of skills and strategies. You can review these on your own or with the help of a peer or supervisor. Compare how you planned to proceed with what actually took place. Look for crisis points, critical incidents, and factors that moved the negotiations forward.

Formal research into your negotiations can make use of various methods: single case design, quantitative evaluation, naturalistic inquiry, and action research. While this is not a research text, the value of various types of research requires at least some mention. Single case study design can help you monitor the effectiveness of your negotiation interventions on a case-by-case basis (Weinbach & Grinnell, 1996). Quantitative program evaluations are useful for determining the effectiveness of a program, where a particular model of negotiation is used on a regular basis (Gabor, Unrau, & Grinnell, 1998).

Naturalistic inquiry is particularly useful for gaining an understanding of the negotiation process from the parties' perspectives (Denzin & Lincoln, 1994). Action research is similar to program evaluation, but combines simultaneous research, evaluation, and program development (Finn, 1994). Often, the research is conducted by practitioners themselves rather than outside research consultants. This allows practitioners greater control over how research is conducted and provides them with ongoing research results rather than one report at the end of the evaluation process (Lewin, 1948). Informal evaluation, as described above, may be sufficient for your individual purposes. Formal evaluation is more costly. However, the results of formal evaluation can be published so that others can also learn from your negotiation experiences.

KEY POINTS

- Helping professionals can approach negotiation from one of four paradigms, separately or in combination: power, rights, interests, and transformation.
- According to the power approach, each party exerts its influence on the other in order to maximize its personal gain, often to the detriment of the relationship between the parties.
- The rights approach suggests that conflicts be resolved in accordance with rights as established by public laws, organizational rules, or community norms.
- Interest-based negotiation is a joint problem-solving process, where parties strive to satisfy their mutual interests, including the opportunity to build a more positive relationship.
- Transformative negotiation is a process designed to provide parties with empowerment and recognition. Empowerment occurs when parties gain a greater sense of self-determination, choice, and autonomy. Recognition occurs when a party gains a better understanding of the other's situation and demonstrates this new-found empathy to the other through words or deeds.
- When negotiating with people from diverse cultures, helping professionals must deconstruct the assumptions underlying various theories and strategies in order to assure that their interventions are culturally appropriate.
- Preparation for negotiation is an iterative process in which helping professionals reflect on negotiation theory, assessment, strategies, and skills at various points throughout the negotiation process.

Discussion Questions and Exercises

1. CONTRACTING: You are working with a psychiatric patient, Pat, who is at risk of committing suicide. Your suicide prevention model suggests that you negotiate a "safety plan" with the client (e.g., Pat will stay with a friend overnight; you will contact the friend by phone to provide the friend with instruction about what to do in case of emergency, Pat will call the 24 hour crisis line if Pat starts to think about committing suicide; Pat will meet with you tomorrow to make further plans). Should this agreement be implicit, explicit and oral, or written? What are the advantages and disadvantages of each type of agreement? Do you or Pat require legal advice before finalizing this agreement? Why or why not? Is this agreement a legally binding agreement? What are the consequences if either one of you breaks the agreement?

2. NEGOTIATION SUCCESS: Consider the four approaches to negotiation described in this chapter: power, rights, interests, transformation. How does each of these approaches view success? Consider the following criteria:

   - I Win (maximize gain for me)
   - Win-Win (maximize joint gain)
   - Satisfies the Interests of the Parties
   - Efficient Process (saves money and other resources)
   - Fair Process (equal bargaining power, neutrality, or impartiality in the process)
   - Fair Outcome (equitable distribution of resources—consider, who decides what is fair?)
   - Better Relationships between the Parties (harmonious, amicable, able to deal with differences)
   - Retributive Justice (appropriate consequences hold people accountable)
   - Restorative Justice (restitution or compensation)
   - Avoidance of Court (e.g., conflicts are settled informally, in negotiation or mediation)
   - Durable Solutions (solutions that last, without new conflict arising)
   - Improve Conflict Resolution Skills of Parties
   - Empowerment
   - Recognition
   - Better Decisions (how do you judge what is "better")
   - Community Enhancement (better off than prior to the intervention)
   - Promotes Diversity
   - Social Control (enforcement of societal norms)
   - Anger is Diffused
   - Other: _____

If you were to design a research project to evaluate success of a CR program, how would you measure success? How do you decide what to measure?

3. POSITIONAL STRATEGIES: Read through the following dialogue between Theodore and Clarabelle. Identify the positional negotiation strategies used by Theodore and Clarabelle. How does this interaction display the power approach? How could Theodore approach this conflict from an interest-based approach?

THEODORE (THERAPIST): *After last week's session, I started to think that there's a problem we have to discuss.*
CLARABELLE (CLIENT): *I don't know what you mean. Let's just forget it.*
THEODORE: *No, I really think that we have to talk about it. What do you think the problem is?*
CLARABELLE: *What do you think the problem is?*
THEODORE: *This therapy is about you. It's important to explore your feelings.*
CLARABELLE: *Well, if you really want to know, I think that you're always trying to lay a guilt trip on me.*
THEODORE: *I'd never do that. I respect you, as I do all my clients.*
CLARABELLE: *Well you asked and I told you.*
THEODORE: *Perhaps you are feeling frustrated about your lack of progress.*
CLARABELLE: *What do you mean? After all I've been through? There you go again, making me feel guilty.*
THEODORE: *Then maybe we should just terminate our relationship.*
CLARABELLE: *I'm not saying that. I just think there has to be more give and take.*
THEODORE: *So, what exactly do you want me to do?*

4. POWER AND ETHICS: In negotiations with a client, when, if ever, is use of power by a helping professional justified? Necessary? Consider your profession's code of ethics, including concepts such as self-determination, respect, safety, and imposition of values.

5. DEALING WITH THREATS: You are working with a drug-abusing client, Dora. Dora is desperate to get into a drug abuse treatment program. You tell her that there is a waiting list of three weeks. Dora threatens to blow up your agency if you cannot get her in the program within two days. You believe that the threats are real and that Dora has the ability to follow through. How will you negotiate with Dora? Consider the four approaches to negotiation and strategies within each approach.

6. RIGHTS AND RELATIONSHIPS: You are working for a gay, lesbian, and bisexual community center. The local government offers funding for programs for street youth. You submit a proposal on behalf of your agency. The government says that it cannot accept your proposal because it does

not want to promote sexual deviance among street youth. You consider your alternatives: assert the rights of the group you represent by challenging the government's decision in a court case (judicial review); assert their rights through demonstrations; try to develop a better relationship with members of government. What are the advantages and disadvantages of each of these alternatives? What other alternatives should be considered? Which alternative is best? Why? (consider use of decision tree analysis)

7. SMOKING POSITIONS, RULES, AND INTERESTS: You are working with a client, Cleo, who asks if she can smoke. You tell Cleo that the office building has a no smoking rule. The two of you get into an argument about whether she has the right to smoke or not. What are each of your positions? If you bargain from a positional orientation, what range of outcomes might you consider? What type of compromise might you reach? Now, analyze the case from an interest-based approach. What are Cleo's underlying interests? What are your interests? Brainstorm 10 to 15 options that might satisfy these interests. How does this interest-based approach differ from the positional approach? (Fisher, Ury, & Patton, 1997)

8. A SLICE OF EVENING PIE: Your supervisor announces that your agency is extending its hours so it can serve clients on evenings and weekends. She suggests that you and three colleagues alternate each week, taking either a weekend or evening shift each week. You have a child who is in school from 9 a.m. to 4 p.m. every weekday. Jules has no children. His commute to the agency takes over an hour, each way. Selma lives close to the agency. She has a physical condition that makes her tire easily, so she needs lots of rest and a regular routine. Whitney wants to go to grad school and work part-time. None of you to like the idea of alternating shifts. What options can you generate for mutual gain? How can the expanded schedule become an advantage rather than a problem?

9. COLD OFFICE: You and a colleague share an office. You find the office hot and stuffy, so you turn on the air conditioner. Your colleague finds the office too cold and wants to turn on the heat. You suggest a compromise, leaving both the air conditioning and the heat off. You colleague asks if there isn't a better solution. What is the nature of this conflict? How else can you resolve this conflict? (Fisher, Ury, & Patton, 1997)

10. CLASS COMPETITION AND COOPERATION: You are in a class where the term project is a paper requiring library research. During the ninth class, the professor will provide the specific research topics. You fear that everyone will rush to the library after that class to take out all of the books. If one or two people horde most of the books, others will suffer. What CR theories can you use to analyzing this situation? What are the incentives favoring competition between students? What are the incentives favoring cooperation? How would you approach negotiations with your classmates?

11. SHARING A DRINK: Have someone bring a bottle of a drink that most people enjoy. Select five people in the class and give them each a glass. The mission for these five people is to identify a method of dividing the drink. All five people would like as much of the drink as possible. The parties agree to following principles for division: fair, practical, and enforceable. Brainstorm alternatives. Once you have an exhaustive list, apply the principles for selection and negotiate an agreement about the process for division. Implement the decision. Evaluate the process and implementation according to the suggestions earlier in this chapter.

12. ROLE REVERSAL: You are working with a client who has a mental illness and is putting others at risk of serious harm. Your supervisor suggests that the client be given sedatives, even though the client does not want them. What is your view on using medication to sedate this client? Write down your reasons. In order to gain a better understanding of someone with a different view, find a partner in the class to do a role reversal. Your partner will play your role in a discussion about this issue. In order to understand your perspective, provide your partner with your list of reasons. You will argue the other person's point of view.

    Debriefing Questions

    What made it difficult for you to assume the other person's role? What did you learn by taking on this role? How might this knowledge help you negotiate about the issue of involuntary use of medication?

13. POWER AND JOINT PROBLEM SOLVING: You are working with an agency that serves youth in conflict with the law. The agency receives referrals from probation officers. Your role is to negotiate a plan with the youth and the youth's parents to deal with underlying problems and to prevent the youth from re-offending. If the youth does not agree to a plan, then the youth will have to return to court to face charges. Consider the ethics of this model. Is it ethically appropriate to use power to push clients into a joint problem-solving process? Is this constructive use of power or an insidious form of social control? How can you construct your negotiation process with the youth in order to minimize the ethical concerns? (cf., Tjaden, 1994)

14. PRESSURE TO AGREE: You have been looking for a job for three months and have just received your first offer. You like the agency and the type of work that the agency offers. Unfortunately, the salary is substantially below your expectations. The agency's position regarding salary is "take it or leave it." Use the Negotiation Preparation Tool to analyse this conflict and to strategize how to approach negotiations. What type of conflict is this? What is your preferred approach? How will you know if your negotiations are successful? Can negotiations be "successful" even if you do not reach an agreement with the agency?

15. NEGOTIATING CONCEPTS OF TIME: You are working with a Native American community. In your culture, as well as that of your agency,

people set appointments for meetings and conduct meetings in offices. The beginning and end times are fixed, with about five minutes of flexibility for lateness or running overtime. Most people from the community you are working with have a different sense of time. People meet when needed and when the time is appropriate, rather than at an artificially predetermined time. Meetings are often held out in the community or in someone's home rather than in an office building. Meetings seem informal to you, with no clear boundary between when the meeting begins and ends. What are the implications of these cultural differences for negotiations between you and members of the community? How do you negotiate a set of norms for meetings that are acceptable to both you and members of the community?

16. DECONSTRUCTING INTEREST-BASED NEGOTIATION: Review Fisher, Ury, and Patton's (1997) model of interest-based negotiation. Identify the underlying assumptions of the model and deconstruct it using a post-modern, feminist analysis. For suggestions on how to deconstruct a model of intervention, see Culler (1982), Lederach (1986), or Pennell and Ristock (1997).

17. TRANSFORMATIVE VERSUS INTEREST-BASED NEGOTIATION: Assume that you adopt the transformative approach to negotiation. Accordingly, you view success as empowerment and recognition. Assume further that your client views success as satisfaction of interests. Are your respective perspectives at cross-purposes? In negotiating with this client, whose perspective will prevail?

Cartoon drawn by Donato Damiano, Montreal artist

18. POLITICAL CORRECTNESS: You work on a committee for advancement of rights of people with disabilities. During a public meeting, a city official refers to people with disabilities as "gimps." The official thinks it is just a joke, but you find the term offensive. What is the nature of this type of conflict? What are your primary goals in negotiating with the official? How can you best achieve them?

19. LEARNING NEEDS: Review the Negotiation Preparation Tool. Identify five or six skills or strategies that you want to focus upon for professional development. These could be areas that you want to explore even though they do not seem to fit with your preferred approach. Alternatively, identify skills and strategies that you believe will be most important for your specific areas of practice. As you work through the role-plays and exercises, remember to practice your chosen skills and strategies.

ROLE-PLAY 3.1: "CONTRACTING WITH CLEM"

This is a role-play between a psychologist, Sylvie, and a client, Clem. Sylvie works for Diversity Plus, specializing in work with men who have been physically abusive with their partners. Clem was referred by his probation officer, following charges of assault against his partner. Clem's probation officer wants to know whether or not Clem is cooperating with the psychologist, one of the conditions of his probation.

The purpose of this role-play is to practice contracting with clients. Since this is the first session between Sylvie and Clem, they need to negotiate the terms of confidentiality and exceptions to it. In order to prepare for this role-play, Sylvie should prepare notes for herself about what issues are negotiable and what issues are not negotiable. Clem should consider, from a client's perspective, what terms would be agreeable to him. Clem is not familiar with the concept of confidentiality, so Sylvie will need to be able to explain what it means, including different options.

During the role-play, first work towards an oral agreement. Once an oral agreement is reached, prepare a written agreement that reflects what you agreed to orally. This role-play takes 15 to 25 minutes.

Debriefing Questions:

What unexpected issues arose in the role-play? What did Sylvie do that helped make contracting more effective? If Sylvie could do the role-play over again, what would she do differently? Does the confidentiality contract between Sylvie and Clem satisfy the needs and expectations of third parties (e.g., the agency, probation, Sylvie's profession; Clem's partner)? If not, what else should be considered? Does either party in this scenario require legal advice before signing the contract? Is this contract a legally binding agreement? If either party breaks the agreement, what are the legal consequences, if any?

ROLE-PLAY 3.2: "NEGOTIATING FOR GRADES"— FOUR APPROACHES

This role-play has two roles—a university professor, Dr. Proulx, and a student, Sandy Simms. Dr. Proulx has given Sandy a grade of 78% for her final term paper. Sandy needed at least 81% in order to achieve an "A" standing for the course. Ordinarily, Sandy would not complain. However, if she gets an A in this course, then she is eligible for a scholarship that will enable her to do research in conflict resolution for her graduate program. Dr. Proulx believes that 78% was a fair grade. Divide the class up into pairs. Each pair will select a different approach for negotiating between Dr. Proulx and Sandy. If possible, have each pair videotape their role-play, so that the class can review the role-plays together and analyze the different dynamics which occur depending on the approaches of the parties.

In order to prepare for this role-play, use parts of the Negotiation Preparation Tool that are appropriate to your chosen approach. Add facts where needed (for example, the university requires a class average of 70%; students have a right to appeal their grades to an appeals committee in the faculty). Remember that one of the best ways to prepare for negotiations is role reversal—put yourself in the other person's shoes in order to identify their positions, rights, interests, and values, as well as how they might be persuaded in negotiation. Set aside at least 40 minutes for this exercise.

DEBRIEFING: If you have ever approached a professor in the past to challenge a grade, what strategies did you use? How were these strategies different from those you used in the role-play? What approaches proved to be most effective? If you were a professor, which approach to negotiation would be most appropriate for this type of conflict? Why?

ROLE-PLAY 3.3: "EXTERNAL EVALUATION CONFLICT"— CONFLICT STYLES AND INTEREST-BASED NEGOTIATION

Rajib works as a researcher who evaluates the effectiveness of publicly funded social services. Ellen is the executive director of the Conflictia Immigration Program (CIP), a branch of Diversity Plus. CIP helps immigrants find housing, training, and employment, as well as develop social supports and other settlement needs. CIP has recently incurred a 20% cutback in funding. This has had a negative impact on morale, as the number of clients is rising and the number of staff has been decreasing. The last thing Ellen needs is a researcher who knows nothing about immigration services to start interfering with clients and staff. Given the cutback in program funding, spending more money on useless research seems ridiculous.

Rajib is not thrilled with this project, having no prior experience in immigration work. He would rather spend more time on a gerontology project he has been doing. Rajib has already picked up on bad vibes from the agency. He is well-grounded in evaluative research and takes great pride in his work.

Ellen and Rajib have scheduled a meeting in Ellen's office for 9 a.m. Monday morning. The ostensible purpose for this meeting is to establish some sort of understanding about how they are going to work together.

In order to prepare, consider the following questions:

(a) How might Ellen respond if her preferred style is competitive? compromising?

How should Rajib respond to each of these scenarios? How can you try to move towards collaboration (if that is desirable)?

(b) How might Rajib respond if his preferred style is accommodating? Avoiding?

How should Ellen respond to each of these scenarios?

(c) What should Ellen/Rajib do to prepare for this meeting? (consider the timing, place, set-up, information.)

(d) What must be watched for in order to separate the people from the problem? (Think of specific comments you can use to address this issue.)

(e) How important is a trusting relationship? If important, what can be done about this?

(f) What are their positions?

(g) What is each party trying to achieve?

(h) What are the interests underlying these positions?

(i) What are their mutual interests?

(j) What are the possible options?

(k) What are the possible outcomes for each of these options? (would a decision tree or other model be helpful)

(l) How do you evaluate the options (what criteria/general principles could be used)?

(m) What is Ellen's BATNA?

(n) What is Rajib's BATNA?

(o) What can each do to improve his/her BATNA?

(p) What might block an agreement?

(q) Who and what is needed to ensure commitment to any agreements?

Discuss these questions in small groups. Identify key strategies that you want to test or practice. Role-play the situation using these strategies.

Debriefing Questions

What strategies seemed to be effective? What strategies seemed ineffective? What did you learn for future negotiations?

ROLE-PLAY 3.4: "JOINT COUNSELING DEBATE" — SKILLS DEVELOPMENT

Chris and Sanchez are two of the clinical supervisors at Diversity Plus. The agency has asked them to develop an agency policy about domestic violence, particularly wife abuse. They have run into a conflict about whether or not to see male and female partners together when there has been a history of abuse. In this exercise, they will debate this issue starting from the following perspectives.

- Chris believes that the only way for couples counselling to be effective is to see both members of the couple together. Chris thinks that safeguards can be put into place to ensure that abuse does not take place during the process of counselling, and that the couples should have the ultimate say in terms of whether or not they should be seen together.
- Sanchez believes that where there is a history of spousal abuse, the two partners should not be seen together. He also thinks there is no way for the worker to ensure safety if both partners are seen together. Sanchez refutes the argument that the couple should have the final say, because it is the counsellor who is responsible for ensuring that counselling is safe and effective.

Use the Negotiation Preparation Tool to prepare for this Negotiation. Identify two strategies that you want to focus upon for this exercise. Consider which skills are needed in order to implement these strategies. The purpose of this exercise is to focus upon skill development. Do not be too concerned about your choice of approaches and strategies.

Give yourselves at least an hour for this role-play, with frequent breaks to debrief. Let the others in your group know which skills you want to focus upon. Ask for suggestions before going into role. When you stop to debrief, begin by identifying what you did well and what you want to improve. Feel free to go back over the same stages of negotiations for practice rather than complete negotiations from beginning to end.

ROLE-PLAY 3.5: "WHAT DO I GET FOR ROLE-PLAYING"— NEGOTIATING CLOSE TO HOME

The question of who participates in role-plays can raise conflicts between students in a class. The following role-play may or may not be close to issues that have arisen in your group. Play the roles as written. When you debrief, consider how similar issues have been dealt with in your group. Remember— separate the person from the problem.

Out of 12 students in the class, only seven have participated in role-plays. Different students have different excuses for why they have not participated. The class needs to decide what, if anything, should happen about the fact that five students have not participated. Consider whether this should be decided by consensus, by one person in the class, by majority vote, or by some other alternative.

The reasons given by the students for not participating are:

- KAREN: My turn to role-play doesn't come up until next week.
- KOBY: I was sick on the day I was supposed to role-play.
- KELLY: I don't like role-plays, so I decided not to come to class.
- KATE: I haven't done role-plays before.
- KYLE: I had to finish writing a paper for the same day as the role-play.

Some of the opinions expressed by other people in the class were:

- BARB: That's not fair.
- BOB: It's their loss.
- BRURIA: Why should I have to do it if they don't?
- BETTY: I don't care one way or another.
- BILLIE: What about the so-called standards of our profession?
- BRAD: I like having more time to role-play rather than watching others.
- BUNNIE: They should not be able to pass unless they role-play.

Assign each of the above roles to twelve people in the class. Use the Negotiation Preparation Tool to prepare for this role-play. Allot 30 to 40 minutes for this role-play.

DEBRIEFING: What types of preparation helped the most? What, if anything, moved each person from the original position? How was negotiating between twelve people different from negotiating between two?

MAJOR ASSIGNMENTS

The following role-plays may be used for major assignments in the course. Each assignment calls for a written analysis of a conflict resolution exercise in which you participated. Include the following content areas for your analysis.

1. Purpose—Define the main purposes of the assignment. What did you want to learn from this assignment? Focus on the educational goals of this assignment, rather than the particular details of the substantive conflict. For example, "The focus of my learning for this assignment was to develop a practical understanding of how game theory (Rapoport, 1974) can be applied in the context of a conflict between professionals in a social agency." Not, "The purpose of the assignment was to get Pam to stop calling Arnie a wimp, and to get Arnie to promise not to slash Pam's tires every time he was mad at her." There may be more than one educational purpose. [1 paragraph]

2. Preparation—Describe the steps that you and the other parties took to prepare for this exercise: reflection or mental preparation; use of instruments to aid in preparation; readings which you planned to apply; steps taken to set up the meeting, issues you expected to deal with; strategies you prepared; etc. Any instruments you used can be attached as an appendix. Use the American Psychological Association (1997) format for references. If you decided to enter the negotiations with little or no preparation, indicate so and note what types of preparation you might have made in retrospect. [1 to 3 pages of description]

3. Narrative—Describe the process of the conflict resolution interaction. Write this narrative in either third person or first person, depending on which you feel will be more clear and concise. Summarize the less important sections of the interaction more generally; focus on the more significant interactions in greater detail. Feel free to provide critical portions *verbatim*[17] (e.g., that wonderful paraphrase that you came up with; or that terribly judgmental comment that you made in the heat of an argument). [3 to 5 pages]

4. Analysis—Provide a detailed analysis of what worked well, what did not work well, and why. Be sure to use non-judgmental, positive, future-focused language. Rather than, "My pathetic attempt to use structured role reversal really sucked," try, "I was trying to use role reversal so that Mable could gain an insight into Garnet's concerns. Mable was not ready to engage in a role reversal, because I had not dealt with her anger (Sibyl, 1995). If I were to be faced with this type of conflict in the future, I would try . . . ." [3 to 6 pages]

5. Follow-up—Describe any follow up that you would suggest for dealing with the conflict in the exercise. [1 to 3 paragraphs]

Some of these sections can be combined. For instance, you can use a split page format for 3 and 4. On the left side of the page, you can provide the

---

[17]Word for word.

basic description of the process. On the right side, provide the critical analysis (see Sample Process Recording in Appendix 2).

Grading will be based upon your ability to synthesize material from the class and your readings with the exercise. Try to integrate skills, theory, values, and reflection. You will not be graded on your actual performance in the exercise, but on your evaluation of the exercise. For example, even if you did not use a certain strategy effectively in the exercise, you can demonstrate in the analysis that you know how it could have been applied. Also, provide a critique of the conflict resolution approaches, skills, and strategies in practice.

You may do assignments individually or as a small group. If you hand in an assignment as a group, then everyone in the group will be assigned the same grade. You do not need to hand in your audiotapes or videotapes, but you should hold onto them until you have received your final grade at the end of the term. Both parties should read the common facts, but the *confidential facts should be read only by the designated party.*

ASSIGNMENT 3A—PHYLLIS'S CASE

Phyllis has recently been admitted to the Conflictia Hope Hospital. She was having auditory hallucinations that caused her to destroy most of the furniture in her apartment. She was seen by a psychiatrist, Dr. Nguyen, who wanted Phyllis to be admitted on an involuntary basis because she was a danger to herself and others. Previously, Phyllis has been diagnosed as having schizophrenia. She has been able to function well when she stays on her medication. However, she does not always take her medication as prescribed.

Sandy is a systems counselor who has been working with Phyllis in the community. Phyllis wants to get out of the hospital right away and has been uncooperative with hospital staff. The hospital has contacted Sandy and asked her to meet with Phyllis, since Sandy has developed a positive relationship with Phyllis.

Assignment 3A: Sandy's Confidential Facts (not to be read by Phyllis)

You do not work for the hospital and you need to define what your role will be in meeting with Phyllis. You believe that she can be returned to the community, but you do not have the power to decide this. You also believe that Phyllis does need some type of monitoring to ensure that she is safe. If she does not follow through on her medication, then she is likely to continue to have more problems.

Try to work out a contract with Phyllis to deal with the conflict.

Assignment 3A: Phyllis's Confidential Facts (not to be read by Sandy)

When Sandy arrives, you are quite angry with her. You think that she is teaming up with the hospital against you. You hate the psychiatric ward at the hospital, because you don't think of yourself as crazy or sick. You acknowledge that things got out of control at home, but you believe that this will not be a problem in the future. You went off your meds for a few days because you thought that they were turning you into a zombie—you've been feeling lethargic and unmotivated. You also feel embarrassed about the nervous twitches that you have developed from the meds. You are scared about having hallucinations again, but the hospital also scares you. Your mother was admitted to a mental hospital when you were 12 and she never got out.

Your main goals are to get out of the hospital and to be left alone. You want Sandy to promise to get you a discharge from the hospital. You want to be treated like an adult and a human being.

In order to prepare for this meeting, think about how Phyllis would present herself and what questions that you might expect from Sandy. You do not have to show great insight into your issues, unless Sandy draws these out during your meeting.

ASSIGNMENT 3B: METHADONE MAINTENANCE CASE

Assignment 3B: Common Facts

You're Off Drugs and Alcohol (YODA) is a substance abuse treatment program at Diversity Plus. Due to concerns about the spread of HIV and AIDS among intravenous drug abusers—through sharing unclean needles—YODA has decided to open up a methadone maintenance clinic. Methadone maintenance is a chemical therapy used for people addicted to heroin. Methadone is a synthetic opiate that is used to prevent heroin users from going through withdrawal. Studies show that methadone maintenance is related to improved social functioning in the family, at work, etc. Darcy is the Director at YODA. One of Darcy's roles is to maintain positive relations within the community.

Not In My Backyard (NIMBY) is a community group which opposes the plans for the methadone program. NIMBY believes the program will attract undesirables to their neighborhood, particularly minorities such as North Americans and Buddhists. NIMBY fears the clinic will put their children at risk. It believes the clinic will lead to increased crime and violence. NIMBY is also opposed to the concept of taxpayers spending money on giving drugs to drug addicts, even if it is methadone. Sidney is the spokesperson for NIMBY. Sidney's position is that YODA must not be allowed to open any type of methadone maintenance clinic.

NIMBY has threatened to go to court for an injunction to prevent YODA from opening its program. In response, Darcy called Sidney for a private meeting in order to try to settle things out of court.

Assignment 3B: Darcy's Confidential Facts

You see NIMBY as a group of rednecks, for whom you have little patience. You find Sidney particularly shallow and abrasive. However, you are responsible for ensuring the best possible services for YODA's target population. That means that you may have to work out an amicable arrangement with NIMBY. You could go ahead with the plans without consulting NIMBY, but at what costs?

There is no other methadone maintenance program in Conflictia and three of your clients have tested HIV-positive in the last two months (one woman and two men). Methadone maintenance is not a cure-all. There is actually a low level of success in terms of detoxification from methadone and all other drugs. However, methadone does work as a means to stopping intravenous drug use and it fits with your agency's philosophy of "harm reduction," as opposed to abstinence.

Assignment 3B: Sidney's Confidential Facts

You represent a group of upstanding citizens in the community. You want to ensure that the streets are safe from drug users and traffickers. The proposed methadone maintenance program was initiated without any consultation with the community. Accordingly, you believe that YODA does not care to hear your views. Darcy appears to show concern, but you think Darcy is just a "bleeding heart liberal."

There are two schools and a day care program within three blocks of the proposed clinic. However, you do not believe that there is any good place for it. You do not agree with the idea of handing out free drugs to anyone. It just encourages more drug use and crime, and does nothing to prevent AIDS. If people are concerned about stopping the transmission of AIDS, then they would be well advised to get off all drugs. You have seen news reports from Zurich where they allowed needle use in a public park, and it attracted drug users from all over Europe. You do not want Conflictia to become a magnet for those types of people.

You are not sure what will happen if the case goes to court. There are 60–40 odds that you can get temporary injunction, and only a 20% chance of gaining a permanent injunction. The costs may be prohibitive, but you may be able to scare off YODA by initiating a court proceeding (even if you have no intention of going through with a full trial). You may also try to solicit political pressure from your local member of the legislative assembly, who happens to be leader of the ROC Party.

MEDIATION

Chapter 1 defines mediation as assisted negotiation. Two or more people involved in a conflict sit down with someone they trust to try to work out their problems. This broad definition encompasses a broad range of possible interventions. Although programs, practitioners, and research studies have produced more specific definitions of mediation (Barsky, 1997d; LeBaron Duryea & Grundison, 1992; Noone, 1996), these definitions are really describing specific models of mediation. Because there is no universally accepted explication of mediation, it is difficult to discern what people are talking about when they say there are mediating. Mediation has been defined differently for different times, cultures, and contexts of conflict.

This chapter focuses on mediation between individuals. It begins with a description of traditional perspectives of mediation among different cultural communities. The bulk of the chapter focuses on four of the more popular models of mediation among helping professionals: structural, interest-based, therapeutic, and transformative. A section on the uses of mediation identifies how helping professionals can use emergent and contractual mediation in a range of contexts. A case study illustrates how each model addresses various phases of the mediation process. An inventory provides a comprehensive list of skills and activities for mediation. As you develop your own model of mediation practice, you can draw from this list and identify which skills and activities to emphasize. The following section contrasts mediation with interventions of other types of helping professionals. Cultural issues are highlighted toward the end of the chapter. Chapter 5 builds on this chapter, moving from mediation between individuals to mediation in the context of communities and groups.

TRADITIONAL PERSPECTIVES ON MEDIATION[1]

1. Philosophical Base

Traditional perspectives on mediation tend to contrast mediation with adversarial approaches to dealing with conflict. An adversarial approach is typified by the notion of a fight or feud. The image of adversarial CR as a "feud" suggests that offenses must be retaliated, people must be separated into friends and enemies, and honor requires more than monetary satisfaction (Bossy, 1983). As Chapter 3 explains, the outcome of adversarial negotiation is dictated by which party possesses the greatest power in terms of legal right, physical might, or other resources.

Whereas the archetypal adversarial approach to CR is seen as a feud, the traditional image for mediation is "love and charity." Under this philosophy, conflicts should be settled amicably. The obligation of love extends to all people, enemies as well as friends (Bossy, 1983). Mediation values the goodness in people, emphasizing their strengths, self-worth, and virtue. Mediation has faith in the capacity of all people to want to resolve conflict in good faith. Mediation focuses on the future. Rather than look for blame for past misdeeds, mediations helps clients build on positives and move ahead.

2. Old and New

Although CR literature frequently describes mediation as a new alternative, the mediation role has existed throughout history in a variety of forms. Mediation is a natural way in which people help others deal with problems. Friends, neighbors, elders, parents, or other family members frequently assume the role of a mediator on an informal basis (Lederach, 1986). Mediation as an institutionalized alternative to court and other dispute resolution systems is relatively new. For example, the first court-based family mediation service in North America began in 1961 at the Los Angeles County Conciliation Court (Landau, Mesbur, & Bartolletti, 1997). The popularity of professionalized mediation programs spread throughout the United States, Canada, the United Kingdom, and other Western countries in the 1980s. Mediation itself, however, has existed in many societies: for example, modern Liberia, sixth-century Gaul, early China, and the Kalahari Desert among the bush people (Capelletti, 1979; Noone, 1996).

---

[1]Parts of this section are derived from Barsky, 1995.

3. Western Perspectives

In western societies, particularly those with strong Christian influence, mediation was based on ideas of forgiveness and charity. In sixth-century Gaul, bishops and other clergy were seen as natural peacemakers. They would be chosen to mediate because of their prestige, wealth, education, diversity of function, knowledge of how to settle particular cases, and ability to inspire confidence. Their role was to guide their flocks from "evil and violence" towards "peace and love." Episcopal courts dealt with matters such as religious offenses, offenses of the clergy, matrimonial and sexual relationships, and cases involving widows, orphans, freedmen, and paupers. In both secular and non-secular cases, the clergy mediated between the law and the parties to the conflict. In some cases where a person adjudged guilty could not afford to pay a fine or compensation order, the church would step in and pay this amount in order to save the person's soul (Bossy, 1983). Clergy as mediators were not neutral, in the sense that they held a degree of bias towards particular types of outcomes. For example, clergy would advocate obedience to religious tenets (e.g., a belief that marriages are immutable and that the possibility of divorce is not recognized). Clergy would also act to balance the bargaining power of disputants where simple negotiations would favor the stronger party (Bossy, 1983).

In the Middle Ages, western European nations made a distinction between settlements resolved by "law" and those resolved by "love." The "law" paradigm refers to rule-centered approaches such as court trials and other adversarial process. The "love" paradigm refers to collaborative, relationship-centered approaches. The preference for love over law is reflected in a number of maxims and biblical quotations. (1) "Agreement prevails over law and love over judgment"; (2) "Love conquers and we must yield to love"; (3) "Judge not, that ye not be judged"; and (4) "He that loveth another hath fulfilled the law".[2] These sentiments were not limited to clergy and officials, as others in the community would also encourage people locked in litigation "to become friends" (Bossy, 1983). The concepts of mediation and reconciliation were enmeshed.

Reconciliation was given strong emphasis in thirteenth-century France and England, where the concept of a "loveday" became part of the dispute resolution process. A loveday was a period of reconciliation fixed by the courts when an action was first presented. The loveday applied to various types of civil disputes. The court would not adjudicate on the matter until the disputants attempted to reconcile on their own. In a sense,

---

[2]Quotes cited in Bossy (1983), pp. 47–49, from the 13th Century *Legis Henrici Prim* and from the New Testament.

the loveday was similar to such modern concepts as pre-trial conferences and mandatory mediation. However, the loveday asked not only that the particular conflict be resolved, but also the quarrel. The goal was for the disputants to become "at one". "Like marriage, a loveday should be sealed with a kiss (a kiss of peace), blessed by a priest, and witnessed by mutual friends and kinsmen" (Bossy, 1983, p. 59).[3] Current mediative approaches used in Native American and Chinese communities still emphasize rebuilding the relationship as part of the process (LeBaron Duryea, 1994; Irving & Benjamin, 1995).

The choice of mediators varies in different times. For example, in eighteenth-century France, the most common mediators were lawyers and notaries, due to their literacy, knowledge of rights, and ability to draft legally binding agreements. The nobility and bourgeois were also popular mediators, due to their status, power, and position of respect. Because these mediators held such positions of authority, they were able to coerce parties into agreement (or even impose settlements) rather than act as neutral facilitators of settlements (Bossy, 1983). These people were still mediators (and not judges) because their role was to help the parties to come to a settlement—albeit with an element of coercion—rather than to adjudicate.

4. Eastern Perspectives

In the traditional Chinese and East Asian form of mediation, village sages or scholars facilitated conflict resolution. These individuals drew on their knowledge, morality, and spirituality to help parties find solutions. Similar to clergy in Europe, these mediators used their positions to encourage parties to settle according to community norms and societal values. This form of mediation continues to be the most popular means of conflict resolution in China, Taiwan, and Japan (Noone, 1996).

5. Back to the Future

Since the 1980s, cultural issues have gained prominence in professional mediation literature (LeBaron Duryea & Grundison, 1992; Hudson, Morris, Maxwell, & Galaway, 1996; LeBaron, 1997). With this newfound awareness of culture, more mediators are looking back to traditional forms of mediation in order to learn how people from various cultures deal with conflict (Barsky, Este, & Collins, 1996; Lederach, 1986; 1995).

---

[3]In modern western institutions, mediated agreements do not require the disputants to kiss and make up, though in many cases the blessings of independent legal advice are required. Either handshakes or signed, sealed, and witnessed agreements continue to be used to formalize and finalize mediated agreements. Mediated agreements may also be brought to court for orders on consent of the parties.

CONTEMPORARY MODELS OF MEDIATION

In contemporary western societies, clergy, elders, and community leaders continue to assume mediative roles. However, there has been an evolution towards professionally trained mediators who ascribe to particular models of mediation and codes of ethics. In this chapter, I focus on four primary models of mediation: structural mediation, interest-based mediation, therapeutic mediation, and transformative mediation. Cultural and feminist perspectives are also interwoven in the analysis.

Structural mediation[4] focuses upon settlement of the basic conflict in an expeditious manner. It is related to the rights paradigm of negotiation, as the mediator encourages parties to resolve their differences according to pre-existing rules and laws (Coogler, 1978; State Justice Institute, 1998). Under this model, mediators are task-oriented and interventionist. They act similarly to an advisor or manager. They may offer explicit advice on how to resolve the conflict. Parties may feel pressured into accepting the advice, given the expertise and stature of the mediator. This form of mediation is often used by judges in pre-trial settlement conferences and by mediators for financial or business disputes (Noone, 1996). Government officials who are mandated by legislation to resolve certain types of disputes in accordance with the law may also adopt this approach.[5]

Interest-based mediation encourages parties to resolve underlying interests, rather than just their overt conflict. Interest-based mediators help parties move away from positional bargaining, selling the merits of a win-win, co-operative approach (Noone, 1996). The role of the mediator is basically to facilitate interest-based negotiation. Among helping professionals, interest-based mediation is more popular than structured mediation because it attends more to relationship issues and encourages parties to make self-determined choices about how to resolve their conflicts.

Therapeutic mediation is designed to help parties deal with psychological and social issues that have contributed to their conflict and have blocked their ability to resolve it. Therapeutic mediators help parties restructure their relationships, enhance communication and problem-solving skills, and deal with underlying emotional issues (Irving & Benjamin, 1987, 1995; Kruk, 1997; Mathis & Yingling, 1998). This model draws extensively from communication theory, ecosystems theory, structured family therapy, and strategic family therapy. Although therapeutic mediation has therapeutic aspects, it is not

---

[4]Sometimes called "rule-based mediation."

[5]Such officials are often called "conciliators" rather than mediators. Conciliation may be used by human rights commissions, labor relations boards, and welfare review tribunals.

therapy, *per se*. The focus of mediation is still to resolve specific conflicts that the parties bring to mediation. While therapeutic aspects occur throughout mediation, key differences from interest-based mediation occur at the beginning and end of the process. In the initial stages, therapeutic mediators conduct an assessment and premediation preparation in order to assure that the clients are ready to participate constructively in mediation. After mediation, therapeutic mediators conduct follow-up sessions to see how the agreement has been working, including its impacts on the parties' relationships with each other and other systems in their environment. Therapeutic mediation was developed for family conflicts, specifically in separation and divorce situations.

Transformative mediation promotes empowerment and recognition between the conflicting parties. This approach is designed to transform individuals by helping them develop mutual understanding and self-efficacy. It downplays the importance of settling specific issues in dispute (Bush & Folger, 1994). Transformation is a humanistic, healing process. Ideally, transformation transcends the immediate parties involved in the conflict. It engenders a philosophy that fosters social harmony and humanism (Kruk, 1997; Lang, 1996).

One of the more common definitions of mediation among helping professionals is that mediation is a voluntary, non-adversarial CR process in which a neutral third party, the mediator, assists clients of relatively equal bargaining power reach a mutually satisfying agreement (Ellis & Stuckless, 1996). This definition underscores a number of assumptions.

1. Mediation is voluntary.
2. Mediation is a non-adversarial process.
3. Mediation is facilitated by a neutral third party.
4. Mediation requires that the parties have equal bargaining power.
5. The function of the mediator is to help the parties reach a mutually satisfying agreement.

On the surface, these assumptions may appear valid, even obvious. However, each has led to significant debate among proponents of mediation. I will review each of these assumptions in light of the four models of mediation presented above.

1. Voluntary

To say that "mediation is a voluntary process" suggests that it is not imposed on people. If they mediate, it is through free and informed choice. While this may be true in some contexts, mandatory and coerced mediation has been used in various circumstances. In some jurisdictions, parties must try mediation before they have access to a court trial. In others, parties are encouraged to go to mediation in order to avoid negative sanctions (e.g., police who advise citizens to go to community mediation[6] in order to avoid criminal charges; misbehaving students who are asked to try peer mediation[7] rather than receive detention or suspension).

Those who advocate for mandatory or coerced mediation suggest that people embroiled in disputes need an incentive to try mediation, particularly if they have had no prior experience with it. If they do not like the way mediation progresses, they can terminate the process without coming to an agreement. Mandatory or coerced mediation fits best with structural or interest-based mediation. Both models view settlement of disputes as primary functions of mediation. They also allow the mediator to use some authority or pressure to move the parties towards settlement. In contrast, therapeutic and transformative mediation place more emphasis on the parties' rights to self-determination, including the right to reject mediation.

One aspect of mediation where consensus exists is that mediators do not decide the outcome for the parties. Rather, mediators encourage clients to take responsibility for making their own decisions about how to handle their conflict. Mediators do not try to suppress or eliminate conflict. Rather, mediators help parties deal with conflict deliberately, consciously, and constructively (LeBaron Duryea & Grundison, 1992).

The assumption of voluntariness raises two important questions for helping professionals: (a) Is it ethical to send people to mediation against their will; (b) Is it effective or will people simply resist the process (Kelly, 1996)?

2. Non-adversarial

Mediation is frequently viewed as an alternative to adversarial processes such as court, arbitration, and adjudicative grievance procedures. This perspective suggests that the mediator's role is to encourage the parties to cooperate rather than compete. If the parties adopt power or rights-based approaches, the mediator may have difficulty moving them away from adversarial positions and tactics. However, the mediator may be able to help them work towards settlement in spite of their adversarial relations. Structural mediation would view settlement as success. The other models, however, suggest that the mediators must also resolve underlying issues and foster more positive relations between the parties.

As noted above, many traditional forms of mediation view reconciliation as the ultimate goal in encouraging more positive relations. The predominant view in professional mediation literature suggests that success in mediation does not require reconciliation. In fact, mediation and reconciliation often

---

[6]For a text on community mediation, see Duffy, Grosch, & Olczak (1991).

[7]See Schrumpf, Crawford, & Usadel (1997).

work in opposite directions. For instance, when a separated couple is involved in mediation over child custody and visitation issues, the purpose of mediation is to come to an amicable resolution whereby parents remain separated from each other. In contrast, reconciliation counseling is designed to help bring parents back together as a couple and as a re-united family. Some writers suggest that mediation is better suited to conflicts requiring some type of ongoing relationship, rather than when there is no prospect of a future relationship (Stulberg & Keating, 1983). Mediation can be used to help the parties renegotiate their roles into a different form of relationship instead of reconciling into the pre-existing one (Emery, 1994).

Consider: Is it necessary for mediators to help parties move towards more amicable relations or is settlement of the immediate issues in dispute sufficient? Will settlements endure if the parties have not resolved their relational problems? Is reconciliation the ultimate goal of mediation?

3. Neutral Third Party

Most mediation literature and codes of ethics suggest that mediators must be independent, neutral, or impartial. However, the authorities differ as to which terms to use and what each of these terms mean (Pruitt & Carnevale, 1993; Stulberg, 1981; Taylor, 1997; Zartman & Touval, 1985).

Independence suggests that the mediator has no economic, emotional, psychological, or authoritative affiliations with any party involved in the conflict. If the mediator is related to one party—for example, as a therapist, parent, lawyer, or teacher—then the other party might have concerns that the mediator will be biased. If the mediator discloses any affiliations to the parties, the parties have the option of accepting or rejecting the mediator.

Some authors equate neutrality with independence, but others go further. *In order to be neutral, the mediator must have no pre-existing biases, no decision-making authority, and no stake in a specific type of outcome. In addition, the mediator must not side with one party or the other during mediation* (Barsky 1997b; 1997d). Each of these aspects of neutrality poses certain difficulties.

First, all mediators have pre-existing biases. At the very least, aren't all mediators interested in helping the parties resolve their conflicts—amicably, constructively, efficiently, fairly, or effectively? Don't all people carry certain values and biases? One response to these concerns suggests that mediators must conduct a self-assessment of their biases. For some biases, a medicator can try to suspend them, so that they do not impose them on the parties. For example, a mediator who believes that religion is important must recognize that clients have a right to make their own decisions about religion. Biases that the mediator intends to bring into the mediation process should be disclosed. During the initial stages of mediation, for instance, mediators describe their model of mediation. If the mediator values promotion of amicable relations, the parties will know this from the start and will have an opportunity to accept or not accept services from this mediator.

In terms of no decision-making authority, most mediators would agree that they cannot mediate if they also have the ability to impose decisions on the parties. However, some conflict resolution practitioners use a hybrid process of mediation-arbitration ("med-arb"). They begin the process as mediators. If the parties do not come to a resolution in mediation, then they become an arbitrator and make a decision for the parties. Similarly, a judge in a pre-trial conference uses mediative strategies to try to bring the parties to a settlement. If the parties do not settle, then the judge hears the case and makes a decision for the parties. In most jurisdictions, the judge who conducts the pre-trial does not hear the case if it goes to trial. If conflicting parties know that their mediator may become their judge or arbitrator, they may act differently in the mediation process. During mediation, a mediator wants the parties to feel free to disclose information, even if it might be embarrassing. If the information may be used in arbitration or court, the parties may be less willing to divulge information.

Although all four contemporary models of mediation say that the parties have a right to make their own decisions, some models allow for greater mediator influence than others. Structural mediators are most likely to use directive techniques in mediation in order to bring about a settlement. Interest-based and therapeutic mediators are less directive, but still adopt strategies where the mediator encourages amicable solutions. Transformative mediators are the least directive mediators. They focus on facilitating communication and understanding rather than facilitating settlements. Still, they cannot deny that they have an influence on how settlements are reached.

The third aspect of neutrality, having no stake in a particular outcome, suggests that the parties are free to make their own decisions about how to resolve their conflicts. Whereas traditional mediators such as clergy and elders were able to influence people to conform to religious or community norms, most contemporary, professional mediators would not find this acceptable.[8] Still, mediators are subject to constraints and incentives created by the systems they work for. For example, if success in mediation is measured by what percentage of cases settle, then mediators may be enticed to pressure

---

[8]Whereas traditional mediators were often chosen because of their position and what they represented in the community, professional mediators are usually chosen because they are viewed to be neutral. They emphasize the rights of the parties to resolve disputes according to their own values and interests. Still, some mediators are chosen not because of professional mediation training, but because of knowledge, status, and experience in a particular field relevant to the type of conflict: lawyers for legal matters; accountants for financial issues; helping professionals for psychosocial, family, and community conflicts; business managers for organizational matters; and former heads of state for international conflicts are some examples.

parties into settling. If a mediator receives funding from a body with a particular political viewpoint, then the mediator may feel pressure to guide the parties to solutions that fit this view.

The final aspect of neutrality is not siding with one side or another. This ensures that the process is fair and perceived by the parties to be fair. In some cases, this means treating the parties equally: giving both parties equal time to speak, ensuring that both parties feel heard, and providing negotiation support to both parties. One of the biggest controversies in mediation concerns how to handle situations where there is an imbalance of bargaining power (described later). If the mediator intervenes to redistribute bargaining power, then is the mediator being neutral? If the mediator does not intervene, then is the process fair?

Some writers suggest that mediators need to be impartial rather than neutral. *Impartiality refers to absence of bias or favoritism to either party.* The mediator must not side with one party or the other. Further, the mediator must not be seen to side for one party or the other. The mediator's background is not relevant as long as the mediator can show by word and by deed that the mediator is not biased. Although this concept deals with some of the issues around neutrality, the question still arises about what it means to be impartial when there is an imbalance of power between the parties. Rifkin, Millen, and Cobb (1991) suggest that a mediator needs to demonstrate "equidistance" as well as impartiality. Equidistance refers to the ability of the mediator to assist all parties express their "sides." Equidistance allows the mediator to align temporarily with each party, so long as the mediator eventually assists all parties equally.

Must a mediator be independent, neutral, equidistant, or impartial? Why are they important? Are they values that are inherent to all forms mediation? Are they simply means to an end? Can mediation be effective if mediators are not independent, neutral, equidistant, or impartial?

4. Equal Bargaining Power

Power imbalances occur when one party has more information, better negotiation skills, greater resources, or more strength than the other party. Power balancing refers to mediation strategies aimed at rectifying power imbalances. These include ensuring that the disadvantaged party has access to information, opportunities to enhance their negotiation skills, or support from others to counter the greater strength or resources of the advantaged party (Ellis & Wight, 1998; Taylor, 1997).

The issue of bargaining power raises important concerns for both proponents and critics of mediation. Basically, four views exist: (a) Mediators should only mediate if there is relatively equal bargaining power between the parties; (b) Mediators should only mediate if there is equal bargaining power between the parties or if they can balance bargaining power through their interventions; (c) Mediators should mediate regardless of bargaining power between the parties and have no obligation to rebalance power when an imbalance exists; and (d) Mediators should never mediate, because they cannot properly assess for power imbalances and because they cannot properly redress power imbalances when they do exist. My own view is, "It depends."

Therapeutic mediators[9] are most likely to view power balancing as an integral role of the mediation process. Therapeutic mediators often deal with family disputes, rather than commercial or public policy disputes. In family disputes, therapeutic mediators are aware that power imbalances frequently exist between spouses, as well as between parents and children. Balancing power is necessary in order to protect spouses or children from coercion, exploitation, and abuse. Accordingly, family mediators must be knowledgeable about how to deal with issues related to safety and power imbalance (Charbonneau, 1994). Challenging power imbalances may also be necessary in conflicts involving social injustices (McCormick, 1997), such as racism, homophobia, and discrimination against people with disabilities.

Those mediators who do not view power balancing as legitimate often specialize in mediating commercial disputes. Although power imbalances exist in commercial relationships, businesses operate in a capitalistic, competitive environment. If the parties do not use a mediator, they would still negotiate under the dynamics of a power imbalance. Many commercial mediators believe that they should not interfere with the parties' relative strength in negotiating with one another. According to this view, power balancing is contrary to neutrality and impartiality. Why would a more powerful party submit to mediation if it knows the mediator will power balance in favor of the weaker party?

Transformative mediators also view power balancing as inappropriate. They emphasize the rights of the parties to make self-determined choices. This includes the right of the parties to choose whether to participate in mediation or not. If a weaker party believes that mediation will not be fair, then that party can refuse to participate in mediation. Transformative mediators do support the use of empowerment interventions, but differentiate these from power rebalancing. The purpose of power balancing is to redistribute power to the weaker party in order to ensure that the mediation process is fair. The purpose of empowerment is to provide both parties with skills and support to enable them to make self-determined, conscious choices (Bush & Folger, 1994). This still raises the ethical dilemma of the mediator's role when self-determination, fairness, and impartiality conflict (Barsky, 1996).

---

[9]Particularly, feminist-informed therapeutic mediators.

The structural and interest-based models of mediation do not specifically indicate how mediators should deal with power imbalances. It may depend on the context of mediation or the values of the particular mediator.

Some feminist critiques suggest that mediation between men and women is inherently unfair given the systemic disadvantages of women in society. Some are concerned that mediators are incapable of assessing for power imbalances, particularly woman abuse. Others believe that mediators are not able to power balance and assure the safety of women, even if mediators were able to assess for such problems (Girdner, 1990; Leitch, 1987; Pearson, 1997). During the 1990s, feminist-informed models began to develop in order to respond to these concerns. Feminist-informed mediators conduct more thorough assessments for power imbalances and abuse. They establish firm ground rules to minimize the risk of exploitation or abuse. They are also very interventionist when abuse or power imbalance issues do arise (Charbonneau, 1994; Ellis & Stuckless, 1996; Irving & Benjamin, 1995; Kruk; 1997).

5. Mutually Satisfying Agreement

While most definitions of mediation suggest that one of the mediator's functions is to help the parties reach a mutually satisfying agreement, this description fits best with the structural and interest-based paradigms of mediation. On the surface, this role seems obvious. Why would parties go to a mediator if not to get help to settle their dispute? If a mediator adopts a transformative approach, however, the role is to facilitate empowerment and recognition. Likewise, if a mediator adopts a therapeutic approach, then reaching a mutually satisfying agreement is not the only role. Therapeutic mediators foster more positive communication and relationships between the parties, as well as help them resolve underlying issues.

Although many mediators view agreement as a central goal for mediation, mediators must ask whether any agreement is sufficient: Must the agreement be fair? Durable? Reasonable? Legal? If the parties are satisfied with an agreement, then why should a mediator question their decision?

In summary, various models of mediation lend themselves to different ways of handling cases. Further research should answer some of the questions about which approaches are most effective and for what purposes (Kelly, 1996; Kressel & Pruitt, 1989). Mediators tend to have different orientations depending upon their professional backgrounds (Kruk, 1998). Mediators with mental health backgrounds tend to focus on family systems, affective issues, needs, and subjective criteria for fairness; mediators with legal backgrounds tend to emphasize the contract, cognitive negotiation, rights, and objective criteria for fairness (Girdner, 1989). Each type of professional can learn from the others in order to develop a balance between perspectives.

Individual mediators and programs must determine which approaches to adopt. As you work through this chapter, consider how you will determine your model of practice. Will it depend upon your values, the agency context, the clients' request, or which approach has proven to be clinically most effective?

USES FOR MEDIATION AMONG HELPING PROFESSIONALS

One area of talent that helping professionals bring to mediation is their ability to deal with process: for instance, facilitation skills, active listening, and helping people express feelings. Helping professionals also have content knowledge and expertise that are advantageous for mediating in specific contexts: divorce and separation, intergenerational family disputes, child abuse and neglect, community conflict, teacher-student conflict, altercations in health care and residential treatment settings, social policy development, workplace harassment, cross-cultural disputes, and criminal justice (Center for Gerontology, 1997; Cummings & Davies, 1994; Kruk, 1997; Wilhelmus, 1998). Some helping professionals focus upon mediation between individuals. Others mediate primarily between groups and larger social systems (Shulman, 1992; Zastrow, 1999).

1. Emergent Mediation

Helping professionals are involved in both contractual and emergent mediation. While the field of contractual mediation is growing, emergent mediation is far more pervasive in practice. In emergent mediation, helping professionals retain their primary professional identification (e.g., as a psychologist, teacher, social worker, therapist, or counselor). They do not become mediators, as such. However, they can draw from a broad range of mediative techniques without becoming a formal mediator. Consider the following examples.

1. Two professional colleagues are debating the ethics of a particular intervention. You offer to help them work through the problem. They see you as a professional peer, rather than a mediator, though you are using a mediative approach.
2. You are a community development worker. Your community is split about its goals. You use mediative techniques to help them build consensus.
3. You are working with a family where the teenager has rejected the parents' religion. In your role as therapist, you employ mediative strategies to help them come to a mutual understanding (Favaloro, 1998).

2. Contractual Mediation

Unlike an emergent mediator, a contractual mediator is hired specifically to mediate. The process begins with an explicit Agreement to Mediate (see below for an example). The Agreement to Mediate specifies the roles of the parties, the role of the mediator, and the parameters of the mediation process. When a helping professional assumes the role of a contractual mediator, it is generally inappropriate to carry on a dual role. Consider whether a conflict of interest exists between your usual helping role and your potential role as a mediator. The following cases illustrate possible conflicts of interest.

- Priscilla is a psychologist who has conducted a battery of psychological tests with a client named Clint. Clint is going through a divorce and asks Priscilla to mediate. If Priscilla accepts the mediation role, what happens to the information from the psychological tests? Can Priscilla use this information in mediation? Does Clint's former spouse have access to this information?
- Charles and Chester are child protection workers. Chester is having a dispute with a family that is upset that Chester has put their children into foster care. If Charles offers to mediate this dispute, what concerns might the family have? (Thoennes, 1991)
- Alex is an anti-poverty advocate. A government official asks Alex to mediate a dispute between two agencies that serve unemployed individuals. If Alex accepts this role, must he relinquish his advocacy role? (Noble, Dizgun, & Emond, 1998)
- Stephanie is a student who has been suspended from school. Her teacher, Tony, is also the chief mediator in the school's education program. If Tony were involved in the original suspension, how could he act as a neutral or impartial mediator in Stephanie's case?

Conflict of interest is particularly problematic in small, isolated communities. In small communities, it is virtually impossible for mediators to have no prior relationships with the parties. While bringing a mediator from outside the community may be the answer, this is not always practical or desirable. Aside from the costs of bringing in a mediator, local mediators have the advantage of understanding the local context of the dispute.

While some helping professionals work exclusively as mediators, most helping professionals mediate as just one part of their practice. Social agencies and court-affiliated services are able to hire full-time mediators if they have sufficient referrals. Mediators in private practice, however, need to build referral sources over time in order to be able to generate sufficient cases to support a practice. In most jurisdictions, mediators cannot expect to simply hang up a shingle and wait for cases to show up at the door. Mediators need to become known in their communities, educating potential referral sources about mediation, generally, and their own services, in particular (Whitten, 1992).

MEDIATION BETWEEN INDIVIDUALS: A CASE ILLUSTRATION

Rather than present a single model of mediation, the following description provides a comparative analysis that incorporates skills and strategies from the four models of mediation presented above. By presenting an integrated framework, you can see how each perspective handles similar issues. When you are mediating a particular conflict, you will need to assess the needs of the clients and make deliberate decisions about which models of mediation to apply.

The basic mediation framework consists of seven phases: Preparation, Orientation to Mediation, Issue Definition, Exploring Interests and Needs, Negotiation and Problem Solving, Finalizing an Agreement, and Follow-up. Structural and interest-based negotiators are more likely to follow these phases in sequence, since one of their primary interests is directing parties towards agreement. Therapeutic and transformative mediators are more likely to use the phases flexibly, since their approaches are more facilitative and less directive. Within each model there is considerable variability.

Consider the following scenario.

> Elvis and Englebert are two employees at Conflictia Software Enterprises (C-Soft). Elvis is 28 years old and has been with the company for five years. He is considered a senior employee in this young, progressive company. Englebert is 22, fresh out of college. In the two months Englebert has been working for C-Soft, Elvis has subjected Englebert to a series of hazing rituals—shaving his head, putting tacky messages on the screen saver of his computer, and filling his mouse with blue pudding.

The next seven sections demonstrate how each phase of mediation could be approached by mediators with various perspectives. A chart is provided after this description, summarizing the skills and activities to be considered at each phase of mediation.

1. Preparation

Cases can find their way into mediation through various avenues: self-referral, referral by third parties, or imposition by third parties. Englebert might request mediation, Englebert's friend might suggest mediation and contact a mediator, or Englebert and Elvis's supervisor might demand that they go to mediation.

The supervisor might decide to mediate the conflict personally, as an emergent mediator. One of the roles of a supervisor is to deal with relations between employees. Emergent mediation is less formal than contractual mediation. The supervisor would abbreviate, omit, and combine many of the skills and activities of mediation. For example, there would be no formal Agreement to Mediate and limited introductions, because the parties already have a relationship with their supervisor.

If the parties go to a contractual mediator, this could be someone who works for the agency (e.g., in their human resources department[10] or employee assistance program[11]). Alternatively, the mediator could be from outside of the agency (e.g., a private mediator, a mediator who works for a human rights tribunal, or a mediator who works for a service that receives cases diverted from court).

Assume that Englebert goes to his supervisor, Sheryl, to file a formal harassment complaint about Elvis. Sheryl suggests that they use the services of a human resources counselor to mediate their dispute. Neither Elvis nor Englebert knows anything about mediation. Englebert says, "You can't force me to go to meditation . . . medication . . . whatever." Sheryl suggests that they each meet individually with the mediator, so they can make informed choices. *Contractual mediation does not formally begin until the parties have signed or orally committed to an Agreement to Mediate.* Sheryl believes that mediation should be voluntary, so she says that there will be no negative consequences from C-Soft if they decide not to mediate.

The mediator, Medina, receives the mediation referral from Sheryl. *The mediator accepts basic information about the conflict from the referral source: who is involved, how can they be contacted, and are there any special concerns such as risk of violence.* Medina does not want to gather too much information at this stage so that the parties can present the information themselves. If Medina accepts more information from the referral source, she risks having the parties believe that she has pre-existing biases when they enter the process.

In order to prepare for mediation, the mediator contacts the parties, conducts preliminary assessments to ensure that the case is appropriate for mediation, arranges for interaction between the parties, and strategizes how to begin the mediation process. Since Medina knows that this case includes a claim about workplace harassment, she inquires whether there are any safety issues: (a) Is the harassment ongoing; (b) Are the parties continuing to go to work during mediation; and (c) Has either party's employment been suspended? Sheryl says that both parties are continuing to work, but they have been placed in separate departments. She does not believe there are any

---

[10]Sometimes called personnel department.

[11]Employee assistance programs traditionally provide counseling, vocational, and therapeutic services. However, some agencies now offer mediation services as part of their employee assistance programs, harassment committees, or legal assistance programs.

safety issues. Medina asks whether either party has an uncontrolled substance abuse problem, mental illness, or other concerns that might hinder their ability to mediate (Barsky, 1997c). Sheryl says she does not know of any problems in these areas.

Medina contacts each party by telephone to arrange for the first mediation session. Structural mediators generally use this stage to schedule meetings, without further assessments. Other mediators, particularly therapeutic ones, assess the parties' willingness and ability to negotiate more thoroughly. Elvis indicates reluctance to mediate. He does not think he did anything wrong, so why should he be punished. Medina assures him that she is not there to judge or punish him. She has no power to judge or sanction either party. Englebert hints that he feels intimidated by Elvis, but says he does not fear face-to-face contact with Elvis.

In order to ensure that both parties can negotiate fairly, Medina decides to meet with both parties individually before bringing them together. If Medina took a structural approach, she would prefer to meet with both parties together right from the start. However, interest-based, therapeutic, and transformative mediators are likely to meet individually first if they are concerned about safety issues.

Medina considers possible legal issues that might arise in this case. Neither party has a lawyer. However, if harassment were proven, C-Soft could fire or discipline Elvis; Englebert could also sue Elvis for damages. Medina informs the parties about the benefits of obtaining independent legal advice and ensures that they have access to legal advice, should they be concerned about their rights or other legal issues. Both parties decline legal advice at this stage. *Mediators from all perspectives need to consider whether legal advice is important.* The extent to which they encourage or direct parties to obtain legal advice often depends more upon the nature of the legal issues than their model of mediation. Still, structural mediators tend to be most directive about legal advice because they view the dispute as based in rights. Transformative mediators tend to be least directive, because empowerment includes the right to reject legal advice.

The mediator considers who should be included in the mediation process: Englebert and Elvis, Sheryl, witnesses, people who have participated in other hazing rituals, and support persons for both parties. She decides to begin with Elvis and Englebert, the two people directly involved in the conflict. Structural and interest-based mediators tend to limit the number of people in order to keep the process simple. Therapeutic mediators are more likely to involve support persons or others who are indirectly affected by the conflict. Transformative mediators tend to give the parties more say about who to include in the mediation sessions. Bringing in additional parties is generally easier than asking parties to leave mediation. Accordingly, mediators can limit the number of people involved at the beginning and bring in others on an as needed basis (for example, to balance power, to offer suggestions, or to help implement decisions made in mediation).

Medina arranges appointments with each party in her office. *The office is arranged in a manner that is conducive to mediation: private, quiet, impartial, and comfortable.* The room has a round table, enabling parties to sit around it and take notes. The light and color schemes are soft. Ventilation is good. The office is housed in the same building that Elvis and Englebert work. This presents two potential problems. First, others in C-Soft can see when they come to mediation, partially infringing Elvis and Englebert's right to confidentiality. Second, the office is affiliated with C-Soft, giving the impression that Medina might use the authority of the employer to influence the outcome of mediation (e.g., pressuring the parties to agree to terms that reflect the norms and policies of C-Soft). Structural mediators are less concerned about this type of issue than other mediators. However, Medina can raise this issue to see if parties are really concerned about Medina's affiliation with C-Soft.

2. Orientation to Mediation

The orientation stage begins with the first meeting with the parties, either jointly or individually, and ends with the parties agreeing to mediate. The primary purposes of this stage are to help the parties understand mediation and to obtain their commitment to a particular process. The mediator tries to establish norms that will ensure that the parties participate constructively. The mediator models effective communication skills and encourages the parties to follow suit. The mediator also strives to build trust by demonstrating impartiality.

For structural mediators, this phase is relatively short. *The mediator provides an introductory statement that explains the goals of mediation, the role of the mediator, confidentiality, what happens if the parties come to an agreement, and what happens if they do not.* Each mediator personalizes the opening statement, so that it feels comfortable to the mediator and so that it is tailored to the needs of the parties. In this case, Medina might begin with the following statement.

> My name is Medina and I have been asked by your supervisor to help you resolve a conflict that has arisen in recent weeks. Sheryl has not given me the details of your concerns except to say that both of you are considering whether you can work things out in mediation. At this point, all you have committed to is today's session. If both of you agree to mediate, I will ask you to sign the Agreement to Mediate [Medina provides copies to the parties].
>
> As a mediator, my job is to help you talk about your concerns and work out a solution that both of you can agree upon. I am not a judge and I am not going

to make decisions for you. I may be able to make suggestions, but it is up to the two of you to decide what you want to do. I will do my best to remain impartial. In other words, I will not take sides with either one of you. If you have any concerns about my ability to be impartial, please feel free to raise these so that we can discuss them. Mediation does not work unless you believe that I am impartial.

If you are able to come to an agreement, then we will work out ways to ensure that both of you are able to follow up on your commitments. This may mean having lawyers draft a legally binding agreement. Most of the time, these types of disputes can be worked out informally and we simply write up a letter of understanding. This letter states your expectations, but it is not a legal document. I understand that you do not want legal advice at this time, but we will talk about it again if any legal issues arise.

If you are not able to reach an agreement, then we can discuss other alternatives. I understand there is a possibility that this conflict could go to the Harassment Committee at C-Soft. However, the Agreement to Mediate that I will ask you to sign says that mediation is confidential. I will not pass on any information to the Harassment Committee, your supervisor, or anyone else at C-Soft. At the end of mediation, you may agree to share certain information in order to implement the decision. C-Soft has assured me that it will honor your right to confidentiality in mediation. The main exception to confidentiality is when someone may be put at risk of physical harm. I have a professional obligation to take reasonable steps to help prevent the harm from occurring. Even if this occurs, I will try to obtain your consent to disclose information before taking further steps.

You probably have some questions about mediation and some of the things I have just said . . .

Other issues that can be included are the credentials of the mediator, the length of time the parties can expect to spend in mediation, and ground rules for the process (e.g., one person speaks at a time; everyone will use respectful language; no smoking during mediation sessions). Some mediators are directive about the ground rules, indicating that the mediator is in control of the process. Other mediators have the parties suggest ground rules, supporting the clients' ownership of the process. If there is a high level of conflict at the outset, the parties may be unable to negotiate ground rules. Accordingly, the mediator may be wise to provide at least basic ground rules at this stage.

Mediators select language that is neutral, positive, and future focused. For example, the introductory statement speaks of "concerns" rather than problems or disputes. The focus is on working out concerns and coming to agreement, rather than finding out what has happened or determining who is to blame.

The introductory statement can be broken down into components to allow the parties to ask questions as the mediator explains various aspects of mediation. Each introductory statement needs to be tailored to the particular situation, including the nature of the dispute, the agency's policies, the clients' level of language, and the mediator's model of mediation. If either party is not fluent in the same language as the mediator, an interpreter should be used from the outset. The interpreter should be independent. Having one party interpret for the other creates a conflict of interest.

Interest-based mediators provide similar information in their introductions. However, they also describe the basics of interest-based negotiation and place more emphasis on collaboration.

> Mediation is a non-adversarial process. In other words, I will encourage you to problem solve together. What are each of your concerns? What interests do both of you share? What types of solutions can we find where both of you are satisfied with the results? There are no winners and losers. Both of you need to be satisfied in order for us to come to an agreement.

Interest-based mediators are less directive than structural mediators. Interest-based mediators emphasize the parties' ownership of the dispute and any agreements they conclude. Mediators often highlight the advantages of mediation over adjudication.

> Mediation is less formal than the hearings conducted by the Harassment Committee. Mediation allows you to come to your own decisions rather than have someone impose them on you. You are the best judges of how to resolve your concerns. If you are happy with the solution, you are more likely to follow through than if the decision is imposed by a third party, such as the Harassment Committee.

Therapeutic mediators do not begin with a formal opening statement. Instead, *therapeutic mediators engage the parties with a brief introduction and more thorough assessment process.* Since the therapeutic model was developed specifically for family mediation, adaptations must be made for mediation in other contexts. Generally speaking, the mediator assesses the following areas:

- The ability of each party to communicate with the others;
- The intensity of the conflict and how the parties seek to resolve differences;
- The nature and extent of any violence between the parties;
- The extent to which the parties trust or mistrust one another;
- The degree to which each party exhibits flexibility;
- The patterns of interaction between the parties and relevant systems;
- The level of dependence or attachment between the parties in their relationship;
- Whether the parties want to continue or terminate their former relationship;
- The extent to which the parties can focus on the future;
- The ability of each party to carry out social functions relevant to the dispute (e.g., parenting, work);

- The financial, social, and emotional resources of each party;
- Ethnocultural issues that are relevant to the issues in conflict; and
- Potential conflicts with third parties that may impinge on the mediation process (Irving & Benjamin, 1995).

In order to conduct this type of assessment, Medina meets separately and then together with the parties. The individual meetings allow each party to ventilate their feelings and tell their stories without escalating conflict with the other party.[12] These meetings also give the mediator an opportunity to offer individualized support. Medina gives Englebert and Elvis some leeway to talk about the history of their relationship, but focuses them on the present context of the conflict. She uses her active listening skills to confirm that she is hearing their perspectives, but is careful to avoid responses which indicate that she agrees or sides with either one.

In this case, Medina discovers that both parties are articulate. There is a moderate level of conflict between the parties. Englebert has acquiesced to the hazing rituals that Elvis has subjected upon Englebert. There may be a power imbalance in terms of their stature in C-Soft and their respective levels of assertiveness. Elvis feels secure in his job. As a new employee on a one-year contract, Englebert fears that his contract may not be renewed. His complaint to his supervisor came with great reluctance, not wanting to look like a "stool pigeon" or complainer. Englebert comes from a cultural background where direct confrontation is not acceptable. Elvis comes from a culture where assertiveness is encouraged.

Medina determines that it would be useful to have a second premediation meeting with both parties to help them prepare for mediation. This will give her an opportunity to rebalance power between the parties, so they can negotiate fairly and fully. For example, she can help Englebert understand that his position in the company is not in jeopardy because he has brought a concern to mediation. She can also offer to teach him assertiveness skills that are consistent with his cultural values.

Elvis is incensed at Englebert for complaining about him. During the first premediation session, Elvis made derogatory remarks about Englebert's nationality. During the second session, Medina allows Elvis to process his feelings. They discuss ways Elvis can communicate his concerns without using bigoted comments or putting Englebert down.

Although therapeutic mediators explain the nature of mediation during pre-mediation, they generally provide a second explanation during

---

[12]The downside of allowing the parties to vent in individual sessions is that they do not hear one another's stories. The mediator may learn information about one party that the mediator believes should be shared with the other. Accordingly, the mediator needs to let both parties know from the outset that the mediator will encourage them to share information with one another. See Exercise 7.

the first joint meeting. This ensures that both parties hear the same messages, supporting the notion of mediator impartiality and encouraging their joint commitment to the process. The opening statement is similar to that of an interest-based mediator. However, therapeutic mediators may give greater emphasis to building a more positive relationship between the parties.

> My job is to help you talk about your concerns and negotiate a solution that works for both of you. We can also look at your relationship. What type of relationship do you have now? What type of relationship, if any, would you like to have in the future?

Transformative mediators use their opening statements to explain empowerment and recognition in terms that are easily understood by the parties. Medina, for example, might begin with this statement.

> My job is to help you talk about your concerns so that you have a better understanding of one another. Each of you has your own view of what has happened in the past and what you would like to do in the future. You do not have to agree with each other about what has happened, but at least you can get a better idea of where the other person is coming from.
>
> In order to decide what to do in the future, we can talk about various options. If both of you agree to some sort of solution, we can put that agreement into writing. If you do not come to an agreement, then you still come away with a better understanding of the one another's positions and the options available to you.
>
> I am not going to make any decisions for you. You decide whether or not you want to mediate. If you agree to mediate, then any decisions made in mediation are ones that you agree upon.
>
> If you have any questions about how to communicate or negotiate more effectively, I can provide some further suggestions.

Transformative mediators encourage the parties to set their own ground rules. Medina asks the parties if they agree to a rule of not interrupting one another. Elvis and Englebert say that this rule is too restrictive. Instead, they agree to give each other equal opportunity to talk, but there may be occasions when one person can interrupt the other. This empowers the parties by giving them greater say over the process. They also learn skills for dealing with conflict on their own. If their rule proves problematic, they can review it and try to come up with a more effective one. They are not completely dependent on the mediator for guiding them through the process.

Most mediators have a standard Agreement to Mediate that they ask parties to sign during the first joint session. This gives them the opportunity to review the Agreement with their lawyers after their individual sessions. The Agreement describes the parties involved, the role of the mediator, the terms of confidentiality, the issues to be mediated, remuneration for the mediator, and important ground rules. Some mediators include a statement about legal advice, so that it is clear they have suggested that the parties obtain independent legal advice from the outset of the process. The signatures of the parties indicate their commitment to the process.

Transformative mediators may encourage parties to build their own Agreement to Mediate or tailor the mediator's standard form in order to meet their needs. Negotiating the Agreement to Mediate may be difficult because of the initial level of conflict between the parties, their lack of experience with mediation, and the possibility that they will insist upon terms that are inconsistent with the mediator's model of practice.

Medina asks Elvis and Englebert to sign the following Agreement to Mediate.

Agreement to Mediate

1. PARTIES: Elvis John Cameron and Englebert Younas are employees of Conflictia Software Enterprises (C-Soft) who agree to mediate a conflict that arose between them at work. They agree to act in good faith and to share all relevant information so that they can work out an agreement in an amicable manner.

2. MEDIATOR: Medina Sellers has been hired by C-Soft to help employees resolve workplace conflicts. Her role is to help the employees discuss their concerns and work towards an agreement that satisfies both of their interests. Medina will act as an impartial mediator, meaning that she will not side with either employee or make decisions for them.

3. VOLUNTARY: Mediation is a voluntary process. Although C-Soft encourages its employees to resolve disputes in an amicable manner, C-Soft will not impose any sanctions on the parties for refusing to mediate or for failure to come to an agreement. Either employee may terminate mediation at any time in the process.

4. CONFIDENTIAL: All information provided by the parties during mediation will be kept confidential, unless the parties provide express written consent or the mediator is required by law to disclose information (e.g., if a person is put at risk of physical harm). The mediator's records will not be shared with other employees of the organization. The parties agree that they will not subpoena the mediator or her records for any trial, hearing, or other legal proceeding.

5. AGREEMENT: If the parties come to an agreement during media-tion, the mediator will write down the terms of the agreement in a letter to the parties. The agreement will not become a legally bind-ing agreement unless the parties agree to have their lawyers draft a formal agreement based on the terms set out in the letter.

6. LEGAL ADVICE: The mediator has explained the benefits of in-dependent legal advice to the parties. They have both chosen not to hire lawyers at this time. The mediator will not provide legal advice to the parties, but will ensure that they have time to meet with a lawyer during mediation, upon their request.

Signed on April 23, 2001 by:

_____   _____

Englebert Younas   Medina Sellers

_____

Elvis John Cameron

This Agreement is relatively simple, making use of plain language. Some mediators use more detailed and legalistic agreements. The Agreement to Mediate should reflect the mediator's approach to mediation and legal issues that may arise in the context of the conflict. Consider which model of media-tion this Agreement seems to reflect. How would you alter the agreement in order to suit each of the other models of mediation?

Parties who have never mediated before often require repeated explana-tions of the mediation process. They may be self-absorbed in their feelings about the conflict, making it difficult to focus on the mediator's explanation of mediation. People frequently confuse mediation with adjudication, think-ing that the mediator will make decisions for them in spite of the mediator's opening statement.

If the parties do not agree to participate in mediation, the mediator can help the parties explore other alternatives to resolving their dispute. Thera-peutic mediators, in particular, view referrals to other resources as an inte-gral part of their role. In any case, mediators can leave the door open for parties to return to mediation if they change their minds in the future.

3. Issue Definition

The issue definition stage begins with storytelling by each party and con-cludes with the parties agreeing upon the specific issues to be dealt with in mediation.

Medina's earlier assessment suggested that Englebert tends to avoid conflict, only responding more assertively when the cause of the conflict has exacerbated. Accordingly, she decides to have him provide an opening statement first. She tells the parties that Englebert will go first since he is the one that originally raised the concerns about what was happening at C-Soft. She reassures Elvis that he will have an equal opportunity to speak. She provides both Elvis and Englebert with paper and pens to allow them to write down any thoughts that come to mind as they are listening to the other person. Elvis expresses concern that he is being put on trial. Medina notes the purpose of this stage of mediation is to allow each of them to hear what the other is concerned about; she is not going to make any judgments.

If Medina adopted a structural approach, she would ask the parties to focus on present concerns. "What concerns do you want to resolve here in mediation?" She would put relatively tight limits on their storytelling or expression of feelings. If Englebert started to discuss why he took a job at C-Soft or how angry he felt when Elvis shaved his head, Medina would acknowledge Englebert's views but quickly refocus Englebert on what needed to be resolved in mediation. A structural mediator wants to get to the crux of the negotiable issues as expeditiously as possible.

If Medina used one of the other models, she would allow for more storytelling, historical detail, and expression of feelings. She might begin by asking each party, "What concerns bring you to mediation?" Interest-based, therapeutic, and transformative mediators are interested in having the parties identify negotiable issues, but they realize the parties may still need to process feelings. People need to feel heard—by the mediator and by the other party—in order to be able to move forward and negotiate solutions. When someone says, "I want my day in court," they mean that they want an objective third person to hear their story. Paradoxically, "getting one's day in court" is more likely to happen in mediation than court. In court, lawyers and judges control what the parties can say and when. A mediator will use active listening skills to demonstrate empathy, without taking sides. The mediator will also encourage each party to use active listening skills, particularly a transformative mediator who wants to foster recognition.

> Englebert, thank you for sharing your concerns with us. Elvis, what were some of the main points that you heard from Englebert? You don't have to agree with him, I am just asking what messages you understood from what he said.

Empathy refers to demonstrating emotional identification or communicating a sense of understanding (Broome, 1993). The active listening skills identified in Chapter 2 form the basis of providing empathy and recognition. Whereas most helping professionals use these skills to demonstrate empathy themselves, the mediator's role is somewhat different. Mediators teach these skills to the parties so they can demonstrate empathy to one another. Each party learns about the other's perspective. In the process, they may develop joint understandings.

An interest-based approach focuses upon clarifying the parties' issues rather than facilitating recognition. Englebert tells of ten different incidents where Elvis harassed him, but does not specifically identify what he wants to deal with in mediation. Medina responds:

> From what you've been saying, I understand that you believe that Elvis has mistreated you ever since you began working for C-Soft. Now, given all that has happened, what specifically do you think we need to work on during mediation?

Note how the language directs Englebert to identify issues for work, not positions or possible solutions. Parties often want to move to solutions early in the process. Unfortunately, this may cause them to become entrenched in positions before trust has been built and before the underlying issues have been identified. For transformative mediators, the process of helping parties clarify interests contributes to their empowerment. If they do not have a clear sense of the issues and their underlying interests, they cannot help but operate out of ignorance.

Therapeutic mediators have already heard the parties' storytelling in pre-mediation. This allows the parties to vent some of their emotions. This also enables the mediator to help them articulate their stories more clearly and rationally. Still, each party needs some time to tell their stories to the other party, rather than have the mediator simply summarize what each party has said. As with narrative therapy (Winslade, Monk, & Cotter, 1998), the process of storytelling in mediation allows each party to explore symbolic meanings of their experiences. For Englebert, the experience of hazing at work may bring back memories of being mistreated at elementary school. Elvis was not previously aware of this. Medina offers emotional support.

For transformative mediators, storytelling is particularly important for recognition. As each person reviews the history of events, the mediator encourages the other person to acknowledge new insights or information. Elvis says that he thought Englebert was consenting to the hazing process. Elvis tells how surprised and angry he was when his supervisor came up to him one day and said a harassment complaint had been laid against him. Englebert believes Elvis is minimizing his actions. Englebert also has trouble believing that Elvis thought Englebert consented to the hazing. Medina responds:

> You think Elvis knew that you were opposed to being hazed. Is there anything Elvis has said today that you did not realize before?

This allows Englebert to acknowledge that he did not know Elvis was shocked and angry when he received the harassment complaint. Elvis has not agreed with Englebert's points, but he has demonstrated some understanding from Englebert's perspective. This helps build trust between the parties.

Maintaining mediator impartiality can be difficult where, as in the present case, one party is the obvious aggressor and instigator. However, mediation is not about blaming. If Elvis feels judged by the mediator, he is likely to withdraw from the process. The mediator might believe that an appropriate solution includes an apology, compensation, or even punishment. The mediator needs to be aware of these biases and allow the parties to come to their own solutions.

Throughout the storytelling, Medina takes notes to help her identify issues and to keep track of important information from one mediation session to the next. She limits her note taking so that she can give the parties generous eye contact. Further, she does not want to appear as though she is gathering evidence. She allows both parties to see her notes. Her notes are not particularly interesting to either of them, since they do not include any of the mediator's interpretations or suggestions.

In order to help the parties clarify the issues to carry forward in mediation, Medina lists both of their concerns on a flip chart. As she lists them, she tries to reframe the issues so that they are more positive, mutual, and future-focused (see Exercise 15 below for a further description of reframing). The issues listed include:

- What to do about the hazing that has already occurred?
- Will Englebert press his concerns forward with the Harassment Committee?
- What type of work relationship do Englebert and Elvis want, if any?
- How will Elvis and Englebert handle any future conflicts at work?

Medina checks to see whether the list of issues is exhaustive, balanced, and clear. The parties say that they have no other concerns. For the first issue, Medina tries to reframe "hazing that has already occurred" to "past treatment between Englebert and Elvis." Englebert objects because he did not mistreat Elvis. Elvis admits to hazing, so he is comfortable with the initial phrasing. Both parties summarize the issues, indicating that they have a common understanding about the issues that need to be resolved in mediation.

They begin to prioritize which issue to deal with first. Englebert says that he is not currently planning to take the case to the Harassment Committee, so that issue is not urgent. They agree that the first issue needs to be dealt with first, before they can move on to the other issues. Medina believes that it would be easier to talk about their relationship first, to help build trust and collaborative spirit. Dealing with easier issues first also fosters momentum of agreement. If she adopted a structural approach, she might be more directive. However, the other models suggest giving the parties greater control over the process, particularly if they can readily agree on process issues. Medina congratulates them on being able to come to a clear and comprehensive agreement about the issues for mediation.

4. Exploring Needs and Interests

Exploring needs and interests is the crux of the interest-based approach. It is also integral to the other approaches, though it may receive less emphasis. *During this stage, the mediator encourages both parties to identify their individual interests as well as interests which they have in common.* Structural mediators move through this stage quickly, giving more time to problem solving than analyzing the problem.

In order to deal with the issue of past hazing, Medina asks each party to identify their own feelings about what has happened. Englebert says he feels embarrassed, degraded, and alienated. Medina explores why he feels embarrassed. Englebert admits that he was not able to confront Elvis directly and had to go to his supervisor for help. He thinks he should have been able to stand up for himself.

Elvis says he is "pissed off" at Englebert for putting his job in jeopardy when all he was doing was fooling around. Medina validates Elvis's feelings and explores what is underneath them:

> I can see you're very angry at Englebert. This tells me that these issues are very important to you. Besides feeling angry at Englebert, what else do you feel?

Elvis says he's not into this "touchy-feely stuff." Medina responds non-defensively:

> You don't need to talk about anything you don't want to. I'm just trying to understand what could make you so angry.

This gives Elvis the opportunity to say that he was scared he might lose his job over a couple of pranks. A therapeutic mediator may have helped Elvis talk about feelings during premediation sessions. If Elvis is still uncomfortable disclosing feelings, the mediator will not push the issue too far.

For a transformative mediator, the previous exchange produces several opportunities to encourage each party to recognize the other's situation. Each has also been empowered to disclose information that they previously found difficult to disclose.

Medina shifts discussion to their self-identities.

> How do you think your co-workers see you? How has this conflict affected their opinions about you?

Elvis says that his co-workers used to respect him. They thought he had a good sense of humor. Once rumors of a harassment case got out, they started to think he was a bully. Englebert, on the other hand, always felt his co-workers thought he was a wimp. Having to go to his supervisor for help probably just confirmed this. Englebert starts repeating his life history of being hazed and bullied. Medina refocuses him on the present issues.

Medina explains the process of interest-based negotiations and asks them to identify their underlying interests.

> We've talked about many different issues. Now, let's focus on your key interests. When you think about what needs to be done to deal with the hazing that's already occurred, what is really important to you?

Elvis responds that he wants Englebert to drop the harassment charges and advise their supervisor that they had worked things out. This is a position or solution rather than an interest. Medina helps him explore what interests underlie his suggestion.

> When you say you want the harassment charges dropped, why is this important to you?

From this line of questioning Elvis identifies "job security" as a primary interest. Medina continues the process of helping Elvis and Englebert identify underlying concerns. Eventually, they arrive at the following list.

- Job security (financial security)
- Respect from co-workers
- Respect from each other
- An end to the dispute, as soon as possible.

They agree that these are mutual interests, although they may have different meanings or levels of importance to each party. Medina writes these on the flipchart and commends them once again for their hard work and good faith.

5. Negotiation and Problem Solving

Negotiation and problem solving are the central foci of the structural approach, as well as integral parts of interest-based and therapeutic mediation. Although negotiation and problem solving also occur in transformative mediation, recognition and empowerment receive greater emphasis. At this point, the mediator has established trust with the parties. They have committed themselves to dealing with particular issues and they have identified their underlying interests. This phase moves them from interests to solutions.

Strategies at this stage include option generation, identifying objective criteria, and drawing the parties' awareness to the cost of non-agreement. These strategies are similar to what was presented in Chapter 3 on negotiation, except that the mediator facilitates the parties through these processes. For example, both parties have expressed an interest in job security. Medina asks them to brainstorm options for solution. She lists their suggestions: both parties continue to work for C-Soft; Elvis quits and finds another job, Englebert quits and finds another job, they start up their own company, they work for different divisions of the same company, they return to their old jobs, or one of them wins the lottery and they split the winnings. They cannot think of any other options at this time.

Englebert thinks Elvis should quit because he was responsible for the conflict in the first place. Elvis thinks Englebert should quit because Elvis has seniority and Englebert is still on probation. Medina explains the need for objective criteria for decision making.

> Each of you has good arguments from your own point of view. What we need is an objective way to analyze this problem. What factors would a complete stranger suggest for how to resolve this issue? Someone who doesn't know either of you and has no stake in the outcome.

They agree that their decision should be based on two factors: fairness and practicality. They define fairness as equal treatment. If one person leaves the job, then both also have to. It would not be very practical for both to leave their jobs, so they agree to work out a solution where both continue to work for the company. They like their jobs and they think that they can work things out where they can work together, side by side.

Englebert says that in order for him to gain respect from his colleagues, Elvis needs to get up in front of all of the employees and make a public apology. Elvis rejects this solution out of hand and threatens to terminate the mediation process. Both parties start to raise their voices. Medina acknowledges their frustration, but notes how hard they have worked to get this far. She suggests a brief break to allow them to regain their composure.

After the break, Medina reviews the process, emphasizing their progress and acknowledging their feelings about the impasse before break. A structural mediator is most likely to be directive at this point, emphasizing the cost of disagreement (their BATNAs). In this case, if the parties do not come to an agreement, Englebert's BATNA is to pursue the case through the Harassment Committee. This process could be lengthy, adversarial, and embarrassing to both parties. Neither one knows how the Committee would decide this case. An interest-based or therapeutic mediator may also draw the parties' attention to their BATNAs, but in a less directive or manipulative manner. The parties themselves would identify the consequences of non-agreement, rather than have the mediator suggest them.

Transformative mediators are the least likely to put pressure on the parties by emphasizing the cost of non-agreement. Rather, they focus the parties on the benefits of agreement. If one or both parties want to terminate mediation, ultimately, that is a choice the mediator must respect.

In this case, Elvis and Englebert agree to move forward in mediation. Englebert is reluctant to back down from his request for a public apology, feeling that he will look like a wimp once more. Medina offers the following metaphor.[13]

---

[13]Source unknown.

Have you ever heard the story about the ship that sees a light shining through the fog? As the ship approaches the light, the captain puts out a call on his radio, "This is the captain of the USS America. You are headed directly towards us. Please turn your vessel portside to avoid collision." The reply comes, "I am sorry we cannot oblige. Please divert your course." As the ship moves closer, the captain becomes more adamant, "We have the right of way. You must alter your course to avoid collision." The reply comes once more, "I am sorry we cannot oblige. Please divert your course." As collision is moments away, the captain says desperately, "You must divert your course. This is the USS America." The reply comes, "You must divert your course. This is a lighthouse."

The parties laugh at the joke and then discuss its lesson. Sometimes it is better to back down. Medina reminds them that there is a difference between backing down from a position and backing down from an interest. She encourages both parties to pursue their interests, in this instance, the respect of their co-workers. A public apology is one option, but not the only one. Elvis says he respects Englebert for reconsidering this issue. He wants to come up with a solution that works for both of them.

They explore various options and come up with one that seems to satisfy both parties' interests. While Elvis was not prepared to make a public apology, he offered Englebert a sincere apology in private. They agreed to send around a memorandum to their co-workers, explaining that they had gone to mediation and come to an amicable agreement. They worked through exactly what would be written and what each of them could disclose orally to their co-workers. They did not want to disclose the full details of the conflict, since both still felt embarrassed about it.

Mediation continues until they come to tentative agreements about all of the issues in dispute. Some issues became immaterial when other solutions fell into place. By this point in the process, the parties are able to work together collaboratively, with less direction from the mediator.

6. Finalizing an Agreement

Once an agreement in principle has been reached, the parties must decide how to finalize it: as an informal understanding, as a legally enforceable agreement, or as an order of a court upon consent of the parties. Since this is not a case that has been filed in court, initiating a case just to secure a court order is not practical. The parties agree that there is no need for a legally binding agreement. They believe that the issues are more about their relationship than about their legal rights. The mediator offers them an opportunity to obtain legal advice, but both decline. They opt for an informal understanding that the mediator will summarize in a letter addressed to both parties.

Medina works through the letter with the parties. A structural mediator is likely to suggest the wording of the informal agreement. A mediator from one of the other approaches is less directive and therefore, more apt ask the parties to suggest its wording. Medina uses plain language, avoiding legalese. Her letter includes the following paragraphs.

> The purpose of this letter is to summarize my understanding of the terms you have agreed to in mediation. This is an informal agreement that is not intended to be legally binding. The agreement will work as long as both of you remain committed to it. If there are any problems with the agreement, you may return to mediation to work these out.
>
> Both of you agree to treat each other with respect. In order to promote a positive working relationship, you have agreed that you will not participate in any hazing rituals at C-Soft. You have also agreed to circulate the attached memorandum to your co-workers. Neither of you will talk to co-workers about other details of matters discussed in mediation.
>
> If either of you has a concern about how the other has treated you, your first step will be to meet with the other in private to discuss your concerns. If the issue cannot be resolved through one-to-one discussions, then either of you can request the help of a supervisor or mediator.

Medina reviews this agreement with the parties to ensure that it reflects their intentions accurately. She asks about potential problems in implementing the agreement. Elvis says that C-Soft needs to consent to distribution of the memorandum before they distribute it to their co-workers. Elvis and Englebert agree to take the agreement to their supervisor to ask for permission to circulate the memorandum. If they cannot work out the arrangements with the supervisor, they will contact the mediator to discuss other alternatives. Ideally, the mediation agreement is self-enforcing; that is, the agreement can be enforced by the parties themselves, without the need for a third party to monitor and enforce agreement. If external monitoring or enforcement is needed, methods of enforcement should be specified.

Many mediators leave it up to the parties to decide upon whether to return for follow-up. Transformative and therapeutic mediators include follow-up as part of their process. Accordingly, they will schedule a specific time and place for follow-up before dismissing the clients.

The mediator concludes this stage by reinforcing the progress that the parties have made and by offering encouragement to move forward. Structural mediators reinforce the fact that the parties have come to their own agreement. Interest-based mediators congratulate the parties on being able to work cooperatively and resolve their underlying interests. Therapeutic mediators emphasize the parties' improved relationship. Transformative mediators encourage their progress towards empowerment and recognition.

7. Follow-up

Follow-up with the parties serves a number of purposes: the mediator can reinforce the parties' progress; new issues can be mediated; the mediator can re-

fer the parties to additional services, as needed; and the mediator can solicit feedback for research and program development purposes. Therapeutic mediators in particular recognize that conflict is not over just because an agreement has been reached. Implementation of the agreement can raise a whole new set of issues: resistance from other people or systems; problems with enforcement; frustration or despair when things do not work out as well as expected; and conflicts around issues that were not previously expected. Conflict is not necessarily resolved, but managed. Ongoing issues are apt to arise, particularly if there is an ongoing relationship between the parties. Ideally, the parties have gained conflict resolution skills through participation in mediation. This enables them to deal with conflict more effectively on their own.

Although follow-up is not emphasized in the other models, follow-up could be used for different purposes. For structural mediation, settlement is key. Accordingly, follow-up could be used to help the parties ensure that settlement endures. The mediator[14] uses follow-up to monitor compliance. If there are problems with compliance, the mediator could help the parties mediate a revised agreement or explore different means of enforcement.

For interest-based mediators, the focal points of follow-up are satisfaction and ongoing collaboration. If the parties are not satisfied with the agreement, the mediator can help them renegotiate. If the relationship between the parties has soured, the mediator can refocus them on the importance of cooperation.

Transformative mediators would use follow-up to continue the processes of empowerment and recognition. By this stage, the parties have learned to take responsibility for their decisions and have learned how to demonstrate empathy to one another. Follow-up acts as a booster session, to provide support for their continued efforts.

In the present case, Elvis and Englebert return for follow-up six weeks after finalizing their agreement. They review implementation of the agreement, including successes and problems. Englebert reports that distribution of the memorandum and responses to it were positive. Elvis also affirms a more positive work environment at C-Soft. Medina cautions them that there may be rough spots in the future, pre-empting possible disappointment if things did not continue to go so well. Medina congratulates them on making their agreement work.

Englebert does have one concern. C-Soft had just issued a policy against hazing new employees. He feels somewhat embarrassed because people were calling this the "Englebert Policy." Elvis demonstrates recognition by ac-

---

[14]Follow-up could also be pursued by an administrative person from the agency, rather than the mediator.

knowledging how these comments singled out Englebert. As Elvis and Englebert talk about the Englebert Policy, they begin to realize that it was nothing to be embarrassed about. Elvis jokes that he is jealous that there was no "Elvis Policy." Elvis and Englebert agree that when people at C-Soft referred to the Englebert Policy, they would add, "You mean the Elvis and Englebert Policy." Medina commends them on the progress they had made since their first mediation session.

This case demonstrates many of the decisions, skills, and activities that comprise mediation. Some aspects of the process have been abbreviated for demonstration purposes. It is not intended to be "the perfect case." Each of your own cases will present you with a different set of issues, level of conflict, and possible approaches.

INVENTORY OF SKILLS AND ACTIVITIES FOR EACH PHASE OF MEDIATION

The following inventory provides a comprehensive listing of skills and activities for each of the seven phases of mediation. Your choice of skills and focal points will depend upon your model of mediation, the dynamics between the parties, and the issues to be resolved.

This inventory can also be used as a checklist for professional development and self-evaluation purposes.[15] Mark "C" for each area of competence, and "W" for each area requiring more work. Use the exercises in this course to practice the W's. If you are using this inventory to give others feedback on their mediation skills, identify positive examples of how they used different skills; in areas where they could use help, suggest alternatives that you might have tried.

The list of skills and activities is presented in a linear fashion for educational purposes. As you are learning to mediate, it is easier to try to master the process one stage at a time. In practice, experienced mediators will not follow the stages in a linear fashion. There are many overlaps between stages. For example, assessment of power and safety issues occurs on an ongoing basis. In addition, mediators often circle back and forth between stages. If, for instance, the parties seem to be getting stuck at one stage of the process, the mediator may loop back to an earlier stage or move ahead to a later stage. As you become more familiar with the various components of mediation, you will learn to integrate them more flexibly.

---

[15]For competencies specific to family mediation, see Family Mediation Canada (1997).

Inventory of Skills and Activities of Mediation

1. Preparation
    a) Receives referral.
    b) Makes contact with the parties.
    c) Screens for safety issues and appropriateness for mediation.
    d) If situation not appropriate for mediation, explores alternatives and develops safety plan, if needed.
    e) Decides whether to meet individually with parties first (for further screening, to allow parties to ventilate in privacy, to help prepare them for negotiation, etc.).
    f) Arranges for interaction between the parties (together, shuttle mediation,[16] use of telephone, or other distance technologies).
    g) Chooses and arranges the meeting space/environment conducive to mediation (quiet, impartial, comfortable, soothing).
    h) Ensures parties have access to legal advice, particularly where the decisions to be made have significant legal consequences.
    i) Speaks with lawyers or other parties who may have an influence over decision making, with permission of the parties (to explain mediation and obtain their support for the process).
    j) Obtains agreement about who will participate in mediation.
2. Orientation to Mediation
    a) Puts clients at ease during introductions to parties.
    b) Opening Statement: Explains the mediation process—structure of the communication; purposes; distinguish from other forms of intervention; role of mediator; credentials; role of the parties; what happens if a tentative agreement is reached or not reached.
    c) Asserts control over process.
    d) Emphasizes parties' responsibility for decision making.
    e) Identifies the timing (beginning; duration; finishing; possibility of future meetings).
    f) Screens candidates for suitability—readiness; balance of power; safety; ability to negotiate fairly (considering impact of any mental illness, substance abuse, etc.).

---

[16]Shuttle mediation refers to meeting with the parties individually and shuttling between them. The two parties could be in separate rooms at the same time, with the mediator moving back and forth between them. Alternatively, the mediator could meet with the parties at separate times. Shuttle mediation may be used when there are safety issues, when the parties refuse to meet face to face, or where slowing down the process is needed to help the parties to cool off.

g) Assesses cultural factors that may affect the process: values, preferred ways of dealing with conflict, traditions related to the subject of the conflict.

h) Determines need for further premediation interventions.

i) Obtains parties' agreement about ground rules for communication and process (e.g., one person speaking at a time, use of notes, use of respectful language, smoking, protocol for calling breaks, and other terms that the parties agree upon).

j) Describes standards of practice in terms understandable to parties:
   - Neutrality or Impartiality
   - Confidentiality (giving permission to speak freely, within limits)
   - Communication with parties, their lawyers, or other parties
   - Use of caucusing (meeting individually with parties during mediation)
   - Safety issues
   - Voluntary Involvement /Ability to withdraw or terminate.

k) Establishes rapport and trust of clients (by demonstrating genuineness, unconditional positive regard, empathic understanding; impartiality, active listening skills).

l) Clarifies the terms of the Agreement to Mediate (the retainer or contract for the mediator's services, including fees or how mediator will be paid).

m) Encourages informed commitment to the process.

n) Reaches agreement to mediate (written or oral agreement)

o) Obtains preliminary information about presenting problem (may do this at beginning or towards end of this stage).

p) Identifies motivations of parties for mediating.

q) Assesses the nature of the conflict: e.g., difference of understandings, ideologies, or interests (see Negotiation Preparation Tool in Chapter 3 for more detailed analysis of conflict)

r) Congratulates or thanks the parties on their decision to commit to the process.

s) Encourages positive expectations of the mediation process.

t) Invites feedback and criticism from the parties.

u) If a party expresses reluctance to mediate, explores why (in joint session or in caucus).

v) If parties do not agree to mediate, explores alternatives with parties and reinforces that the parties are in the best position to decide upon how to proceed.

(continued)

Inventory of Skills and Activities of Mediation (Continued)

    w) Empowers clients (e.g., supporting their negotiating skills, giving each a fair opportunity to speak, reinforcing their strengths).

3. Issue Definition
   a) Provides rationale for "who goes first."
   b) Allows each party the opportunity to identify their concerns.
   c) Allows parties to ventilate feelings.
   d) Puts appropriate limits on storytelling and expression of feelings.
   e) Assures each party hears and understands the others (e.g., encourages each party to use active listening skills to reflect back or summarize what the other has said).
   f) If a party seems surprised about information provided by another party, explores how this new information changes the first party's understanding of past events.
   g) Identifies key interests of each party (summarized/clarified), including relationship issues.
   h) Identifies areas of agreement and mutual interest.
   i) Develops a list of concerns that is balanced, exhaustive, and clear.
   j) Obtains consensus about how to proceed (priorities of parties; order of issues to be addressed: e.g., by most important; least important first; most urgent, easiest, or most difficult first).
   k) Responds appropriately to different conflict styles.
   l) Validates identity and role of each party.
   m) Avoids taking sides (e.g., uses neutral statements to demonstrate active listening).
   n) Conducts own analysis of underlying concerns.

4. Explores Interests and Needs
   a) Asks parties to identify their feelings around their own issues.
   b) Asks parties to identify their perceptions of the other's feelings around the issues in conflict.
   c) Helps parties explore underlying interests and needs.
   d) Helps parties explore their self-images and how these contribute to the conflict and its possible resolution.
   e) Asks clear and relevant questions.
   f) Encourages parties to share information.
   g) Maintains safe environment for clients.

   h) Maintains appropriate level of control over emotional climate (e.g., exhibiting relaxation through body language, calling for a breather, exploring immediacy, using humor).

   i) Keeps parties focused on one issue at a time.

   j) Maintains control over disruptive behavior.

   k) Partializes issues.

   l) Establishes priorities with parties.

   m) Achieves understanding or closure on relevant feelings.

   n) Interventions are appropriate for:
  - Balancing power,
  - Maintaining problem-solving focus,
  - Responding to emotional needs, and
  - Resolving impasses.

5. Negotiation and Problem Solving

   a) Clarifies the goal or purpose of coming to an agreement.

   b) Helps parties develop objective criteria.

   c) Moves from broad principles to more specific topics.

   d) Encourages cooperative problem solving.

   e) Encourages generation of options for each issue.

   f) Makes substantive suggestions and proposals.

   g) Avoids imposing mediator solutions.

   h) Avoids moving to solutions prematurely.

   i) Provides a structure for problem solving.

   j) Narrows issues in dispute (if full agreement not reached).

   k) Uses pre-emptive strategies.

   l) Reframes parties' statements to be positive, mutually acceptable, future focused, non-judgmental and interest-based [rather than positional].

   m) Maintains appropriate control over process—may turn over more control to the parties as they begin to work more collaboratively.

   n) Uses decision trees, charts, notes, or other visual aids.

   o) Encourages parties to use lateral thinking (viewing problems from different angles to try to come up with innovative solutions).

   p) Uses caucusing, meeting individually with both parties, where appropriate.

   q) Proposes possible concessions (as options rather than as advice).

   r) Rewards party concessions.

   s) Links the parties with outside experts or resources to help enlarge their perceived option set.

(continued)

Inventory of Skills and Activities of Mediation (Continued)

t) Identifies information that needs to be produced.

u) Supplies and filters missing information, or obtained agreement on how parties will obtain it.

v) Pre-empts or corrects counterproductive negotiation behavior.

w) Praises constructive negotiation behavior.

x) Identifies the function or effect of parties' behaviors or attitudes on negotiation.

y) Allows all interests of the parties to be discussed.

z) Recognizes or legitimizes the rights of others to be involved in the process.

aa) Explores cultural differences and misunderstandings.

bb) Adapts language and behaviors to fit with culture(s) of parties

cc) Explores power dynamics and concerns for fairness.

dd) Encourages parties to remain at the table.

ee) Helps parties save face or undo a commitment.

ff) Educates the parties about constructive negotiation skills and principled negotiation strategies.

gg) Changes the parties' expectations (e.g., through reality testing questions, role reversals, metaphoric storytelling, looking at hypothetical situations)

hh) Focuses the parties on the future, rather than on the past.

ii) Focuses on one issue at a time (or a manageable number of issues).

jj) Explores relationship issues.

kk) If parties express judgmental statements, helps them see one another in a more positive frame of reference.

ll) Asks parties to consider possible changes in future circumstances.

mm) Helps parties separate personality issues from the substance of the negotiations.

nn) Takes responsibility for concessions.

oo) Prescribes homework tasks for parties to carry out between sessions.

pp) Asks parties to consider the interests of parties affected who may not be at the mediation table.

qq) Brings others into the mediation process to contribute to agreement.

rr) Uses constructive confrontation (e.g., helps a party to identify incongruencies between two pieces of information the party has given, or between a statement and the party's behavior).

ss) Draws parties' awareness to the cost of non-agreement (e.g., what is the best alternative to a mediated agreement).

tt) If parties have forgotten issues raised earlier, gives parties an opportunity to put them back on the table.

6. Finalizing an Agreement

a) Uses appropriate language in the agreement:
   - Oral / Written
   - Plain language / Legal language
   - Impartial / Mutual
   - Clear and concise

b) Tests agreement with parties to ensure it is realistic.

c) Deals with contingencies.

d) Clarifies the roles and obligations of each party.

e) Ensures commitment.

f) Explores doubts expressed by either party.

g) Ensures access to independent legal advice.

h) Deals with how the tentative agreement will be finalized (drafted by lawyers, court order on consent of parties, informal letter rather than legally binding agreement).

i) Helps devise ways to monitor and enforce the agreements (defining terms of implementation, evaluation, follow-up and review; including sanctions or other provisions that take effect if certain of the terms are broken).

j) Summarizes the process that has taken place.

k) Reinforces the parties' efforts and decisions (end on a positive note; shake hands, have a meal together, have a drink, or some other ritual).

l) Arranges for follow up (date, time, place, who responsible).

m) If no agreement is reached:
   - Summarizes areas of agreement and disagreement.
   - Explores possible alternatives for resolution of outstanding issues.
   - Explores parties' feelings and frustrations.
   - Links parties to desired resources.
   - Reinforces parties' efforts and successes (including empowerment and recognition).
   - Offers opportunity to return to mediation at future date.

(continued)

Inventory of Skills and Activities of Mediation (Continued)

7. Follow-up
    a) Contacts the parties (by mediator or other person; sets up face-to-face meeting, conducts the interview by telephone, or asks for written feedback by mail).
    b) Solicits feedback (research, evaluation forms; informal feedback).
    c) Provides mediation reviews at specific time intervals (e.g., to look at short-term or trial agreements, to consider longer-term arrangements; to consider progress and problems since finalizing the agreement).
    d) Reinforces positive outcomes.
    e) Offers further services.
    (Bercovitch, 1992; Bush & Folger, 1994; Family Mediation Canada, 1997; Irving & Benjamin, 1995; McMan Youth Services, 1996; Slaikeù, Pearson, Luckett, & Myers, 1985; State Justice Institute, 1998)

In addition to the skills that can be used to advance the mediation process, mediators must also consider what types of behaviors to avoid. "Dysfunctional mediator behaviors" are mediator responses that impede effective mediation. Many of these are the inverse or opposite of the positive skills and activities described above. For example, if "allowing all parties to discuss their interests" contributes to the process, then "failing to provide all parties with an opportunity to discuss their interests" impedes the process. The following list highlights some of the most important dysfunctional behaviors to avoid:

Dysfunctional Mediation Skills

- Demonstrates bias to one party.
- Follows agenda too rigidly.
- Allows assumptions and misunderstandings.
- Allows threats or blaming.
- Uses inflammatory language.
- Lacks genuineness (sounds artificial or disinterested).
- Exhibits lack of confidence (in self as mediator or in mediation process).
- Focuses on the parties' positions.
- Judges or blames parties for their role in the conflict.

- Glosses over serious problems to try to reach settlement.
- Denies opportunity for parties to discuss feelings.
- Mismanages information provided by the parties.
- Leads parties into a settlement that pleases the mediator.
- Pressures parties into agreement.
- Tries to solve problems for the clients.
- Moves parties through stages too quickly.
- Allows one party to take control of the process.
- Becomes defensive when challenged by a client.
- Assumes a non-mediator role (e.g., crosses boundary into therapy, law, etc.).
- Asserts own reality rather than allowing parties to express their own realities.
- Offers advice rather than information or suggestions.

As you try to develop your skills, focus upon skills that you want to master, as well as dysfunctional skills that you want to relinquish.

COMPARING MEDIATION TO OTHER HELPING PROFESSIONS

One way to gain a better understanding of mediation is to learn how it is similar to and different from other helping professions. For example, how is therapeutic or transformative mediation different from therapy (Favaloro, 1998)? Is structural mediation simply a form of legal practice? To what extent do you have to change your skills, strategies, and values when you switch hats from your original professional identification to that of a mediator? Table 4.1 provides a comparison of three professions: mediation, social work, and law. I use the interest-based model of mediation and Germain and Gitterman's (1996) Life Model of Social Work[17] for the purposes of demonstrating these comparisons.

Both law and social work view mediation as one of the possible roles that these professions include. However, when you analyze the orientations, values, and methods of the three disciplines, significant differences emerge. The traditional role of a lawyer is that of an advocate. Advocates (described in more detail in Chapter 6) pursue the rights and interests of one party involved in a conflict. In order to assume the role of a mediator, lawyers must

---

[17]The Life Model of Social Work is one of the more popular models of practice taught in schools of social work. This model encourages social workers to effect change in the interactions between individual clients and their social environments. One of the reasons that this model is useful for comparison is because it views mediation as one of the roles of a social worker.

TABLE
4.1

COMPARISON OF MEDIATION, SOCIAL WORK, AND LAW

	Mediation Interest-based Model	Social Work Life Model[18]	Law
Definition	A problem-solving process in which a neutral third party helps disputing parties try to reach a mutually acceptable settlement, by facilitating communication and negotiation between them.	A conceptual framework and practice method consistent with a dual focus on the individual's needs and capacities, and on the adaptive tasks imposed by the environment (Germain & Gitterman, 1996).	A principle or rule of conduct so established as to justify a prediction with reasonable certainty that it will be enforced by the courts if its authority is challenged (Cardozo, 1924). A system of conflict resolution (Vayda & Satterfield, 1997).
Domains, Philosophy	Assists people deal with conflicts in a manner that satisfies their underlying interests. Focuses on relationships rather than rules. Encourages joint problem solving. Focuses on future. Avoids assigning blame (restoration; remediation). Makes parties responsible for deciding how to deal with the conflict. Contexts include: family, community, commercial, and international conflicts.	Enhances social functioning (prevention, restoration, remediation). Remedies personal dysfunction (something that impairs ability to use resources that are available). Promotes social justice. Strengthens adaptive capacity and increases environmental responsiveness (Germain and Gitterman, 1996; Hepworth and Larsen, 1993).	Regulates relationships between individuals, institutions, and the state. *Civil Law:* Remedies damages and loss caused by wrongful acts (compensation). *Criminal Law:* Punishes and rehabilitates wrongdoers; deters crime (retribution) *Promote Justice:* Balances individual rights (social rights to a lesser extent). *Family Law:* special rules and principles designed to protect people who may be in vulnerable, non-commercial situations. *Administrative Law:* protection of human rights, social assistance (welfare), etc. Legislatures make laws; Courts interpret and enforce laws.

---

[18]The framework of this chart and the social work column are drawn from Mandell (1991), with permission of the author.

	Mediation Interest-based Model	Social Work Life Model[18]	Law
Objectives	Two views: 1. Satisfaction and settlement: Resolves conflict amicably, consensually, informally, and collaboratively. Fosters win-win outcomes. Avoids court and saves money. 2. Social justice: Strengthens the weak by helping establish alliances among disadvantaged groups; looks at community of interest rather than individual rights; redistributes power to correct imbalances. (Bush & Folger, 1994)	Helps people enlarge their competencies and increase their problem-solving and coping skills. Obtains access to resources and makes organizations responsive to people. Facilitates interaction between individuals and others in their environment. Influences interactions between organizations and institutions, particularly for the benefit of oppressed or disadvantaged groups.	Promotes justice, defined as individual rights, equality, freedom, democracy, and security of the person. Promotes certainty and efficient transactions.
Assumptions and Perspectives	Conflict is a natural phenomenon, dealt with effectively through collaborative processes. People should be responsible for making decisions over matters affecting themselves. People are more likely to follow through on arrangements that they have discussed and agreed upon. Conflict should be resolved based on ways to satisfy the parties' interests (rather than rights or precedents).	People and environments form an ecosystem in which each shapes the other. Human needs and problems are generated by the transactions between people and their environments. These transactions are located in the life course (role demands, conflicts, etc.), environmental pressures, and interpersonal processes.	Society is governed by the rule of law. Like acts should be treated alike (rule of precedent). The rule of precedent must be tempered with judicial discretion based on principles of fairness (exceptions). Truth is most likely to emerge in an adversarial process with specific rules of evidence. Positive behavior, including avoidance of negative behavior, may require coercive enforcement.

(continued)

TABLE 4.1 (CONTINUED)

	Mediation Interest-based Model	Social Work Life Model[18]	Law
Roles	Impartial facilitator, intermediary, negotiation coach, coordinator, educator (information, not advice).	Enabler, broker, advocate, activist, mediator, negotiator, educator, initiator, coordinator, group facilitator (Zastrow, 1999). One of the primary roles as a mediator is to enhance interactions between individual clients and systems in their social environments.	Advocate, mouthpiece, draftsperson; interviewer, assessor, advisor, counselor. Alternative roles include arbitrator, judge, mediator, law maker. Help avoid problems (creating and maintaining social order). Help resolve problems (a full court trial is one of the least frequent means of settling disputes).
Values and Ethics	Self-determination. Empowerment. Respect for all people; non-judgmental. Neutral/impartial. Disclosure; sharing information between parties. Confidentiality. Fair negotiation. Voluntariness. Right to legal advice. Professional integrity. Safety of parties. Clients have a right to competent mediators.	Self-direction. Belief in the problem-solving capacities of clients. Respect for uniqueness and individuality of clients. Acceptance of and belief in the worth and dignity of human beings. Confidentiality. Access to resources and opportunities to realize one's potential. Professional integrity. Clients have a right to competent social workers.	Autonomy and freedom. Equality. Procedural rights (fair trial; innocent until proven guilty; justice is blind). Confidentiality; privacy. Justice. Ambivalence—tolerates coexistence of different and opposing attitudes or beliefs. Professional integrity. Clients have a right to competent lawyers.
Focus	Conflict between the parties and others affected by the conflict. Future. Objective criteria.	Interface between the person and environment. Reciprocal and adaptive processes.	Legal rights and obligations. Individual entitlements and social responsibilities. Accountability for one's actions.

	Mediation Interest-based Model	Social Work Life Model[18]	Law
Focus (continued)	Problem solving. Collaboration.	Combating oppression and abuses of power in social structures (Germain & Gitterman, 1996).	
Client-Professional Relationship	Clients agree on the definition of the problem and on the solution—mediator is impartial. Mediator neutrality is crucial to establishing trust and fairness of the process. Mediator is a reflective practitioner. Uses empathy to build trust. Debate as to whether the mediator needs to ensure a balance of power between the parties (Taylor, 1997).	Client and social worker must agree on the definition of the problem and on the solution (mutuality). Worker neutrality and impartiality as part of "professionalism" are rejected. Worker self-awareness is necessary to minimize distorted or maladaptive communication. Uses empathy to build trust. Worker must be aware of socially induced barriers to communication and the impact of social forces on the relationship, especially those coming from the agency. (Germain & Gitterman, 1996).	Client defines the problem and decides upon the solution, with advice of the lawyer. Lawyers advocate for one party; neutrality is rejected unless lawyer is acting as a mediator rather than as an advocate. Ability to think like a lawyer requires objectivity, but self-awareness is not emphasized. Trust depends on integrity and expertise of lawyer. Lawyers have special obligations to serve and protect those who are disadvantaged or subjected to discrimination.
Structure/ Phases	Preparation. Orientation. Issue definition. Exploring interests and needs. Negotiation and problem solving. Finalizing an agreement. Follow-up.	Beginning: Entry, exploration, assessment and Planning. Middle: Implementation and goal attainment; work on problems. Ending: Termination, planning, maintenance strategies and evaluation (Hepworth & Larson, 1993).	Lawyer helps identify problem from client's perspective. Lawyer actively involves client in the process of exploring potential solutions. Lawyer encourages client to make any decisions that are likely to have a substantial legal or non-legal impact.

(continued)

TABLE 4.1 (CONTINUED)

	Mediation Interest-based Model	Social Work Life Model[18]	Law
Structure (continued)			Lawyer provides advice based on client's values.
			Lawyer acknowledges client's feelings and recognizes their importance.
			Lawyer repeatedly conveys a desire to help.
			(Client-centered model—Binder, Bergman, & Price, 1991).
Methods	Emphasis on relationship.	Dual emphasis on individual and situation.	Emphasis on problem rather than people; deductive reasoning.
	Attends to cognitive and affective elements, but focuses on rational decision making.	Attends to cognitive and affective elements.	Attends to legal issues and rational decision-making.
	Historical material may be part of storytelling and ventilation, but focus is on the future.	Historical material explored as it becomes relevant to the client.	Historical information may be relevant to assigning blame, guilt, or responsibility for compensation.
	Mediator controls the process, clients responsible for the decisions—clear role boundaries.	Client relationship is integral part of the helping process. Moderate degree of mutuality is required.	Client relationship requires trust in lawyer as expert with professional integrity. Does not require mutual understanding of the problem and what needs to be changed.
	Focus on the parties' understanding of the problem and what needs to be changed.	Mutual understanding of the problem and what needs to be changed.	
	Contracting is used to submit to the process—voluntary; consent to ground rules, etc.	Contracting is essential to client-worker mutuality.	Lawyer receives instructions from client about how to act, but ideal situation may be compromised by power differentials (clients often defer to expertise of the lawyer).
	Intervention geared to change of roles, relationships, and concrete issues.	Intervention geared to both personal adaptation/change and change in environment.	
	Negotiating, cognitive restructuring, action, and problem solving.	Cognitive restructuring, action, and problem solving.	Intervention geared to relationship between disputing
		Understands and acknowledges differences in age,	

	Mediation Interest-based Model	Social Work Life Model[18]	Law
Methods (continued)	Cultural issues addressed if they pertain to underlying interests of the parties.	class, race, and sex.	parties, or parties with conflicting rights.
			Negotiating, problem solving—instrumental orientation.
			Remedies available for discrimination.

suspend their orientation as advocates and become impartial facilitators. Conversely, most social workers are used to advocating for particular clients or causes. Mediators allow clients to advocate on their own behalf. Although mediators support each party's ability to negotiate, they do not support a particular position or solution. Impartiality is one of the most difficult transitions for helping professionals to make when they become mediators.

In terms of values, law, social work, and mediation each emphasize the right of clients to make self-determined choices. They respect individuality and the self-worth of all people. Some people view law as contrary to self-determination, because courts impose solutions on parties. However, court is an avenue of last resort, even for lawyers. Preferably, conflicts are resolved through informal or lawyer-led negotiations (Ellis & Stuckless, 1998). Court is used only when the parties are unable to come to a solution on their own.

The similarities and differences between professions depend upon the models of intervention being compared. For example, the therapeutic and transformative models of mediation adopt methods that are similar to those used by clinical social workers, psychologists, and other mental health professionals. The structural model of mediation focuses more on rights and resolving legal issues, similar to the traditional practice of law. As mediation continues to evolve, helping professionals must consider how it relates to their original professional identities and what changes they need to adopt in order to assume the role of a mediator.

CULTURAL ISSUES

Cultural issues affect mediation from a number of perspectives:

- If the conflict is between parties from different cultural backgrounds, the conflict may be based on cross-cultural miscommunication, conflicting cultural values or beliefs, or dividing resources between people from the different cultures.

- If the parties are from a different culture than the mediator, the mediator needs to determine which knowledge, values, and skills are necessary in order to be a culturally competent mediator.
- Each model of mediation has a number of assumptions that may or may not be valid when working with people from different cultures.

The following two sections deal with these concerns by exploring cross-cultural issues between clients, as well as between mediators and clients. Sections 3 to 5 re-examine the value, knowledge, and skill bases of mediation in light of cultural factors.

1. Clients from Differing Cultures

Mediators must be prepared to explore whether the nature of a conflict is rooted in cross-cultural issues. Some mediators are reluctant to explore issues such as prejudice and power because they are afraid about exacerbating the conflict. However, if cultural issues are left brewing below the surface, the parties cannot deal with the real basis of the conflict. On the other hand, mediators must be careful not to assume that a conflict is caused by cultural issues simply because the parties come from different cultures. The following strategies may be useful in dealing with cross-cultural issues.

- Uses recognition strategies from the transformative paradigm to facilitate understanding and to reconcile past miscommunications.
- Emphasizes dialogue as a means to understand one another and gain mutual respect (Dubinskas, 1992).
- Validates different cultural beliefs, values, and ways of doing things, since many conflicts do not have a right and a wrong; reinforces that conflict is a part of diversity (Rabie, 1994).
- Separates interests and values; helps the parties understand the conflict between their values and focus the problem-solving component of mediation on satisfying interests that exist regardless of their difference in values.[19]
- Uses cultural interpreters to help each party gain better understandings of one another. If clients have lived most of their lives in a homogenous culture, they may have difficulty explaining cultural norms to others in language that they can understand. Cultural interpreters have had experi-

---

[19]Because values are so deep-rooted, they are difficult if not impossible to change in a brief intervention such as mediation. However, parties can learn to respect one another's values without having to agree with them.

ence with more than one culture, so they have learned how to translate cultural norms from one culture to another.

- If the conflict is based on inter-group conflict, consider group approaches rather than mediation between individuals (see Chapter 5 for mediation in group contexts).

The cross-cultural approaches to negotiation described in Chapter 3 are also useful for mediators.

2. Mediator's Culture

Some proponents of mediation suggest that one of the advantages of mediation is that the parties can select mediators who come from the same cultural background as themselves. While this may be true, it is not necessarily an advantage nor a given. Some individuals do prefer to deal with a mediator from their own cultural background: such mediators bring an understanding of cultural issues into the mediation process. Further, some people do not like to air their conflicts in the general community. For example, if the parties come from a discriminated group in society, they may distrust mediators from outside of their group. Others prefer to take their conflicts to professionals outside of their community. The cultural group may be small and closely knit. If the parties are concerned about confidentiality, they may believe that their privacy is easier to protect with an outside mediator.

Mediators can and do come from a variety of backgrounds. In many regions, however, the vast majority of professional mediators are people from middle class, western cultures. To some extent, this reflects access to professional education and mediation training programs. In some jurisdictions, mediators require a law degree or a graduate degree in one of the helping professions in order to be eligible for certification. These requirements block access to those who are not interested in or who cannot afford such education (See Appendix 3).

Since all mediators can expect to work with people from different cultures, cultural-specific education and experience is an integral part of professional development. Competence to work with people from one culture does not ensure competence to work with people from other cultures. Cultural competence requires specialized values, knowledge, and skills (Barsky, Este, & Collins, 1996).

3. Values

Two values that are particularly important for mediation with clients from different cultures are cultural relativism and respect for individuality. Cultural relativism suggests that no one culture is better or worse than another; they are simply different. Accordingly, mediators must demonstrate respect for cultures that are different from their own, rather than judge or impose values on them. Respect for individuality suggests that individual differences among people from the same culture must also be respected. Mediators need to caution against stereotypes or other generalizations that ignore diversity within the cultural group.

As noted in the discussion of traditional models of mediation, neutrality is not a universal value for mediation. Within some cultural traditions, mediators provide moral guidance or encourage the parties to resolve their conflicts in accordance with particular values or laws (Green, 1998). The parties trust these mediators because of their moral authority, rather than because of their neutrality. Although professional mediators from outside the parties' culture must be wary of imposing values on the parties, a mediator from within the culture may have greater latitude to refer clients to moral principles accepted within their group. Such mediators should indicate their value biases to the clients up front. If the parties consent to a mediator's biases, then neutrality may not be essential.

4. Knowledge and Process

Knowledge required for cultural competence depends upon the context of the conflict. In general, the mediator needs to inquire into how the parties and their cultures view each of the following.

- What constitutes a conflict?
- How should conflict be approached?
- Which process is most appropriate for intervention?
- What constitutes resolution? (LeBaron, 1997)

Consider the following case.

Conflictia High School recently suspended Raphael Florez for acting violently in the schoolyard. The Florez family believes that Raphael, subjected to racist taunting, was justified in defending himself.

In order to answer questions about conflict with this particular family, the mediator can draw on a number of sources: the family members themselves, cultural interpreters, other helping professionals from their community, readings, and research. Mediators tend to view conflict as something to be resolved. Members of the Florez family, however, have experienced ongoing racism. They believe that conflict of this sort needs to be confronted and challenged. To them, resolution sounds as if they are being told to accept the *status quo*.

In terms of who to involve in mediation, the mediator needs to identify how the family members would identify the parties. This family views the affront to Raphael as a family issue rather than an individual one. Accordingly, the mediator should consider involving family members, not just Raphael. In some cases, conflict is viewed as a group issue. The mediator may need to involve leaders or representatives of the group.

In terms of how to approach the conflict, the mediator needs to accommodate the school and the family. In this case, the school prefers to deal with conflict through a rational, structured dialogue. The family is accustomed to more open expression of emotion and informal discussions. The family wants to have a public forum, whereas the school wants to keep the process confidential.

With regard to developing an appropriate process, mediators have three primary options: (a) use their general model of practice and try to be sensitive to the needs of people from different cultures within the general model; (b) adapt their model to meet the specific needs of the specific cultures; or (c) create a new model of conflict resolution by learning about the means of conflict resolution used traditionally within the culture. For the last alternative, the mediator works in partnership with the culture in order to develop the culturally specific approach to conflict resolution (Lederach, 1995; LeBaron, 1997). The process is complicated where, as in the present example, the parties come from different cultures.

In this case, the mediator begins by having separate meetings with the family and with the school. This enables the mediator to explore their values and beliefs about conflict and the way it should be resolved. The mediator finds that the parties share some values: both want the conflict to be resolved, they are looking for a process that is fair, and they define fairness as having a mediator who does not take sides. Where the mediator identifies contradictory values and beliefs, the mediator will have to make tough choices. Believing that it will be more difficult to engage the family, the mediator decides to tailor some of the process to their needs. Also, the school is represented by teachers and the principal, professionals who should be willing to make accommodations for the family. The mediator develops and proposes a hybrid process to the family and the school. The mediation process is voluntary. Mediation only proceeds if both parties consent to the process.

5. Skills

Culturally competent mediators adapt their use of skills to the needs of different groups. This requires an understanding of the group's norms of communication and conflict resolution styles (Irving & Benjamin, 1995). The following mediator skills are particularly useful for situations where the parties' culture is different from that of the mediator.

1. Checks out assumptions on meanings of terms and phrases;
2. Presents issues or ideas as they are perceived from the parties' perspectives;

3. Uses short, clear sentences;
4. Uses concrete examples and specific language;
5. Avoids idiomatic expressions, mixed messages, abstractions, or unfamiliar terms;
6. Indicates appreciation and respect for the dignity of the parties and the groups to which they belong;
7. Promotes an environment that allows for sharing of selected (appropriate) cultural information;
8. Tolerates ambiguity;
9. Upon making an interactive mistake, acknowledges it in a non-defensive manner (e.g., apologize, acknowledge your limitations, indicate your intent to learn how to avoid mistakes in the future);
10. Acknowledges differences in beliefs, values, and norms;
11. Makes tentative suggestions ("I wonder if . . . .");
12. Acknowledges interest in and unfamiliarity with the parties' culture;
13. Recognizes that the parties knows more than the mediator about their culture;
14. Provides positive feedback for how the client has helped you to understand;
15. Asks about the parties' natural or informal support systems (including who is involved in making different types of decisions); and
16. Uses appropriate self-disclosure to help build a positive working. (Barsky, Este, & Collins, 1996; Greey, 1994; Kavanaugh & Kennedy, 1992)

Mediators can expect to invest considerable time in order to learn how to work effectively with people from a different culture. Cultural competence develops over time through experience, feedback, reading, and reflection. Conflict occurs not only between the two parties, but between each of the parties and the mediator. Mediators can make positive use of conflict with the parties by modeling conflict resolution skills for the parties.

KEY POINTS

- The role of a mediator is to provide parties with support so that they can negotiate more effectively.
- Although mediation has only become popular among helping professionals since the 1980s, traditional forms of mediation have existed in different cultures throughout history.
- A mediator's choice of intervention models depends upon how the mediator views success.
- Structural mediators emphasize expedient resolution of manifest conflict.

- Interest-based mediators engage the parties in a joint problem-solving process in order to help them resolve the conflict and their underlying interests in a mutually satisfactory manner.
- Therapeutic mediators assist parties with emotional and relational issues in order to be able to resolve their conflict more effectively.
- Transformative mediators foster empowerment and recognition between the parties.
- When selecting or developing a model of mediation, mediators need to consider the following issues: voluntary or coerced participation, neutrality, impartiality, fairness, power imbalances, confidentiality, and definitions of successful mediation.
- Helping professionals can act as emergent or contractual mediators in a range of contexts, including family, mental health (Schwebel & Clement, 1996), cross-cultural, criminal justice, workplace, public policy, and community conflicts.
- Mediation can be broken down into seven phases: Preparation, Orientation, Issue Definition, Exploring Interests and Needs, Negotiating and Problem Solving, Finalizing an Agreement, and Follow-up.
- In order to switch from one's conventional helping role to the role of mediator, a helping professional needs to identify key differences in skills, strategies, values, and manners of interaction with clients.
- When working with people from different cultural backgrounds, mediators need to decide whether to use a standard model of mediation, to adapt their standard model, or to develop a culturally specific model of mediation.
- Cultural competence in mediation requires that mediators develop knowledge, values, and skills to be able to work with people from specific cultural groups.

DISCUSSION QUESTIONS AND EXERCISES

1. MEDIATION SUCCESS: Identify a conflict situation where you see yourself as a potential mediator. As a mediator, what would your goals for mediation be in these circumstances? Refer back to your answers to "Exercise 2—Negotiation Success" in Chapter 3. Are there any differences between how you view success as a mediator and success as a negotiator? Does it depend upon the context of the conflict?
2. MEDIATOR VALUES: As a mediator, what are your primary values? Consider the following: safety, fairness, respect for all individuals; accepting, nonjudgmental, empowerment, impartiality, neutrality, self-determination.

3. IMPARTIALITY DILEMMA: You are facilitating a play therapy group for six year olds who have experienced physical abuse from their parents. During the third session, two of the children start to fight over one of the puppets. You decide to use your mediative skills to help them resolve this conflict. You encourage them to come up with their own decision, rather than impose one on them. You are able to help them work toward a mutually agreeable solution: rip up the puppet into small pieces so that neither of them can fight over it any more. You personally find this solution troubling because it is violent and destructive. Still, you have encouraged the children to come up with their own solution. Do you support their decision or direct them to a different type of solution? What factors do you consider in making your decision?

4. OTHER MODELS: This chapter focuses upon four models of mediation. There are many other models of mediation and mediation-like interventions; for example, Native North American Healing Circles (Green, 1998; Stuart, 1997), Family Group Conferencing in New Zealand and Australia (Hudson, Morris, Maxwell, & Gallaway, 1996), Ho'opono pono in Hawaii (Wall & Callister, 1995), of Sulha in Arab communities (Jabbour, 1996). Select one of these models. Conduct a literature review on this model to identify its key assumptions, components, and strategies. Compare this model to one of the models analyzed in this chapter.

5. CRITIQUING MEDIATION: Review the mediation case illustration between Englebert and Elvis. Select one phase of the process. Identify the

strengths and limitations of how Medina handled this phase. What other issues and alternatives could have been considered?

6. OPEN OR CLOSED: The examples of an opening statement and Agreement to Mediate in Elvis and Englebert's case describe "Closed Mediation."[20] Closed Mediation means that information from the mediation cannot be used for court or other purposes. The parties are agreeing that the mediator and the mediator's files cannot be subpoenaed. If the parties agree to "Open Mediation," then either party can use information from the mediation in other processes, particularly if the parties do not come to a full agreement. In Open Mediation, the mediator provides a report at the end of the process, summarizing the issues, underlying interests, and final offers or positions on the issues. The mediator does not provide recommendations. What are the advantages of Open Mediation? What are the advantages of Closed Mediation?

7. CAUCUSING DILEMMA: Some mediators never meet individually with the parties. Others meet with the parties individually to screen for safety issues, to help with power balancing, or to help parties resolve an impasse. What happens if a party shares important information with the mediator but refuses to allow the mediator to disclose it to the other party? Under what circumstances should the mediator disclose the information? When should the mediator keep the information confidential? How can the mediator pre-empt this sort of dilemma?

8. POWER PLAYS: What is the difference, if any, between "empowering" and "power balancing?" How do mediators using different models view the appropriateness of each?

9. STORYTELLING: Compare the process of storytelling in mediation with the use of stories in Narrative Therapy.

10. CONTRASTS: Earlier in the chapter, I provided a comparison between mediation, social work, and law. In order to conduct a similar analysis, select a model of mediation and a model of intervention from your own profession (e.g., cognitive restructuring, solution-focused therapy, strategic family therapy, structured family therapy, psychoanalysis, radical social work, andragogy [adult education], feminist counseling). Compare these two models in terms of their definitions, domains and philosophies, objectives, assumptions, roles, values and ethics, focus, client-professional relationship, structure, and methods. What can you transfer from your original profession to mediation? What are the key changes you need to make when you take on the role of a mediator?

[20]The terms "Open" and "Closed" mediation originated in the province of Ontario and may not be used in other jurisdictions.

11. CO-MEDIATION: Co-mediation refers to mediation conducted by two or more mediators. Identify the advantages and disadvantages of co-mediation. Under what circumstances is co-mediation advisable?

12. DEAL WITH THE DEVIL: Andrew is addicted to alcohol. One evening, he finds himself without cash or alcohol. Suffering from withdrawal symptoms, he screams out, "I'd sell my soul for a 12-pack of beer." Suddenly, the Devil appears. The Devil says, I'll give you 6 beers for your soul." They haggle back and forth, but are unable to come up with an agreement. They decide to hire you as their mediator. What ethical issues are raised by this case? How would you handle them? What techniques could you use if you wanted to balance power between the parties?

13. CULTURAL VALUES DILEMMA: As a mediator you respect your clients' right to self-determination and their cultural diversity. You also believe in cultural relativism. Consider a case where all the clients come from the same culture, but that culture is different from your own. The conflict is a noise-related dispute between two couples that live in adjacent apartments. During mediation, the husbands speak on behalf of their wives, even though the primary conflict occurred between the women. According to their culture, women are not permitted to speak directly with the mediator or with men other than their husbands. You find this offensive. How do you reconcile your values and deal with this situation? (cf., Freshman, 1997)

14. CULTURAL HETEROGENEITY: In #13, you are asked to consider "clients who come from the same culture." While there are similarities between people from the same culture, there are also differences: e.g., people from different subcultures, people with different personalities, people with different life experiences. Conversely, there are often more similarities between people from different cultures than differences. How can a mediator use information about culture without falling into the traps of stereotyping and over-generalizing?

15. MEDIATION AND GENDER: Kolb (1992) suggests that women have certain attributes that help them perform more effectively than men as peacemakers in organizations. Why might this be true? What attributes associated with men might contribute to their abilities to act as peacemakers? (cf., Gilligan, 1990)

16. REFRAMING: Reframing refers to looking at a situation from a different perspective (Bandler & Grinder, 1982). Consider how a painting changes appearances when you change its frame, or how different people look if you view them face-to-face as opposed to from an aerial view. To illustrate, consider the following figure:

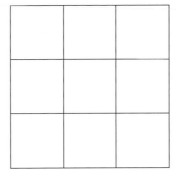

Count the number of squares in this figure and write down the number. Ask others in the class to do the same.

Compare answers. If there are any differences, how do you account for these? Is there only one right answer?

17. REFRAMING, THE SEQUEL: Reframing is a key skill in mediation. One format for reframing is to restate what someone has said (a) in positive terms, (b) to eliminate blame or accusation, (c) to identify underlying concerns, fears, interests, needs, values, or goals, or (d) to identify common ground. One format to follow in order to reframe is:

> "You seem to feel . . ." (*underlying concern or fear*)
> "Both of you/All of us . . ." (*mutual interest, need, value or goal*)
> "Why don't we . . ." (*problem-solving approach*)[21]

The following statements have been made by one client to another during mediation. You are the mediator. Provide an example of reframing for each statement.

   a. You're wrong. The children need to live with me.
   b. If we can't offer service to this client, then we might as well close up shop.
   c. Two thousand therapists in this city and I ended up with you!
   d. If you're not going to cooperate, then I really can't help you.
   e. What do you mean there's a six month waiting list?
   f. Who made you dictator?
   g. I get A's in all my other classes.
   h. The Student Representative Council is useless.
   i. You're a racist, male chauvinist pig.

---

[21]Source unknown.

18. MEMORANDUM OF UNDERSTANDING: Consider the following Memorandum of Understanding, written by a mediator in a case between a mental health patient and a long-term care facility.

> The parties of the first part and of the second part hereby agree that Mr. Paul Paterson will stop harassing the nursing staff by calling them in the middle of the night for trivial matters. If Mr. Paterson continues this immature behavior, he will be immediately discharged from the Shady Firs Residence. The residence accepts no responsibility for Mr. Paterson's welfare should the Residence need to discharge Mr. Paterson.

Critique this memorandum according to the suggestions provided in this chapter. Analyze both strengths and limitations. Re-write the memorandum in a way that deals with the limitations you have identified. Feel free to use your creativity.

ROLE-PLAY 4.1: "PARKING PERILS"—OPENING STATEMENT

You are a volunteer mediator for a community dispute resolution program in Conflictia. A police officer, Sgt. Poile, refers two neighbors—Nora and Nelly—who have been feuding over parking problems. Over the past month, Nora has called the police on six occasions to complain that Nelly was parking in front of Nora's driveway. Nelly responded that Nora would let the air out of her tires if she parked within 12 feet of her driveway. Prepare an opening statement that you could use for the first joint session. Create crib notes to help you cover key points. Practice the opening statement with two others in the class. Do not read a script. Ensure eye contact with both parties as you go through the statement. Remain flexible, answering questions of the parties that may arise.

ROLE-PLAY 4.2: "MUTUALLY NOISY NEIGHBORS"—AGREEMENT TO MEDIATE

Ms Thibault and Mr. Omar have been embroiled in a 60-day dispute, ever since Ms Thibault moved into the apartment unit directly above Mr. Omar's apartment (genders of the disputants can be changed without affecting the nature of the dispute). Mr. Omar is a 71-year-old widower who has lived in the apartment for over 20 years. Ms Thibault is a 22-year-old university student. Ever since she moved into the building, she has been disturbed by noise coming from Mr. Omar's apartment. Mr. Omar has a hearing impairment and needs to turn up the volume on his TV or radio in order to be able to hear them. Mr. Omar likes to go to bed early and wake up early. The TV or radio are kept on when Mr. Omar is up because he likes the company; also, it is his only way of keeping up with what's going on in the community.

Ms Thibault is away at school during the afternoon, but likes to work at home in the morning and in the evening. She finds it difficult to study with Mr. Omar's noise, but she needs to work at home because that is where her computer and her books are. She is also awakened early (about 5:30 a.m.) when Mr. Omar gets up and turns on the radio. Ms Thibault has told Mr. Omar about the problem several times, but he continues to leave the volumes at the same levels. In frustration, Ms Thibault has begun to respond by playing her stereo at high levels or by stamping on her parquet floors. When this happens, Mr. Omar just raises the volume of his TV or radio. With the escalating noise war, other neighbors have complained to the building manager. The manager has told Mr. Omar and Ms Thibault to get together to work it out themselves. Management does not want to hear anymore problems from either of them. Ms Thibault and Mr. Omar agree to go to the Conflictia Mediation Center, on neutral ground, to try to work out a solution.

This case can be role-played using a variety of negotiation styles: hard, soft, positional, chicken, compromising, tit-for-tat, interest-based. Each party should select a style and not disclose it to the others. In preparing for the role-play, write down some of the tactics and strategies you will use in playing your designated negotiation style.

The main purpose of this role-play is to give the person playing the mediator practice at the initial phases of the mediation process. The mediator should select a model of mediation and use the Inventory of Skills and Activities for Each Phase of Mediation to prepare for this role-play.

ROLE-PLAY 4.3: FOUR CASES OF EMERGENT MEDIATION

The following cases involve emergent mediation. For each case, identify the issues in dispute and the nature of the conflict. What challenges do they pose for the third party? What strategies would you use to deal with them? Would it be appropriate for you to act as an emergent mediator? If so, what would you need to do to improve the chances that the parties accept you as a mediator? Try role-playing these situations.

a. Family Feud

Richard and Jane are adult siblings who come from a family that deals with conflict by slamming doors, screaming, or throwing things. You are a long-time friend of both of them. During dinner at a restaurant, Richard and Jane start to argue about who is going to pick up the tab. You are caught in the middle. You are embarrassed about making a scene, and offer to pay the bill.

Jane says, "No way! It's Richard's turn. Don't let him walk all over you." Richard replies to Jane, "You're full of it! You're the one who's always bragging about how much money you make!"

As a friend, what strategies would you use to help mediate the dispute? What if you were Jane and Richard's counselor, rather than their friend: How would you help them deal more effectively with this conflict? How is your role similar to that of the friend? How is it different?

b. Crabby Co-Workers

Bea and Jay work as receptionists in Diversity Plus. Jay always complains that Bea is late, takes long lunches, and leaves early. Jay thinks Bea is lazy and is taking advantage of Jay's good nature. Bea has a number of excuses—having to drop off and pick up the kids at daycare, needing time to do the shopping, and being tired from working too hard. Besides, Bea says that she's more efficient than Jay and makes up for the time off. Jay finally can't put up with Bea and goes to you (the office manager) to "fire Bea and get someone competent." Because of Bea's seniority and position, you are reluctant to fire Bea and would prefer to work it out amicably. Also, it is not Jay's decision about who to hire and who to fire. You have arranged for a meeting with both of them.

c. Gossipy Group

Ashley and Gerry are members of a recreational softball team that you play on. In fact, you've been nominated captain. In recent weeks, Ashley has been saying that Gerry is having an affair with someone 15 years older. The team is out on the playing field. Gerry has just caught wind of this story from the shortstop and decides to throw the next ball that comes his way at Ashley's head. Gerry has a bad arm, so the ball misses Ashley. The two start cursing and threatening each other. As captain, you intervene and get them into the locker room to "talk it out."

Would it make any difference if your softball team were a group of social workers, nurses, and doctors who worked together in a hospital setting? How are the roles of baseball team captain and interdisciplinary team leader similar regarding conflict management roles? How are they different?

d. Catch 22 Couple

You are a family therapist who has been seeing Andy and Michele over the past three months for couples counseling. Andy and Michele are trying to decide what to do for their 5th anniversary. Andy wants them to go on a nostalgic trip back to their birthplace, where they also met and married. Michele wants to throw a big party here in Conflictia. They do not have the time or money to do both. They come to you, their trusted therapist and friend, to tell them what to do or where to go. If you side with one, then you will offend the other. If you give them a third option, then they will both get angry with you. If you refuse to help, then they'll think you're "a whus."[22]

Do you respond as a therapist or as a mediator? How would your responses differ?

ROLE-PLAY 4.4: "ANTI-DISCIPLINARY TEAM"— SKILL DEVELOPMENT

Norman is a nurse. Sonia is a social worker. Phyllis is a psychologist. These three professionals work on a specialized, interdisciplinary team at Conflictia Hope Hospital. The team provides assessments and supportive interventions for children who are suspected of having been sexually abused. Norman and Sonia personally cannot stand one another. Norman sees Sonia as arrogant, non-co-operative, and indecisive. Sonia sees Norman as petty and backstabbing. Recently, they returned a child (Chelsey) home with her parents. Chelsey was abused further. Norman told administration that he had nothing to do with the case, laying blame at Sonia's feet. During a case conference regarding another family (the Farquhars), Norman and Sonia start arguing about Chelsey's case. Phyllis gets caught in the crossfire and tries to use her mediative skills.

The person playing Phyllis can use this role-play for skill development. Use the inventory of skills and activities to identify mediation skills that you want to practice and dysfunctional behaviors that you want to extinguish. Focus on no more than four skills at a time.

ROLE-PLAY 4.5: "CONFLICT IN THE RANKS"— CONTRASTING MODELS

An alliance of agencies advocating for women's interests decides to hold a demonstration walk through downtown Conflictia to Conne Servativ's house, the official residence of the Head of State. Three people are present at an organizational meeting: Sofia (a supervisor from a women's shelter); Winnifred (representing a black women's advocacy group), and Carole (a community organizer who works with families living in public housing). The agenda for the

---

[22]A derogatory term, suggesting that you are a coward.

meeting is to establish a list of demands from the provincial government. Winnifred suggests that concerns for women of color should be given high priority. Sofia believes that this would be divisive and that they should push for the common interests of all women. Winnifred accuses Sofia of racism. Sofia responds that Winnifred is being over-sensitive. Carole tries to use her mediative skills.

This situation can be role-played using different models of mediation: structural, interest-based, therapeutic, and transformative. Assign different models to different people who will play Carole's role.

DEBRIEFING: What skills and strategies did Carole use effectively? What were the key differences in the process when different people used different models of mediation? Which model of mediation seems most appropriate for this case situation?

ROLE-PLAY 4.6: "TOUCHY ISSUE"— EMPOWERMENT AND POWER BALANCING

Diversity Plus has a special unit that provides support services to people with cognitive disabilities. Victor is a vocational counselor. Clara is one of Victor's clients. Clara has moderate cognitive impairment related to brain damage that occurred during birth. During a meeting with Victor, she believes that he has touched her in an inappropriate manner: He touched her shoulder, without her permission. Although he did not mean to do this in a sexual manner, Clara took offense. As Clara came out of Victor's office, Don (the director of CYB) saw she was distressed and asked her what was wrong. Don tries to mediate the conflict.

Ordinarily, the person playing a mediative role would not have time to prepare, but for learning purposes, try to strategize in advance. Consider, should Don assume a mediative role? What must he do to gain acceptance in this role? What stages and strategies might be useful? What potential pitfalls should Don watch for? This exercise can be used to practice empowerment and power balancing. Consider having individual meetings with the parties.

ROLE-PLAY 4.7: "FAMILY PLANNING"— CULTURAL INTERPRETER

For this role-play, team up with a person from a different cultural background (if possible, someone who is also from a different professional background). One of you will role-play a mediator. The other will play a cultural interpreter. The mediator is helping a couple negotiate a pre-nuptial agreement. The couple wants to mediate the following issues: the number of children and approximate timing for having children; will one or both spouses work outside of the family home; and how will they make decisions about parenting issues. The couple is from a different background than the mediator, so the mediator arranges to meet with a cultural interpreter in order to gain a better understanding of cultural issues that may be raised in this case.

The mediator should plan what types of questions to ask the cultural interpreter in order to prepare for this meeting (e.g., what are the norms within this culture about parenting; what happens within the community if people do not follow the norms). During the meeting, the cultural interpreter should draw from his or her culture in order to answer the mediator's questions. The role of the cultural interpreter is to educate the mediator. The interpreter may not feel comfortable making generalizations about his or her culture. If so, the mediator can validate these concerns and negotiate what types of information that the interpreter would be willing to share.

Debriefing Questions
What did the mediator learn about the family's culture? How would this information affect the way that you mediate with the couple? What ethical issues does this scenario raise for the mediator?

MAJOR ASSIGNMENTS

The following role-plays can be used for major assignments. See the section on Major Assignments in Chapter 3 for instructions on how to prepare a written analysis. These role-plays give you broad latitude about how to prepare and how to intervene. You can use theory from this chapter or from other books and articles.

ASSIGNMENT 4A—GUN PROHIBITION CASE

Assignment 4A: Common Facts

The three roles to choose from in this case are Adele (who will take on a mediator role), Faith, and Connie. If any of the role-players are male, they could be Arnie, Foster, or Constantine.

Adele is an administrator for Conflictia's Seniors' Center (CSC). At CSC's last annual meeting, many of the members said that they were concerned about their safety on the streets of Conflictia. They believed that the elderly were especially vulnerable to violent crime because of concerns such as physical frailties, dementia, and lack of awareness about potentially dangerous situations. A motion was passed at the meeting that the Center should send a position paper to each of the three major political parties in Conflictia: ROC,

LOC, and SIM. The LOC party has recently proposed that Conflictia ban possession and sale of all guns and rifles.

Among members of CSC, there is rift between: 1) those who believe prohibiting guns would go a long way to promoting safety, and 2) those who believe that prohibiting would not only be ineffective; it would be a gross infringements on the rights and freedoms of law abiding citizens. In order to try to resolve their differences, Adele suggested that they try a two-party mediation process, in which she would act as mediator.

Each side of the debate has met as a group and appointed a leader to represent its viewpoint. Faith will represent those who favor the proposed gun laws. Connie will represent those that oppose the proposed gun laws. They will meet with Adele to try to work out a joint position paper that they will present to the three political parties. They believe that their Center will have a stronger voice if it submits a single, consensus report, rather than have members with different viewpoints submitting their own suggestions. They also believe that this process can bring the members of the community closer together if the process is successful; on the other hand, an unsuccessful process could be alienating and divisive.

Assignment 4A—Connie's Confidential Facts

Connie is a member of a rifle association and has a collection of guns, some of them antiques. She doesn't hunt and they stay in a special locked case. If the gun prohibition laws are passed, Connie would not turn in her guns as a matter of principle. This is just another attempt by bureaucrats in government to come into the bedrooms and basements of law-abiding citizens. Money could be better spent on food for the hungry or housing for the homeless. Although Connie does not agree, most people at CSC who oppose gun prohibition believe that the government should be spending more money on law enforcement and prisons in order to make the streets safe for all citizens.

Connie does not like conflict—at least conflict where there are fights and raised voices. She is concerned that Faith might get carried away and start yelling. If this happens, Connie will withdraw into silence. Better to avoid this type of trouble. In addition, Connie isn't sure the mediator (Adele) can handle Faith.

Assignment 4A—Faith's Confidential Facts

Faith tends to express feelings openly, verbally, and with broad hand gestures—perhaps it is a cultural thing. The issue of gun control is an emotional issue for Faith, having been mugged at gunpoint only 18 months ago. Faith realized that she represents a group from her agency, and will try to keep her personal experiences in check—most of the time.

Faith believes that the purpose of government is to keep peace and order. She sees gun prohibition as a legitimate way to try to reduce the incidence of violent crime and injury. She is also aware of suicide statistics, showing that the availability of guns is associated with a higher incidence of completed suicides. If people having suicidal thoughts have direct access to an effective means of killing themselves, then they are more likely to kill themselves. Also, unplanned murders (committed in the heat of passion) are more likely when guns are accessible. Spousal violence, in particular, can result in death rather than lesser injury.

Faith is subject to *occasional*, short-term memory lapse. She is embarrassed about this, and will try to cover it up—perhaps pretending she has a hearing problem.

Consensus is very important to Faith. She likes to get along with everyone and doesn't want this debate to leave any scars on CSC.

Assignment 4A—Adele's Confidential Facts (Mediator)

Adele is an old navy admiral and likes to deal with people straight on; i.e., no nonsense. Adele personally favors gun prohibition, not just for the public but for the police. Only the national armed forces should have access to guns. Adele has seen the damage that people can do when they do not know how to use a gun properly.

The only other case facts that you have are the "Common Facts." You may want to meet with another person from your class who is playing the mediator to help you prepare and plan out a process. Brainstorm some of the issues that you might expect and try to identify strategies that will help you deal with them.

ASSIGNMENT 4B: MESSY ESTATE DISPUTE (THE MED CASE)

Assignment 4B: Common Facts

The three roles to choose from are Suzie, Selma and Mona. Mona will play the mediator. If any of the role-play participants is male, he could be Sheldon, Simon, or Malcolm.

Suzie (38) and Selma (41) are siblings. Their parents died five months ago, leaving them shocked, angry, and saddened. The sisters have not gotten along very well for years, dating back to their envy and competitiveness in high school days. However, they somehow managed to act "good" in front of their parents. Relations have soured further given their reaction to the loss of their parents, and the present task of how to divide their parents' estate.

Neither parent had a valid will. Selma and Suzie are the only children, and (now that Selma has paid off the parents' bills) there are no other parties making claims in the estate.

The main assets include a joint bank account with $15,000.00, life insurance and pension benefits worth $20,000.00, a condominium (purchased five years ago for $120,000 with an outstanding mortgage of $80,000.00; present market value unknown); mom's diamond engagement ring; two wedding rings; a gold bracelet; grandma's brooch (low monetary value, but sentimental to both); six photograph albums; a china set (serves 12); furniture (bedroom/living room/dining room); and a 1993 Buick (which neither daughter wants due to car repair needs). Selma is the more financially secure of the two women and has threatened to take Suzie to court (mostly out of spite). Suzie is only working part-time now and rents an apartment; she would like to move into the condo to save money. Besides, the market value is currently depressed due to the recession in Conflictia. Suzie believes it would be best to wait before selling. Selma thinks that Suzie is already living in the condo and that she has started to sell off pieces of furniture.

Both Selma and Suzie have independent legal advice; the lawyers referred them to mediation to try to work out a memorandum of understanding. If/when the issues are resolved, the lawyers will draft the final agreement. Selma and Suzie have agreed to try to work things out with Mona, a family mediator recommended by one of Selma's friends.

Assignment 4B: Suzie's Confidential Facts

Suzie is not sure that she can trust Mona, the mediator. Mona seemed to know Selma from before, and Suzie is worried that Mona and Selma are good friends. Suzie does not want to make any accusations, because her lawyer said that she should try to make a good impression with the mediator.

Suzie is not very knowledgeable about real estate values or investments. Her parents used to help her budget and told her what to do with her money. Suzie was quite dependent on them, emotionally, as well as for concrete support and advice. When she found out her parents were killed in a car crash, she was devastated.

Suzie is not living in her parents' condo. She has mixed emotions about doing so. On the one hand, she could save rent money. On the other hand, she would be living with a constant reminder of her parents and their recent tragedy.

Suzie can be accommodating, but she will become competitive if backed into a corner. She might even start to decompensate or regress into childish name-calling if she feels threatened. Suzie may be willing to compromise on some of the monetary items in her parents' estate, but if there's one thing that she wants—whether through litigation or through mediation or whatever—it's grandma's brooch. Grandma promised it to her when she was 12.

Assignment 4B: Selma's Confidential Facts

Selma is the older, wiser, and stronger sibling. She has mixed emotions about dividing her parents' estate—on the one hand, her parents always told her to take care of Suzie; on the other hand, she hated that; and on the other hand, Selma is still in shock about her parents' sudden death in a car accident. She was supposed to meet them earlier that day. She still feels guilty for backing out at the last minute.

Selma may approach the mediation in a "tit-for-tat" manner, willing to trade off one item for another. However, if Suzie rubs her the wrong way, Selma will shoot back. There are some items that Selma must have: Grandma's brooch, the entire china set, and the diamond engagement ring. She does not think that Suzie should get anything of value, since she is not good with money. Selma believes Suzie is likely to lose any investments and sell off family heirlooms to pay for her day-to-day needs. She spoke to the superintendent at her parents' condo. He thought that Suzie had already emptied out most of the furniture.

Selma wants to get things settled in one session. She is quite willing to go to court. She is only mediating because her lawyer strongly suggested it. She has difficulty maintaining attention for long periods. She may get up once in a while to wander around. Selma has never met a mediator before. She finds that Mona can sometimes be "too nice."

Assignment 4B: -Mona's Confidential Facts (Mediator)

The only case facts that you have are the "Common Facts." You may want to meet with another person in your class who is role-playing the mediator, to help you prepare and plan out a process. Brainstorm some of the issues that you might expect. Identify strategies that will help you deal with them.

MEDIATION WITH GROUPS

Whereas Chapter 4 focuses on mediation between individuals, this chapter concentrates on mediation with groups. These areas of practice certainly overlap, as groups are composed of individuals (Picard, 1998). Many of the skills and strategies transfer well from one context to the other. However, some models have been developed specifically for inter-group conflict.

This chapter is broken down into four primary topics: types of inter-group mediation; complexities; skills and strategies for group facilitation; and models of inter-group mediation and related processes.

TYPES OF INTER-GROUP MEDIATION

Inter-group mediation refers to mediation between two or more groups in the community. Within each group, individuals have shared values, common beliefs, or mutual interests. Between groups, there are conflicting values, beliefs, or interests. As noted in Chapter 1, conflict exists whether the difference in values, beliefs, or interests is perceived or real. Perceptions of conflict often arise because of miscommunication, stereotyping, or other types of mis-understandings.

One of the more common forms of inter-group conflict is between people from different cultural backgrounds, for example, Mexicans and Americans, Hindus and Moslems, middle-aged and elderly people, men and women, disabled and able-bodied people. However, some of the fiercest conflicts arise between people of the same culture (within-group or inter-subgroup conflict). Although any conflict can be laden with emotions, people tend to feel particularly angry, betrayed, or hurt when conflict escalates with people from their own family, clan, or culture.

Within a community, mediation can be used to facilitate a range of public policy processes that require consensus from the community. For example, does the community support euthanasia; what are the community's priorities in terms of how government allocates tax revenues to social programs; or how does the community balance interests between environmentalists and business leaders (Dukes, 1996; Mayer, 1997)? Inter-group mediation is also useful within social agencies and other organizations. As with mediation between individuals, inter-group mediation can be a formal, contractual process or an informal, emergent process.

Just because conflict exists between two or more groups does not mean that mediation is either necessary or welcome. First, conflict can be desirable. The fact that different groups possess different beliefs and values contributes to the color and diversity of society. When people can accept and respect differences, resolution of conflict may not be necessary. When conflict brings about negative consequences—violence, exploitation, subjugation, and so on—various interventions need to be considered. Mediation is just one alternative. Other roles, such as administrator, buffer, and healer (described in Chapter 1) should also be considered.

As an inter-group mediator, you can assist groups (or subgroups) as they negotiate based on any of the four paradigms of negotiation: positions, rights, interests, or transformation. A mediative role is sometimes referred to as "consensus building," "peace building," or "participatory decision making." Unfortunately, there is no consensus about whether these roles are the same, and if they are different, what the differences really are.

Whether a helping professional self-identifies as a mediator, facilitator, chair, or peace builder depends upon the image and role the professional wants to project. The term "mediator" conveys impressions of impartiality and assisted negotiation. "Facilitator" suggests that the primary role of the intermediary is to help the parties communicate, though not necessarily to negotiate specific issues and solutions. "Chair" implies that the role of the third party is to conduct a meeting or guide the group through a planned agenda. "Peace builder" highlights the professional's orientation toward peace and harmony. As you work through this material, consider what types of processes should be called "mediation" and which should be given different names.

For community-based social workers and other community organizers, mediation in a group context probably sounds like community development work. In both community development and mediation, the role of the professional can include helping community members communicate, building collaborative relationships, identifying common goals, and working through problem-solving processes. In spite of the similarities between community development and mediation, literature in each field has remained largely separate (Campfens, 1997; Kaminsky & Yellott, 1997).

COMPLEXITIES

Mediation between groups can be complex because the mediator must simultaneously attend to conflict at many different levels: between the key conflicting groups, between individuals within each group, and between various parties and the mediator. Lines between who is a member of each group are often blurred because various groupings of people have both shared and diverse interests, values, and beliefs. The relationships between individuals and groups may be in a continuous state of flux, given the dynamic nature of human interaction. The following strategies can be used to deal with these complexities: use co-mediators; meet with group delegates rather than the entire group; or frame the conflict as communal conflict, rather than a conflict between groups.

1. Co-Mediation

Using more than one mediator is particularly advantageous when there are many parties and difficult issues to address. More mediators means more people to watch, listen, and assess the interaction in progress (Picard, 1998). Co-mediators can offer one another both instrumental and moral support. They can either divide or share responsibilities. Some co-mediators prefer to have one lead mediator, with others who take on supportive roles: for example, note-taking, timekeeping, or monitoring process. Other co-mediators prefer a more fluid sharing of responsibilities. In either situation, the mediators must have a clear understanding of their roles.

Another advantage of co-mediation is that the parties can be broken up into small groups, each having its own mediator to facilitate small group discussion. Small groups allow individuals more time to provide direct input. In addition, people who have difficulty speaking in front of large audiences may find it easier to participate in small groups.

Co-mediation can be challenging. Because co-mediators are individuals, they will often have different opinions about how to proceed. When conflict occurs, they must ensure that they model constructive CR behaviors: agreeing upon process in advance; checking out assumptions; demonstrating trust and respect for one another; and dealing with private matters in a private setting. Co-mediators must be particularly aware of situations where one party tries to play one mediator off against another. This requires continuous communication between mediators.

2. Delegates

For some inter-group conflicts, mediators meet with delegates of each group rather than with all group members. Fewer people at the table can simplify the process and reduce the costs of bringing people together. Where conflict is heated and protracted, groups may wish to choose delegates who can convey their interests effectively, without getting caught up in counterproductive patterns that have maintained the conflict in the past (e.g., blaming, positioning, or insulting one another).

Meeting with delegates tends to be most appropriate where there are clearly defined groups with clearly defined needs or interests. In order for mediation between delegates to work, the members of each group need to trust their delegate and empower this delegate with decision-making authority. If there are differences within the group, these are ideally resolved be-fore the meeting between delegates. A mediator could meet with each group as a prelude to the mediation between delegates. The purposes of within-group meetings are to provide individuals with an opportunity to provide input and to identify what issues the group wants its delegate to take to mediation. The mediator discourages parties from sending their delegates to the table to fight for a particular position, so that the process is not set up to be adversarial.

When mediation extends over days or weeks, delegates need to meet periodically with their groups. This allows delegates to keep their constituencies apprised of the progress in mediation, as well as to gather their input. If a delegate does not keep the group involved, the group may withdraw its support or refuse to comply with any decisions that are made in mediation. During mediation, the delegates and mediators need to attend to the concerns of those not present in the room. For example, the delegates might come to a solution that will be a hard sell to one group. The mediator will encourage all delegates to work toward a solution that can win favor with all groups. If one delegate might be seen to have made to great a concession in mediation, then other delegates may find ways to support that delegate: for example, offering concessions in other areas, making positive public statements about the hard work and good faith of all delegates, or rethinking their proposed solution to ensure that it has broad support from all interested groups.

In many situations, use of delegates is inappropriate. As noted above, if groups are not clearly defined, then mediating between delegates is not a valid method of ensuring that everyone's interests are brought to the table. Mediation between delegates may also be inappropriate when you want to involve the whole community in responding to a problem. Assume, for instance, that a community is trying to decide how to deal with child prostitution. If delegates are used, then individuals will tend to feel less ownership over the problem and its solution. By involving the whole community, more points of view will be raised and more people will feel committed to solutions reached in mediation.

3. Reframe as Communal Conflict

Framing a problem as a conflict between groups tends to push people into positional stances. In order to foster collaboration, the mediator could frame the problem as one that affects the entire community, rather than groups within the community. Using this approach, the mediator encourages everyone to look at the conflict from non-partisan perspectives. People speak as individuals and not simply on behalf of a particular group.

The primary advantage of this approach is that people will look at the conflict more holistically. The primary disadvantage is that minority viewpoints and disadvantaged individuals may become even more disempowered. If only two out of a hundred delegates come from a particular minority, then the mediator may have to use power-balancing techniques to ensure that they can participate fully and fairly. As Chapter 4 notes, this raises questions of how a mediator can balance power without being viewed as biased.

FACILITATION

Facilitation refers to helping people communicate more easily. Mediators use facilitation skills, though they are not the only type of facilitator. Essentially, a facilitator uses the basic communication skills described in Chapter 2—active listening, questioning, and making statements—to pre-empt or remove barriers to effective communication. The following analysis deals with some of the more common obstacles to inter-group communication: individuals have different agendas; the discussion has no focus; the discussion is dominated by certain individuals; some individuals keep interrupting; some individuals remain silent; individuals lose their attention; individuals have difficulty listening to other's ideas; statements or questions put some people on the defensive; individuals are not saying what they really think; and individuals are confused about the agreements (Kaner, 1996; Kraybill, 1987). To illustrate facilitation strategies for each of these obstacles, I use a mediation situation between various helping professionals with conflicting ideas about how to regulate their professions.

1. Different Agendas

In a room full of 50 people, you might have 51 different opinions about the purpose of the meeting. If people come into a meeting with different agendas, at least some of them will come away feeling disappointed. Conflict resolution begins well before the first joint meeting, particularly with large groups. Everyone must be prepared ahead of time with the following types of information: what are the goals for the meeting; who will be attending; who will be facilitating the process; what are the roles of various participants; and what materials or information do people need to bring to the meeting. Proper preparation means pre-empting surprises. Although surprises can be entertaining, they are generally not conducive to constructive decision-making and conflict resolution.

In order to prepare for a joint meeting, the mediator must decide whether to meet with individuals or subgroups that will be participating at the larger meeting. Meeting with individuals or small subgroups is particularly desirable when the level of conflict is high and there are many different points of view. In some cases, the mediator can meet with representatives of each group in order to develop an agenda. The representatives for each group are responsible for ensuring that their members are prepared and in agreement with the agenda prior to the larger meeting.

Where the relevant parties do not agree upon the agenda, the mediator must use mediation skills to help them develop a mutually acceptable agenda. The mediator may need to shuttle back and forth between the parties until an agreement is reached. Often, the toughest negotiations go on before the parties ever agree to an agenda and sit down together. Each party may be positioning for certain advantages: e.g., a time and place that is favorable to their own group, a wording of the issues for discussion that limits the possible solutions in their favor, or a conflict resolution process that is biased in their favor. The mediator must recognize these tactics and promote more constructive negotiation strategies (see Chapter 3 for examples).

Some mediators are more directive at the beginning of the process. They suggest a specific agenda and process, ask the parties for comments, and try to move quickly for consensus on these issues so that they can move more quickly to dealing with the substantive issues.

2. No Focus

Once an agenda is set, the mediator needs to keep the parties focused on the agenda. If necessary, the parties can renegotiate parts of the agenda. However, this should be a deliberate process. Too often, the mediator and the parties wander from one issue to another without any clear focus.

"Punctuation" refers to the skill of clearly separating each issue from other issues. The facilitator lets the participants know which issue is up for discussion and when it ends (Kraybill, 1987).

> We are now moving on to the issue of standards for accreditation. We have 45 minutes to discuss the proposal put forward by the Accreditation Committee. We will then take a five-minute break. After the break, we will move on to the issue of professional discipline.

Punctuation emphasizes the transitions from one topic to another. Topic separation can be enhanced by making conscious changes in time and environment: taking a break between topics, moving to a different room, moving people from large groups to small groups, changing the lighting in the room, and so on.

When people stray from the topics on the table, the mediator uses refocusing skills. The mediator can remind the parties that they have agreed to a specific agenda, that they have limited time, and that they have made time for all issues to be discussed.

> I understand that you're concerned about professional discipline. We'll get to that after the break. I'll make a note that you want to speak to this issue. Did you want to add anything to our discussion on accreditation?

If people perceive that they have ownership of the agenda, they are more likely to keep focused. If the mediator notes a certain pattern to the interruptions, the mediator should assess the reasons for the interruptions; for example, individual difficulties maintaining focus or attention; tactic to prevent constructive problem-solving; or underlying emotional needs that require attention.

In the current example, one participant, Paul, keeps talking about how he was brought up on charges of professional misconduct. Other participants are getting frustrated because the issue is not about Paul, but professional issues more generally. The mediator assesses that for Paul, the issue is about Paul. He has unresolved anger about how he was treated. In order for Paul to participate more constructively as a group member, he needs help with this issue. The mediator needs to decide whether to allow Paul time within the structure of the group or to meet with Paul outside of the group in order to help him work through the anger. In this case, the mediator finds a way to mesh Paul's needs with the needs of the group. With the group's approval, the mediator sets aside a specific time for professionals to share horror stories; the group will use the stories to identify common themes about problems in the current regulatory system.

3. Domination

In any group interaction, certain people might dominate discussion. This may be due to individual or cultural differences: some people speak more loudly than others, some require less time to think before they speak, some demonstrate more passion, and some are more articulate. In order to ensure that everyone is able to participate fairly in the process, the mediator can use empowerment and power balancing strategies described in Chapter 4: giving everyone in the room a turn to speak, giving less empowered people the opportunity to speak first, teaching people effective communication skills during preparation for the meeting, slowing down the pace of the discussion, or using a combination of written and oral presentations so that all parties can communicate in their preferred modes.

In the regulation illustration, a group of vocational counselors has not prepared for the meeting. A group of family therapists has prepared thoroughly and tends to dominate the discussion. The mediator recognizes the imbalance and asks the parties to consider adjourning the meeting so that everyone can contribute. The family therapists may perceive a bias against them: everyone had the same chance to prepare, why should they have to come back for another meeting just because another group was negligent? The mediator acknowledges their frustration and gives the other groups an opportunity to do the same. The mediator then encourages the parties to consider the purpose of the meeting: to come up with the best decisions possible. In order to do this, each group must be prepared.

Competitive groups or individuals use domination as a strategy—to win. Mediators can recognize this tactic when people are arguing positions rather than needs or interests. As with mediation between individuals, the mediator must encourage the parties to look at interests and needs rather than positions. In addition, the mediator can move the parties toward cooperation by helping them understand the costs of adversarial relations and non-agreement.

When a mediator tries to prevent or remedy domination by a few individuals, the mediator must be careful not to shut people down. One of the essential purposes of the interaction is to promote a full discussion of the issues, with everyone's input.

4. Interruptions

Group participants may interrupt the discussion by switching topics, speaking over top of another person, making noises, or behaving in a distracting manner. With occasional interruptions, the mediator can simply use focusing skills.

> Excuse me, Sharon. If we can finish hearing what Paul has to say, I'll put your name down to speak next.

The difficulty is how to deal effectively with an interruption without putting the person who interrupted on the defensive. Some mediators use a process called stacking, listing people who want to speak and then recognizing them in the order that they asked to speak (Kaner, 1996). If one person is talking and another wants to respond, the second person raises a hand and the mediator adds that person to the list. This prevents interruptions. Unfortunately, it formalizes the process and can make the flow of discussion artificial. By the time a person gets a chance to speak, the topics may have changed. As noted earlier, linear problem solving, where one person speaks at a time and the focus is on one issue at a time, works better for some cultures than for others. The mediator needs to determine how flexible to be about interruptions and the flow of communication. Some groups can tolerate interruptions and still work constructively. In fact, sidetracking can lead to creative solutions.

When certain people constantly interrupt the process, this may indicate that they have a different agenda or that they are using interruptions as a competitive tactic. They may also have emotional needs that require addressing (as discussed above).

Some facilitators use a "talking piece" to discourage interruptions and to promote more equal participation. A talking piece, originally used in Native healing circles, is a feather, stone, stick, or other object that participants pass between them. Whoever has the talking piece is allowed to speak without interruptions. When finished, the speaker passes the talking piece to the next person.

5. Silence

Silence among certain participants is difficult to assess. Sometimes people assume that if someone is silent, they are agreeing with what is being said. However, silence could also mean the person is not comfortable speaking in front of a group; the person disagrees but does not know how to respond; the person does not feel safe presenting a contrary point of view; the person is not paying attention; or the person does not understand what is being said. Since sharing information is vital to small group decision making (Schittekatte, 1996), mediators need to address any issues related to silence.

Mediators can establish several ground rules at the beginning of the process to pre-empt some problems related to silence.

- All participants will be given an opportunity to speak.
- Everyone's needs and interests are important to the group and its decisions.
- Diverse opinions will be valued and respected.
- If anyone has difficulty speaking in front of the group, they can discuss alternatives with the mediator (e.g., practicing communication skills in order to prepare, using an advocate, submitting a written brief).
- Although participation in discussion may be encouraged, nobody will be forced to speak.
- The group will not assume that silence means agreement.

Some people do not bother to speak up at meetings because they do not believe that their input will have any bearing on decisions to be made. In order to avoid this problem, the group needs to know how decisions will be made from the outset. In some cases, the group will operate on a consensus model. That is, decisions will require general agreement of the group. For some decisions, the group may require unanimity. For others, it may require majority or supermajority votes (e.g., over two-thirds of the people present). Voting procedures ensure that everyone has a say in the outcome; consensus approaches are more likely to encourage win-win solutions and collaborative problem-solving. If voting procedures are used, they can be open voting or secret ballot. Secret ballot allows people to vote their conscience without fear of recriminations from others. The downside of secret ballot is that no one knows why people voted a particular way. This allows individuals to vote a particular way without ever letting others know of their true concerns.

One of the best ways to find out why a person is remaining silent is to ask, either in the group or in a private caucus. The mediator should allow the person to speak, without feeling pressure or embarrassment.

> Veronica, we haven't heard from you for a while. I'm not sure whether this is because you're agreeing, disagreeing, or just need more time to think this through.

Asking people a direct question and looking at them as though you expect an answer generally provokes a response. However, you may also want to respect a person's right not to speak. For some individuals, observing and listening is a sufficient form of group participation. Their body language may indicate whether they are agreeing or disagreeing with the direction of the meeting.

People who are silent may have difficulty expressing themselves. In order to draw them out, the mediator can use reflective listening skills and exploration skills.

> You seem to agree that higher standards are needed. Can you please say more about that?

In spending time to draw out particular individuals, the mediator must be careful about losing impartiality. Often, mediators are tempted to draw out people whose opinions fit with their own or whose ideas that mediator believes might lead to a speedy solution. The mediator must ensure that all people have an opportunity to speak, regardless of whether the person's ideas are interesting or realistic (Kaner, 1996).

In some instances, people do not actively participate in the group process because they do not believe that their input will be valued. For example, at the end of the discussion, a small group will be responsible for actually making the decisions. In such a case, the mediator needs to ensure that the decision-makers will actually take everyone's input into account. The mediator could ask the decision-makers directly, "Why are we having this discussion with 50 people when only five of you will actually decide what happens?" The decision-makers can explain that they value the knowledge and opinions of all group members. They can also note that the decisions will need to be implemented by the membership; therefore, a decision that does not reflect their needs and interests cannot be implemented effectively.

6. Lost Attention

Group participants can lose their attention for a number of reasons: the content is not interesting to them, the process is long or dull, there are outside distractions, or they have a relatively short attention span.

If the parties have agreed to the agenda and the mediator keeps discussion focused on the agenda, then the content should be of interest to the participants. If some participants seem disinterested in the topics being discussed, the mediator could ask directly whether this is so. The agenda may require renegotiating in order to focus on what really matters.

In order to ensure that the process does not drag on for participants, keep meetings to less than 90 minutes or have breaks at specified intervals. Use a variety of formats for discussion: small group discussion, panel discussion, brainstorming session, keynote presentation, written submissions, experiential exercises, etc. Make use of audiovisual equipment, such as flipcharts, overhead projectors, compact discs, and videotapes. Allow for humor to lighten up the discussion.

External distractions could be physical or emotional. Physical distractions include noise, hunger, and discomfort because it is too hot or too cold. Simply assuring that participants are well fed and comfortable goes a long way to ensuring that they can participate constructively. Dealing with emotional distractions may not be so easy. People may have a number of things on their mind that distract them from the process, many of which have nothing to do with the issues for mediation. Ideally, try to set a time for meetings when people are less likely to have emotional distractions (e.g., not when a key participant is dealing with a family emergency or not just before a major holiday). If a person seems distracted, this may be occasion for the mediator to approach the person privately, during a break, to see if there is a problem.

Another method to ensure that people remain attentive during mediation is to provide everyone with a specific role: meeting chair, timekeeper, recorder, and so on. Some people could be designated in advance to present on particular topics within their realm of expertise (e.g., social work, psychology, vocational counseling). This gives people something to do and shows that their participation will be valued. Avoid assigning people to represent particular positions or interests. This tends to push people into polarized positions. For example, a person trying to represent the interests of vocational counselors might push their agenda to the exclusion of the interests of human service workers. Instead, encourage people to draw from their own area of expertise, but to explore the conflict from a global perspective.

> Each one of us comes from a different professional background, with different views and areas of interest. The issue of professional regulation, however, cuts across all professions. Perhaps we can focus on our common concerns.

The mediator tries to foster joint problem solving. This encourages participants to listen to one another because the discussion affects all of them, regardless of whether the speaker is a psychologist, family therapist, or pastoral counselor.

7. Difficulty Listening to Others

One of the most common causes of conflict is miscommunication. Often, this means that people involved in the conflict have had difficulty listening to the others. People involved in destructive conflicts tend to focus on their own needs and their agenda. As noted in Chapter 4, one of the mediator's roles is to facilitate recognition; i.e., helping conflicting parties listen to one another. This can be done through modeling or teaching people active listening skills.

> Frank, you're scheduled to speak next. Before you tell us your ideas, would you mind providing a brief summary of what you understood Sharon to say?

The mediator encourages participants to hear what others have to say, from their point of view. This does not mean that they have to agree with one another. However, mutual understanding can go a long way to resolving conflicts.

The mediator needs to accept that misunderstandings are virtually inevitable. The mediator can acknowledge that misunderstandings are stressful for all parties, but every group member has potential to gain a better understanding of one another (Kaner, 1996).

8. Others Put on Defensive

Insults, insinuations, and direct attacks can put participants on the defensive. Often such remarks are unintended. Where a high level of conflict exists, people often impute negative connotations to remarks that the speaker did not intend. In order to prevent problems of this kind, the mediator can establish ground rules with the parties.

- Everyone will speak to one another with respect.
- If individuals feel slighted or harassed by another person, they can state how they feel and ask what the other person intended.
- Participants will act in good faith and take responsibility for what they say.

If participants breach such ground rules, the mediator can remind them of their previous agreement and explore whether the ground rules need to be renegotiated. This encourages positive interaction without embarrassing specific individuals. Another strategy is to involve the group in a discussion of the costs of non-cooperative relations.

9. Not Saying What They Think

One of the most difficult issues for a mediator to assess is whether participants are saying what they think. People may self-censor themselves in order to avert conflict, to fit in, or to look good. This may be because they are conflict avoiders, conflict accommodators, or naturally shy. The mediator's role is to ensure that the environment for discussion is safe for all of its members. Mediators can foster such an environment through certain ground rules.

- The group encourages all individuals to express their opinions, even if they may sound contrary or unpopular to others.
- All participants will try to understand diverse opinions expressed by others, before making any comments about them.
- People can disagree on various issues, while still maintaining respect for those they disagree with.

The mediator can also encourage participants to use active listening skills with one another in order to build a sense of trust.

> Veronica, Sharon . . . the two of you seem to have different opinions about disciplinary procedures, but I'm not sure I understand what the difference really is. Veronica, could you try to restate what Sharon is saying? After, I'll ask Sharon about Veronica's statement.

Since each person knows that the other will be paraphrasing their statements, they will try to restate what the other has said in a respectful and accurate manner.

10. Confusion about Agreements

Toward the conclusion of a group mediation, the group needs to know what they have agreed upon. The fact that there are many individuals involved in group mediation means that there is greater opportunity for confusion than in individual mediation. Record-keeping or note-taking is vital. The mediator, or someone else who has been designated, should take notes throughout the process and periodically ask for feedback to ensure that the notes accurately reflect what the group agrees.

Records or notes can take various forms. A video or audio-recording of a meeting can be used to prepare a "*verbatim*[1] transcript" of the meeting. "Minutes" of a meeting include the topics discussed, key issues, votes taken, and decisions made. A "summary of agreements" only lists the agreements that the parties reached during the process. Transcripts are the most detailed and accurate, since the recorder does not have to make any interpretations of what has been said. However, they are lengthy and costly to produce. In addition, few people have time to spend reviewing transcripts. Minutes require the recorder to make interpretations. Tentative minutes can be passed around the group for feedback to ensure their accuracy. A summary of agreements is less detailed than minutes. The group can work through the wording of the agreements as they are being reached. The recorder can use a flipchart or overhead transparency to record agreements in a manner that the group can respond to immediately. The agreements are the most important parts of the meeting to record. Transcripts or minutes of the process often generate further conflict between the parties (e.g., "I didn't say that," "That's not what I meant," or "Why didn't you include my suggestions?")

In order to avoid future misunderstandings, the notes from a meeting should include at minimum: what the group agreed to do, who is responsible

---

[1]Word-for-word.

Group Facilitation Skills

1. Obtains agreement on agenda.
2. Establishes ground rules to promote effective communication.
3. Keeps participants focused on the agenda.
4. Punctuates topics and transitions between topics.
5. Allows for flexibility in the agenda to meet specific needs of the group.
6. Provides all participants with an opportunity to contribute to the process.
7. Assists individuals needing support to communicate without losing impartiality.
8. Constructively confronts people who dominate or interrupt, without putting them on the defensive.
9. Promotes safe environment for expressing divergent or unpopular opinions.
10. Establishes clear understanding about how decisions will be made (e.g., by group, by certain individuals, by consensus, or by majority vote).
11. Shares facilitation tasks, where appropriate (e.g., note-taking, time-keeping, sharing expertise).
12. Uses reflective listening skills or exploratory questions to draw out nonverbal participants.
13. Makes use of various formats for discussion in order to ensure the process is interesting.
14. Paces the meeting, balancing time constraints with the needs of various participants to express themselves.
15. Pre-empts or attends to external distractions (e.g., noise, uncomfortable environment, hunger, emotional distractions).
16. Encourages participants to use active listening with one another to foster mutual understanding and recognition.
17. Clarifies misunderstandings between participants.
18. Encourages participants to demonstrate respect to one another, regardless of expressed differences of opinion.
19. Provides participants with constructive responses for dealing with potential insults, insinuations, or attacks.
20. Ensures agreements are accurately recorded.

for doing what, what is the expected time frame for getting tasks accomplished, and how the group will monitor and follow-up on the agreements.

INVENTORY OF GROUP FACILITATION SKILLS

The inventory list on the facing page summarizes group facilitation skills identified earlier. As with previous inventories, this one can be used as a checklist to help you prepare for a specific intervention or to help you identify skills that you want to work on.

MODELS OF INTER-GROUP MEDIATION AND RELATED PROCESSES

In addition to having a command over group facilitation skills, mediators must select a model of mediation. In this section, I describe four contrasting models: debate, dialogue, problem solving, and identity-based mediation. Each model provides a different framework for interaction. Whether each of these models is truly a form of mediation is a contentious issue. However, I leave that question for you to consider as you work through this chapter.

To illustrate each model, consider the following conflict scenario.

> Amanda is a woman of African descent living in an area of Conflictia where the majority of the residents are of European descent. On her way to and from work, she passes the high school. Often, she is confronted by a group of teenagers who taunt her with racial slurs. One day, she hears about a new Center for Community Mediation. She decides to call the Center to see what it can offer. The Center says it could offer to mediate between Amanda and the specific group of teenagers. However, it has received similar complaints from others and believes that the issue should be dealt with on a community basis.

1. Debate

A debate is a forum for discussion where conflicting parties advocate for particular positions. In a formal debate, the mediator guides the parties through a particular sequence of presentations.

- The mediator introduces the question for debate, often in the form of a statement that requires the parties to take a stand, pro or con. In the present example, the statement to be debated could be, "Students who commit racial slurs should be suspended from school."
- People who agree with the statement (the Pro side) present a brief introduction to their argument.

- People who oppose the statement (the Con side) present an introduction to their argument.
- The Pro side presents its full argument.
- The Con side provides a response to the Pro side's argument.
- The Con side presents its full argument.
- The Pro side provides a response to the Con side's argument.
- The Con side summarizes its case.
- The Pro side summarizes its case.
- A decision is made by a panel of judges or a vote by the stakeholders.

With regard to the question of whether this is a form of mediation, consider the role of the facilitator. The facilitator in a debate helps the parties communicate with one another and guides the parties through a conflict resolution process. The facilitator establishes ground rules and keeps the parties to them. The facilitator has no decision-making power. The decision is generally left to a panel of judges or a vote of the stakeholders. The structure of the debate is designed to inform participants about a range of issues and arguments. On the other hand, the facilitator does not help the parties work toward a mutually satisfactory agreement, does not try to foster amicable relations between the parties, and does not promote transformation. The debate format tends to be adversarial, similar to court proceedings or positional negotiation. The facilitator of a debate is often called a "moderator." Consider: Is a moderator a specific type of mediator or is a moderator a distinct CR role?

Public discussions often take on the qualities of a debate, even if the forum is not set up as a formal debate. For example, the Center for Community Mediation decides to set up a town hall meeting to discuss the issue of racial taunting among students. Various stakeholders are invited: Amanda and other recipients of harassment, students, parents, directors from the school board, teachers, guidance counselors, community workers, police, and equal rights advocates. During the meeting, the mediator asks people to respond to this issue. Some people suggest that the students should be suspended. Others reject this idea. The two groups become polarized, each arguing its own point of view without considering the other's perspective. The mediator acts as a referee or peacekeeper, encouraging the parties to demonstrate respect, speak in turn, and focus on the key issues. However, the mediator does not help them negotiate a mutually acceptable agreement.

One of the primary advantages of a debate is that a decision is guaranteed at the end of the process. The judges or participants make a decision by majority vote. Consensus is not needed. Debates also tend to simplify the issues. The options for solution are typically narrowed into a clear choice: e.g., to suspend or not to suspend. Debates highlight the issues and the areas of disagreement. They also allow for a broad range of participation. All stakeholders can have an opportunity to express their point of view—having one's day in court, so to speak.

The downside of debating is that people become entrenched in positions. Debates encourage participants to use rhetoric to support their positions, rather than look at underlying interests and ways of working toward creative, win-win solutions (Chasin, Herzig, Roth, Chasin, Becker & Stains, 1996). Often, debates become provocative, rather than simply thought provoking (Tannen, 1998). The question for debate is posed as "pro" or "con," meaning that alternative solutions are often ignored. Although the parties are encouraged to look at issues from the other group's perspective, this is only for the purpose of being able to counter their arguments. While debates lead to final decisions, these are not necessarily decisions that both parties can live with. If follow-through on the decision requires cooperation of the parties, this may not be forthcoming from a group that is not happy with the decision.

Debates certainly have a place in determining inter-group and community conflicts. A helping professional's choice of models will depend on the type of issue in dispute, the nature of the conflict, the willingness of the parties to engage in a particular type of process, and the type of outcomes that are desired. Sometimes a combination of models can be used.

Consider: In the racial taunting case, is a debate really appropriate? If so, what is the most germane question for the debate? If not, what are the problems with this process for Amanda and the other interested parties?

2. Dialogue[2]

Whereas debates tend to place people on opposite sides of issues and foster adversarial relations, dialogues are designed to build cooperation and positive relationships. The dialogue model draws a number of its elements from family therapy.

- The mediator works in a non-hierarchical manner with the participants, establishing a collaborative relationship with each of them as they endeavor to realize their conflicting desires.
- The mediator conducts much of the work prior to bringing the participants together: assessing their skills, hopes, and fears; preparing them with constructive communication skills; obtaining commitment to the dialogue process; and identifying old, destructive patterns of relating that they need to discontinue for the dialogue to be effective.

---

[2]Some people use the word multilogue rather than dialogue to connote that there are many different parties and perspectives rather than just a competition between two.

- During the dialogue, the mediator promotes an atmosphere of safety, where people can express divergent points of view and still demonstrate respect for one another. (Chasin et al., 1996)

Whereas participants in a debate represent a position, side, or stereotype, participants in a dialogue are encouraged to speak as individuals, from their own personal experience. In debates, advocates or representatives are often selected as spokespeople for each group. The dialogue model encourages broad participation, as individuals speak on their own behalves rather than through designated leaders. The dialogue model encourages participants to listen to one another in a way that builds insight and mutual understanding. In this sense, the dialogue model is similar to the transformative model of mediation (Chasin et al., 1996).

If the Center for Community Mediation decided to set up its town hall meeting as a dialogue, the first step is to meet with each of the various stakeholders. The mediator encourages the victims of harassment to speak on their own behalf, rather than through lawyers or human rights advocates. The mediator helps Amanda and others like her so that they can articulate their personal experiences of how the harassment affected them. Likewise, the mediator works with the students to speak on their own behalf, rather than through their parents or teachers. The students are reluctant to engage in the dialogue, believing that they are being set up in a process bent against them. The mediator needs to ensure the process is fair and that the students feel safe participating. The participants agree to the following ground rules: participants will speak to one another in respectful terms; the focus of the discussion is not to establish fault or blame, but to promote understanding; and the dialogue will not result in any decisions about the students' status at the school.

The issue for the dialogue is not "to suspend or not to suspend," but "how have each of the participants experienced this conflict?" This question opens up the discourse and allows participants to explore the conflict from a broader perspective. Those who have experienced harassment will learn about the views and motives of the students. The students, in turn, will learn how their actions have affected the people they have taunted. As a result of this exchange, the students may apologize for their actions or the group may come to an agreement about what to do from now on. However, success of the dialogue does not depend on coming to an agreement. Success may occur through healing.

The primary goals of the dialogue are to provide everyone with an opportunity to speak and to gain a better understanding of one another. Although a dialogue might help parties work toward resolution of conflicts, it might also make differences between parties more pronounced. Given that reaching agreement is not a primary goal, is a facilitated dialogue a form of mediation?

The dialogue model is particularly useful when reaching agreement is not a realistic goal. If people have conflicting values, for instance, these are difficult to reconcile. Consider the controversy over euthanasia. Those who support the use of euthanasia value individual autonomy over the sanctity of life. Those who oppose euthanasia value sanctity of life over individual autonomy. Because these values are deeply held, a conflict resolution process designed to reconcile these values is likely to fail. Dialogue, however, allows the parties to learn more about one another's perspectives, without expecting them to compromise their own values. By establishing mutual understanding, the participants learn to respect one another, including their differences.

In some instances, dialogue can be used as a prelude to an agreement-oriented CR process. Where the level of conflict between participants is high and level of understanding is low, dialogue provides the participants with an opportunity to engage with one another in a non-threatening process. They know coming into the dialogue that they are not being asked to "compromise with the enemy." Dialogues ask people to sit down and talk, without requiring any further commitment. Since mistrust builds over time, rebuilding trust also takes time. Dialogue can be structured as a process that occurs over time, rather than as a one-time event. The helping professional develops a sequence of opportunities for conflicting groups to engage in dialogue. During initial stages, the structures for dialogue tend to be more formal. As trust builds, the structures become less formal. Decision-making may emerge from the process, but the CR professional does not try to force it on the parties.

3. Problem Solving

A problem-solving approach to inter-group mediation parallels the interest-based approach to mediation between individuals in Chapter 4. The mediator guides the parties through a series of phases: preparation, orientation to mediation, issue definition, exploring interests and needs, negotiation and problem solving, finalizing an agreement, and follow-up.

In order to highlight some of the issues in a problem-solving process between groups, consider the harassment scenario again. At the beginning of the preparation phase, the Center for Community Mediation needs to *consider who are the parties and how will they participate.* If this were mediation between individuals, the primary parties would be Amanda and the students that she claims harassed her. However, the Center has decided to approach this as an inter-group conflict. The primary groups are the students and the various complainants against the students. Teachers, parents, counselors, etc. could also be brought into the process. Some mediators prefer to limit the number of participants in order to streamline the process. Others prefer larger groups because of the advantages of pooling information and expertise from a broad range of participants (Stewart & Strasser, 1998). In this case, the Center decides that the conflict pervades the community and requires broad participation. Participants will act as individuals, rather than representatives of particular groups. Any decisions will be made by consensus of the participants.

Given the large number of participants, the Center opts for two mediators to co-mediate. They select one mediator of African descent and one mediator of European descent, hoping to pre-empt any fears that the process is biased toward one group.

The mediators meet with each group separately, in order to hear their concerns, explain mediation, obtain their commitment to mediation, and help them prepare. Preparation is particularly important in inter-group mediation because of the numbers of people and potential for the process to get out of control. Smaller meetings also provide the parties with a chance to vent feelings, so that they may be able to focus more on problem solving during the joint meetings.

Of all the groups involved in the process, the students are the most reluctant participants. Upon meeting with them, the mediators offer suggestions about how to articulate their needs and interests. This empowers the students and helps the mediators establish trust with them.

The group complaining of harassment expresses concern about how to deal with racist comments that may arise during the joint meetings. The mediators offer ground rules to try to pre-empt this type of conflict from escalating. They also describe techniques such as "I statements" and constructive confrontation that can be used to respond to hurtful remarks.

During meetings with the teachers, the mediators discuss how the teachers can contribute to the process without taking a dominant role. The teachers are used to resolving conflict on their own. The mediators acknowledge the teachers' expertise in conflict resolution. Following some negotiations, the teachers agree to act as constructive participants—looking for mutual interests, focusing on the future, brainstorming options for solution, etc. However, they will leave facilitation of the process to the mediators.

The pre-mediation meeting with the parents is marked by a high level of conflict between them. Various parents accuse one another's children of being racist, rude, or degenerate. *Mediation between individuals within a group is often more important than mediation between groups.* The mediators do not try to get the parents to agree on who was or was not responsible for the problem. Instead, the mediators focus the parents on their mutual interests. All of the parents agree that they do not want past incidents to interfere with their children's ability to complete their education. They also agree that they do not want their children or community to be known as racist.

By the time the first joint meeting takes place, the parties are oriented and committed to the process. The mediators review the process and comment on the positive level of participation from all groups during the premediation meetings. The mediators review an agenda that has previously been distributed to the participants. Today's meeting will last three hours. The first ninety minutes is designated for an open dialogue about the concerns that brought people to this meeting. The mediators have prepared the parties with ways of expressing concerns from personal perspectives, without inflaming conflict. After a break, the discussion will turn to identifying issues and exploring underlying interests. A follow-up meeting is scheduled a week later to work through the later stages of the problem-solving process. The mediators keep the parties to a relatively fixed time schedule. They also tend to be more directive about the agenda than for mediation between individuals, in order to maintain control over the process. Still, they need to ensure that they have consensus with the agenda before moving forward.

The storytelling portion of the process goes ahead as planned. Various individuals describe what has been happening. Others start to focus on the future. The group is too large for everyone to have as much say as they would like, so the mediators need to place limits and keep the parties focused. Some students seem intimidated, so the mediator tries to draw them out with exploration questions.

After the break, the parties begin to identify issues. Some participants begin to offer solutions, such as suspending the students, having the students do community service, or having the complainants avoid passing by the school. The mediators explain that it is too early to focus on solutions, since the issues have not even been clearly identified. Some of the teachers take the lead, helping others understand the difference between issues and solutions: how to hold students accountable for their behavior; how to make amends to those who have suffered from harassment; and what the school can do if similar incidents arise in the future. The big issue that emerges is what to do about racism in the school and in the general community. To the mediators' surprise, everyone seems to coalesce around this one issue. The students are not singled out as the problem. Rather, the community seems prepared to look at racism as a broad community issue. The people who originally complained of harassment are encouraged that people are accepting responsibility for what has happened.

The mediators move the participants into a discussion of their interests. Initially, individuals focus on their own interests. The mediators remind them of their primary issue: racism in the school and the community. This helps them focus on mutual interests. Once the participants get going, they start to flood the mediators with ideas. The mediators list the ideas on a flipchart. Once an exhaustive list is completed, the mediators help them draw out themes and common interests. The participants achieve consensus on three key interests: respect for all individuals and groups, regardless of race or ethnic background; racist-free education; and the ability to walk down the streets without being harassed. The mediators congratulate the participants on their progress in this first meeting. In order to prepare for the next meeting, the mediators ask them to brainstorm ideas for how to satisfy these interests. The mediators advise everyone to keep their ideas tentative: during the next meeting they will explore a broad range of options before deciding how to proceed.

During the second meeting, the mediators review the process to date, remind everyone about the ground rules, and confirm everyone's commitment to the agenda. Notes on flipcharts list the issues and interests identified at the last meeting. The mediators engage the parties in brainstorming by going around the room and asking each person to identify one possible solution, not necessarily their favorite one. The mediators write each idea on the flipchart, as it is suggested.

At one point in the brainstorming, a parent uses the term, "colored people." Some participants jump all over him for using such an offensive term. Others come to his defense, saying they do not believe in political correctness. The mediators suggest that they suspend brainstorming for 15 minutes in order to discuss this issue. One of the mediators takes the parent through a series of questions: what did you mean when you said "colored people;" where did you learn this term; did you mean it to be offensive; do you understand how others might find it offensive? The mediator asks for a volunteer who is offended by the term. The mediator asks the volunteer the following questions: when you heard someone say "colored people," how did it make you feel; why do you think you felt this way; do you think that it was intended to be a racist remark; what words could you suggest other than "colored people?" The mediator uses this exchange to promote mutual understanding. The mediator also models how to confront racist comments in a constructive manner. Not everyone is satisfied that the issue has been resolved. The mediators validate their concerns and suggest that this may be one of the issues for the group to deal with over the longer term. The mediators did not intend to put closure to this issue.

The mediators make a transition back to brainstorming. Once an exhaustive list has been ascertained, the mediators divide the participants into three groups. Students, teachers, complainants, and others are randomly dispersed through the groups. Each group is assigned responsibility for one of the key underlying interests. They are allotted 30 minutes to review the list of options and to develop a general plan to deal with this issue. Each mediator facilitates one group. They have also prepared one of the teachers to facilitate the third group. One advantage of smaller groups is that individuals have greater opportunity to participate. Another advantage is that they can tackle more than one issue at a time.

Each group reports back to the full forum. Following each presentation, individuals are invited to provide comments. The mediators encourage them to build on the ideas of subgroups rather than offer completely different options. Eventually, the group comes to consensus on the following plans.

- A joint teacher-parent-student committee will be established to review the curriculum at the school to ensure that racism, discrimination, and other forms of bigotry are dealt with effectively in all grades.
- The school will develop a Harassment Committee to deal with any complaints about student harassment or racism.
- The community will develop a public campaign to raise awareness about the effects of racism and to promote greater respect for people from different backgrounds.

The mediators ask questions to ensure that these plans are feasible. They explore who is responsible for what; how will they secure sufficient resources to do what they want; and how will they ensure that people follow up on the tasks they accept. They also encourage broad participation in these tasks so that the whole community takes ownership of the solutions. Certain people accept leadership roles. The mediators offer to provide these leaders with further information and support about how to facilitate the implementation of their decisions. The work has just begun.

4. Identity

Identity models of inter-group mediation are designed for identity-based conflict. In contrast to conflict based on miscommunication or division of limited resources, identity-based conflict is rooted in the ways that conflicting groups view themselves and the other group. Archetypal examples of identity-based conflicts include the conflicts between Roman Catholics and Protestants in Ireland, Jews and Arabs in the Middle East, and Blacks and Whites in South Africa, Europe, and the Americas. Identity-based conflicts may originate as disputes over land, money, values, or power, but develop into identity issues as the conflict becomes protracted. Each group tends to view itself as innocent victims. In addition, each group imputes blame to the other group as the oppressors, transgressors, or evil adversaries. Stereotypes and discrimination can also develop through lack of contact and inter-group ignorance.

Identity-based models of CR (Bargal & Bar, 1992a; Halabi, 1998; Rothman, 1997) are based on Kurt Lewin's (1948) identity theory. Lewin studied the issues of majority-minority relations in democratic, pluralistic societies. He posited that inter-group hostilities are often grounded in identity issues. A significant portion of individual behavior is determined by group membership. Therefore, the manner in which people from a majority group perceive and respond to a minority group depends upon how the majority group views itself and the minority. The same applies to the way that a minority group perceives and responds to the majority group. If a conflict is rooted in identity issues, then it is difficult to redress unless the CR process helps individuals change within the context of their social groups (Bargal & Bar, 1997).

According to role theory, each individual in a social group has a particular position, similar to an office or job. People come to expect certain behaviors of the individual associated with that job. If the individual does not behave as expected, then stress occurs in the system: others in the system punish or alienate the person; alternatively, they reward the person for taking steps back toward the expected behaviors for the role (Bargal & Bar, 1992a). In order for inter-group mediation to be effective, the mediators help each group alter its role expectations.

Changes in self-perception and role expectations require experiential workshops rather than just educational lectures. Accordingly, the mediator needs to design interactions that enable participants to see themselves in new roles. The mediator helps them re-evaluate perceptions of themselves as powerless victims or innocent bystanders. Each group challenges the other's stereotypes, generalizations, and self-perceptions. In a sense, each group acts as a mirror for the other group, allowing group members to see themselves in a different light (Halabi, 1998).

Groups tend to define themselves by similarity of background, experiences, or values. Accordingly, groups with different backgrounds, experiences, or values often find themselves at odds with one another. One method of altering identity-based conflict is to encourage different groups to see themselves as one group, bound together by an interdependence of fate (Lewin, 1948). Conflicting groups must come to the realization, "Whether we like it or not, we are in this together." Rather than focus upon past differences or present crises, focus upon the opportunity to build better relations in the future.

Common obstacles to improving inter-group relations are low self-esteem and lack of confidence among people from a minority group. The mediator can help the minority group by teaching CR skills and by fostering ethnic pride. Some mediators do this by meeting individually with the minority group. Others refer the minority group to community developers or advocates for this type of support.

When inter-group conflict is deeply entrenched, the goal for mediation may not be to resolve conflict, but to alter its course. At the end of mediation, for example, the two groups will likely retain their core values. However, they will have a greater appreciation of their respective roles in maintaining or alleviating their conflicts. They can focus their energies on resolving pragmatic problems rather than philosophical ones. They can also establish ongoing interactions to help them build the sort of trust needed to handle larger issues over the long run.

The focus of identity-based mediation is an encounter between groups rather than between individuals. In sharp contrast to the dialogue and problem-solving frameworks, participants are encouraged to see themselves as group members (Halabi, 1998). They must take responsibility for themselves, as well as others in the group. For example, European participants might agree that Africans have been mistreated but claim that they are not personally responsible for this. By focusing participants on group issues rather than personal ones, the European members are compelled to look at their role in discrimination against Africans.

Identity models use either a "cultural island approach" or a "community-based approach." In the cultural island approach, the mediator selects certain members from the conflicting groups to participate in a series of interactions. These may be structured as weekly meetings or as a concentrated retreat. The advantage of a concentrated retreat is that the parties live together in a controlled environment for a period of a few days. This helps them learn about one another's cultures, including food, music, and religious rituals. The two groups are treated as a microcosm of the dynamics that occur in broader society, including oppression, anger, and other manifestations of the inter-group conflict. The mediator helps participants relate their issues to external influences, but the primary focus of the intervention is on the participants in the cultural island (Halabi, 1998).

In a community-based approach, the interventions take place in the community rather than in a controlled environment. The mediator extends invitations to the whole community rather than to selected individuals. The participants focus upon current community conflicts and each group's roles in these conflicts (Fisher, 1997).

Arguably, neither the cultural island nor the community-based approach is mediation. The cultural island approach is sometimes referred to as an "encounter group" or a "conflict management workshop."

> "Organizational arrangements [are] devised to bring together two opposing groups (on ethnic, political or interpersonal grounds) in a relatively isolated situation. Through the use of interpersonal, group, and organizational means, the two parties come to know each other's members closely. Some of the roots and manifestations of the conflict are brought out in the open, discussed, and clarified in order to enable them to get along more satisfactorily" (Bargal & Bar, 1992a, p. 6).

The community-based approach might be defined as community development, rather than inter-group mediation (Campfens, 1997; Rothman, 1997). Structured dialogues are used to promote understanding and trust between groups (Dubinskas, 1992). The focus of the intervention is to help community members interact more constructively.

In both approaches, the role of the intervenor includes CR training and facilitating. However, are they forms of mediation?

Identity-based models tend to be less structured than problem-based models. Although the mediator leads participants through a series of stages, the mediator does not advise the participants of these stages. Instead, the mediator lets the participants know the purpose of the interaction in general terms. The mediator guides the participants through a series of stages, but does not make the transitions between stages explicit.

In Halabi's (1998) cultural island model, the mediator facilitates the participants through group formation, storytelling, confrontation, and resolution.

- Group Formation: When the groups are brought together, the mediator and participants introduce themselves. Initially, no direct reference is made to the conflict. The participants tend to be courteous and pleasant toward one another. The group is permitted to set the agenda, at which point the dominant group tends to take control of the process and dynamics.
- Storytelling: The oppressed group begins to tell stories of the oppression and discrimination they have experienced in society. The polite relations between groups begin to become more tense. The oppressed group starts to feel a moral advantage in the discussion. The dominant group starts to lose its tolerance and respond more defensively, offering rationalizations for the suffering endured by the oppressed group. The two groups begin to challenge one another's versions of events.
- Confrontation: The dominant group raises concerns about the oppressed group's role in the conflict, trying to assert its control. Anger and frustration among both groups start to emerge. The oppressed group maintains greater strength and does not back down. When the smoke begins to clear, there is a possibility for a more equal relationship between the groups.
- Resolution: The dialogue becomes more equal. Rather than rationalize oppression, the dominant group becomes more willing to recognize the legitimate rights of the oppressed group. Better understandings emerge and each group has developed a different sense of its role in the broader conflict (pp. 4–5).

According to this model, success is measured by a change in each party's self-perceptions. Participants need not make decisions or take specific actions, though these may occur as incidental results. Other variations of identity-based models, however, add components of the problem-solving model to the end of the process (Rothman, 1997). Following the resolution stage, the parties go on to action planning: i.e., given their new understandings of themselves and the others, what actions can they take in order to deal with community issues or other problems?

Consider the conflict between Amanda and the students. Assume the Center for Community Mediation views this as an identity-based conflict. The roots of the conflict extend beyond the parties directly involved in the harassment. The Center decides to use the cultural island model, bringing a selected group of African and European students together for a two-day retreat. The Center opts to invite students who teachers have identified as troublemakers and antagonists. Even though these may be the most difficult people to work with, they represent the greatest need.[3] Co-mediators are used, one African and one European, in order to demonstrate balance and to model positive relations between people from the two groups.

The mediators explain that the purpose of this retreat is to explore issues between the African and European communities in Conflictia. Neither group really knows what to expect. Participants are nervous and look to the mediators for guidance. The mediators encourage the participants to set the agenda, giving them ownership over the process. At first, everyone is reluctant to suggest agenda items. Eventually, informal leaders emerge. Europeans tend to take control with well-intentioned suggestions: to improve African-European relations; to deal with complaints of racial harassment; and to deal with discrimination in the community.

Some European participants rebel. They think this is turning into an exercise in European bashing. They make claims about crime, drug use, and unemployment in the African community. They lay blame squarely with the Africans. The mediators do not take sides on the issues, but try to balance the dialogue by encouraging African participants to respond.

The mediators ask the African group to share their experiences of African-European relations. Various participants begin to tell personal stories of discrimination: being pestered by police, being thrown out of stores, and being scolded by teachers, for no reason other than being African. Initially, the Europeans are hesitant to contradict these stories. They become uncomfortable and eventually start to challenge the credibility of the stories they are hearing.

The mediators allow the conflict to escalate. Members from each group become defensive and make verbal attacks on the other side. The mediators maintain certain ground rules to ensure that the conflict does not escalate into violence, but provide them with significant leeway for arguing. During breaks, the mediators notice that each group sticks together. The mediators encourage participants to continue their dialogue and interactions with each other during breaks in the formal discussions.

The mediators provide a summary of the concerns raised by both groups. They label the anger and frustration that each side has expressed indirectly.

---

[3]Other writers suggest inviting the people most amenable to the mediation process, because they are easier to engage and the process is more likely to be successful. This may sound like "preaching to the converted," but the hope is that participants will go back to their communities with greater skills and abilities to influence others.

This encourages both sides to talk about their feelings. The level of conflict begins to de-escalate as both groups come to realize that they have much in common. By allowing both sides to vent their prejudices, anger, and frustration, catharsis occurs. They are ready to start dealing with issues in a more constructive fashion.

The mediators place more structure on the dialogue, guiding the participants through various issues they have raised. One of the stereotypes, for example, is that Africans are lazy. The mediators explore where the Europeans learned this stereotype. The mediators ask the Africans questions that allow them to speak to the stereotype, from their perspectives. Other inter-group stereotypes are discussed in a similar fashion. The mediators encourage each group to re-assess its own role in perpetuating myths and prejudices.

Throughout the process, the mediators strive to maintain their objectivity and impartiality. They check with one another to ensure that neither is demonstrating sympathy, anger, or other biases toward either group. The mediators also ensure that each mediator contributes equally, rather than have one mediator dominate control over the process.

The dialogue tends to become more constructive and balanced between the parties. They begin to appreciate one another's perspectives and question their own biases. The mediators ask how the confrontations during this process relate to dynamics in the broader community. Although the groups in mediation have gained a new sense of their roles in the inter-group conflict, they realize that the old conflicts will still exist when they return to the community.

The mediators in this situation did not intend to take the groups to the next level—action planning. Their primary goal was to have members of each group redefine their identities in relation to the other group. Some of the participants decide on their own to carry the process forward. They plan an ongoing committee at the school to work on inter-group relations. The committee will develop educational materials to promote better understandings. In addition, it will develop forums for further dialogue between the groups. The mediators offer consultation and support, but allow the participants to take the lead.

Identity-based interventions have had varying success. They tend to be most successful in dealing with specific disputes and developing better relationships between people from antagonistic groups (Rabie, 1994). Eradicating racism and prejudice on a larger scale is difficult. There is no quick fix. Mediation may be part of a solution, but expectations for mediation must be realistic. Social change at a grassroots level is more likely to be successful when accompanied by support from political powers and other structures in society. Accordingly, mediators must work with community leaders in order to secure ongoing political, financial, and moral support.

KEY POINTS

- Inter-group conflicts are caused by differences in values, beliefs, or interests; such conflicts are often complicated by stereotyping, prejudice, miscommunication, and other forms of misunderstanding.
- Inter-group mediators need to attend to conflict at three levels: between groups, within groups, and between groups and the mediator.
- The facilitation role of an inter-group mediator is to improve the flow of communication between participants.
- A facilitator helps participants decide who speaks when and what issues to focus upon.
- Models for dealing with inter-group conflict include debate, dialogue, problem-solving, and identity-based interventions. Whether or not these models constitute mediation depends upon one's definition of mediation.
- In the debate model, each group takes a stance and presents arguments to support its position. The mediator facilitates discussion but does not try to guide the groups toward consensus. Group members or a panel of judges make decisions based on majority votes.
- The dialogue model encourages people from conflicting groups to communicate with one another as individuals. The mediator coaches participants on how to speak and listen to one another. The primary goal of dialogue is to promote understanding rather than to come to agreement on the issues.
- The problem-solving model is specifically designed to help conflicting groups come to agreement on the identified problems. The mediator facilitates interest-based negotiations between the parties and encourages the groups to work toward mutually satisfactory solutions.
- Identity-based models of mediation are designed to change the way that members of each group view their roles in relationship to members of the other group. The mediator helps participants confront stereotypes, myths, and prejudices that exist between the groups.
- In order to determine which model of mediation to employ, the mediator should consider the type of conflict, the goal for mediation, and the readiness of each party to participate in a particular type of process. In some situations, different models can be used in combination.

DISCUSSION QUESTIONS AND EXERCISES

1. ASSESSING CONFLICT: Identify an inter-group conflict that has persisted in your community for several years. Who are the key players in the conflict? What is the nature of the conflict? How could each group be

persuaded to participate in an inter-group mediation process? How could the parties select a mediator? Would it be better to have a mediator or co-mediators who come from within the community or from outside?

2. DELEGATES: A community health board is trying to decide whether to reduce funds for hospitals and mental health institutions, so that it can commit more resources to community-based services. What groups are affected by this issue? Given the nature of this conflict, should the person designing a mediative process work with delegates or with all members of the affected groups? What criteria inform your decision?

3. FACILITATION SKILLS: Compare the facilitation skills required for mediating between groups with the facilitation skills required for mediating between individuals. What are the key differences?

4. MEDIATION-LIKE INTERVENTIONS: Select one of the following terms: consensus building, peace building, participatory decision making, or community development (Susskind, McKearnan, & Thomas-Larmer, 1999). Conduct a literature search of your chosen term using CD ROM data bases such as *PsychINFO, Sociofile, Social Work Abstracts*, and *ERIC*. How does the literature define your chosen term? Compare and contrast your chosen term to one of the models of inter-group mediation. Try to isolate differences in assumptions, values, and methods.

5. OPPRESSED WITCHES: Witches comprise one of the most oppressed groups in Conflictia. Their religion is not recognized by the state. They have no elected representation. Most of the people in Conflictia are ignorant about Wicca—some fear that Witches cast evil spells, use children for witchcraft experiments, and bring Satan into the community. Construct an inter-group mediation process to deal with the conflict between Witches and the rest of the community: what is the nature of the conflict; what is the purpose of the intervention; what model best suits this purpose; what are the main barriers to communication between these groups; how can a mediator deal with these?

6. DISRUPTIVE MINORITY: You are mediating a community conflict involving over 80 people. Most participants are trying to be cooperative, but five people seem bent on disrupting the process. How would you assess the cause of this problem? What facilitation skills could you use to redress the problem?

7. LOBBY GROUP CONFLICT: A group of mental health counselors is lobbying Conflictia's government for more funding for mental health services. A group of probation officers is asking the same government to invest more money in the criminal justice system. Each group believes that more money to one cause means less money for the other cause. What is the nature of the conflict between the groups? Which model of inter-group mediation would be most appropriate for dealing with this conflict? Why?

8. DEFINITIONS: Write down your preferred definition of mediation. Consider each of the models of inter-group mediation presented above. Which models fit your definition? Which do not? Why does it matter whether a model of intervention is called mediation or has a different name?

9. CRITIQUING FACILITATION: Review the problem-solving example described earlier in this chapter. Identify each of the facilitation skills used by the mediators. What other skills would have been useful and for what purposes?

10. TV CONFLICT: Videotape a television news program involving a facilitator and two or more parties who are discussing a controversial issue. What is the purpose of the discussion? Which model of mediation does it resemble more closely—debate or dialogue? How could the facilitator change the format in order make the process more constructive?

11. CONFIDENTIALITY: Chapter 4 discusses the issue of confidentiality in mediation between individuals. Does confidentiality apply in a mediation process that involves large community groups? If it does apply, how would you explain confidentiality and obtain agreement from all participants?

Role-play 5.1: "Professionals and Paraprofessionals"—Skill Development

This role-play involves the entire class: two people to play the mediators and the rest of the class divided into two groups of equal size. One group comprises the professionals who work for Diversity Plus. The other group comprises paraprofessionals who work for the same agency. Identify the type of helping professionals and paraprofessionals based on who is in your class (e.g., social workers, educators, counselors; human service workers). The purpose of this exercise is to practice facilitation skills in an inter-group conflict situation.

A severe rift has developed between the employees at Diversity Plus. The paraprofessionals believe that they are being mistreated: their wages are lower; they carry higher caseloads; and they have no room for advancement in the agency. The professionals believe that the *status quo* is necessary and desirable. The agency cannot afford to pay everyone the same rate of pay, so salaries are based on educational background and level of experience. The professionals have at least a graduate degree, whereas the paraprofessionals have college diplomas. The professionals justify their smaller caseloads because they deal with the more difficult cases. They suggest that the paraprofessionals can go back to school if they want to advance their careers. Doing graduate work is not feasible for most of the paraprofessionals: some cannot afford to go back to school; others do not have sufficient grades.

The two emergent mediators for this role-play are actually two of the senior supervisors of the agency. Prior to the role-play, the mediators will ask certain members of the class to introduce one of the following obstacles into the dynamics: individuals have different agendas, the discussion has no focus, the discussion is dominated by certain individuals, some individuals keep interrupting, some individuals remain silent, individuals lose their attention, individuals have difficulty listening to other's ideas, statements or questions put some people on the defensive, individuals are not saying what they really think, or people are confused about the agreements. This will enable the mediator to identify and practice facilitation skills that can be used to deal with this sort of challenge.

This role-play can be conducted in 15 minute segments. Switch mediators for each segment and try to deal with a different type of obstacle.

Debriefing Questions

How did the mediators attempt to deal with the prescribed obstacle? What worked? What other methods could be used to deal with this type of problem? What were the underlying causes of the problem behavior? What strategies could be used to deal with these underlying causes?

ROLE-PLAY 5.2: "WEIGHTY PROBLEM"— DEBATE AND DIALOGUE

Conflictia Police Services have a policy that all employees must be within 15 pounds of their ideal weight for their height, according to guidelines established by the Health Department of Conflictia. This applies to all employees, regardless of their age, sex, or position in the Police Services. Proponents of this policy say that it is necessary to protect the image of the Police Services in the community. The guidelines also promote good health, reducing costs for sick leave, early retirement, and accidents related to obesity.

A group within the police force opposes this policy. They find it discriminatory and unduly restrictive. Many positions within the organization do not require peak physical condition. Different people have different metabolisms, making it impossible for some people to fit within the policies. Also, as police officers age, they should not be fired from the police force because they are gaining weight.

For this role-play, divide the class into two groups. One group will role-play this exercise as a debate. The other will role-play this as a dialogue. Within each group, assign one mediator and divide the group into proponents and opponents of the policy.

Each group can prepare for this exercise by reviewing suggestions from the negotiation chapter: start off as positional negotiators. The mediator may or may not move you from this style, depending on the model the mediator is using.

The mediators can prepare for this exercise by reviewing the description of their respective models, debate or dialogue. Also, identify two or three skills from the Inventory of Group Facilitation Skills that you want to remember to incorporate.

Each of the two role-plays require approximately 45 minutes. Ideally, the two groups will have separate rooms and videotape the role-play to show to the other group.

Debriefing Questions

How were the two role-plays similar? How were they different? What impressed you the most about how each mediator carried out the mediation role? In this type of conflict, what model of mediation seems most appropriate? Why?

ROLE-PLAY 5.3: "CLIENTS AND STAFF"— PROBLEM-SOLVING AND IDENTITY

This role-play takes place in the Conflictia Group Home, a residential treatment facility for teenagers with emotional and behavioral problems. Select two people from the class to act as group home supervisors (in the role of emergent mediators). Divide the rest of the class into two equal groups: one group will play teenaged clients; the other group will play residential staff.

In recent weeks, turmoil has erupted at the Group Home. The residential staff is unionized. The union is currently negotiating a new collective agreement with the Group Home. Staff is unhappy with the way negotiations are proceeding, so they have begun a work-to-rule campaign: they are performing all of their required duties, but they are not taking on the additional jobs that they normally assume. For the clients, this has meant fewer recreational activities, more house chores, skimpy meals, and earlier curfews (because staff will not perform any overtime activities). The clients have responded by acting out in various ways: refusing to do chores, sleeping late, messing up the house, and making verbal threats toward Staff.

The Staff feels like double victims. First, the Group Home pays little, expects lots, and provides little support for them to do a tough job. Now, they are being attacked by the clients when they are just doing their jobs. The clients also feel like victims. They do not want to be in the Group Home to begin with. With the work-to-rule campaign, they feel like they are caught in the middle of someone else's fight.

In order to respond to this conflict, the supervisors call a house meeting. One supervisor will begin the process using the problem-solving model. At 20 minutes into the role-play, the other supervisor will take over using strategies from the identity-based model. This segment will also take 20 minutes. During the role-play, both clients and staff will begin with positional styles.

Both supervisors can prepare by reviewing the materials on their respective models of mediation. Two or three of the clients and staff can be designated to introduce special challenges into the process (e.g., silence, disturbances, demonstrating anger).

Debriefing Questions
Which skills did the problem-solving supervisor successfully employ? Which skills did the identity-based supervisor successfully employ? What changes did the staff and clients notice when the mediators switched from one model to the other? Which model was more appropriate for this situation? Why?

Major Assignments

This chapter has no major assignments. The major assignments at the end of Chapter 6 are geared toward issues from Chapters 5 and 6.

ADVOCACY

Advocacy refers to influencing decisions that affect the welfare or interests of another individual or group. Whereas a mediator is an impartial third party who assists both parties negotiate, an advocate is partial to one party or cause. The word advocate derives from the Latin "avocare," meaning to summon one's help (Hopkins, 1994). An advocate can work with clients in order to help them negotiate more effectively, on their own behalf. Alternatively, an advocate can act on their behalf, representing or defending them in a conflict resolution process. Working with clients tends to be more empowering. Acting on their behalf may be necessary or more efficient, depending on the circumstances. In many cases, an advocate combines both methods.

FORGET EMPOWERMENT... YOU DEAL WITH MY WELFARE WORKER AND I'LL JUST STAY HERE.

All helping professionals have an obligation to advance the interests of their clients. Most codes of professional conduct also impose an obligation to advance the causes of justice, health, or social wellbeing. Many professionals engage in advocacy because of their personal values, wanting to advance causes that they support. The greatest needs for advocacy generally come from disadvantaged groups in society, for example, children, the elderly, people with mental illnesses or disabilities, people with low incomes, victims of abuse, people charged with crimes, and minority groups who are subjected to discrimination (Ezell, 1994; Lurie, Pinsky, Rock, & Tuzman, 1989).

This chapter encompasses the following topics: approaches to advocacy, the relationship between advocates and decision makers, advocacy activities, using power, advocacy skills, and ethical issues. As you read through the chapter, note the similarities and differences between advocacy, negotiation, and mediation.

APPROACHES TO ADVOCACY

The manner in which helping professionals advocate partially depends on their theoretical orientation: what influences people and how do social institutions change? For helping professionals with a systems orientation, change occurs by altering the transactions between people. Accordingly, one means of advocating is to teach clients communication and assertiveness skills. In contrast, Marxist or radical feminist helping professionals believe that change occurs when the disenfranchised and divided proletariat band together. In this instance, one of the key means of advocacy is coalition building, mobilizing people to work together for a common cause (Wood & Middleman, 1991). Social exchange theory suggests that negotiation is a process of trading resources. Applying this theory, an advocate would try to bolster a client's resources prior to entering into a negotiation process with competing parties. Similarly, advocates could adopt many of the other theories underlying conflict resolution described earlier in this book.

Advocacy can target three different levels: individual, administrative, or policy. Individual advocacy[1] helps a specific client or group deal with a single, concrete conflict; for example, advocating for an HIV-positive client to receive service from an agency that traditionally restricts service to people with full-blown AIDS. Administrative advocacy is directed at changes in an agency's policies. Rather than advocating for an exception for a particular client, one advocates for a change in the general procedures of the agency.

---

[1]Individual advocacy is sometimes called "case advocacy," as opposed to "cause advocacy," which includes both administrative and policy advocacy.

Policy advocacy is directed at changes in rules or laws that go beyond a single agency (Fowler, 1989; Sosin & Caulum, 1983). In the HIV example, a policy advocate might seek to change the way that government funds social agencies so that clients with HIV have greater access. Helping professionals often focus on one level of advocacy in their work; however, advocacy coordinated at all three levels is advantageous in many situations.

RELATIONSHIP BETWEEN ADVOCATES AND DECISION MAKERS

The strategies of an advocate depend upon the type of relationship between the advocate and the decision makers: alliance, neutrality, or adversarial. *In an alliance situation, the decision makers view the advocate as someone who is on the same side.* They tend to have common beliefs, goals, or mandates. *In a neutral situation, the decision maker views the advocate as an objective source of information or opinion.* The decision maker does not see the advocate as an ally or an adversary. *In an adversarial situation, the decision maker views the advocate as an enemy.* Typically, the level of disagreement is so large or so fundamental that the decision makers view the advocate with little legitimacy (Sosin & Caulum, 1983). The easiest situation for an advocate to have influence is as an ally.

Often, decision makers have certain preconceptions about advocates. For example, "This professional can be trusted," or "This person is biased." The advocate can either try to foster a different type of relationship or employ strategies that are most likely to be effective given the confines of the existing relations. Consider the following scenario.

> Mr. and Mrs. Pinder are proud new parents of a baby girl. Both parents use cocaine and other drugs. The hospital called child protective services when the baby was born. The child protection worker, Warren, needs to determine whether to allow the baby to go home with her parents. He speaks with three helping professionals at the hospital: an addictions counselor, a nurse, and a parent support worker.

1. Ally

The addictions counselor happens to have a previous relationship with Warren, who sees the addictions counselor as an ally. They share similar views about the needs of children and their right to proper parenting. The addictions counselor believes that the baby would be put at risk of abuse and neglect if the Pinders took her home. In order to advocate for the baby's welfare, the addictions counselor builds on the values she has in common with

Warren. Since Warren already trusts the addictions worker, the worker does not have to put much effort into building the relationship. She can focus on providing cogent arguments that substantiate the need for intervention required to safeguard the welfare of the baby.

2. Neutral

The nurse happens to have no prior relationship with Warren. Accordingly, he has no initial bias towards or against her. In order to build credibility as an advocate, the nurse tries to demonstrate her professionalism. She is knowledgeable, articulate, conscientious, and objective. She believes that the baby can be returned home with the Pinders, provided that they agree to cooperate with in-home support to monitor the situation and ensure that the baby's needs are met. She bolsters her credibility by showing that she has considered all of the possible options (Barsky, 1997a). She reviews the advantages and risks of both options before showing how she arrived at her conclusion. Although Warren initially views the nurse a neutral, he begins to see her as more of an ally (someone with shared interests who wants to help him carry out his mandate effectively).

3. Adversary

The parent support worker has a reputation for supporting the rights of parents over the rights of the child. Warren views the support worker as an adversary who will try to push him into releasing the baby to the Pinders, even if there are substantial protection risks. The support worker can choose between two different courses of action. The first is to try to move towards a relationship of neutrality or alliance. How can we work together; what are our common interests; how can I demonstrate that my opinions are valid and reliable? With this alternative, the support worker focuses on establishing a more positive relationship before advocating a particular position. The second approach is to remain in an adversarial relationship and make use of competitive strategies. For example, the support worker could engage Warren in a debate and try to provide stronger arguments (e.g., moral or factual arguments). The worker could also try to coerce Warren by threatening to go to his supervisor or to take the case to court.

In deciding which course of action to take, an advocate should first consider more collaborative and peaceful approaches (discussion, persuasion, joint problem solving, and mediation). Only when these have been exhausted or ruled out as infeasible, should the advocate consider more competitive or coercive approaches. Collaborative approaches reflect professional values such as peace, non-violence, respect, and partnership. Before adopting competitive or coercive methods, an advocate must consider the potential costs. Even if a coercive strategy works in the short run, there may be a price to pay at a later date; for example, harmed relationships, retaliation, and backlash. An advocate's selection of approaches is essentially the same as a negotiator's BATNA analysis, as described in Chapter 3: what is the Best Alternative to a Negotiated (or Collaborative) Agreement? Too often, advocates fall back on adversarial approaches when more constructive and creative approaches have not been fully explored.

ADVOCACY ACTIVITIES

The range of advocacy activities is virtually limitless. The following lists encompass the more common means of helping clients advocate and advocating on their behalf (Ezell, 1994; Nicol, 1997; Panitch, 1974; Chetkow-Yanoov, 1997). Consider which activities are more collaborative and which activities are more competitive.

1. Helping Clients Advocate on their Own Behalf

- Helping clients set reasonable goals.
- Educating clients about their rights.
- Informing clients about how the system works.
- Training clients how to negotiate the system.
- Facilitating access to information for your clients.
- Helping people listen to your clients.
- Teaching advocacy skills to clients.
- Teaching problem-solving skills to clients.
- Organizing coalitions among clients.
- Helping clients write an advocacy brief.
- Role modeling advocacy skills and techniques.
- Facilitating opportunities for your clients to influence (e.g., setting up meetings between clients and professionals in the system; promoting mediation or other CR processes that involve clients in decision making).
- Supporting client self-confidence.
- Supporting risk-taking by client if this is required to pursue a worthwhile cause.
- Providing practical support (e.g., use of space and computers).
- Accompanying client during negotiations or hearings.
- Being available for clients and patient even when they seem to reject your help.
- Providing constructive feedback.

2. Advocating on Behalf of Clients

- Educating the public on an issue.
- Negotiating with agencies or other social systems (for access to services, better services, honoring client rights, etc.).
- Monitoring other agencies' performance (including follow-up on their promises).
- Appealing to an external ombuds.
- Preparing an advocacy brief (Kaminski & Walmsley, 1995).
- Giving testimony to decision makers (Barsky, 1997a).
- Encouraging decision makers to pay attention to the client's demands (e.g., lend credibility to client group by demonstrating your support).
- Creating or sustaining a crisis environment in order to stimulate conditions for change (e.g., organizing boycotts, demonstrations, street dramas, vigils, or nonviolent civil disobedience).
- Lobbying individual policy makers (conveying demands, placing pressure on decision makers).
- Mobilizing constituent support (facilitating petitions, organizing community groups).
- Directing complaints to the agency's funding body.
- Litigating or seeking legal remedies.
- Conducting research in order to produce information required for decision making.
- Instituting demonstration projects to show the effectiveness of certain types of interventions.
- Representing a client in a case conference or at an administrative hearing.
- Influencing administrative rule making in other agencies.
- Political campaigning.
- Influencing media coverage of an issue (raising awareness of issues or manipulating public opinion).
- Conveying positive attitudes to the community about your clients (counter negative stereotypes).

Deliberate and controlled advocacy processes are generally more effective than unplanned ones. A problem-solving process can be used to help strategize:

1. What is the nature of the problem?
2. What are the objectives for the advocacy?
3. What levels should be targeted for advocacy—individual, agency, policy?
4. What resources can the helping professional and client draw upon for advocacy?

5. Given the range of advocacy activities, which are most likely to lead to a satisfactory resolution of the conflict?
6. Who will take which responsibilities for implementing the advocacy plan?
7. How will the results be evaluated and fed back into the problem-solving process?

Empirical studies have begun to identify factors associated with effectiveness of advocacy interventions. One of the keys to successful advocacy is leadership. Leaders initiate advocacy organizations, establish organizational track records, and revitalize stagnant organizations. Advocates often operate with limited financial resources. Accordingly, they must find ways to use resources in a cost-effective manner. Many advocates depend upon volunteers, donations, and creative use of non-financial resources to advance their causes (for example, by linking advocacy and service delivery activities). Working in coalitions with like-minded organizations also contributes to effectiveness. Finally, advocates must balance organizational flexibility with this with consistency and continuity (Reisch, 1990).

POWER

Power, the relative capacity of different parties to influence one another, plays a significant role in advocacy. As mentioned earlier, helping professionals often work on behalf of disadvantaged groups in society. In order to advance their concerns, helping professionals need to know how to affect the balance of power between individuals or groups involved in a conflict situation. Professionals familiar with systems and structural theories can use these theories to assist their analysis of power and the reciprocal influences that individuals or systems have on one another (Goldberg-Wood & Middleman, 1991). This section provides a means of analyzing power and intervening based upon the ten sources of power: expertise, associations, possession of resources, control of procedures, legitimacy, sanctions, nuisance, habit, morality, and personal attributes (Mayer, 1987).

To illustrate how the various sources of power can be used, consider the following scenario.

> Stella is a 12 year old student with a learning disability. She has been going to a mainstream school. Although she takes regular classes, she also has a special education teacher who provides extra support. Because of budget cuts, the Board of Education now says she must go to a school specifically designed for students with disabilities. The Board says it can no longer afford to have special education instructors in all of its schools. Stella and her parents believe that Stella is better off in her mainstream school.

1. Expert Power

Expert power derives from having expertise or special knowledge. Expert power is sometimes called information power because expertise is based on possessing certain wisdom, facts, or data. Helping professionals can lend their support to clients by providing them with access to information (Freire, 1970) or by providing information on their behalf.

Some helping professionals see themselves as experts; others reject this title. For example, feminist counselors try to reduce the distance between counselor and client by presenting themselves as facilitators rather than experts. They prefer to help clients gain access to information rather than directly provide expertise to clients. Still, all helping professionals have knowledge that they can make available to clients.

One of the key areas of knowledge required for advocacy is knowledge about agency policies, procedures, and structures. In the case example, an advocate could provide Stella's family with information about the structure of the Board of Education, how it makes decisions and whether there are any avenues for appeal (e.g., administrative or court challenges). Many bureaucracies are complicated systems, with their peculiar jargon and norms. Advocates who are familiar with these norms and jargon can act as interpreters for clients. *An advocate may also have knowledge about the formal and informal power structures: who are the people who make the decisions and what tends to influence their decisions?* If the Board of Education is accountable to the municipal council, an advocate may suggest that Stella's family try to find an ally from this council. If there are upcoming elections for the Board of Education, Stella's family might be able to use the campaign to raise their concerns. *Clients also need to know about the probable consequences of escalating issues.* If Stella's family decides to appeal the Board's decision, what are the potential benefits and risks? Will Stella have to face the media? What are the chances they will succeed? Decision tree analysis can help the family view its alternatives and make informed choices. *Advocates can provide access to government documents and other data sources* (Kirst-Ashman & Hull, 1993). Unless family members have been educated about social research, it is unlikely that they will know how to conduct a literature review on special education. An advocate can help locate studies comparing students who are mainstreamed versus those who go to specialized schools.

Advocates can teach clients advocacy strategies, tips, and tricks. For example, get everything in writing and date your notes in order to improve their credibility. If Stella's family documents all of its interactions with the school and the Board of Education, it can use these documents to support its case in any future hearings. Advocates can also help clients recognize problems and suggest CR strategies for dealing with them. For example, representatives from the Board of Education may be using stalling tactics, not returning telephone calls, or saying they do not have the authority to make decisions. An advocate informs the family that they can move up one level and speak to a supervisor, rather than wait for a response (Nicol, 1997).

2. Associational Power

Associational power comes from having a relationship with other people who have power. Also called referent power, associational power allows clients to combine resources, build alliances, and gain moral influence.

One way to bring clients together is through consciousness raising. Individual clients often feel alone in their problems and believe that their plight is caused by personal deficits. Advocates can help clients understand how various sociopolitical systems limit and devalue them. By working in concert, clients are in a better position to challenge existing power structures (Wood & Middleman, 1991).

In Stella's situation, an advocate could develop associational power by bringing families together who share similar concerns. They can speak with a collective voice and share the cost burden of pursuing their cause. One of the downsides of a narrowly based interest group is that the group is seen as self-interested and biased. If the advocate can attract individuals and families who do not have children with disabilities, then the group no longer looks self-interested.

Advocates can also foster associational power by bringing specific individuals into the cause. People with high profile, special expertise, moral reputation, or other desirable characteristics help to raise awareness and lend credibility to an advocacy plan. Stella's family would benefit, for instance, from associations with leading experts on special education who support mainstreaming. Some advocacy groups connect with sports or entertainment celebrities to advance their cases. A celebrity spokesperson can be very influential, particularly among groups that identify with the celebrity. Unfortunately, associational power can work in two directions. If a celebrity's reputation falters, an association with the fallen star will also have a negative impact on the advocacy group and its cause.

Advocacy within a group is generally safer than "going it alone." Suppose one teacher speaks up in defense of Stella's wish to remain in the school. In effect, he is going against the position of his employer. The Board of Education might impose sanctions to keep teachers from opposing the Board's decisions. If several teachers banded together in support of Stella, it would be more difficult for Board to impose sanctions.

Another aspect of associational power is emotional support. If Stella's parents had to testify at an administrative hearing, for instance, the experience could be daunting. An advocate can offer emotional support by being there for the clients, escorting them to the hearing, sitting through the hearing with them, and helping them debrief afterwards (Barsky, 1997a). This type of support provides clients with confidence and a sense of hope.

Associational power can be used for "power with" another party, rather than "power over" another party. In the previous examples of associational power, the advocate is making use of associational power to gain influence over another party. In order to move toward a more collaborative approach, the advocate could try to facilitate a joining of power between conflicting parties. Instead of using their power to try to gain favor over the other, they can form an association to gain power to pursue goals that meet both their interests.

3. Resource Power

Resource power stems from control over valuable assets; for example, money, materials, labor, or other goods and services. The inverse version of resource power is the ability to deny needed resources or to force others to expend them. In many situations, this is the primary area where clients are at a disadvantage. If the conflict is with a social agency, for instance, the agency is likely to have access to greater resources, both professional and monetary.

Advocates can help clients gain resource power by helping them secure assets from external sources. Clients may not know of social assistance benefits, legal aid funds, or other entitlements they can claim. In Stella's situation, there may be a charitable foundation that could provide financial support for her cause. Lawyers, educators, or other helping professionals may be willing to donate their time. When resources are scarce, advocates also need to explore creative ways to make better use of what they have.

A growing area of power imbalance concerns technology. People with more money and better education are more likely to have access to technology. In public policy, for example, interest groups are using fax and e-mail to convey opinions to governmental decision-makers. Other groups use Web sites to solicit memberships and fundraise for their causes. Advocates can relieve these types of inequities by promoting broader access to education and equipment in schools, libraries, and other public institutions. Advocates may also need to promote literacy programs, since many of the new technologies require higher rates of literacy for people to participate.

4. Procedural Power

Procedural power refers to control over the processes by which decisions are made. Procedural power is not the same as control over the decisions themselves. Consider various CR alternatives: negotiation, mediation, administrative hearings, and court trials.

In negotiation, the parties have control over the process as well as over the decisions to be made. They can decide to have informal meetings, formal meetings, long meetings, short meetings, and so on. If one party is more powerful than the other, it may be able to dictate some of the terms of the process. For example, the Board of Education might insist that any discussions about Stella's case take place at the Board of Education's offices. This gives the Board "home field advantage." By having the meeting in their offices, they have access to secretarial support, computers, etc. Stella's parents may also feel intimidated since they are not familiar with the surroundings. The Board might also say that Stella's parents cannot bring a lawyer. An advocate could assist Stella's parents by helping them negotiate a more equitable process: if the Board can bring its professionals to the meeting, then Stella's family should be able to bring its own.

In mediation, the mediator controls the process and the clients control the decisions. As noted in Chapter 4, a mediator has an ethical obligation regarding impartiality. Accordingly, the process should not be biased towards one side or another. If there is an imbalance of power between the parties, the mediator could make use of power balancing strategies.[2] Essentially, the mediator could manipulate any of the ten sources of power described in this section in order to redistribute power. For instance, if the problem were caused by an informational imbalance, the mediator could refer the less powerful party to an advocate who could ensure equal access to relevant information.

In an administrative hearing, the administrative board typically has control over both the process and the decision. In order to maintain its moral authority, the board must try to ensure that its process is fair and seen to be fair. The Board of Education, for example, might have an appeals process that allows parents to make written submissions. Stella's parents want an opportunity to present their case at an oral hearing. An advocate may be able to push for changes in the procedure by negotiating with the Board or by advocating that the government establish mandatory regulations. If an administrative process is unfair, legal advocates could also explore the possibility of going to court to have the case reviewed.

In a court hearing, the judge has control over the process and the decision.[3] Court procedures are established by government and the court has an obligation to ensure that the process is fair. Judges are less likely than administrative boards to have a stake in the outcome. If, however, a judge demonstrates bias or conducts the process contrary to the law, the decision can be

---

[2]This raises the ethical issue concerning the appropriate role of a mediator when there is a power imbalance: Should the mediator balance power to ensure fairness or reject power balancing in order to remain impartial? Refer back to Chapter 4 for further discussion of this dilemma.

[3]There is an exception for jury cases, where the jury makes findings of fact (Barsky, 1997a).

appealed to a higher court. Only lawyers can represent clients in court. Non-lawyer advocates can provide support for clients; however, providing legal advice or representing them in court would constitute unauthorized practice of law.[4] Clients and non-lawyer advocates have little control over the court process.

Advocates can help clients make informed choices about CR alternatives, as well as helping them negotiate processes that treat them more fairly. If legal issues are involved, then the advocate should also refer them for legal advice.

5. Legitimate Power

Legitimate power derives from having an official position or authority, as from legislation or policies of an organization. The Board of Education, for example, is mandated by regulations to make decisions about how to use funds targeted for education. Teachers are authorized to discipline students who do not act in accordance with school policies. A broad range of helping professionals and government officials have these types of power over clients. For the most part, helping professionals try to limit their use of legitimate power. Even if a helping professional has the ability to impose decisions, codes of ethics dictate that clients have a right to self-determination. Exploiting a client is not in the professional's best interests. It is generally easier to work with clients on a voluntary basis than try to impose authority (see nuisance power, below).

Advocates may be able to intervene at a peer level with other helping professionals or officials who are making inappropriate uses of their authority. Ideally, the issues can be resolved informally and collaboratively. If necessary, an advocate can bring in a supervisor, administrator, mediator, or other professional to help resolve the conflict in a constructive manner. If the law or policy authorizing legitimate power is problematic, then the preferred target of advocacy may be at the policy level.

6. Sanction Power

Sanction power emanates from the ability (or perceived ability) to inflict harm or to interfere with a party's ability to realize its interests. A typical sanctioning problem for clients occurs when an agency threatens to refuse services or impose other sanctions if the clients do not acquiesce to the agency's demands. For example, Stella's parents might fear that teachers would sanction Stella if the conflict is escalated.

---

[4]The helping professional could be fined, sued by an unsatisfied client, and risk professional accreditation.

When sanctions are legitimate, they are difficult to counteract. For example, if Stella becomes violent, then the school would have legal authority to suspend her. If the sanctions are not legitimate, then an advocate could counteract them by surfacing the issue. Initially, the advocate could discuss the issue of inappropriate sanctions with the party trying to impose them. If informal negotiations are unsuccessful, then the advocate could raise the issue in a more public forum (e.g., with elected politicians or the media).

7. Nuisance Power

Nuisance power is based upon the ability to cause discomfort to a party, falling short of the ability to apply direct sanctions. Nuisance power is often used by people who are at a disadvantage in terms of sanction and legitimate power. Clients who feel oppressed by agencies or other systems may rebel, using nuisance power without being conscious about it. Bureaucratic systems often respond more quickly to individuals who are causing them distress. Unfortunately, this teaches clients to use confrontational approaches to CR rather than collaborative ones.

Advocates can help clients use nuisance power in a deliberate manner. Nuisance power is risky, because the other party may respond by trying to reimpose its power. If the Board required Stella to go to a special school, she could rebel by misbehaving at the new school. The school might decide that it is easier or better for Stella to be returned to her old school, where she did not pose problems. However, the school might just decide to suspend her. Advocates can help clients assess the risks and benefits of using nuisance strategies. Generally, nuisance strategies should be used only after other strategies have been exhausted.

Protests, strikes, boycotts, and non-violent civil disobedience are examples of nuisance strategies. In addition to the risk of negative consequences, advocates must also consider ethical issues (discussed below).

8. Habitual Power

Habitual power rests on the premise that it is generally easier to maintain a particular arrangement or course of action than to change it. Decision makers may also be persuaded by arguments in favor of maintaining traditions.

In Stella's case, the *status quo* suggests that Stella should remain in her old school. An advocate could argue that it is unfair to disrupt her education and have her move to a new school. The Board of Education might be persuaded to phase out special education in general schools, allowing students currently enrolled to complete their education.

Prolonging the *status quo* is a common tactic in positional negotiations. If Stella is in her old school while the decision about special schools is being considered, Stella's family might want to prolong the decision-making process. The longer the process takes, the longer the *status quo* is maintained and the more difficult it is to make changes.

9. Moral Power

Moral power extends from appeals to widely held values; for example, family, charity, freedom, privacy, fairness, and democracy. In order to finesse moral power, advocates use language that frames their cause in a positive light; for instance, groups which support women's rights to abortion call themselves "Pro-Choice" rather than "Pro-Abortion." Stella's parents could lay claim to values such as equality and respect. All they want is for their daughter to have the same friends and opportunities as everyone else's child.

At its best, using moral power helps people make decisions based upon values and interests, rather than positions. Unfortunately appeals to morality often turn into positional bargaining. Each party claims moral superiority: "We stand for everything good; the others stand for evil." Once people establish values, it becomes difficult for them to compromise. Advocates may be able to intervene by helping the parties focus upon common values. Demonizing another party also runs contrary to professional ethics, such as respect for individuals and diverse groups.

Some groups claim moral power by presenting themselves as victims. This may be effective in gaining public sympathy and support. In fact, they may actually be victims (of oppression, abuse, etc.). Over time, however, victim mentality can be damaging. When people see themselves just as victims, they may not take responsibility for helping themselves. They operate on fear and mistrust. They become unable to consider constructive CR processes, even when safety and fairness can be ensured (Chetkow-Yanoov, 1997). Advocates can support such clients by validating their concerns, but also helping them build confidence and self-efficacy in their identities.

10. Personal Power

Personal power is based upon a variety of individual attributes. Characteristics that contribute to a client's personal power include self-assurance, the ability to articulate one's thoughts and understand one's situation, determination, and endurance (Mayer, 1987). Some aspects of personal power come naturally. Others can be learned. Advocates can help clients raise their level of personal power by teaching them advocacy skills (see Inventory of Advocacy Skills below). In the case example, an advocate might help Stella's family gain comfort using political processes and speaking in public forums. If they have a low tolerance for conflict, an advocate can teach them strategies for dealing with it more effectively (Kirst-Ashman & Hull, 1993).

Power issues are pervasive in conflict resolution. As the forgoing discussion indicates, there are a number of ways in which advocates can use power bases in order to advance the interests of their clients. This does not mean, however, that advocates must rely upon positional and competitive strategies for conflict resolution. Wherever possible, advocates should promote collaborative strategies. By doing so, they can foster win-win solutions, improved relationships, mutual understanding, and client empowerment. Using the least force necessary to achieve advocacy objectives also minimizes unwanted counterforces (Wood & Middleman, 1991).

INVENTORY OF ADVOCACY SKILLS

Skills for advocates include many of the same skills that are used by mediators and negotiators. The following inventory highlights some of the key advocacy skills. The inventory is broken down into three parts: preparation, oral advocacy, and written advocacy.

In order to provide feedback to colleagues during role-plays, make photocopies of the inventory and put each advocate's name at the top of the page. Use the following scale to give feedback on specific skills. Also, add descriptive comments on the reverse side of the photocopies.

1—Demonstrated in Exceptional Manner
2—Demonstrated Effectively
3—Demonstrated, but could use Practice to be more Effective
X—Not Demonstrated

Name of Advocate: _____

Person giving Feedback: _____

Preparation for Advocacy:

_____ Becomes informed with all sides of the issues.

_____ Understands who must be persuaded.

_____ Becomes familiar with a range of advocacy techniques.

_____ Takes steps to improve power dynamics before primary intervention.

_____ Plans agenda and structure.

(continued)

Oral Advocacy:

_____ Identifies own and mutual purposes of the meeting.

_____ Isolates key issues to be decided.

_____ Seeks consensus on process and issues to be determined.

_____ Provides relevant and persuasive information.

_____ Identifies information that needs to be produced.

_____ Asks questions to raise consciousness or insights.

_____ Encourages positive expectations for the process.

_____ Facilitates linkages between people and resources.

_____ Joins with others (using associational power).

_____ Identifies common values and entitlements (using moral power).

_____ Articulates specific needs and interests.

_____ Separates people from the problem.

_____ Generates options.

_____ Identifies legitimate or objective criteria for evaluation.

_____ Uses clear and concise language.

_____ Checks out assumptions.

_____ Uses visual aids or other presentation devices.

_____ Uses active listening to demonstrate empathic understanding and build trust: paraphrase, summary, reflection of emotions, appropriate body language to show attending.

_____ Identifies specific commitments for self and other.

_____ Uses emotional appeals appropriately.

_____ Demonstrates respect for diversity and difference of opinion.

_____ Presents with confidence.

_____ Presents in an assertive manner (rather than passive or aggressive).

_____ Uses creative strategies (indicate example: _____).

_____ Keeps focus on the issues being discussed.

_____ Narrows issues in dispute (if full agreement not reached).

_____ Helps other parties save face or undo a commitment.

_____ Uses devices to change other parties' expectations (e.g., through reality testing questions, role reversals, metaphoric storytelling, looking at hypothetical situations).

_____ Uses constructive confrontation (e.g., helps a party to identify incongruencies between two pieces of information the party has given, or between a statement and the party's behavior).

_____ Draws parties' awareness to the cost of non-agreement.

_____ Uses flexibility and rigidity for tactical purposes.

_____ Arranges for necessary follow up (date, time, place, who responsible).

Written Advocacy:

_____ Writes clearly and concisely.

_____ Presents arguments in logical manner.

_____ Presents facts to support opinions.

_____ Uses non-judgmental language.

_____ Clarifies the issues or problems.

_____ States goals and objectives.

_____ Appeals to concerns of the decision-makers.

_____ Provides balanced evaluation of various options for solution (demonstrating understanding of the positions of various parties).

_____ Suggests preferred options for solution.

_____ Highlights areas of mutual interest.

_____ Offers concrete plans for implementation, follow-up, and evaluation.

_____ Uses creative techniques to ensure written brief captures the interest of its target audience (e.g., metaphors, vivid language, pictures, case examples).

ETHICAL ISSUES

Ethical issues are pervasive in advocacy. Helping professionals need to be aware of potential problems and consider the following factors: legal restrictions, agency mandate, individual—group interests, authorization, professional values, and futile causes.

1. Legal Restrictions

Although helping professionals have an ethical obligation to advocate for clients and social causes, their advocacy role is also subject to many legal and ethical restrictions. For example, defamation laws limit what one can say about another person in a public forum. In the heat of advocacy, helping professionals might be tempted to discredit another person with verbal or written attacks. If the information is untrue and causes the person harm (including harm to personal or professional reputation), the helping professional could be sued for damages.

2. Agency Mandate

Advocates who work in an agency context are limited by the mandate and policies of their agencies. If an agency is designated as a charitable foundation for tax purposes, that agency may be prohibited from engaging in legislative or political advocacy. Likewise, many agencies that receive government funding have restrictions on whether and how they can criticize government policies or services. Advocates who act on their own behalf may have more latitude than advocates who act on behalf of the agency. Still, it may be difficult for a helping professional to take a stand as a personal citizen when that person also works as a professional for a public agency.

Ethical dilemmas for advocates frequently arise when there is a conflict between the interests of the agency and the interests of the client (Loewenberg & Dolgoff, 1996). Although many helping professionals would like to give precedence to the interests of their clients, this may put them at risk of dismissal or other sanctions from their agencies. By using collaborative CR approaches, advocates may be able to avoid ethical dilemmas. In other words, by focusing on the mutual interests of the client and agency, an advocate may not have to choose between them.

3. Individual—Group Interests

Another type of dilemma arises when advocating for one client takes away resources from another person or group. How should advocates prioritize? Unfortunately, codes of ethics give little guidance. If the only obligation of helping professionals is to pursue their own clients' best interests, then helping professionals may be depriving others who may be more needy or deserving. If helping professionals do not act as staunch advocates for their clients, then whom can clients look to for support? Once again, helping professionals can use CR processes to work towards win-win solutions. In some situations, consensus may be possible. If not, at least the parties can analyze the issues and develop mutual understanding of one another's positions.

Advocacy can be directed at different levels: to produce change for a specific client or to produce change for broader causes. This may present professionals with a number of difficult choices.

- Advocating for an individual client is generally faster and less expensive than trying to advocate for broader change—at least in the short run. However, if resources are continuously used for individual clients, then how will broader change ever occur?
- How does a helping professional determine how to advocate when an agency is mandated to act on behalf of specific clients, but the professional's code of ethics obliges the professional to advocate for broader social change?
- Does a client have a right to advocacy, even when the client's wishes contravene values or causes that the agency and helping professional represent?

4. Authorization

When professionals advocate on behalf of clients, the professional should have the clients' consent to act their behalf. Unfortunately, many professionals advocate for clients without gaining explicit consent to do so. Although the professional may be well-meaning, advocacy engenders many risks: costs in time and other resources; potential backlash; and the chance that advocacy will not bring about the expected changes. If a client is not informed or the professional does not have the client's consent, then the professional may be putting both the client and the professional at risk. The client could also claim breach of confidentiality. Advocates must be aware of issues related to the capacity of certain clients to consent: e.g., young children and people with severe cognitive impairments (Linzer, 1999). In such instances, the advocate may need to secure consent from a parent, guardian, or other representative.

Authorization for cause advocacy can be even trickier than consent for individual advocacy. Ideally, the professional seeks informed consent from all of the people in the group or community affected. If members of the community or group have disparate views on how the advocate should proceed, then the advocate may need to use mediative skills to bring the group to consensus. Often, a helping professional derives authority to advocate for a certain cause from the agency or organization that pays the professional. This type of authority provides the professional with some safeguards should the professional's work be challenged.

5. Professional Values

Advocates must develop an awareness of their own values and priorities (refer back to your values inventory from Chapter 2, Exercise 3). When helping professionals do not feel right about their advocacy work, they should ask themselves: (a) Why they are doing it; (b) Is their goal ethical, and (c) Are the means of attaining the goal also ethical? Ethical decisions should not be made in isolation. Consulting with others allows professionals to explore various alternatives and how others might deal with difficult decisions.

6. Futile Causes

Some helping professionals question whether they should become involved in causes that seem overwhelming or futile. Too often, this excuse is an easy way out. One person can make a difference, even when the odds seem enormous. Remember the Chinese student in 1989 who stood before a row of tanks in Tiananmen Square? The Chinese government brought in the military to quash pro-democracy demonstrations by the students. One young man, standing alone, stopped the progression of the tanks. In doing so, he captured the imagination and support of a world audience. Although the demonstrations were eventually stopped, his image lives on to inspire others.[5]

KEY POINTS

- The role of an advocate is to promote changes in favor of particular clients or causes.
- Helping clients advocate on their own behalf is generally more empowering than advocating for them.
- Advocates can influence change at three levels: individual, agency, and policy.
- Advocates who have a positive relationship with decision makers are able to use collaborative approaches to influence change; advocates with an adversarial relationship with decision makers may need to build a more constructive relationship before trying to influence decision making.
- If competitive strategies are required, advocates should use the least force necessary to achieve key objectives.
- Selection of advocacy strategies depends upon the following factors: the nature of the problem, the objectives of the client, the theoretical orientation of the helping professional, available resources, and the likelihood of success among various alternatives.

---

[5]When I raised this example in one of my classes, a student asked, "You're telling us we have to put ourselves in front of a line of tanks?" Perhaps. Can you think of a cause that is very important to you? What would you be willing to risk in order to defend this cause?

- Advocates can make use of ten sources of power in order to influence change: expertise, associations, possession of resources, control of procedures, legitimacy, sanctions, nuisance, habit, morality, and personal attributes.
- An advocate's choice of skills will vary depending upon the forum for conflict resolution: for example, private negotiation, mediation, administrative hearing, and public campaign.
- In order to analyze whether an advocacy intervention is ethical, advocates must consider both the means and objectives of the intervention.

DISCUSSION QUESTIONS AND EXERCISES

1. OBLIGATIONS: Refer to the code of ethics of your professional association. What does it say about your professional obligation to advocate? Identify three causes that you value as a helping professional.
2. ADVOCATES AND NEGOTIATORS: Compare and contrast the role of an advocate with the role of a negotiator.
3. ADVOCATES AND MEDIATORS: Compare and contrast the role of an advocate with the role of a mediator (cf., Barsky, 1993).
4. LEVELS OF ADVOCACY: You work in a family counseling agency in a remote community with a large indigenous population. About two-thirds of your clients suffer from depression. Eighty percent of your clients with depression are unemployed. What are the advantages and disadvantages of advocating for clients individually versus advocating at a policy level? What type of advocacy strategy would be most effective?
5. POWER AND PROFESSORS: Review your notes for Role-play 3.2— "Negotiating for Grades." What are the power issues raised by this scenario? Having read this chapter, what would you do differently? How could you use different sources of power in an ethical and effective manner? What are the short- and long-term implications from using power in this situation?
6. POWER ANALYSIS: Identify a client who could use assistance in advocating. Consider the sources of power identified in this chapter. What are your client's strengths as a negotiator? What are your client's limitations? As an advocate trying to help the client negotiate on the client's own behalf, what types of interventions would you suggest?
7. VENUS/MARS: What are the differences, if any, between the ways that men and women tend to approach advocacy? (cf., Palczewski, 1996) When dealing with conflicts between women and men, what is the relevance of power, patriarchy, and privilege?

8. ROLE REVERSAL: Select one of the following issues where you have strong feelings:

> Euthanasia—Right to Die with Dignity vs. Sanctity of Life
> Abortion—Pro-Life vs. Pro-Choice
> Mandatory Prosecution of Wife Assault Allegations
> Legalization of Marijuana/Heroin
> Sterilization of the Mentally Challenged

With the help of at least one other person, identify and write down the following:

(a) What is my position on this issue?
(b) Why do I hold this position? What values, attitudes, or beliefs is this position based upon?
(c) What other points of view could one have on this issue?

Select the point of view which is furthest (most polar) from your own preferred perspective. Role-play a debate with another person, where you are defending the point of view that you have just identified as most polar to your perspective. Take note of your arguments. Which types of arguments were most effective in persuading you? Which types of arguments were most effective in persuading the person taking your original position? What were the three most important things you learned from this exercise?

9. ADVOCACY RELATIONSHIPS: The Society for the Protection of Fruits and Vegetables (SPFV) is concerned about violence towards non-animal food products. People slice, dice, chomp, boil, and otherwise annihilate fruits and vegetables without concern for their feelings. SPFV is advocating for greater respect for fruits and vegetables as living, benevolent sources of vitamins, protein, and fiber. Assume the role of an advocate for SPFV. Develop three advocacy strategies based on influencing three target groups: carnivores (who share a deep alliance with you), omnivores (who see you as a neutral), and herbivores (who view you as an adversary).

10. CULTURAL ACCOMMODATIONS: Assume you are working with a client who has been mistreated by another social agency in your city. Your client comes from an eastern culture that values peace, harmony, and non-conflictual relationships. She does not want to confront the agency in order to assert her rights. You assess that a linear problem-solving approach to advocacy is inappropriate. How would you adjust the intervention strategies in this chapter, if at all, in order to ensure that your approach respects the client's culture?

11. ETHICAL ISSUES: Select one of the following situations. Analyze the ethical issues and suggest how you might try to resolve them. How would your approach differ if you adopted a conflict resolution approach versus a framework for ethical decision making from the literature (e.g., Corey, Corey, & Callahan, 1993; Loewenberg & Dolgoff, 1996; Rave & Larson, 1995)?

    (a) One of your clients self-identifies as a neo-Nazi. She wants you to help her get into a social work program at a local college. Personally, you do not believe she is an appropriate candidate. Your job, however, is to help clients apply to school programs.

    (b) A group of elderly clients asks you to help them advocate for a new recreation center for seniors. You do not believe that this center has much of a chance of succeeding. You would prefer to focus upon more feasible advocacy projects.

    (c) A man suffering from cancer has been denied social assistance because he has parents who are able to support him. The man does not have a good relationship with his parents and does not want to receive their support. There is an internal appeals procedure for social assistance; however, you would have to establish a new precedent. The stress of going through with the appeals procedures might take its toll on this client, already quite ill from cancer. He is unsure about how to proceed and seeks your advice as an advocate. You think it would make a great test case, but the likelihood of success is relatively low.

    (d) You work with an advocacy group that promotes the interests of women who have been abused by husbands or partners. During a public awareness campaign, one of your colleagues publishes information that grossly exaggerates the extent of abuse in the community. She also makes up fictitious stories about clients who have been abused. When you confront her, she says, "Exaggerating is necessary in order to make a point. Besides, it's for a good cause."

12. RESEARCH AS ADVOCACY: You are working with a client who is claiming refugee status because of emotional torture he suffered in his country of origin. He claims to have post-traumatic stress disorder as a result of threats to himself and family over a three-year period. The tribunal hearing his case is skeptical about his claims. They question whether someone can be a victim of torture if there are no signs of physical abuse. Conduct a literature review in order to gather information that may be helpful in advocating for the client (Mnookin, Susskind, & Foster, 1999). Develop an advocacy brief that could be provided to the refugee tribunal.

ROLE-PLAY 6.1: "ICE CREAM ALIENS"—
ASSESSING DECISION MAKERS

This role-play allows you to practice assessing decision makers in order to determine what types of advocacy affect their decision making. The whole class takes part. Assign two people to role-play Aliens. The rest of the class role-plays Earthlings.

Chafe and Veej are from another planet, Huggendaz. Their supreme master, Benjer, has sent them down to earth to advocate for a certain type of ice cream: Chafe must advocate for chocolate ice cream. Veej must advocate for Strawberry. These just happen to be the flavors that they actually like best. In order to prepare for this exercise, Chafe and Veej will be sent out of the room. Each of them will write down a list of reasons why they like their flavor of ice cream best. Their role is to advocate for their favorite type of ice cream, persuading as many earthlings as possible to vote for their flavor. The ice cream with the fewer votes will be banished from Huggendaz forever. Chafe and Veej will have 13 minutes to do their advocating.

Confidential Facts for both Chafe and Veej (not to be read by Earthlings)

In order to prepare for this case, consider various ways of influencing the Earthlings. Try to assess how each person might be persuaded: Consider which groups of earthlings view you as an ally, a neutral, or an adversary. Ensure that your tactics are appropriate for each of these groups. How can you win over people who view you as adversaries? Consider both ethical and unethical tactics. Have fun.

Confidential Rules for Earthlings (not to be read by Aliens)

Each of you will only have certain ways of being persuaded:

- People with glasses: You are affected by emotional appeals. You view both aliens as neutrals.
- People with contact lenses: You are affected by rational appeals. You feel an alliance with Veej and adversarial relations with Chafe.
- People with neither glasses nor contact lenses: You are affected by humorous appeals. You feel an alliance with Chafe and adversarial relations with Veej.
- Females: You tend to be more persuaded by loud voices.
- Males: You tend to be more persuaded by soft voices.

- People with detached ear lobes: You are persuaded by bribes (particularly subtle ones)
- People with joined ear lobes: You are turned off by bribes.

Check off the rules that affect you and try to remember them. Do not disclose them directly to either of the Aliens. Engage in normal conversation with the aliens and cooperate with any of their questions. When a vote is taken at the end of the exercise, vote according to the above rules.

Debriefing Questions
(After taking a vote by show of hands among the Earthlings) *To each Alien:* Which people viewed you as allies? as neutrals? as adversaries? How did you find out? As an advocate, what seemed to work? What did not seem to work? *To each Earthling:* How did it feel to be a decision-maker in this case? What influenced you the most?

ROLE-PLAY 6.2: "PERRY'S PAROLE"— ORAL AND WRITTEN SKILL DEVELOPMENT

This role-play involves one person playing a therapist (Therma) and three people playing members of a parole board. The purpose is to provide the therapist with an opportunity to practice advocacy skills.

Therma is a therapist on contract with the Criminal Justice Department of Conflictia. She has been working with Perry, a 34-year-old man who has been convicted of sexual assault of a minor. He is coming up for parole. Therma has been asked to prepare a report for the parole board. Therma believes that Perry now has a low risk for re-offending, as he has developed insights and empathy regarding the impact of sexual abuse on children. He has consented to the use of drug therapy to control his sexual drive and wants to continue in counseling.

Confidential Facts for Therma

In order to prepare for the role-play:

(a) Write down a list of concerns/criteria that you believe the Parole Board will be considering when they read your report.
(b) Draft a report advocating for Perry's Parole—separate the facts from your expert opinions; address the concerns that you have identified in 1; and consider language that would be most persuasive.
(c) Consider how to handle information that may go against Perry's application for parole. Do you present both sides of the issue?
(d) Prepare how you will present your case as an advocate in front of the Parole Board.

When you role-play, you will be making submissions to the members of the Parole Board. One of them will facilitate the process. The Parole Board will be making a decision about whether to release Perry on parole, and if so, with what conditions.

Confidential Facts for Parole Board

Prior to the oral hearing, consider the therapist's written advocacy brief. In order to prepare for the role-play, consider the following questions.

1. What criteria will you use to make your decision about Perry's parole?
2. What information do you need to make a decision based on these criteria?
3. Where will you get this information from (aside from what you will get from the therapist)?
4. How important will the therapist's information be? Why?
5. What types of strategies could the therapist use in order to make her submission to you most persuasive?
6. What types of strategies would turn you off?
7. Review the Inventory of Advocacy Skills, so that you can give Therma feedback on her use of skills following the role-play.

During the role-play, your function will be to hear submissions. You will be in control of the process (appoint one member to be the facilitator). You will have the task of making the decisions at the end of the process: Will Perry be released on parole? If so, under what conditions?

Debriefing Questions
What are the strengths of the written brief? What oral advocacy skills did the therapist demonstrate most effectively? What other strategies could an advocate use under similar circumstances?

ROLE-PLAY 6.3: "WORKFARE CASE"—SKILL DEVELOPMENT

The Right of Center (ROC) Government of Conflictia has proposed a Workfare Program, where people will be required to work in state-sponsored jobs in order to be eligible for welfare payments. The Left of Center (LOC) party opposes this proposal. The Somewhere in the Middle (SIM) party has not decided its position.

For this role-play, work in groups of three. One person will play an advocate who opposes the Workfare proposal. The second person will role-play a member of one of the three parties (to be decided by your group). The third person will act as an observer, to provide feedback. During the interaction between the advocate and the party member, the advocate will try to develop a positive relationship with the party member and then try to influence the way the member votes in the upcoming vote on the Workfare proposal. The advocate should identify three or four advocacy items from the Inventory of Advocacy Skills that the advocate wants to practice.

The position of LOCs who oppose Workfare can be summarized as follows.

- Mothers on welfare are already working: They are raising children.
- Many others on welfare are also working outside of the home. They supplement their inadequate welfare payments by working "under the table." However, they are not reporting their incomes to avoid being cut off welfare.
- It is mean to require welfare recipients to train for tedious jobs that do not offer career advancement or benefits (such as health insurance or vacations).
- These jobs pay so little that many would remain on welfare rolls even if they retained their jobs following the Workfare program.
- Where good jobs are offered through Workfare, employers are displacing regular salaried employees with a cheaper, "second class" workforce.
- Previous work-training programs have not worked.
- Governmental policy makers should quit "blaming the victim." Instead, reform the inequitable education system; banish racism; pay a living wage; and provide decent housing, adequate nutrition, health care, and child care.
- In terms of welfare reforms, substantially raise benefits and allow welfare mothers to choose whether they will work or not. Offer them incentives and opportunities to work (e.g., through subsidized day care or job training for meaningful careers).

The position of ROC members who favor Workfare can be summarized as follows.

- Work is inherently good. It is a core value of life in this society.
- Most parents today, even those with children, are in the labor force.
- Welfare recipients act as a drain on the economy and are exploiting taxpayers who work.
- Getting rid of people on welfare who exploit the system will allow tax revenues to be used for other public purposes.
- Benefits for the truly needy can be increased if those on Workfare enter the productive economy.
- People who work have better self-esteem and will be more likely to find productive places in the community than those who stay home collecting welfare.
- Public sector jobs could be given to those on welfare.
- If people cannot depend on welfare, they will be more likely to pull themselves up by the bootstraps.

Role-play for about 45 minutes. Break up the role-play into short segments, so that you have ample opportunity to provide feedback during the role-play.

Debriefing Questions

What were the objectives of the advocate? What skills did the advocate use to work towards these objectives? Which skills did the advocate use most effectively? Which skills does the advocate want to prioritize for future practice?

MAJOR ASSIGNMENTS

The following role-plays can be used for major assignments. See the section on Major Assignments in Chapter 3 for instructions on how to prepare a written analysis.

These role-plays are designed to be conducted during class. Each person in the class will be assigned an advocacy role in one of the role-plays. In another role-play, you will play a person on a panel to which others will be advocating. One person on the panel will act as a neutral facilitator; the others will be decision makers. During the role-plays where you are not an advocate or a panel member, you will be an observer. Your job will be to observe the role-play and complete a feedback form for each of the people playing an advocacy role. Make photocopies of the Inventory of Advocacy Skills and use these to provide detailed feedback to colleagues in your class.

Each role-play will last 45 to 50 minutes. You may decide to have orientation or preparatory meetings outside of class time. There will be a few minutes before each role-play for setting up, as well as 20 minutes after each role-play for debriefing and filling out the feedback forms. During debriefing, the advocates will be asked to identify some of the strategies they used and how effective they were. They may also explain why they did not use certain types of strategies (e.g., if their assigned role asked them to take a positional stance, then they may have chosen not to focus on interests).

You will have the option of videotaping these exercises. Upon permission from each of the participants, copies could be made by your instructor as a resource for future classes.

All parties should read the common facts for their role-plays. In addition, read the confidential facts for your specifically assigned role.

ASSIGNMENT 6A—CONFLICTIA PROTEST CASE

Assignment 6A: Common Facts

A coalition of advocacy groups has requested permission from the Municipality of Conflictia to conduct an anti-racism demonstration this Saturday. The date was chosen to commemorate the internment of Japanese families during

World War II and a recent decision by government rejecting a request for compensation. The elected officials of the Municipality acknowledge that discrimination, social disenfranchisement, and poverty are problems that affect visible minorities disproportionately. They are also aware that "freedom of expression" is not only an integral value in a free and democratic society, it is constitutionally entrenched in the Conflictia Declaration of Rights and Freedoms. However, given the negative experience of other municipalities with protests and conflicts, some people think this request should be denied. They believe that while there are issues that legitimately deserve demonstrations, the potential for violence and hooliganism is too great. In an effort to involve the community in the decision-making process, the Municipality has invited the following people to participate in a think tank.

1. Collette: a representative of the coalition requesting the demonstration.
2. Stonewall: a store-owner, on the proposed route of the demonstration.
3. Sgt. Polgat: a representative of the police force.
4. Arabella: The president of a student run Anti-Racism Group from Conflictia University.
5. Socrates: A social worker who works in an agency that serves elderly people from the Japanese-Conflictian community.

The panel conducting the hearing will consist of Miranda (the mayor and facilitator); Miguel, Mavis, Martin, and Maureen (Municipal Councilors). They have decision-making authority over whether to grant a permit for a public demonstration.

This group has been brought together for a 45-minute meeting. Its task is to make recommendation to the Municipality about what it should do in response to the coalition's request for a demonstration permit. No one knows for sure what consequences will result, whether or not a permit is granted.

Assignment 6A: Confidential Facts for Collette

You would like to see the demonstration go ahead, with approval of the city. The members of your coalition, however, may go ahead with their demonstration regardless of whether it is approved. You are their spokesperson, although you do not have a lot of influence over them. The coalition represents a variety of interests and does not agree about how best to proceed with their "anti-racist" agenda. Moving the demonstration to a less commercial or less trafficked area is not a good solution for you. You want high visibility. Further, people will only start to listen to your concerns if you cause them some discomfort. You are particularly offended by those who want ethnic minorities to be out of sight or silenced.

Assignment 6A: Confidential Facts for Stonewall

You believe that having the demonstration would be a big mistake. You do not agree that racism is a big issue, but you are also unsure about how people would react to your saying so. You are mostly concerned about the loss of business and the potential risk to your property if the demonstration goes ahead. Saturday is your best day for sales. A protest would keep shoppers away. You have spoken to people in Sydney, Los Angeles, London, and Montreal about riots they have had. Even well-planned demonstrations can spark fires. Other businesses on the demonstration route share your concerns.

Assignment 6A: Confidential Facts for Sgt. Polgat

You have a lot of experience working with people from diverse backgrounds. You can empathize with their concerns. You do not, however, believe that the cost of policing a demonstration is justified. Demonstrations in public places can put the interests of a few above the interests of the majority. People have a right to freedom of expression, but do not have the right to inconvenience others, particularly at the expense of taxpayers. A demonstration would require keeping on extra police for a Saturday, paying overtime, and putting the riot squad on alert. If there is a riot, it is your head that is put on the line.

Assignment 6A: Confidential Facts for Arabella

You have never been the victim of racism yourself, but your education has raised your awareness of such issues. You have a large student group behind you. You have also started to prepare for the demonstration in conjunction with the Coalition. You have lined up a number of celebrity speakers, including Sasha Lizte (leader of the LOCs). The local newspapers and radio stations have also received copy to promote the demonstration. If the demonstration is blocked, considerable time and effort will have gone for naught.

Assignment 6A: Confidential Facts for Socrates

The agency and client group you represent feel angry and hurt about the treatment from many levels of government—at the time of internment, as well as whenever they have been asked for reparations. You believe that the demonstration would be a great way to raise the awareness of the plight of Japanese-Conflictians. You believe that the people of Conflictia owe Japanese internees and their descendants an apology, an admission of wrongdoing, and monetary compensation for property that was lost or expropriated.

Assignment 6A: Confidential Facts for Committee Members: Miranda (the mayor and facilitator), Miguel, Mavis, Martin, and Maureen (Municipal Councilors)

Try to put yourselves into the roles of mayor and Municipal Councilors. Jot down some of your concerns, questions, and biases. During the role-play, try to be sensitive to the types of arguments and strategies that would persuade you. Remember, there is an election coming up next year.

ASSIGNMENT 6B—TO HOLD OR NOT TO HOLD

Diversity Plus operates three group homes for children with emotional distur-bances. The ages of the children range from 7 to 16 years old. The Office of the Ombud in Conflictia has recently received complaints from three children in the group homes. Each stemmed around a different incident in which group home staff used physical force to discipline children. The Ombud has initiated a conflict resolution process in which it will hear from all interested parties before rendering its recommendations. Ideally, the parties will come to a consensus on how to proceed. At present, consensus does not seem possible.

The current policy of the group homes allows staff to physically restrain children who pose a risk to themselves, others, or property. Three or four staff members hold down a child who is acting out. Both arms and legs are restrained in order to ensure that the child is safe. Agency staff say that "hold-ings" are a therapeutic intervention, providing the child with structure, bound-aries, and a sense of being cared for (similar to a hug from a parent). Staff are not permitted to strap, hit, or otherwise discipline children with physical force.

This role-play involves four advocates.

1. Chet—A child advocate who opposes the use of holdings in group homes.
2. Urania—A union steward who represents the group home staff.
3. Amelia—The administrator of the group homes.
4. Dr. Parker—a psychologist who is advocating for a group of parents whose children have laid complaints against the group homes.

The Office of the Ombud has appointed four people to hear the case: Orillia (who will facilitate the process), Ovide, Omer, and Opra.

Assignment 6B: Confidential Facts for Chet

As a child advocate, you value the civil liberties of children. You believe that holdings infringe the autonomy of children. Staff can use other methods in order to ensure the safety of themselves and others. Many staff are poorly trained, leading to frequent crises in the group home that could be avoided with more effective verbal interventions. You realize that the group homes are under-resourced and have a difficult time retaining good staff.

About 45% of the children in the group homes have a history of being sexually abused. Holdings are particularly scary and demeaning for this group. Consider alternatives to empower the children.

Assignment 6B: Confidential Facts for Urania

You have a background in social work and organizational behavior. As a representative of the union representing child care staff at the group homes, you are concerned about the charges that have been laid against child care staff by various children. The group homes have used holdings for over 25 years, with no complaints until this past year. You believe that the children have raised charges against staff as a way of manipulating them. Some of the children have been violent: punching walls, throwing dishes at staff, and bullying smaller children. The staff is paid not much more than minimum wage, even though most of them have 2-year diplomas in childcare or early childhood development. There is a high rate of turnover, which is not good for the union, the agency, or the children. Personally, you are unsure about the therapeutic value of holdings.

Assignment 6B: Confidential Facts for Amelia

As Administrator for the group homes, you strongly believe in the use of holdings. Under certain circumstances, you also advocate for the use of reasonable physical force to discipline children. Otherwise, the children you serve will have no respect for staff and will become uncontrollable. You believe so strongly in this that you are prepared to resign if the Office of the Ombud recommends prohibition of holdings. You have worked in this field for 30 years. In that time, you have never seen a child who has been injured by a holding. On the other hand, many staff have come away from holdings with significant cuts and bruises.

You are particularly concerned about how complaints from children have been portrayed in the media. You believe that this infringes on the privacy of others in the group home. Also, charitable donations to the group homes have dropped since the publicity started.

Dr. Parker conducts groups for parents, as part of his contract with your agency. You respect his professional opinion, but believe that he does not have the right to advocate against the policies of Diversity Plus.

Assignment 6B: Confidential Facts for Dr. Parker

You are a psychologist who has worked with many of the parents now complaining about the group home. Parents are concerned about the competence of the group home staff. Some parents report that the behavior of their children has been deteriorating, not getting better. You may want to review the literature, to look at the impact of holdings or other physical discipline on children with emotional disturbances.

You have a contract with Diversity Plus, so you have concerns about how your stance on this issue will affect your future relationship with the group homes.

Assignment 6B: Confidential Facts for the Ombuds: Orillia, Omer, Ovide, Opra

As members of the Office of the Ombuds, you would like to see the parties resolve this matter themselves. Set up a process that will allow you to gather information from the parties, share it with one another, and determine whether there is common ground. If the parties cannot reach an amicable resolution, then your mandate is to make suggestions about how the group homes should proceed.

ASSIGNMENT 6C—HELGA'S HEART

Helga is a 15 year old girl who was born with a moderate case of Down's Syndrome. She functions at the level of a five-year old, but is generally a happy child. Helga has recently been diagnosed as suffering from a heart condition requiring a heart transplant. Her doctors believe that she cannot survive beyond the next 40 days without a transplant. Transplant surgery is expensive. However, the main concern is that hearts appropriate for this type of surgery are in short supply. Even if Helga's name is put on the top of the list, there is no guarantee that a suitable heart will be found for her in time (in fact, the chances are about 40%). If she is put at the middle of the list, her chances are 15%. If she is placed at the bottom of the list, then her chances are zero. Some of the other people already on the list include a 40-year-old single actress, a 24-year-old married mother of two (ages 2 and 4), and a 62 year old retired army sergeant who is a heavy smoker. The hospital administration and representatives from the Department of Health need to decide how to handle Helga's situation. The have assembled a panel to hear the views of a number of interested parties. The parties that they will hear today include:

1. Seth—a social worker who is acting as an advocate for Helga and her family.
2. Rhonda—a medical researcher, specializing in heart transplant surgery. She believes that Helga is a poor candidate for this surgery.
3. Praba—a psychiatric nurse who advocates for people with cognitive impairments. The group she represents believes that they should be treated with the same respect and rights as anyone else.
4. Cwan: a counselor from the Department of Defense, advocating for the retired army sergeant.

The panel listening to these representations includes: Dr. Hadad (hospital administrator and designated facilitator), Drs. Dudley and Doright (two doctors), and Ms. Holloway (a representative from the Conflictia Department of Health).

Assignment 6C: *Confidential Facts for Seth*

You are personally unsure about whether Helga is a good candidate for this surgery, given that she lacks the basic abilities to take care of herself. Even if the surgery goes well, she will always be highly dependent on others. You do share Helga's family's concern for her and will advocate for her to be given high priority for a heart transplant. You may lapse into name calling—out of anger at the insensitivity of some of the others who are advocating against Helga. Otherwise, you can use whichever strategies you believe will be most effective.

Assignment 6C: *Confidential Facts for Rhonda*

Your research shows that the effectiveness of heart surgery depends significantly on the post-operation cooperation of the patient. The patient must be able to follow strict instructions in terms of diet, activities, cleanliness, and rehabilitation therapy. Your information about Helga is that she has bad nutritional habits and that she is not very cooperative with being given instructions. Given the shortage of hearts, you believe that tough decisions have to be made and that the best candidates for surgery need to be the ones selected. You do not want to play God or evaluate which person is more deserving.

You expect some sort of trouble from Cwan. About a year ago, you applied for a position with the Department of Defense and Cwan was responsible for torpedoing your chances. You think Cwan feels defensive with you because you have such strong academic credentials.

Assignment 6C: *Confidential Facts for Praba*

You believe that all people who need surgery should be given equal consideration. No one has the right to judge which of two or more people should live or die. If there is such a choice to be made, then your initial solution would be to use a random generating device (e.g., drawing names whenever a suitable heart became available). You are particularly incensed by people who would rate a girl with Down's Syndrome as a second class citizen. You know Helga personally and believe that her life is as worthy as anyone else's on the list.

Assignment 6C: Confidential Facts for Cwan

You have nothing against Helga. You do not even know her. However, your role is to advocate for Amy Salk, an army sergeant who has served her country and deserves high priority on this decision. You (and Amy) fear that her age and smoking will be held against her. In fact, you have seen research that shows that people in her situation are not as good candidates as younger, non-smokers. Your focus, however, is that the decision should be made on the basis of merit—or at least respect for all people. You never know which individual will actually make the best candidate.

You do not have a lot of respect for Rhonda. You believe that her research methods are not very good. You also know she is angry because you did not hire her for a research position at the Department of Defense.

Assignment 6C: Confidential Facts for the Hospital and Ministry of Health Panel: Dr. Hadad, Drs. Dudley and Doright, and Ms. Holloway

Try to put yourselves into the roles of the Hospital and Department of Health Representatives. Jot down some of your concerns, questions, and biases, based on your professional views. During the role-play, try to be sensitive to the types of arguments and strategies that would persuade you. None of you actually has decision-making authority. You will be using this consultation to develop a report to another body that will make the ultimate decisions. There is precedent for assigning priority based on who is expected to have the best quality and longevity of life, post-operation. You have already had input from other advocates who made a strong case for giving the 24-year-old mother top priority, based on these criteria.

ASSIGNMENT 6D—ARCHIE'S ADOPTION

Peabody's Adoption Services (PAS) is a privately based agency acting as an intermediary to facilitate voluntary adoptions. Archie is a 38-year-old single male, who has applied to PAS to be considered as an adoptive parent. Archie is willing to adopt a boy or a girl. Although he would prefer to adopt an infant, Archie realizes that the waiting list for infants is long. He would be willing to adopt an older child (for which there is greater need).

Slobodan is the social worker for PAS who conducted the intake interview with Archie. During the intake interview, Archie explained that he is a gay man, who is financially secure given his job as an architect for the city. Archie has always wanted to raise children, but he had decided to wait until he was in a relationship of some permanence. He believes that given his age, now would be a good time to adopt. Although he does not have a partner, he does have support from family and friends. Slobodan advised Archie that before going further in the adoption process, he would have to consult with the agency. Although there is no law against a gay, single man adopting, Slobodan was not aware of any prior situations where a gay, single man had adopted through PAS. Archie gave Slobodan permission to discuss his situation, but was concerned about whether the agency would discriminate against him. Slobodan said that he did not have a problem with Archie's application. However, Slobodan did not have final say for the agency. Personally, Slobodan is not sure about the right way to deal with this situation because he feels he does not have enough knowledge about the relevant issues. He does not want to hurt Archie.

Clarice is Slobodan's clinical supervisor. She was glad that Slobodan brought this case to her attention, because it was long past due that the agency developed a policy about these issues. She believes strongly that sexual orientation should not be a factor in eligibility criteria for adoption. She also believes that the biological parent should not have any say about whether a child goes to a heterosexual or homosexual adoptive parent. She believes homophobia should not be tolerated.

Elvira is the Executive Director of PAS. Elvira believes that the agency does not have any obligation to serve gay men or women who want to adopt, because the agency is a private agency. Elvira thinks that the agency should restrict its eligibility to legally married couples. In support of this position, Elvira notes that same sex couples are not legally sanctioned relationships and that many biological parents may not want their children raised by homosexual parents. Elvira fears that biological parents may not use the agency if it starts to work with gay adoptive parents. Elvira states there is no research about whether gay men make good adoptive parents. Elvira says this is not being homophobic; it is just being pragmatic.

Colleen is a child psychologist who does assessments for PAS. Colleen believes that it may be advantageous for gay children to be placed with gay adoptive parents, for modeling and for support. However, most of the children that PAS deals with have not clearly developed a sexual orientation. Colleen believes that there are far more important factors than a parent's sexual orientation that would determine whether someone would make a good adoptive parent. Colleen does feel strongly that couples have more time and resources to provide for a child's needs than does a single parent. Also, older children should have some say about the sexual orientation of their adoptive parents.

Father Connel is a Catholic Priest. He believes that homosexuality is immoral; accordingly, gay men should not be considered as potential adoptive parents. He is not an employee of PAS, but believes that his input is important. Clarice respects Father Connel as a spiritual leader in the community, but objects to his presence in private agency meetings.

The decision about how to deal with Archie's adoption application is being referred to the agency's Board of Directors. Boris, Betty, Bruce, Brandy and Bob serve on PAS's Board. During past, informal discussions, they came to a consensus that adoptive parents had the right to decide whether a child is adopted by gay or straight parents. In a local survey by another agency considering this issue, less than 8% of biological parents would consent to having their child adopted by a gay couple. The figure would be even lower for a single gay man. Because of this, very few children would be placed with gay parents. They believed that it would be misleading to gay men to say they are eligible, when in fact, they would just sit on the waiting list forever.

These professionals have come together for a consultation to decide whether Archie should be considered further as a potential adoptive parent. Elvira, as Executive Director of PAS, will facilitate the process. Elvira may start out by setting ground rules and asking everyone to agree to them.

There are no confidential facts for this case.

CONCLUSION

chapter 7

The "conclusion" of a book usually tries to resolve unanswered questions and bring outstanding issues to closure. Hopefully, the readings and exercises in this text have raised many questions, and hopefully, you have begun to find answers for yourself. As when you practice CR with clients, finding answers for yourself is more empowering and respectful than having others impose their answers. Given the enormity of issues raised in this text and the fact that many have no universal truths, trying to bring closure to all issues would be infeasible. Instead, this conclusion focuses upon four questions.

1. Is conflict resolution a collection of techniques, a group of practice models, or a distinct profession?
2. What type of qualifications are required to practice CR?
3. When developing a CR system, what criteria should be considered with respect to choosing a particular CR process for dealing with different types of conflict?
4. How can helping professionals develop their own approaches to CR practice?

Although this chapter answers some questions, it is likely to raise even more. After all, learning CR is an ongoing process.

TECHNIQUES, MODELS, OR PROFESSION

Conflict resolution is a dynamic and growing field. Although many aspects of CR can be found in the longstanding practices of the helping professions, these were not always viewed as CR interventions. Some writers question whether CR is a collection of techniques, a group of practice models, or a distinct profession. Perhaps it is all three.

First, CR offers a range of techniques that helping professionals can use in various contexts: clinical interventions, interactions with co-professionals,

256

advocacy for clients, and systems negotiation. Viewed in this way, CR allows practitioners to select various methods or skills based on their own models of practice.

CR could also be seen as a bundle of practice models: for example, interest-based negotiation, therapeutic mediation, and rights-based advocacy. A practitioner assesses a situation with a client and they determine which CR model is most likely to be effective. The practitioner's choice of techniques is driven by the framework of the chosen CR model.

Finally, some helping professionals not only adopt CR models or techniques, they adopt the persona of a CR professional. This includes a distinct value system and knowledge base. Helping professionals possess a variety of skills and attributes that allows them to move smoothly into CR roles. Although this book focuses upon negotiation, mediation, and advocacy, helping professionals are also well suited to other CR roles, for example, ombuds, assessors, facilitators for public dialogues, and family group conference coordinators. New CR models are evolving and opportunities for helping professionals are growing.

In spite of the optimistic trends in CR, this field does face a number of serious challenges. Although the evolving nature of CR is dynamic and exciting, CR does need to define itself more clearly. What does it stand for; what does it mean in practice; and is it really distinct from other models of practice among helping professionals? Among CR approaches, mediation and negotiation possess the most advanced levels of theoretical development, ethical codification, standards for accreditation, and empirical research. Practitioners, ethicists, and researchers need to continue to work together to refine CR, ensuring that it is value driven and clinically effective.

QUALIFICATIONS

The interdisciplinary nature of CR encourages helping professionals to work together and learn from one another. However, CR professionals are not immune to turf wars as various groups lay claim to different areas of practice. In order to deal with such problems, CR professionals need to use CR skills, not only with clients, but among themselves.

One of the key issues is the question of what standards, if any, should be required for a practitioner to qualify as a specific type of CR professional. Family mediators and lawyers have already developed systems for accreditation and licensing. While some people view mandatory regulation as a way of ensuring competent, responsible CR practice, there are some areas of CR where restricting practice to "qualified professionals" may not be appropriate. These include peer mediation in schools, informal or emergent CR roles assumed by helping professionals as part of their ordinary practice, and lay advocacy to promote health, justice, and other social causes.

When determining what types of qualifications, if any, are needed to practice CR, the following guidelines should be considered.

- In order to provide broad access to CR services, restricting CR practice to certain groups should be avoided unless the risks of unregulated practice are too high (where there are severe legal issues or safety concerns, where CR users are particularly vulnerable because of mental capacity, etc.).
- Any requirements for qualification should be based on what a practitioner needs in order to practice in a competent manner: that is, what values, skills, and knowledge must a practitioner possess in order to provide effective CR services.
- Different qualifications are required for different CR processes and different contexts of practice. A victim-offender mediator, for example, needs to know about the effects of victimization, whereas a patient advocate needs to know about hospital procedures.
- If practice in certain areas of CR is restricted to "qualified" professionals, ensure that the qualifications do not have any systemic biases against particular cultural groups.
- Any association that establishes standards for CR should have broad-based representation to ensure that it does not become self-serving or biased. Include users of the CR services, if possible.
- Any association that regulates CR professionals should adopt CR processes that are consistent with CR values and knowledge; for example, using mediation to try to resolve client concerns before moving toward more adversarial processes, such as disciplinary hearings (Feld & Simm, 1998).

Recent trends suggest greater movement toward professionalization and accreditation of CR practitioners. When considering whether to regulate CR, heed concerns about who regulation benefits and how.

CHOOSING A PROCESS

Although the CR movement places high value on peace and harmonious relations, helping professionals also value mental health and social justice. In many situations, these values coincide. In situations where these values collide, helping professionals need to establish guidelines for how to proceed. When designing a system to deal with conflict, consider a staged approach.

1. *Pre-emptive CR*: Be pro-active. Consider potential conflict situations and employ systems that can address them before they arise: (a) scheduling periodic planning meetings; (b) providing clients with clear policies, indicating the expectations, services, and limitations of the agency; and (c) providing CR training so that people know how to manage conflict in constructive manners, before critical problems arise.

2. *Informal CR:* When conflict arises, encourage parties to deal with it informally, on a face-to-face basis. Third party intervenors may be unnecessary and disempowering. Parties may need help with communication skills and informal problem-solving frameworks. Otherwise, this level of the system should be easy to access and unfettered by bureaucracy. Unless there are significant power imbalances, encourage people to first try to negotiate on a one-to-one basis, without the use of advocates.

3. *Formal Collaborative CR:* If informal CR is ineffective or inappropriate, a more formal process may be necessary. This does not mean, however, that the process has to be adversarial. Interest-based negotiation, transformative mediation, and structured dialogues are some examples of collaborative processes to consider. Helping professionals may assume roles as mediators, advocates, or facilitators. Decision-making power rests with the parties. Still, helping professionals may assume power-balancing roles, to ensure that the process is fair.

4. *Formal Adjudicative Processes:* The next stage in a system removes decision-making power from the parties and gives it to an impartial, third party. Judges, arbitrators, assessors, and investigators are examples of adjudicators. Helping professionals can assume the roles of arbitrators, assessors, investigators, witnesses, and advocates in such processes. Since most helping professionals value client self-determination, they may be reluctant to assume a role where they make decisions for clients. Such a role can be justified if other processes have failed.

5. *Separate Power-based Action:* More forceful interventions may be necessary in order to secure mental health, social justice, or other client needs (Germain & Gitterman, 1996). Using the least force necessary to achieve such results minimizes costs and risks of retaliation. Even if one must resort to competitive strategies, consider the possibility of healing relationships in the future (Pruitt & Carnevale, 1993).

In some situations, parties should progress through the earlier processes, before trying the more adversarial ones. For example, a client who has a complaint about a helping professional should be encouraged to deal directly with that professional first. If, however, the client has concerns about the safety of meeting that professional in a one-on-one meeting, the system should allow the client to move to a more formal stage where safety strategies can be employed. Offer clients as much choice as possible, so they gain a sense of empowerment.

OWNING AN APPROACH

Choice is also important for helping professionals. CR training materials often prescribe what to do and how to do it. As a reflective practitioner, you will want to understand the theory and values underlying various models of CR intervention. Refer back to the values and beliefs about CR that you identified for yourself in Chapters 1 and 2. Reflect on whether these have changed given your readings and experiences throughout this course. As you continue to work with client systems, you will develop greater skills in assessing conflict situations and determining the most appropriate models and strategies. For educational purposes, you have focused on learning one model or a few skills at a time. Once you have mastered a number of models and techniques, you will be able to develop your own model of practice, drawing from a range of CR theories, skills, and strategies.

Conflict is inevitable. The challenge is to turn what could be antagonizing, frustrating, and stressful, into something that is energizing, exciting, and constructive . . . for you and your clients.

DISCUSSION QUESTIONS AND EXERCISES

1. REFLECTION: Review your written exercises from throughout the course. Summarize the changes that have occurred in terms of your values and attitudes toward conflict. Identify your strengths in the field of CR. Describe the skills and models of intervention that you want to improve upon. Identify readings, training programs, conferences, or practical experiences that you could use for next steps in professional development (note resources in Appendix 2).
2. AGENCY CRITIQUE: Identify an agency that has a CR component. Meet with a practitioner from the agency who incorporates CR into practice. Develop a critical analysis of the CR component, including strengths and recommendations. Describe the extent to which the agency and practitioner base their practice on CR theory, research, and values. Consider whether and how to give feedback to the agency.
3. CR PROGRAM: Identify an agency that you believe could use a CR element to its programming. Describe the existing concerns and a rationale for developing a CR service. Construct a CR system that fills the agency's needs. Identify how to evaluate success of the proposed system.
4. PUBLICATION: Review your writings and assignments from this term. Consider whether any of your work is publishable in an edited form. Appendix 2 includes a list of journals that publish CR articles. If you

intend to submit an article for publication, ensure that it meets the terms of reference (guidelines) set out in the journal.

5. EVALUATION: Identify an agency that has a CR program. Develop a proposal for evaluating the effectiveness of the CR program. Your proposal should include:

   a) description of the program, its goals, and objectives;
   b) literature review examining the theoretical bases of the program and evaluative research results for similar programs;
   c) research design;
   d) description of sample;
   e) methods and instruments for collecting data;
   f) how data will be analyzed; and
   g) how ethical issues will be handled.

   Ideally, the agency will want to implement your proposal. Maintain a journal to log any conflicts that arise between you and the agency, as well as how you and agency staff handled these conflicts. How well were you able to implement what you have learned about CR?

APPENDIX

Glossary

1

accommodative a style of conflict resolution where a party tries to satisfy the other person's interests, without trying to satisfy their own; relationship oriented.

adjudication a form of CR where the parties present evidence and arguments to a neutral third party who has power to decide how the conflict will be resolved. Adjudicators are generally required to base their decisions on objective standards, laws, or precedent cases. Arbitration and litigation are forms of adjudication.

administrator a professional who assists with implementation of the resolution of a conflict.

adversarial a style of CR where the party sees itself in competition; a process in which there is a winner and a loser.

advocacy the act of providing CR support to a particular party or cause.

anecdotal storytelling using narratives to demonstrate a point; using analogies or metaphors to help parties gain insight into their own conflict situation.

arbitration a CR process where the parties select and agree upon a neutral third person to resolve their dispute through an adjudicative process. Arbitrators receive oral and/or written evidence and arguments from the parties and issue a decision. The arbitrator's decision could be binding or non-binding, depending on prior agreement of the parties. The parties may also have input into the rules of the arbitration process. Most arbitration processes are closed to the public.

avoidant a style of CR in which a party denies the existence of the conflict or backs away from conflict; not wanting to confront conflict directly.

balance of power the relative capacity of two or more individuals or groups to influence one another.

bargaining communication between two or more conflicting parties who are trying to work towards an agreement; sometimes used to describe a positional approach to negotiation.

bias favoritism, perceived or objective; siding with one party or cause in a conflict.

bicultural having sufficient experience in two cultures, so that one is able to understand and interpret both effectively.

brainstorming generating ideas on a topic by asking participants to list as many options as they can imagine, regardless of whether they are realistic or reasonable.

buffer   an individual or agency that separates conflicting parties during an intense, destructive phase of conflict.

case advocacy   supporting a particular client or client system in a CR process.

cause advocacy   supporting a particular set of values or goals in a CR process.

Chance Fork   used in Decision Tree Analysis to denote the possible outcomes from various courses of action (e.g., a negotiation process might result in a favorable settlement, an unfavorable settlement, or no settlement); marked by a small circle with one line extending from the circle for each possible outcome.

collaborative   to work together to satisfy one another's interests; joint problem solving.

competitive   focused upon self-interest or individual success.

compromise   to make concessions; to reduce goals or demands in return for the other party also reducing its demands; a form of positional bargaining.

conciliation   a problem-solving process similar to mediation, but focused upon settlement of the presenting issues rather than dealing with underlying concerns, relational, or process issues (contrast with "reconciliation").

conflict   see social conflict.

conflict resolution   any means used by people to deal with conflict situations; for example, negotiation, mediation, fighting, and debating (sometimes referred to as "conflict management").

conflict style   an individual's preferred way of dealing with conflict (accommodating, avoiding, compromising, competing, collaborating).

consensus building   any CR process that works towards agreement among all of the parties directly involved in the conflict. Consensus building includes negotiation, mediation, community development, and therapeutic processes that give the parties the power to make decisions for themselves. General consensus may not require that all parties agree; the group can agree to a certain level of consensus required to take an action.

contract   an exchange of promises between conflicting parties. A contract can be binding (enforceable in court) or non-binding (an informal commitment that the parties intend to follow, although it is not enforceable in court).

contractual conflict resolution   a formal CR process in which the parties agree to a specific process, as established by contract (in contrast to emergent CR, below).

cultural relativism   valuing all cultures, without making assumptions about one culture being better than another.

culture   a system of values, language, customs, and beliefs among a group that shares a common nationality, ethnic origin, gender, sexual orientation, disability, or other background.

debate   a form of discourse in which participants take a stance and argue for their preferred outcomes (contrast with "dialogue").

Decision Fork   used in Decision Tree Analysis to denote the alternative courses of action that a decision-maker can choose between (e.g., go to court, negotiate, initiate war); marked by a small square with one line extending from the square for each alternative.

dialogue   a constructive form of discourse in which participants listen to one another and try to gain a higher level of mutual understanding.

directive   an interventionist approach to CR, particularly mediation; in contrast to a facilitative approach in which the intermediary encourages the parties to communicate, but avoids guiding them towards specific solutions.

emergent conflict resolution   an informal CR process which emerges from a situation without an explicit contract; the person who facilitates the process is not necessarily recognized as a CR professional (in contrast to "contractual mediation").

empower   facilitate self-determination, choice, and autonomy (Bush & Folger, 1994).

Endpoint Value   used in Decision Tree Analysis to denote the value of a particular chance outcome (e.g., if you negotiate and two possible outcomes are settling for $100 compensation and settling for $2,000, then the endpoint values are $100 and $2,000).

equilibrium   according to systems theory, a balanced state between individuals in a family or other social system, where each person in the system has a complementary role; according to game theory, a situation where two or more parties have a singular best strategy, regardless of how the other party behaves.

ethics   principles which tell individuals, groups, or organizations what is right and what is wrong; a system of studying the morality of behavior.

Expected Value   the weighted average of a series of chance events; used in Decision Tree Analysis to decide which decisions are most likely to bring about the best result. For example, if you negotiate and there is a 20% chance of settling for $100 compensation and an 80% chance of settling for $1,000, then the Expected Value is:

$$[20\% \times \$100] + [80\% \times \$1,000] = \$820.$$

expert/consultant   a professional who provides information, expertise, or advice to one or both interested parties to help them resolve a conflict.

facilitate   to assist parties communicate with one another; e.g., through mediation, family counseling, supervision, or group therapy.

healer   a facilitator who helps parties work through the underlying causes of a conflict.

homeostasis   see "equilibrium."

impartial   free from bias or favoritism, as perceived by the parties or objectively true.

impasse   a deadlock in negotiations; a point in the process when it looks as if there is no negotiable solution or room for agreement.

independent legal advice   the right of each party involved in a conflict to advice from a separate lawyer before entering into an agreement.

interests   concerns, needs, or underlying motivations; the reasons that a certain position matters to a party involved in a conflict.

interest-based negotiation   an alternative to positional negotiation where parties are encouraged to look at their underlying interests (concerns) and work towards solutions that satisfy all parties' interests.

interpreter   a person who can help parties understand one another, particularly if they speak different languages or have different cultural interpretations of the language being used; an interpreter conveys the meaning of language, rather than simply translate word-for-word.

interventionist   see "directive."

investigator   a professional who gathers information in order to determine what has happened or what should happen in order to resolve a conflict.

judicial process   a CR approach where an independent third party decides how to resolve a conflict for the parties (see also, "adjudication").

jurisdiction   a municipal, state, provincial, or national government which has the power to make laws. In Canada and United States, provinces and states generally have the legislative authority to regulate helping professions, including CR.

lateral thinking   using cognitive processes in a creative manner; viewing a problem from various angles in order to consider innovative options for solution; an alternative to linear thinking.

learning styles   preferred ways of learning; the predominant manner in which individuals acquire knowledge, skills, and understanding.

litigation   a trial, where conflicting parties bring their dispute to court to be decided by a neutral judge or panel of judges; the parties have the right to present evidence and arguments, but the judge's decision is binding on the parties. Most trials are open to the public.

mediation-arbitration (med-arb)   a hybrid model of CR, where the practitioner first attempts to mediate a resolution; if the parties are unable to reach their own agreement, the mediator becomes an arbitrator and imposes a decision.

mediation   assisted negotiation:

> *open mediation*   mediation where the parties agree to limited confidentiality; the mediator cannot disclose information from mediation to the general public, but either party may ask the mediator to disclose information to a court or other tribunal, particularly if the conflicts are not resolved in mediation.

> *closed mediation*   mediation where the parties agree the process is completely confidential; information shared in the process cannot be disclosed by the mediator to a court or other process.

> *comprehensive mediation*   in divorce or separation mediation, used to describe mediation of both financial concerns (alimony, child support, and division of property) and parenting concerns (custody, access, and visitation).

> *therapeutic mediation*   mediation designed not only to resolve the overt conflicts, but to heal relationships, deal with underlying problems, and enhance the abilities of the parties to deal with future conflicts.

mediative   a process that has some of the qualities of mediation, but does not fit the strict definition of mediation.

metaphoric storytelling   a parable that provides an analogy or lesson, used in CR to help one or both parties gain insight into their conflict (see also "anecdotal storytelling").

mutual   for the benefit of all parties; for joint or shared interests.

negotiation   communication between two or more parties involved in a conflict; could include joint or independent action.

neutral   unbiased; fair; disinterested; having no stake in final outcome.

ombud   an official designated by government or another institution to investigate complaints about the institution, particularly those concerning discriminatory practices or unfair treatment. The ombud (or the ombud's staff) may try to mediate a solution or offer suggestions; however, they have no power to adjudicate or impose a solution. Sometimes, the recommendations will be made public. This puts pressure on the parties to follow up on the recommendations.

participants   individuals or groups who are involved in a CR process; the parties are always included as participants; however, other participants might include advocates, support persons, people required to help implement decisions, and experts.

parties   individuals or groups who are involved in a conflict. "Interested parties" are directly involved in the conflict and have a stake in its outcome; "Third parties" are not directly involved in the conflict and typically have no stake in a particular outcome; however, they can be brought in to facilitate resolution of the conflict.

peace building   fostering collaboration and co-operative relations between conflicting parties (e.g., through mediative processes).

peacekeeping   refereeing; maintaining peace by buffering the parties or by enforcing ground rules to avoid violence.

peer mediation   assisted negotiation, where the mediator comes from a similar background as the conflicting parties (e.g., a student who mediates disputes between other students in their school).

penalizer   an individual or agency with the power to impose sanctions on parties for misconduct.

position   the preferred outcome or solution stated by a party involved in a conflict.

positional negotiation   bargaining by trying to advance one's own preferred solution.

power   the relative capacity of individuals or groups to influence one another.

power balancing   redistributing power between the parties; helping a disadvantaged party participate fairly in a CR process (contrast with "empowerment").

power base   sources of power; ways of garnering greater capacity to have influence over others.

pre-empt   using a strategic intervention to avoid a problem; identifying potential barriers to CR and designing interventions to prevent the problem from occurring.

professional   a person who uses a specific set of knowledge, skills, and values to guide practice (e.g., professional teachers, social workers, nurses, psychologists, counselors, human service workers, clergy).

radical   perspectives that challenge the *status quo* in society, including power structures, patriarchy, and various forms of systemic discrimination.

recognition   understanding and demonstrating empathy to another party's situation (see "transformative mediation").

reconciliation   process of returning a relationship to its prior state; repairing or healing a relationship.

resolution   dealing effectively with the underlying issues in a conflict situation; reaching an agreement that truly satisfies the parties (contrast with "settlement").

restitution   returning a situation to its prior state (e.g., repairing damaged property).

restorative justice   CR perspective based on compensation or restitution; encourages parties to restore losses and repair relationships.

retributive justice   CR perspective based on punishment for wrongdoing; holds people accountable for their actions and deters future wrongdoing.

settlement   an agreement that deals with the surface issues, but does not necessarily resolve the parties' emotional or underlying issues; for example, an agreement allowing the parties to avert a trial, fight, or strike, but not fully resolving the parties' underlying concerns.

shuttle mediation   assisted negotiation, where the third party meets with each party in a different place, moving back and forth between them.

social conflict   an expressed difference in values, beliefs, or interests between two or more parties (as opposed to intra-psychic conflict, which occurs when an individual has conflicting values, drives, beliefs, or behaviors).

stake   a personal or monetary interest in the resolution of a conflict.

structural   see "radical."

system   a group of inter-related parties.

transformative mediation   assisted negotiation, where the third party facilitates empowerment and recognition between the parties; bringing the parties to a settlement of their conflict is not a primary goal.

values   deeply held preferences or priorities; principles which individuals or groups believe are good or worthy of aspiration.

Resources

The following lists provide information about locating additional resources for professional development, accreditation, and training. The topics include conflict styles instruments, journals, research institutes, professional associations, World Wide Web sites, videotapes, practice opportunities, metaphoric storytelling, sample process recording, and sample codes of ethics.

CONFLICT STYLES INSTRUMENTS

Contact one of the following organizations to inquire about obtaining instruments to assess conflict styles.

- Thomas-Kilmann Conflict Mode Instrument, Xicom Incorporated, Sterling Forest, Tuxedo, NY, USA 10987. Tel.: 800-75-XICOM (toll free in USA) or 914-351-4735.
- Myers Briggs Type Indicator, Consulting Psychologists Press, PO Box 10096, Palo Alto, CA, USA 94303-0979. Tel.: 800-624-1765 (Toll free in USA)
  Or in Canada: Psychometrics Canada Ltd., Room 103—Student Union Building, University of Alberta, Edmonton, AB, Canada T6G 2J7. Tel.: 800-661-5158

JOURNALS

- *Mediation Quarterly*
- *Negotiation Journal*
- *Family and Conciliation Courts Review*
- *Journal of Dispute Resolution*
- *Argumentation and Advocacy Journal*
- *Peace, Environment and Education*

RESEARCH INSTITUTES AND DATA BASES

- ADR Mediation Resources Web: http://www.adrr.com
- Campaign for Equity-Restorative Justice, 740—15th Street NW, Washington, DC, USA 20005-1009. Tel: (202) 662-1680 Web: http://www.cerj.org (including Victim-Offender Mediation)

- Canadian International Institute of Applied Negotiation, 200 Elgin Street, Suite 701, Ottawa, ON, Canada, K1P 1L5. Tel.: (888) 244-2637 E-mail: Conciian@intranet.ca Web: http://www.canadr.com
- CDR Associates, 100 Arapaho Avenue, Suite 12, Boulder, CO, USA 80832. Tel.: (800) MEDIATE or (303) 442-7367; Web: http://www.mediate.org
- Conflict Research, Resolution and Education Group, c/o Dr. A. Barsky, Faculty of Social Work, University of Calgary, Calgary, AB, Canada T2N 1N4. Tel.: (403) 220-7550 Email: barsky@ucalgary.ca Web: http://www.ucalgary.ca/UofC/research/CRREG
- Conflict Resolution Resources Web: http://www.nova.edu/adr/ssss/DR/resources.html
- CPR Institute for Dispute Resolution. Tel.: (212) 949-6490 Web: http://www.cpradr.org
- George Mason University, Institute for Conflict Analysis and Resolution, Fairfax, VA, USA 22030-4444. Tel.: (703) 993-1300 Web: http://www.gmu.edu/departments/ICAR
- Institute of Peace and Conflict Studies, Conrad Grebel College, Waterloo, ON, Canada, N2L 3G6. Tel.: (519) 885-0220 http://grebel.uwaterloo.ca/pacs/pacs.htm
- National Institute for Dispute Resolution and National Association for Community Mediation, 1527 Hampshire Avenue NW, Washington, DC, USA 20036. Tel.: (202) 667-9700 E-mail: nidr@nidr.org Web: http://www.crenet.org; http://www.nafcm.org
- National Multicultural Institute, 3000 Connecticut Avenue NW, Suite 438, Washington, DC, USA 20008. Tel.: (202) 483-0700 Web: http://www.nmci.org
- Peace and Conflict Studies, University of Colorado, Tel: (410) 367-8723 Web: http://csf.colorado.edu/peace/index.html (lists peace studies journals)
- Program on Conflict Management and Negotiation, University of Toronto, 252 Bloor St. West, 8th Floor South, Toronto, ON, Canada, M5S 1V6. Tel.: (416) 978-6498 Web: http://learn.utoronto.ca/business/dispute/index.asp
- Program on Negotiation, 518 Pound Hall, Harvard Law School, Cambridge, MA, USA 02138. Tel.: (617) 495-1684 Web: http://www.pon.org
- Team Management Briefings. Web: http://www.briefings.com
- UVic Institute for Dispute Resolution, Begbie Building, University of Victoria, PO Box 2400, Station CSC, Victoria, BC, Canada. Tel.: (250) 721-8777 Web: http://www.finarts.uvic.ca

PROFESSIONAL ASSOCIATIONS

- Academy of Family Mediators, 4 Militia Drive, Lexington, MA, USA 02173. Tel.: (781) 674-2663 E-mail: afmoffice@igc.apc.org Web: http://www.mediators.org
- American Bar Association Section of Dispute Resolution. http://www.abanet.org/dispute
- Arbitration and Mediation Institute of Canada (AMIC), Suite 2600, 160 Elgin Street, Ottawa, ON, Canada K1P 1C3. Tel.: (613) 786-8650
- Association of Family and Conciliation Courts, 329 West Wilson Street, Madison, WI, USA, 53703. Tel.: (608) 251-4001 Web: http://www.afccnet.org
- Colorado Conflict Research Consortium, University of Colorado, Campus Box 327, Boulder, CO, USA 80309-0327 Tel: (303) 49202154 Web: http://www.Colorado.EDU/conflict
- Family Mediation Canada, 528 Victoria St. N., Kitchener, ON, Canada N2H 5G1. Tel: (519) 585-3118. E-mail: fmc@fmc.ca Web: http://www.fmc.ca
- Mediation Information and Resource Center, http://www.mediate.com [includes links to various codes of ethics]

- Network: Interaction for Conflict Resolution, Conrad Grebel College, Waterloo, ON, Canada, N1H 3Y8. Tel.: (519) 885-0880 x274 E-Mail: nicr@watserv1.uwaterloo.ca Web: http://www.nicr.ca/index.asp
- The Ombudsman Association, Suite 104-265, 5521 Greenville Avenue, Dallas, TX, USA, 75206. Tel: (214) 553-0043 Web: http://www.igc.org/toa
- Public Education for Peace Society, 405—825 Granville Street, Vancouver, BC, Canada V6Z 1K9. Tel: (604) 687-3292
- Society of Professionals in Dispute Resolution (SPIDR), 1527 New Hampshire Ave. NW, 3rd Floor, Washington, DC, USA 20038. Tel.: (202) 667-9700 Web: http://www .spidr.org
- Victim-Offender Mediation Association c/o Marty Price, J.D., 2315 NE Mason Portland, Oregon, USA 97211. Tel.: (503) 281-5085 E-mail: martyp@hevanet.com Web: http://www.voma.org

VIDEOTAPES

The following animated films are useful educational tools for children aged 5 to 12. Creative and humorous, these videotapes help children explore conflict resolution and learn how to deal with anger and conflict more effectively. Adults will also find the presentations entertaining and insightful.

- National Film Board of Canada (1997). *Dinner for two* (videotape). Toronto: Author.
- National Film Board of Canada (1997). *When the dust settles* (videotape). Toronto: Author.[1]

For Peer Mediation Videotapes for students in grades 6 to 12, consider the following.

- Schrumpf, F., & Crawford, D. K. (1994). *The peer mediation video: Conflict resolution in schools.* (1996 Program Guide and Student Manual come separately). Waterloo, ON. Research Press.[2]
- Hawaii Research Center for Future Studies (1991). *Cultural approaches to conflict resolution* (Videotape). Honolulu, HA: Author.

The following videotape provides a good introduction to interest-based mediation, in the context of a dispute between developers and environmentalists:

- Gibson, M. (Ed.). *Mediation: An introduction* (Videotape). Toronto: MGI Film & Television, Mackenzie Group International.

For an introduction to adult guardianship mediation, consider:

- The Center for Gerontology (1999). *Adult guardianship mediation: An introduction.* Ann Arbor, MI.[3]

---

[1] To order or to look for other resources in the ShowPeace series of films, see http://www.nfb.ca

[2] E-mail orders may be made through: order4csl@aol.com, or call 800-265-3375

[3] Order form available at http://www.tcsg.org

Conflict Resolution Practice Opportunities

One of the primary concerns of newly educated CR professionals is where to gain practice experience. If practice opportunities are not readily available, you may need to be creative. Consider the following possibilities:

- Practicum—some training programs and professional degree programs offer supervised internships as part of the program.
- Volunteer mediation—contact neighborhood community dispute resolution services, victim services (possibly located in the criminal court), or volunteer service listings.
- Co-mediate—mediate together with a more experienced mediator; some mediators charge trainees who want to co-mediate with them.
- Private supervision—obtain your own cases and hire an experienced mediator to provide feedback, suggestions, and support.
- Peer consultation—meet periodically with other mediators to discuss cases and offer one another support (be careful to protect client confidentiality).
- Career development—practice CR skills in your traditional practice on an emergent basis or work with others in your agency to develop CR programming.

Metaphoric Storytelling

Metaphoric storytelling refers to the use of narratives, anecdotes, or analogies to change perceptions and move parties towards agreement. Conflicting parties can also use them to gain insight into their own conflict situation. The following examples are provided to illustrate the types of stories that can be used in conflict resolution. When creating your own anecdotes for CR, use humor, creativity, and common wisdom.

1. "Seeking Creative Solutions"

A man died, leaving seventeen camels to his three sons. The first son was to receive one-half, the second son was to receive one-third, and the third son was to receive one-ninth of their father's camels. They were unable to figure out how to divide the camels fairly. After arguing among themselves, they consulted a wise woman for a solution to this difficult problem. She offered to lend them her one camel. Of the eighteen camels, the first son took nine, the second took six, and the third took two. One camel was left over, so the sons gave it back to the woman.
(From a Middle Eastern parable, cited in Rothman, 1997, p. 53)

2. "Strength from Weakness" or "Collaboration Wins Over Competition"

The director of an agency announced that she was going to retire. The obvious choices to replace her were the three senior supervisors: Jodie, Frank, and Beatrice. Everyone assumed that Jodie would be chosen, since she had the greatest experience and was a strong administrator. Frank seemed to be the second favorite, given his capacity to raise funds and develop new programs for the agency. Beatrice did not think she had a chance against the others, so she just went about her job as usual.

Frank really wanted the director's position, so he decided to do whatever Jodie did, but better: he stayed late, worked harder, and tried to do everything faster. Jodie quickly saw what Frank was trying to do and she responded in kind. Everything she did had to be perfect and she would always go the extra step to ensure that her performance would exceed Frank's. Frank and Jodie were so anxious to impress, they even asked Beatrice if they could do her work for her. Reluctantly, Beatrice offered each of them some of her most tedious responsibilities.

Decision time came and Beatrice was selected for Director. She demonstrated that she could delegate work and collaborate with her colleagues.
(drawn loosely from Game Theory)

3. How Fear Sounds Like Anger

I was driving to work one morning, when I saw the driver of a van cut in front of a car. The car driver had to slam the brakes in order to prevent a collision. The car driver honked and the van driver honked back, but even louder. This seemed to enrage the car driver, as the car sped ahead and passed the van. The van then raced up and passed the car as if to play a game of chicken. By this point, both were going so fast that I lost sight and never did find out who won.

As I pondered what happened, I tried to figure out how these folks could get so angry at each other. Then I wondered if it really was anger. When the car first honked, perhaps the driver was saying, "Hey, we almost crashed. That really scared me." The van driver must have interpreted the honk as, "You idiot. You almost killed me!" The van driver honked back meaning to say, "I didn't mean it. It was an accident." Now the car driver probably heard this honking differently, "What are you honking at me for, jerk!" And on they went. I wonder if we need to develop a new car horn that communicates different sounds for "I'm angry" and "I'm scared." I wonder if people could benefit from the same sort of thing.

SAMPLE PROCESS RECORDING

This abbreviated sample illustrates a format for assessing process in your role plays, as well as actual interventions in your regular practice.[4] See the guidelines for Major Assignments in Chapter 3 for further explanations of how to analyze your work.

Purpose: In my previous work placements, I have had difficulty dealing with strong emotions and clients who are not acting rationally. I have chosen this role play to work on my affect management skills using the Dilbert & Sullivan (2001) model of "evacuative mediation." In addition, I plan to use the analysis to reflect upon my affective and behavioral responses to repetitive victimization of one party . . .

Preparation: For this role exercise, I play a budgie named Tweety B. I perform community mediation services for an agency called Diversity Plus. In recent months, Conflictia has witnessed a marked increase in gang violence among its pet population. I have been assigned to mediate between two gangs: the Felines and the Canines. Each gang has over 30 members, so I decide to begin the process by meeting with representatives of the two groups: Tiger and Felicia who are top cats of the Felines, and Buddy and Spike who are top dogs of the Canines. Although meeting with delegates for two groups can simplify the process, I will need to attend to the interests and feelings of all gang members (Snowball, 1999). Prior to the first joint meeting, I meet separately with the dogs and cats to screen for risks of scratching, clawing, and biting . . .

---

[4]To protect the privacy of clients, change identifying information or include a covering statement to indicate that the process recording is confidential.

The four representatives each come from a different ethnic constituency: Siamese, Calico, Labrador, and Irish Setter. I have reviewed literature describing some of the cultural preferences of these groups in relation to conflict resolution (Sylvester, 2002; Tom, 1958). I know that I could get eaten up by this group if I am not adequately prepared, so I set an agenda (Dino, 1999) and arranged the meeting room with a round table, separate drinking bowls filled with warm cream, and soft blue lights (Fido, 2005). The stated purposes for this meeting are: (1) to identify areas of individual concern, and (2) to identify areas of common concern. The following transcription begins with introductions:

Narrative (Verbatim)	Observations & Interpretation	Reflections (Thoughts/Feelings)	Skills/Theory
Me (Tweety): Chirp. I'd like to thank you for your time and commitment in coming to this very important meeting. Perhaps we can begin by introducing ourselves, and stating our reasons for being here. Spike, would you care to start . . .	Everyone arrived promptly and is sitting attentively around the table. Spike is tapping his left front paw—looks anxious. Maybe I should start with him.	I think I forgot to use mouthwash this morning. Maybe I better not sit too close to anyone today.	We are a task group (Heidi, 1964) and at the forming stage (Alvin, 1998)—I need to use listening skills and gain their trust if I want to be an effective chair.
Spike: I'm Spike and I'm tired of all these nasty fat cats who provoke us all the time and then complain that they're innocent victims.	Spike hasn't touched his warm cream.	Perhaps I wasn't culturally sensitive to his dietary needs. I feel embarrassed. Underlying value—respect for diversity.	I don't know what theory or skill I can use to deal with someone who is so belligerent and bigoted towards felines. Perhaps I'll just ignore the insults.
Me: What are you hoping that we can accomplish here today?	The others have moved onto the edge of their seats—Felicia's tail is straight up—a sign of anger?	I have to control my anger towards Spike—he's been hard to deal with, but he represents a large segment of the community.	Setters and Calicos have had a long history of conflict (Muttley, 1998). Skill: Open-ended question; nonjudgmental and concrete.
Felicia: Spike just wants to lock us up in a cage and throw away the key. Who invited him anyway?	Felicia's tone of voice is high and quivering. She sounds bitter, but she's likely nervous underneath.	Now I'm being attacked. I just wanted to help out.	I think we've gone into the "storming stage" too quickly. Haven't these folks read the book? (Sparky, 2001)
ETC.			

Analysis: Everyone joined the argument. I lost control for about 10 minutes. At this point, Tiger stepped in and settled everyone down. Tiger told a sad, personal story about losing two kittens in a recent gang fight. This was a turning point, as we talked about the need to work together. Spike acknowledged that turf wars and other negative reactions to overcrowding in the neighborhood were not just feline phenomena. Buddy and Spike noted that there is a lot of dogchismo (pride) in the canine community, making it difficult to admit problems to outsiders. We decided that we needed to develop some type of forum to discuss the needs of the community. We divided up tasks. Buddy said he'd do some research into methods of conducting "town hall meetings" (Beast, 2002). I agreed to bring information about the use of surveys for a needs assessment (Snoop, 1998). Tiger said she'd contact associates in Bassetville to obtain information about their "Pets Against Violence" campaign. Felicia and Spike agreed to bring refreshments.

I was able to implement the first three steps of the "Evacuative Approach" quite effectively, but the fourth step proved difficult because the parties were reluctant to share affective information. Perhaps I need to find a different way to introduce this step . . .

Follow-Up: At one point, I was hanging on by a wing and a prayer, but my prayers must have been answered. I'm not sure if I had any positive influence—Tiger did most of the work. My biggest fear is that what happened at the beginning of the meeting today is only a small sample of what would/will happen when we get the whole community together. I had better read Robins (2000), *A Bird's Eye View to Community Development Work with Dogs and Cats* . . .

SAMPLE CODES OF ETHICS

The codes of ethics for the Academy of Family Mediators and for the Society for Professionals in Dispute Resolution are provided below. Various jurisdictions, agencies, and contexts of mediation practice have their own codes of ethics.

Academy of Family Mediators[5]

Standards of Practice for Family and Divorce Mediation

I. Preamble

Mediation is a family-centered conflict resolution process in which an impartial third party assists the participants to negotiate a consensual and informed settlement. In mediation, whether private or public, decision-making authority rests with the parties. The role of the mediator includes reducing the obstacles to communication, maximizing the exploration of alternatives, and addressing the needs of those it is agreed are involved or affected.

(continued)

---

[5] © 1988. Academy of Family Mediators, www.mediators.org. Reprinted with permission.

Standards of Practice for Family and Divorce Mediation (Continued)

Mediation is based on principles of problem solving that focus on the needs and interests of the participants; fairness; privacy; self-determination; and the best interest of all family members.

These standards are intended to assist and guide public, private, voluntary, and mandatory mediation. It is understood that the manner of implementation and mediator adherence to these standards may be influenced by local law or court rule.

II. Initiating the Process

A. Definition and Description of Mediation. The mediator shall define mediation and describe the differences and similarities between mediation and other procedures for dispute resolution. In defining the process, the mediator shall delineate it from therapy, counseling, custody evaluation, arbitration, and advocacy.

B. Identification of Issues. The mediation shall elicit sufficient information from the participants so that they can mutually define and agree on the issues to be resolved in mediation.

C. Appropriateness of Mediation. The mediator shall help the participants evaluate the benefits, risks, and costs of mediation and the alternatives available to them.

D. Mediator's Duty of Disclosure

   1. Biases. The mediator shall disclose to the participants any biases or strong views relating to the issues to be mediated.

   2. Training and Experience. The mediator's education, training, and experience to mediate the issues should be accurately described to the participants.

III. Procedure

The mediator shall reach an understanding with the participants regarding the procedures to be followed in mediation. This includes but is not limited to the practice as to separate meetings between a participant and the mediator, confidentiality, use of legal services, the involvement of additional parties, and conditions under which mediation may be terminated.

A. Mutual Duties and Responsibilities. The mediator and the participants shall agree upon the duties and responsibilities that each is accepting in the mediation process. This may be a written or verbal agreement.

IV. Impartiality and Neutrality

A. Impartiality. The mediator is obligated to maintain impartiality toward all participants. Impartiality means freedom from favoritism or bias, either in word or action. Impartiality implies a commitment to aid all participants, as opposed to a single individual, in reaching a mutually satisfactory agreement. Impartiality means that a mediator will not play an adversarial role. The mediator has a responsibility to maintain impartiality while raising questions for the parties to consider as to the fairness, equity, and feasibility of proposed options for settlement.

B. Neutrality. Neutrality refers to the relationship that the mediator has with the disputing parties. If the mediator feels, or any one of the participants states, that the mediator's background or personal experiences would prejudice the mediator's performance, the mediator should withdraw from mediation unless all agree to proceed.

C. Prior Relationships. A mediator's actual or perceived impartiality may be compromised by social or professional relationships with one of the participants at any point in time. The mediator shall not proceed if previous legal or counseling services have been provided to one of the participants. If such services have been provided to both participants, mediation shall not proceed unless the prior relationship has been discussed, the role of the mediator made distinct from the earlier relationship, and the participants given the opportunity to freely choose to proceed.

D. Relationship to Participants. The mediator should be aware that post-mediation professional or social relationships may compromise the mediator's continued availability as a neutral third party.

E. Conflict of Interest. A mediator should disclose any circumstance to the participants that might cause a conflict of interest.

V. Costs and Fees

A. Explanation of Fees. The mediator shall explain the fees to be charged for mediation and any related costs and shall agree with the participants on how the fees will be shared and the manner of payment.

B. Reasonable Fees. When setting fees, the mediator shall ensure that they are explicit, fair, reasonable, and commensurate with the service to be performed. Unearned fees should be promptly returned to the clients.

C. Contingent Fees. It is inappropriate for a mediator to charge contingent fees or to base fees on the outcome of mediation.

D. Referrals and Commissions. No commissions, rebates, or similar forms of remuneration shall be given or received for referral of clients for mediation services.

VI. Confidentiality and Exchange of Information

A. Confidentiality. Confidentiality relates to the full and open disclosure necessary for the mediation process. A mediator shall foster the confidentiality of the process.

B. Limits of Confidentiality. The mediator shall inform the parties at the initial meeting of limitations on confidentiality, such as statutorily or judicially mandated reporting.

C. Appearing in Court. The mediator shall inform the parties of circumstances under which mediators may be compelled to testify in court.

(continued)

Standards of Practice for Family and Divorce Mediation (Continued)

D. Consequences of Disclosure of Facts Between Parties. The mediator shall discuss with the participants the potential consequences of their disclosure of facts to each other during the mediation process.

E. Release of Information. The mediator shall obtain the consent of the participants prior to releasing information to others. The mediator shall maintain confidentiality and render anonymous all identifying information when materials are used for research or training purposes.

F. Caucus. The mediator shall discuss policy regarding confidentiality for individual caucuses. In the event that a mediator, on consent of the participants, speaks privately with any person not represented in mediation, including children, the mediator shall define how information received will be used.

G. Storage and Disposal of Records. The mediator shall maintain confidentiality in the storage and disposal of records.

H. Full Disclosure. The mediator shall require disclosure of all relevant information in the mediation process, as would reasonably occur in the judicial discovery process.

VII. Self-Determination

A. Responsibilities of the Participants and the Mediator. The primary responsibility for the resolution of a dispute rests with the participants. The mediator's obligation is to assist the disputants in reaching an informed and voluntary settlement. At no time shall a mediator coerce a participant into agreement or make a substantive decision for any participant.

B. Responsibility to Third Parties. The mediator has a responsibility to promote the participants' consideration of the interest of children and other persons affected by the agreement. The mediator also has a duty to assist parents to examine, part from their own desires, the separate and individual needs of such people. The participants shall be encouraged to seek outside professional consultation when appropriate or when they are otherwise unable to agree on the needs of any individual affected by the agreement.

VIII. Professional Advice

A. Independent Advice and Information. The mediator shall encourage and assist the participants to obtain independent expert information and advice when such information is needed to reach an informed agreement or to protect the rights of a participant.

B. Providing Information. A mediator shall give information only in those areas where qualified by training or experience.

C. Independent Legal Counsel. When the mediation may affect legal rights or obligations, the mediator shall advise the participants to seek independent legal counsel prior to resolving the issues and in conjunction with formalizing an agreement.

IX. Parties' Ability to Negotiate

The mediator shall ensure that each participant has had an opportunity to understand the implications and ramifications of available options. In the event a participant needs either additional information or assistance in order for the negotiations to proceed in a fair and orderly manner or for an agreement to be reached, the mediator shall refer the individual to appropriate resources.

A. Procedural Factors. The mediator has a duty to ensure balanced negotiations and should not permit manipulative or intimidating negotiation techniques.
B. Psychological Factors. The mediator shall explore whether the participants are capable of participating in informed negotiations. The mediator may postpone mediation and refer the parties to appropriate resources if necessary.

X. Concluding Mediation

A. Full Agreement. The mediator shall discuss with the participants the process for formalization and implementation of the agreement.
B. Partial Agreement. When the participants reach a partial agreement, the mediator shall discuss with them procedures available to resolve the remaining issues. The mediator shall inform the participants of their right to withdraw from mediation at any time and for any reason.
C. Termination by Participants. The mediator shall inform the participants of their right to withdraw from mediation at any time and for any reason.
D. Termination by Mediator. If the mediator believes that participants are unable or unwilling to participate meaningfully in the process or that a reasonable agreement is unlikely, the mediator may suspend or terminate mediation and should encourage the parties to seek appropriate professional help.
E. Impasse. If the participants reach a final impasse, the mediator should not prolong unproductive discussions that would result in emotional and monetary costs to the participants.

XI. Training and Education

A. Training. A mediator shall acquire substantive knowledge and procedural skill in the specialized area of practice. This may include but is not limited to family and human development, family law, divorce procedures, family finances, community resources, the mediation process, and professional ethics.
B. Continuing Education. A mediator shall participate in continuing education and be personally responsible for ongoing professional growth. A mediator is encouraged to join with other mediators and members of related professions to promote mutual professional development.

XII. Advertising

A mediator shall make only accurate statements about the mediation process, its costs and benefits, and the mediator's qualifications.

(continued)

Standards of Practice for Family and Divorce Mediation (Continued)

XIII. Relationship with Other Professionals

A. The Responsibility of the Mediator Toward Other Mediators/Relationship with Other Mediators. A mediator should not mediate any dispute that is being mediated by another mediator without first endeavoring to consult with the person or persons conducting the mediation.

B. Co-mediation. In those situations where more than one mediator is participating in a particular case, each mediator has a responsibility to keep the others informed of developments essential to a cooperative effort.

C. Relationships with Other Professionals. A mediator should respect the complementary relationship between mediation and legal, mental health, and other social services and should promote cooperation with other professionals.

XIV. Advancement of Mediation

A. Mediation Service. A mediator is encouraged to provide some mediation service in the community for nominal or no fee.

B. Promotion of Mediation. A mediator shall promote the advancement of mediation by encouraging and participating in research, publishing, or other forms of professional and public education.

Society of Professionals in Dispute Resolution[6] Model Standards of Practice for Mediators

Preface

The model standards of conduct for mediators are intended to perform three major functions: to serve as a guide for the conduct of mediators; to inform the mediating parties; and to promote public confidence in mediation as a process for resolving disputes. The standards draw on existing codes of conduct for mediators and take into account issues and problems that have surfaced in mediation practice. They are

---

[6]Reprinted with the permission of the Society of Professionals in Dispute Resolution, Washington, DC.

offered in the hope that they will serve an educational function and provide assistance to individuals, organizations, and institutions involved in mediation.

I. Self-Determination: A Mediator Shall Recognize that Mediation is Based on the Principle of Self-Determination by the Parties.

Self-determination is the fundamental principle of mediation. It requires that the mediation process rely upon the ability of the parties to reach a voluntary, uncoerced agreement. Any party may withdraw from mediation at any time.

COMMENTS:

- The mediator may provide information about the process, raise issues, and help parties explore options. The primary role of the mediator is to facilitate a voluntary resolution of a dispute. Parties shall be given the opportunity to consider all proposed options.
- A mediator cannot personally ensure that each party has made a fully informed choice to reach a particular agreement, but it is a good practice for the mediator to make the parties aware of the importance of consulting other professionals, where appropriate, to help them make informed decisions.

II. Impartiality: A Mediator Shall Conduct the Mediation in an Impartial Manner.

The concept of mediator impartiality is central to the mediation process. A mediator shall mediate only those matters in which she or he can remain impartial and evenhanded. If at any time the mediator is unable to conduct the process in an impartial manner, the mediator is obligated to withdraw.

COMMENTS:

- A mediator shall avoid conduct that gives the appearance of partiality toward one of the parties. The quality of the mediation process is enhanced when the parties have confidence in the impartiality of the mediator.
- When mediators are appointed by a court or institution, the appointing agency shall make reasonable efforts to ensure that mediators serve impartially.
- A mediator should guard against partiality or prejudice based on the parties' personal characteristics, background or performance at the mediation.

III. Conflicts of Interest: A Mediator Shall Disclose all Actual and Potential Conflicts of Interest Reasonably Known to the Mediator. After Disclosure, the Mediator shall Decline to Mediate unless all Parties Choose to Retain the Mediator. The Need to Protect Against Conflicts of Interest also Governs Conduct that Occurs During and After the Mediation.

A conflict of interest is a dealing or relationship that might create an impression of possible bias. The basic approach to questions of conflict of interest is consistent with the concept of self-determination. The mediator has a responsibility to disclose all actual and potential conflicts that are reasonably known to the mediator and could reasonably be seen as raising a question about impartiality. If all parties agree

(continued)

Society of Professionals in Dispute Resolution Model Standards of Practice for Mediators (Continued)

to mediate after being informed of conflicts, the mediator may proceed with the mediation. If, however, the conflict of interest casts serious doubt on the integrity of the process, the mediator shall decline to proceed.

A mediator must avoid the appearance of conflict of interest both during and after the mediation. Without the consent of all parties, a mediator shall not subsequently establish a professional relationship with one of the parties in a related matter, or in an unrelated matter under circumstances which would raise legitimate questions about the integrity of the mediation process.

COMMENTS:

- A mediator shall avoid conflicts of interest in recommending the services of other professionals. A mediator may make reference to professional referral services or associations which maintain rosters of qualified professionals.
- Potential conflicts of interest may arise between administrators of mediation programs and mediators and there may be strong pressures on the mediator to settle a particular case or cases. The mediator's commitment must be to the parties and the process. Pressure from outside of the mediation process should never influence the mediator to coerce parties to settle.

IV. Competence: A Mediator Shall Mediate Only When the Mediator has the Necessary Qualifications to Satisfy the Reasonable Expectations of the Parties.

Any person may be selected as a mediator, provided that the parties are satisfied with the mediator's qualifications. Training and experience in mediation, however, are often necessary for effective mediation. A person who offers herself or himself as available to serve as a mediator gives parties and the public the expectation that she or he has the competency to mediate effectively. In court-connected or other forms of mandated mediation, it is essential that mediators assigned to the parties have the requisite training and experience.

COMMENTS:

- Mediators should have information available for the parties regarding their relevant training, education, and experience.
- The requirements for appearing on the list of mediators must be made public and available to interested persons.
- When mediators are appointed by a court or institution, the appointing agency shall make reasonable efforts to ensure that each mediator is qualified for the particular mediation.

V. Confidentiality: A Mediator Shall Maintain the Reasonable Expectations of the Parties with Regard to Confidentiality.

The reasonable expectations of the parties with regard to confidentiality shall be met by the mediator. The parties' expectations of confidentiality depend on the circumstances of the mediation and any agreements they may make. The mediator shall not disclose any matter that a party expects to be confidential unless given permission by all parties or unless required by law or other public policy.

COMMENTS:

- The parties may make their own rules with respect to confidentiality, or other accepted practice of an individual mediator or institution may dictate a particular set of expectations. Since the parties' expectations regarding confidentiality are important, the mediator should discuss these expectations with the parties.
- If the mediator holds private sessions with a party, the nature of these sessions with regard to confidentiality should be discussed prior to undertaking such sessions.
- In order to protect the integrity of the mediation, a mediator should avoid communicating information about how the parties acted in the mediation process, the merits of the case, or settlement offers. The mediator may report, if required, whether parties appeared at a scheduled mediation.
- Where the parties have agreed that all or a portion of the information disclosed during a mediation is confidential, the parties' agreement should be respected by the mediator.
- Confidentiality should not be construed to limit or prohibit the effective monitoring, research, or evaluation of mediation programs by responsible persons. Under appropriate circumstances, researchers may be permitted to obtain access to the statistical data and, with the permission of the parties, to individual case files, observations of live mediations, and interviews with participants.

VI. Quality of the Process: A Mediator Shall Conduct the Mediation Fairly, Diligently, and in a Manner Consistent with the Principle of Self-determination by the Parties.

A mediator shall work to ensure a quality process and to encourage mutual respect among the parties. A quality process requires a commitment by the mediator to diligence and procedural fairness. There should be adequate opportunity for each party in the mediation to participate in the discussions. The parties decide when and under what conditions they will reach an agreement or terminate a mediation.

COMMENTS:

- A mediator may agree to mediate only when he or she is prepared to commit the attention essential to an effective mediation.
- Mediators should only accept cases when they can satisfy the reasonable expectations of the parties concerning the timing of the process. A mediator should not allow a mediation to be unduly delayed by the parties or their representatives.

(continued)

Society of Professionals in Dispute Resolution Model Standards of Practice for Mediators (Continued)

- The presence or absence of persons at a mediation depends on the agreement of the parties and the mediator. The parties and mediator may agree that others may be excluded from particular sessions or from the entire mediation process.
- The primary purpose of a mediator is to facilitate the parties' voluntary agreement. This role differs substantially from other professional-client relationships. Mixing the role of a mediator and the role of a professional advising a client is problematic, and mediators must strive to distinguish between the roles. A mediator should, therefore, refrain from providing professional advice. Where appropriate, a mediator should recommend that parties seek outside professional advice, or consider resolving their dispute through arbitration, counseling, neutral evaluation, or other processes. A mediator who undertakes, at the request of the parties, an additional dispute resolution role in the same matter assumes increased responsibilities and obligations that may be governed by the standards of other processes.
- A mediator shall withdraw from a mediation when incapable of serving or when unable to remain impartial.
- A mediator shall withdraw from a mediation or postpone a session if the mediation is being used to further illegal conduct, or if a party is unable to participate due to drug, alcohol, or other physical or mental incapacity.
- Mediators should not permit their behavior in the mediation process to be guided by a desire for a high settlement rate.

VII. Advertising and Solicitation: A Mediator Shall be Truthful in Advertising and Solicitation for Mediation.

Advertising or any other communication with the public concerning services offered or regarding the education, training, and expertise of the mediator shall be truthful. Mediators shall refrain from promises and guarantees of results.

COMMENTS:

- It is imperative that communication with the public educate and instill confidence in the process.
- In an advertisement or other communication to the public, a mediator may make reference to meeting state, national, or private organization qualifications only if the entity referred to has a procedure for qualifying mediators and the mediator has been duly granted the requisite status.

VIII. Fees: A Mediator Shall Fully Disclose and Explain the Basis of Compensation, Fees, and Charges to the Parties.

The parties should be provided sufficient information about fees at the outset of a mediation to determine if they wish to retain the services of a mediator. If a mediator charges fees, the fees shall be reasonable, considering among other things, the mediation service, the type and complexity of the matter, the expertise of the mediator, the time required, and the rates customary in the community. The better practice in reaching and understanding about fees is to set down the arrangements in a written agreement.

COMMENTS:

- A mediator who withdraws from a mediation should return any unearned fee to the parties.
- A mediator should not enter into a fee agreement which is contingent upon the result of the mediation or amount of the settlement.
- Co-mediators who share a fee should hold to standards of reasonableness in determining the allocation of fees.
- A mediator should not accept a fee for referral of a matter to another mediator or to any other person.

IX. Obligations to the Mediation Process: Mediators have a Duty to Improve the Practice of Mediation.

COMMENT:

- Mediators are regarded as knowledgeable in the process of mediation. They have an obligation to use their knowledge to help educate the public about mediation; to make mediation accessible to those who would like to use it; to correct abuses; and to improve their professional skills and abilities.

Supporting Development of Mediation

3

Helping professionals can promote development of mediation through a number of roles:

- Training mediators;
- Providing public education and promotion about mediation;
- Planning and developing community-based mediation programs;
- Working with mediation associations; and
- Public policy development for mediation.

This section provides an overview of each of these roles.

1. Training Mediators

One of the burgeoning areas of practice for mediators is training other mediators. On the upside, this means that the people who train mediators generally have significant mediation experience. On the downside, few jurisdictions have set standards of competence for trainers, meaning that the quality of mediation training varies greatly. In some instances, mediators go into training to supplement their incomes because they have few mediation cases themselves. If the trainers have difficulty attracting cases, then imagine how difficult it is for mediators fresh out of training to attract cases.

Competence in mediation is a prerequisite for competence in training mediators. Since one of the ways people learn mediation is through observation, trainers must be able to model effective mediation. Mediation is a practice-based profession. Trainers must be able to help their students translate mediation values and theories into skills and direct interventions. The role of a trainer is similar to that of a coach: to provide knowledge, strategies, constructive feedback, and motivational support.

Most mediation training courses are 40 to 60 hours long. The length may be determined by mediation accreditation bodies. Some courses provide certificates for completion of the course, without any testing to ensure that students have actually learned what they were supposed to learn. Other courses use written tests, live role-plays, or videotaped role-plays to test student knowledge and skill. Standards for competence have been most highly developed for family mediation courses (English et al., 1995).

Ideally, training is individualized to meet the needs of the particular trainees: (1) the trainer identifies the core competencies required for practice; (2) the trainer assesses which competencies each participant possesses and which each needs to work upon; (3) the course is tailored to provide knowledge and experience where needed; and (4) the participants are tested at the end of the training to determine whether they have reached required levels of competence. For example, helping professionals may enter mediation training with excellent facilitation skills. If they do not know the legal issues relevant to their proposed area of mediation practice, the course should focus on filling this need. Interdisciplinary classes are useful, so that people from different professional backgrounds can learn from one another (Severson, 1998).

Written materials for training programs generally focus upon one model of mediation practice. Preferably, this model has a theoretical basis and empirical research support. Mediation associations in some jurisdictions identify specific areas of content to be included in the course, for example, stages of the mediation process, code of ethics, cross-cultural issues, and how to deal with power imbalance and safety issues. Case examples and illustrations are used to demonstrate how the model is put into practice. Supplementary readings can be used to broaden the scope of the training.

One of the most important parts of training is a mediation internship or practicum. Lectures, discussions, and role-plays provide trainees with the basics of mediation. An internship ensures that trainees are ready to practice on their own. Typically, an internship involves a series of mediations in which there are two mediators—the trainee and an experienced mediator (sometimes one of the primary trainers). During the first two or three mediations, the experienced mediator takes most of the responsibility for facilitating the process. Gradually, the trainee takes more and more responsibility. The experienced mediator provides feedback and support and is able to intervene to help out the trainee where necessary. This type of co-mediation ensures that clients receive competent mediation services, even when one of the mediators is inexperienced.

Unfortunately, many training programs do not offer internships. Internships can be time-consuming and costly. In addition, trainers with private mediation practices are often reluctant to expose their clients to inexperienced trainees. An alternative to internships is for the newly trained practitioners to hire experienced mediators to act as consultants during their first few mediation cases. New mediators can also volunteer at community mediation centers in order to gain mediation experience.

In addition to training people to be professional mediators, some trainers teach people conflict resolution skills that they can use as emergent mediators. Some courses are designed for groups such as business managers, clergy, politicians, or community leaders from different cultural groups.

In order to develop as a professional trainer, consider taking courses in teaching and learning, as well as reading adult education literature (MacKearcher, 1997; Severson, 1998). Obtain feedback from trainees and co-trainers. If resources permit, conduct follow-up research so that you can receive more structured feedback.

2. Public Education and Promotion

Unless mediation has already been entrenched in your community and culture, public education and promotion are crucial to the development of any mediation service. Public education informs people about the mediation process, its uses, its advantages, and its disadvantages. Rather than presenting mediation as a panacea, presenting a balanced view of mediation has greater credibility. Public education can take many forms: articles in newspapers or local newsletters, speaking engagements with community groups, or workshops for lawyers and helping professionals. Two of the best ways for the public to learn about mediation are to see it in action and to participate in role-plays. Radio, television, the World Wide Web, and other media can be used to reach mass audiences. Court-TV broadcasts trials 24 hours a day. Why not at least one weekly spot on mediation?

Promotion can be aimed at the general public or specific referral sources (e.g., teachers, physicians, counselors, community leaders, lawyers, clergy). Business cards, brochures, posters, telephone book advertisements, and other promotional materials should be customized for each intended audience: language should be clear; claims about mediation should have empirical support, and the format should project professionalism. Promotional materials generally include a description of mediation, the mediator's credentials, the types of cases that are appropriate for mediation, and how to contact the mediator for further information or referral. Some mediators offer a free information session for each party. Referral sources and prospective clients often find it useful to have the mediator's *curriculum vitae* in order to determine the mediator's level of training and experience. Reputation and word-of-mouth tend to be the most powerful forms of promotion.

Some mediation associations produce listings of mediators and promotional materials for their members. Public education and promotion are time-consuming and expensive. In order to share the burden, some private mediators work in partnership.

3. Planning and Developing Programs

Mediation has a certain allure that gets people excited about creating new programs. Mediation promotes peace, collaboration, and self-determination. Who can argue with an idea like that? However, successful implementation of mediation requires more than just a good idea and well-intentioned enthusiasm. Many programs have failed due to lack of planning and follow through.

When planning a mediation program, developers should consider the following issues: program goals and objectives, target population, mediatable issues, models of mediation, qualifications of mediators, program policies, and research. To illustrate, consider a mediation pilot project designed for students at Conflictia Elementary School. The guidance counselor, Ms Gandy, establishes a team of teachers and students to help her develop the program.

Goals are the broad aims of the program. In this case, the committee decides that the primary goal of the program is to promote peaceful resolution of conflicts among students. *Objectives are desired, measurable outcomes that are based on the program goals.* Objectives for the school program include: students will resolve their own conflicts; they will learn conflict resolution skills; they will deal with anger and other emotions constructively; they will communicate feelings about violence, and they will think creatively about alternative solutions (Morse & Andrea, 1994).

The target population refers the individuals or groups the program hopes to attract to its services. The target population for the school program includes all students who are involved in conflict at Conflictia Elementary. Some school-based mediation programs include teacher-student conflict, but this does not fit with the program's initial goal and objectives. This is a peer mediation program, since both the mediators and the parties are students. The program is intended to be a voluntary program. Although teachers and fellow students may refer the parties to mediation, the parties are free to reject mediation without fear of negative consequences for refusing to mediate. In practice, students may feel pressured to participate, because teachers maintain authority over them, including the power to discipline them for inappropriate behavior during school hours. Initially, the program will be offered to Grade 4 and 5 students, with plans to expand the program to the whole school within two years.

The term "mediatable issues" refers to the types of conflicts that the mediation program is designed to help parties resolve. The planning committee provides broad latitude for mediatable issues: cross-cultural conflicts, gang-related issues, disputes in the classroom or on the sports fields, and bullying complaints between students. The mediation program will insist that there are no immediate risks to either students' safety. The program will not mediate cases involving drugs and weapons, because such cases need to be handled by teachers or school administration.

The models of mediation chosen should reflect the goals of the program and the needs of the target population. The committee reviews the literature on mediation in schools (Girard & Koch, 1996; Hessler, Hollis, & Crowe, 1998; Kaplan, 1997). Since the primary goal of the program is "peaceful resolution," the committee selects an interest-based model. In this case, the mediators will be Grade 4 and Grade 5 students. The model will be simplified in order to tailor it to their cognitive abilities and levels of social skills. At a very basic level, mediation can be reduced to three questions.

- What happened?
- What did you hear ___ say?
- How can we work out this problem so both of you are happy and friendly to each other?[1]

The first question facilitates storytelling. The second question helps the parties develop mutual understandings. The last question focuses the students on collaborative problem-solving.

For some settings, having a choice of mediation models is desirable. Different models can be used for different circumstances. Because of the age of the mediators in the school program, the committee decides to focus on one model.

Mediator qualifications include knowledge, skills, and values. Some school programs select peer mediators according to who already possesses the best conflict resolution skills. These tend to be the "keenest," the "brightest" and the "most well-behaved" students. Other schools select the "bullies" and "trouble makers" to be their mediators. First, these are students who have the greatest need to learn constructive conflict resolution skills. Second, if the school can enlist their help, then other students with similar backgrounds will be more likely to use the services. Ms. Gandy's committee decides to allow the students themselves to determine who the mediators will be. Each class will elect six peer mediators. The mediators will participate in a training program conducted by experts from the Board of Education. Role-plays will be used to evaluate each mediator's level of competence. If a mediator falls below the desired level, further training and coaching will be offered.

Policy issues include terms of confidentiality, impartiality, payment, and participation of people who are not directly involved in the conflict. Because this program is offered within the context of a school system, blanket confidentiality cannot be assured. Teachers will not participate directly in the mediation sessions; however, the mediators will report back to the two teachers responsible for the program for supervision and consultation. Issues pertaining to drugs and safety must be reported. Information from mediation will not be shared with other students, unless the parties agree. Because this is a peer mediation program, mediators will know the parties and may even be friends with one or both. If the parties do not believe that a certain mediator can be impartial, then they can request another mediator. Students will not be permitted to bring a lawyer to the mediation session (Yes, some have asked to do so). The mediation program will not charge any fees and the mediators will not receive any payments for their services.

The mediators will use an oral Agreement to Mediate, in order to keep the process

---

[1] For another example of teaching children constructive conflict resolution skills see Kraybill, 1985.

informal. Any agreements reached in mediation will not be legally binding agreements, also to keep the process informal.

Evaluative research explores the extent to which the program is meeting its objectives. In this case, the school enlists the help of a graduate student at the local university to design and conduct the research component. The researcher establishes measures and questionnaires for each of the objectives identified. The researcher also conducts interviews with mediators and parties in order to obtain qualitative feedback. This information will be used for further program development. The school and the Board of Education will not allocate staff time and other resources to the program unless it can demonstrate its effectiveness.

Program start-up requires a lot of time and energy: to get stakeholders on side, to secure funding, to set up a location, to select and train mediators, and to publicize for cases. Once a program is in place, continuity requires that mediators and support staff have sufficient resources and support. Because conflict tends to be emotional, mediation can be very taxing. In order to reduce the risk of stress and burnout, mediators should have opportunities for debriefing in supervision or peer consultation.

4. Mediation Associations

With the professionalization of mediation since the 1970s, mediation associations have developed across North America, Europe, Australia, and New Zealand. Most of these associations are voluntary organizations. However, some jurisdictions have passed laws requiring that mediators be licensed or accredited by a specific organization in order to practice certain types of mediation. Licensing or certification are most common for family mediators, commercial mediators, and labor mediators. Regulation of mediators is intended to ensure competence and accountability: by establishing standards for education and supervised internships; by establishing a binding code of ethical conduct; and by establishing grievance procedures for clients who have complaints against mediators.

In areas where the state does not require regulation, voluntary associations often try to fill the void. For mediators, there are a number of incentives to join: to show support for the professionalization of mediation; to show potential clients that they have met certain standards and are willing to be held accountable for their practice; and to have a say in the further development of the profession.

Some mediation associations act as regulatory bodies, representing the public interest. Other mediation associations provide advocacy and support for mediators (e.g., to promote the profession with government and in the community). In order to avoid a conflict of interest, these functions should be separated. In situations where the association takes on both roles, clients bringing complaints may sense the grievance procedure is biased towards the mediator.

Grievance procedures in mediation associations vary. Some try to model mediation practice and offer to mediate solutions between the mediator and the aggrieved client (Feld & Simm, 1998). Others hold formal disciplinary hearings, paradoxically similar to those in the court system.

Some proponents of mediation oppose the development of professional mediation associations. They believe that professionalizing mediation deprecates the value of traditional mediators. As noted in Chapter 4, educational standards set by associations limit access to the profession to those who can afford the requisite courses. Professionalization also encourages conformity to certain models of practice. In the absence of research to show which models are superior, society may be better off with mediators offering a broad range of models. Still, concerns about competent, ethical, and accountable practice seem to dictate the ongoing professionalization of mediation.

5. Public Policy Development

Individual mediators and mediation associations have advanced the cause of mediation with varying degrees of success in different jurisdictions and areas of practice. Mediation has been sold to public policy makers as a money saving venture, a way to resolve labor disputes without strikes or work stoppages, a means of diverting cases away from court, and as a more humane way of resolving disputes than the adversarial processes that exist in many social institutions. To some extent, research backs up each of these claims (Kelly, 1996; Kressel & Pruitt, 1985, 1989). More recently, some proponents claim that the true promise of mediation is its ability to transform individuals and society (Bush & Folger, 1994).

Public policy issues include:

- Whether to support mandatory or voluntary registration of mediators;
- Whether to support mandatory or voluntary mediation for conflicts that may be headed towards court, arbitration, labor strikes, grievance procedures, or other adversarial processes; and
- Whether to subsidize the cost of mediation with public funding.

Once again, the context of mediation—family law, mental health, labor, community, and so on—has an impact on how these issues will be decided. In Chapter 6, I present advocacy techniques that can be used to advance the causes of mediation with public policy makers.

DISCUSSION QUESTIONS AND EXERCISES

1. PROMOTION: Identify a segment of your community that you want to educate about mediation: e.g., teachers, politicians, lawyers, children, the elderly, immigrants. Develop a 15 minute educational videotape that you could show to this audience. As you prepare this videotape, consider what your audience already knows about mediation (if anything), what messages you want to convey, and how to convey these messages in suitable language and format. Consider using humor, role-plays, special effects, or other devices to make the videotape interesting and persuasive.
2. PROGRAM PLANNING: Diversity Plus has decided to establish a mediation program for conflicts between children who have run away from home and their parents. The Director has asked you to develop a plan for this program. Identify the goals of the program, which model(s) of mediation will be used, how mediators will be selected, and key issues for implementation of the program.
3. LICENSING: What are the advantages of requiring licensing for professional mediators? What are the disadvantages? What are the differences between licensing and accreditation?
4. PROFESSIONAL ASSOCIATIONS: Identify a field of mediation that you are considering for your professional practice: e.g., family mediation, labor relations, community mediation, victim-offender mediation. In order to practice in this field, is licensing or accreditation required? If so, what are the requirements for licensing or accreditation? If licensing or accreditation is not required, what voluntary associations could you consider joining? What services do these associations offer to mediators and to the public?
5. MANDATORY MEDIATION: What are the advantages and disadvantages of "mandatory mediation?" Consider values issues and research comparing the effectiveness of mandatory versus voluntary mediation.

Decision Trees

As Chapter 1 noted, most disciplines use some type of structured problem-solving process. A generic problem-solving model includes the following steps:

- identify problems,
- canvass a broad array of alternative courses of action,
- identify objectives and values to be taken into account,
- gather information relevant to the choices to be made,
- evaluate the alternatives,
- select the best alternative given the identified objectives and values,
- implement the decision, and
- evaluate its execution to identify any further problems (Zey, 1992).

Decision Tree Analysis is basically an extension of this type of problem-solving process. Decision trees offer a specific structure for exploring alternative courses of action to resolve a conflict (Elangovan, 1995; Walls & Fullmer, 1995). They are commonly used in business and law to evaluate various courses of action: for example, is it better to go to court or negotiate a settlement privately; should the company invest in research and development or use its funds for marketing and promotion? Generally, these types of decisions are based on monetary factors. However, non-monetary factors such as emotions, values, communication, and relationships can also be factored into Decision Tree Analysis. For helping professionals, these "soft factors" are often more important than monetary ones.

Decision Tree Analysis follows six basic steps:

1. Depict the decisions to be made and possible outcomes for each decision.
2. Assign probabilities to each of the uncertain events.
3. Assign values to each of the possible outcomes.
4. Calculate the Expected Values for each possible alternative.
5. Identify soft factors that are relevant to the decisions to be made.
6. Decide upon the best alternative.

In order to demonstrate these steps, consider a situation where you are trying to decide whether to confront a client, Clifford, about paying his bill for your services. To simplify for the purposes of demonstration, consider two courses of action, ignoring the late payment or confronting Clifford the next time you see him for a counseling session.

In Step 1, depict the decision to be made and possible outcomes for each decision. To depict a decision, draw a small square with lines (or branches) extending to the right for each possible alternative. Label each alternative on this Decision Fork as follows.

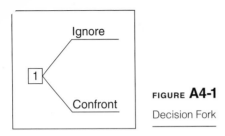

FIGURE **A4-1**

Decision Fork

Each decision or "alternative" is a potential course of action. The decision maker has control over these. In this case, you can decide whether to confront your client or ignore the issue of late payment. When you select an alternative, you do not know the specific outcome or solution. *Possible outcomes or "options" for solution are dependent upon the other person's response to your decision.*[1] If you confront Clifford, he will either pay his bill or refuse to pay. To depict each of these possible outcomes, draw a small circle at the end of Decision Fork 1 and draw one branch for each possible outcome. Label each outcome as follows.

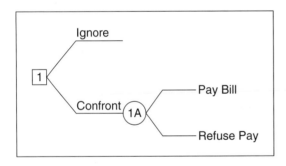

FIGURE **A4-2**

Decision Fork and Outcome Fork

For Step 2, probabilities are assigned for each uncertain event. Probabilities for outcomes are often best estimates, rather than precise percentages. If you believe that there is a high likelihood of a particular outcome, then the percentage will be in the range of 70 to 100%. If you believe there is a moderate likelihood, then the percentage will be in the range of 40 to 70%. If you believe there is a low likelihood, then the percentage is in the range of 0 to 40%. You could also identify conservative and optimistic estimates in order to perform the calculations. To keep the illustration relatively simple, I will use just one set of reasonable estimates. Assuming you believe there is a 70% likelihood that Clifford will pay and a 30% chance that he will not pay, the decision tree looks as follows.

---

[1]To remember the difference between an "alternative" and an "option", remember that "alternative" and "action" both begin with the letter "a". "Option" and "outcome" both begin with the letter "o".

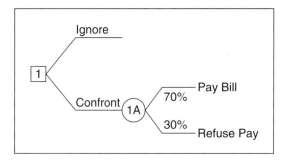

FIGURE **A4-3**

Decision Tree with Percentages

Note that the percentages for each Outcome Fork add up to 100%, indicating that all possible outcomes have been identified.

Step 3 requires one to insert Endpoint Values for each possible outcome. The Endpoint Value is the difference between the benefit and cost of each outcome (i.e., the net benefit). Assuming Clifford owes $500, then his paying is worth $500 and his refusing to pay is worth $0. If you incurred any costs in order to collect these amounts, then the costs would be subtracted. If the costs exceed the benefits, then the Endpoint Value will be negative.

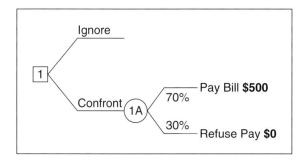

FIGURE **A4-4**

Decision Tree with Dollar Values

Step 4 requires calculating the Expected Value for each Outcome Fork. The Expected Value is the weighted average of the End Values for each Outcome Fork. To calculate the Expected Value, multiply each probability with the End Value, and add the results together. In the sample case, the Expected Value of decision 1A (EV1A) is:

$$EV1A = (70\% \times \$500) + (30\% \times \$0) = \$350$$

To complete the decision tree, insert the Outcome Fork, End Values, and Expected Values for the second decision alternative, ignoring the issue of late payments. Assume that there is only a 20% chance that Clifford will pay what he owes if you do not confront him. The decision tree looks as follows.

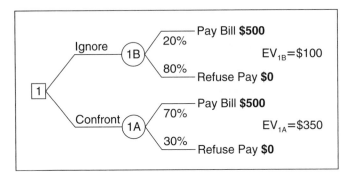

FIGURE **A4-5**

Decision Tree with All Branches and Expected Values

Step 5 says to identify soft factors. For example, you might find it difficult to confront a client about money. Alternatively, you might believe that confronting Clifford at this time is inappropriate since Clifford is dealing with a crisis situation. If you are averse to taking risks, you might be particularly concerned about whether confronting Clifford about the money will put him over the edge. Once you label these concerns, the decision tree looks as follows.

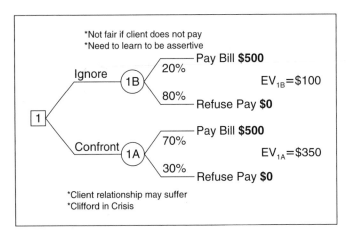

FIGURE **A4-6**

Decision Tree with Soft Factors

I describe other soft factors, including moral sentiments about justice, in greater depth below.

Step 6 concludes the analysis by determining which course of action is preferable, given the monetary and non-monetary concerns identified. When evaluating each decision alternative, the branch with the largest Expected Value represents the choice with the greatest economic benefit. Based on monetary concerns, confronting Clifford is preferable because the Expected Value for confronting ($350) is higher than the Expected Value for ignoring ($100). However, you also identified that Clifford is in a crisis. If you determine that helping Clifford through the crisis is more important than collecting fees owed by Clifford, then you will choose to ignore the late payments (at least for the present time).

This example begins to show how Decision Tree Analysis can help you make reasoned decisions about how to proceed in conflict situations. Many other alternatives could also be considered: write Clifford a letter; confront Clifford at a later date; refuse to provide services for Clifford; or help Clifford apply for financial support to pay for counseling.

You can also analyze a sequence of alternatives and possible outcomes. For instance, if you confront Clifford and he does not pay his bill, you need to decide what to do next: write a letter, confront him again, ignore the problem, etc. For each successive decision fork, the tree will expand to the right with further Outcome Forks.

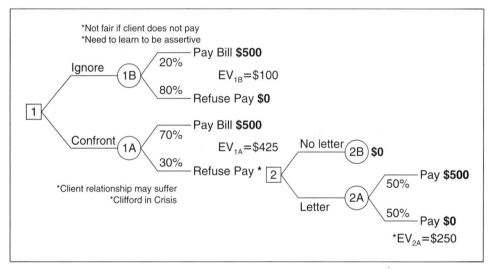

FIGURE **A4-7**

Decision Tree with Second Series of Decisions

When calculating Expected Values, begin with the Outcome Forks furthest to the right and work back toward the left ("folding back the tree"). In this example, the highest Expected Value for decision 2 is EV2A = $250. This suggests that you should write Clifford a letter if he does not respond to your initial request for payment. The Expected Value for Decision 1A now becomes:

$$EV1A = (70\% \times \$500) + (30\% \times \$250) = \$425$$

This amount is higher than in the first example, indicating that the best course of action financially is first to confront Clifford in person. If he does not pay his arrears, then follow up with a letter. You have increased your chances of collecting your fees by using a staged approach. Once again, soft factors need to be considered.

Some helping professionals are turned off by the use of mathematical equations to determine how they will intervene. Keep an open mind when you are working through the exercises in this book, since monetary factors are important for many types of decisions. For other kinds of conflict situations, the numbers and calculations are not essential. Even without the numbers, Decision Trees are useful because they:

- clarify the decisions to be made;
- help to brainstorm alternatives in a structured manner;
- indicate the possible outcomes of alternate courses of action;
- identify factors that are critical to decision making;
- encourage the decision maker to consider rational factors as well as emotions, traditions, and moral sentiments;
- provide visual representations to guide the decision-making process, enabling one to see both the broad picture and the finer points;
- help one strategize and prepare for how to deal with a conflict; and
- help two or more parties work through a conflict jointly.

The example with Clifford demonstrates how you can use decision trees to make your own decisions about how to respond to conflict. You can also use decision trees to help clients decide how to respond to their own conflict situations (Aaron, 1995). For instance, in working with a battered woman, you can use a decision tree to help her explore her alternatives. Often, such clients are so used to a particular pattern of interaction that they do not see other available choices. The client may see her choices as leaving her spouse and home versus staying in an abusive relationship. If she leaves, then she gives up the security of her home and familiar surroundings. She may believe she has no place to go except for the streets or a hostel for battered women. If she stays, she continues to be abused. By helping her look at other alternatives, she broadens her choice set and becomes more empowered to make self-determined decisions (Dan-Cohen, 1992).

For an example of using decision trees for joint decision making, consider an interdisciplinary committee meeting where the participants are deciding how to regulate their professions. Ordinarily, each professional might submit a separate plan. This sets them up to have to decide whose plan is best. In a joint problem-solving exercise, the participants develop a decision tree together. Various alternatives are canvassed and evaluated without any individual owning a particular idea. The tree belongs to the whole group and the group comes up with a mutually acceptable course of action.

When analyzing a decision tree, one of the key questions is, "What do the decision makers want?" A common theme in conflict situations is that parties want "justice." Each party feels wronged by the other and wants a solution that is just. Definitions of justice vary from person to person and culture to culture. Some want retribution or punishment. Others want restitution, compensation, deterrence, healing, or protection (Umbreit, 1997b).

Retributive justice demands that people receive appropriate punishment for their misdeeds. Criminal courts focus on retributive justice. If someone commits murder, then the punishment (typically incarceration) must be commensurate with the crime. The Biblical adage, "an eye for an eye, a tooth for a tooth," also suggests that punishment must be equivalent to the harm done. If, for example, Ingrid pokes out Dilbert's eyes, then Ingrid deserves to have her eyes poked out. Vengeance is based on the concept of retribution. You hurt me, so I need to hurt you back. The archetypal blood feud between the Hatfields and McCoys seems irrational, until you factor in each side's desire for revenge (Frank, 1992). After three decades of fighting, it hardly mattered what originally caused the feud. Each side was bent on retribution. After a series of atrocities are committed against one another, however, can there ever be justice?

Compensation and restitution are related concepts of justice. Under the notion of compensation, when one person incurs a loss caused by another, the person who caused the loss is expected to make up for the loss. Compensation could be a monetary payment or replacement of the loss "in kind." Restitution refers to putting the situation back to how it was prior to the loss. Exact restitution may not be possible, so a next best replacement may be necessary.

Ho'opono pono ("making right the wrong") is traditional conflict resolution method among Hawaiians that is partially based on the concept of restitution (Wall & Callister, 1995). It is also based on the notion of healing. Healing is an emotional or spiritual process that enables the people to move on with their lives and relationships in a more positive fashion.

Whereas retribution, restitution, and compensation focus on making up for past wrongs, deterrence and protection focus on the future. Under these latter notions of justice, people are concerned about preventing harm from recurring.

Consider Clifford's case again. If he is late on paying his bill, what do you really want—retribution? Compensation? Restitution? Deterrence? Rehabilitation? Your decision about how to deal with this conflict depends on the type of justice you are seeking. The type of justice you choose depends, in turn, on your values and moral sentiments. There is no universally correct formula for justice.

When selecting between various models of conflict resolution, different models are better suited to definitions of justice. Mediation, for instance, is future focused, making it well-suited for rehabilitation of relationships. The public court system is better suited to assigning blame, imposing punishment for past misdeeds, and setting precedents for future cases.

Certainly, Decision Tree Analysis does have its drawbacks and limitations (Zey, 1992). First, decision trees and calculations become cumbersome in complex situations. If there are many choices and possible outcomes, you may need to simplify the facts in order to make the analysis manageable. This may not reflect the full reality of the situation. On the other hand, decision trees help decision makers cut through complex details and focus upon the most important issues. Computer software designed to illustrate decision trees and calculate Expected Values makes it easier to depict and synthesize complex situations (Walls & Fullmer, 1995).

The second criticism is that Decision Tree Analysis (and all reasoned choice models) assume that the decision makers have perfect information (Goldstein & Hogarth, 1997). In most social conflict situations, the decision makers do not know all of the possible alternatives or all of the possible options for solution. Probabilities of various outcomes are particularly difficult to predict. Decision trees help decision makers identify gaps in information. To the extent that they can fill in gaps, the quality of the choices improves. Still, decision makers must acknowledge lack of perfect information, limitations of subjective factors, and possibilities of error. Conflict resolution and decision making are not exact sciences.

The third criticism is that Decision Tree Analysis suggests that rational choices are preferable to ones based on emotional, moral, or other criteria. The terminology implies that someone who is not rational is "irrational" or "crazy." To avoid this connotation, the converse of rational could be termed "non-rational." Non-rational choices can be perfectly valid choices. Whether Decision Tree Analysis actually has a bias towards rational choices depends upon how one employs it. The examples above demonstrate how soft factors can be considered in making decisions. Decisions need not be based solely on monetary factors or economic efficiency. The focus of Decision Tree Analysis is "informed choice" rather than "rational choice." In order to respect a client's right to self-determination, a practitioner must respect the client's ultimate decision—even if it goes against what the practitioner believes is a rational choice. However, the practitioner does have a role in helping the client explore a range of alternatives and options so the client can make an informed choice. As with any model of practice, helping professionals must be careful not to impose personal values on clients.

The fourth criticism is that there is no formula for how to take soft factors into account. Soft factors could be quantified; for example, how much is revenge worth to you? Would you be willing to engage in a fight, knowing it would cost you $10,000, as long as it satisfied your yen for vengeance. Quantification of soft factors is not easy or required. Even if there is a subjective element to considering soft factors, it is better to identify them rather than leave them out of the analysis altogether. Once monetary and soft factors are identified, decision makers are in a better position to make informed decisions about their priorities.

In spite of their limitations, decision trees can assist with various types of CR. Trees are a tool which can be used in combination with other tools and strategies. No one tool is perfect for all types of situations nor as an exclusive strategy for CR.

Bibliography

Aaron, M. C. (1995). The value of decision analysis in mediation practice. *Negotiation Journal, 11,* 123–133.

Academy of Family Mediators (1998). *Standards of practice for family and divorce mediation.* Available: www.mediators.org/afmstnds.htm.

Adler, R. S., Rosen, B., & Silverstein, E. M. (1998). Emotions in negotiation. How to manage fear and anger. *Negotiation Journal, 14,* 161–179.

Alberta Agriculture, Food and Rural Development (1997). *Finding common ground: negotiating agreements.* Edmonton, AB: Author.

American Psychological Association (1997). *Publication manual of the American Psychological Association* (4th ed.). Washington, DC: Author.

Aponte, H. J. (1991). Structural family therapy. In A. S. Gurtman (Ed.), *Handbook of family therapy.* New York: Brunner/Mazel.

Auerbach, J. S. (1983). *Justice without law?* Toronto: Oxford University Press.

Bandler, R., & Grinder, J. (1982). *Reframing: Neuro-linguistic programming and the transformation of meaning.* Moab, UT: Real People.

Bargal, D., & Bar, H. (1992a). The encounter of social selves: Intergroup workshops for Arab and Jewish youth. *Social Work with Groups, 17*(3), 39–59.

Bargal, D., & Bar, H. (1992b). A Lewinian approach to intergroup workshops for Palestinean-Arab and Jewish Youth. *Journal of Social Issues, 48*(2), 139–154.

Bargal, D., & Bar, H. (1997). *Living with conflict: Encounters between Jewish and Palestinian youth.* Jerusalem: Jerusalem Institute for the Study of Israel.

Barone, J. T., & Switzer, J. Y. (1995). *Interviewing: Art and skill.* Boston: Allyn and Bacon.

Barsky, A. E. (1993). When advocates and mediators negotiate. *Negotiation Journal, 9,* 115–122; 273–274.

Barsky, A. E. (1995). *Mediation in child protection cases.* Unpublished doctoral dissertation. University of Toronto, Toronto.

Barsky, A. E. (1996). Mediation and empowerment in child protection cases. *Mediation Quarterly, 14*(2), 111–134.

Barsky, A. E. (1997a). *Counselors as witnesses.* Aurora, ON: Canada Law Book.

Barsky, A. E. (1997b). Neutrality in child protection. In Y. A. Unrau, J. L. Krysik, & R. M. Grinnell (Eds.), *Student study guide for Social Work Research and Evaluation* (5th ed.). Itasca, IL: F. E. Peacock.

Barsky, A. E. (1997c). Mental illness, mental capacity, and negotiation competence. *Conflict Resolution Notes, 14*(3), 23–24.

Barsky, A. E. (1997d). Child protection mediation. In E. Kruk (Ed.). *Mediation and conflict resolution in social work and the human services.* Chicago: Nelson-Hall.

Barsky, A. E., Este, D., & Collins, D. (1996). Cultural competence in family mediation. *Mediation Quarterly, 13,* 167–178.

Barsky, A. E., & Trocmé, N. (1998). Essential aspects of mediation in child protection cases. *Child and Youth Services Review, 20,* 629–656.

Barsky, M. (1983). Emotional needs and dysfunctional communication as blocks to mediation. *Mediation Quarterly, 2,* 55–66.

Bercovitch, J. (1992). Mediators and mediation strategies in international negotiations. *Negotiation Journal, 8,* 99–112.

Binder, D. A., Bergman, P., & Price, S. C. (1991). *Lawyers as counselors: A client-centered approach.* St. Paul, MN: West.

Birkhoff, J. E., & Warfield, W. (1997). The development of pedagogy and practicum. *Mediation Quarterly, 14,* 93–110.

Bodine, R. J., Crawford, D., & Schrumpf, F. (1994). *Creating the peaceable school.* Champaign, IL: Research Press.

Bossy, J. (Ed.) (1983). *Disputes and settlements: Law and human relations in the west.* Cambridge: Cambridge University Press.

Bratton, L. B. (1997). Themes of conflict theory: An integrative model for practitioners. *Journal of Teaching in Social Work, 15*(1/2), 131–146.

Brett, J. M., Adair, W., Lempereux, A., Okumura, T., Shikhirev, P., Tinsley, C., & Lytle, A. (1998). Culture and joint gains in negotiation. *Negotiation Journal, 14,* 61–84.

Brinkman, R., & Kirchner, R. (1994). *Dealing with people you can't stand: How to bring out the best of people at their worst.* Toronto: Ryerson-McGraw-Hill.

Broome, B. J. (1993). Managing differences in conflict resolution: The role of relational empathy. In D. J. D. Sandole & H. van der Merwe (Eds.), *Conflict resolution theory and practice: Integration and application.* Manchester, UK: Manchester University Press.

Brossart, D. (1980). *Creative conflict resolution in religious education and church administration.* Birmingham, AL: Religious Education Press.

Burstow, B. (1992). *Radical feminist therapy.* Newbury Park, CA: Sage.

Bush, R. A. B., & Fogler, J. P. (1994). *The promise of mediation: Responding to conflict through empowerment and recognition.* San Francisco: Jossey-Bass.

Campfens, H. (Ed.) (1997). *Community development around the world: Practice, theory, research, training.* Toronto: University of Toronto Press.

Cappelletti, M. (1979). *Access to justice* (Vol. III). Milan, Italy: Sijthoff and Noordhoff-Alphenaandenrijn.

Carniol, B. (1995). *Case critical: Challenging social services in Canada* (2nd ed.). Toronto: Between the Lines.

Cardozo, B. N. (1924). *The growth of law.* New Haven, CN: Yale University Press.

Center for Social Gerontology (1997). *Adult guardianship mediation manual.* Ann Arbor, MI: Author.

Charbonneau, P. (Ed.) (1994). Report from the Toronto Forum on Woman Abuse and Mediation. Guelph, ON: Network Interaction for Conflict Resolution.

Chasin, R., Herzig, M., Roth, S., Chasin, L., Becker, C., & Stains, R. R. (1996). From diatribe to dialogue on divisive public issues: Approaches drawn from family therapy. *Mediation Quarterly, 13*, 323–344.

Chetkow-Yanoov, B. (1992). *Social work practice: A systems approach*. Binghampton, NY: Haworth Press.

Chetkow-Yanoov, B. (1997). *Social work approaches to conflict resolution: Making fighting obsolete*. Binghampton, NY: Haworth.

Chisholm, B., & McNaughton, (1990). *Custody/access assessments: A practical guide for lawyers and assessors*. Toronto: Carswell.

Conley, J. M., & O'Barr, W. M. (1990). *Rules versus relationships: The ethnography of legal discourse*. Chicago: University of Chicago Press.

Coogler, O. J. (1978). *Structured mediation in divorce settlement*. Lexington, MA: Lexington.

Corey, G. (1996). *Theory and practice of counseling and psychotherapy*. Pacific Grove, CA: Brooks/Cole.

Corey, G., Corey, M. S., & Callahan, P. (1993). *Issues and ethics in the helping professions*. Pacific Grove, CA: Brooks/Cole.

Culler, J. (1982). *On deconstruction: Theory and criticism after structuralism*. Ithaca, NY: Cornell University Press.

Cummings, E. M., & Davies, P. (1994). *Children and marital conflict. The impact of family dispute and resolution*. New York: Guilford.

Dan-Cohen, M. (1992). Conceptions of choice and conceptions of autonomy. *Ethics, 102*, 221–243.

Dana, D. (1996). *Managing differences: How to build better relationships at work and home*. Overland Park, KS: MTI.

Denzin, N. K., & Lincoln, Y. S. (Eds.) (1994). *Handbook of qualitative research*. Thousand Oaks, CA: Sage.

Deutsch, M. (1973). *The resolution of conflict*. New Haven, CN: Yale University Press.

Deutsch, M. (1991). *Education for a peaceful world*. Amherst, MA: National Association for Mediation in Education.

Douglas, A. (1962). *Industrial peacemaking*. New York: Columbia University Press.

Druckman, D. (1993). An analytical research agenda for conflict and conflict resolution. In D. J. D. Sandole & H. van der Merwe (Eds.). *Conflict resolution theory and practice: Integration and application*. Manchester, UK: Manchester University Press.

Dubinskas, F. A. (1992). Culture and conflict. In D. M. Kolb & J. M. Bartunek (Eds.). *Hidden conflict in organizations* (pp. 187–208). London: Sage.

Duffy, K. G., Grosch, J. W., & Olczak, P. V. (Eds.) (1991). *Community mediation: A handbook for practitioners and researchers*. New York: Guilford.

Dukes, E. F. (1996). *Resolving public conflict: Community and governance*. Manchester, UK: Manchester University Press.

Dworkin, R. M. (1977). *Taking rights seriously*. Cambridge, MA: Harvard University Press.

Edelman, J., & Crain, M. B. (1993). *The Tao of negotiation.* New York: Harper.

Elangovan, A. R. (1995). Managerial third-party dispute intervention: A prescriptive model of strategy selection. *Academy of Management Review, 20,* 800–830.

Ellis, D., & Stuckless, N. (1996). *Mediating and negotiating marital conflicts.* Thousand Oaks, CA: Sage.

Ellis, D., & Wight, L. (1998). Theorizing power in divorce negotiations: Implications for practice. *Mediation Quarterly, 15,* 227–244.

Emery, R. E. (1994). *Renegotiating family relationships: Divorce, child custody, and mediation.* New York: Guilford.

English, P., Neilson, L., The Board of Directors, & The Standards and Ethics Committee of Family Mediation Canada (1995). *Report on practice standards, training, and certification of competent family mediators & standards for the FMC endorsement of family mediation training programs.* Kitchener, ON: Family Mediation Canada.

Erikson, E. H. (1950). Eight stages of man. In *Childhood and Society* (pp. 219–234). New York: Norton.

Ertel, D. (1991). Conflict resolution/negotiation styles. In *Negotiation Course Materials.* Toronto: University of Toronto Faculty of Law.

Evans, D., Hearn, M., Uhlemann, M., & Ivey, A. (1997). *Essential interviewing: A programmed approach to effective communication* (5th ed.). Pacific Grove, CA: Brooks/Cole.

Ezell, M. (1994). Advocacy practice of social workers. *Families in Society: The Journal of Contemporary Human Services, 75*(1), 36–46.

Family Mediation Canada (1996). *Code of Professional Conduct.* Kitchener, ON: Author.

Family Mediation Canada (1997). *Family mediator skills assessment manual.* Victoria, BC: British Columbia Ministry of the Attorney General.

Favaloro, G. J. (1998). Mediation: A family therapy technique? *Mediation Quarterly, 16,* 33–36.

Feld, L., & Simm, P. A. (1998). *Mediating professional conduct complaints.* Waterloo, ON: Network—Interaction for Conflict Resolution.

Finn, J. (1994). The promise of participatory research. *Journal of Progressive Human Services, 5*(2), 25–42.

Fisher, R., & Brown, S. (1988). *Getting together: Building relationships as we negotiate.* New York: Penguin.

Fisher, R., & Urtel, D. (1995). *Getting ready to negotiate.* Toronto: Penguin.

Fisher, R., Ury, W., & Patton, B. (1997). *Getting to yes: Negotiating agreement without giving in* (3rd ed.). New York: Penguin.

Fisher, R. J. (1997). *Interactive conflict resolution.* Syracuse, NY: Syracuse University Press.

Fook, J. (1993). *Radical casework: A theory of practice.* St. Leonards, Australia: Allen & Unwin.

Fowler, M. D. M. (1989). Social advocacy. *Heart & Lung, 18*(1), 97–99.

Frank, R. H. (1992). A theory of moral sentiments. In M. Zey (Ed.) *Decision making: Alternatives to rational choice models* (pp. 158–184). Newbury Park, CA: Sage.

Freire, P. (1970). *Pedagogy of the oppressed.* New York: Continuum.

Freshman, C. (1997). Privatizing same-sex "marriage" through alternative dispute resolution: Community enhancing versus community-enabling mediation. *University of California Los Angeles Law Review, 44,* 1687–1771.

Freud, S. (1963). *The complete works of Sigmund Freud.* London: Hogarth.

Fulghum, R. (1988). *All I really need to know I learned in kindergarten.* New York: Villard.

Gabor, P. A., Unrau, Y. A., & Grinnell, R. M. (1998). *Evaluation for social workers: A quality improvement approach for the social services* (2nd ed.). Needham Heights, MA: Allyn & Bacon.

Gadlin, H., & Ouelette, P. (1986). Mediation Milanese: An application of systemic family therapy to mediation. *Mediation Quarterly, 14/15,* 101–118.

Germain, C. B., & Gitterman, A. (1996). *The life model of social work practice: Advances in practice and theory.* New York: Columbia University Press.

Gilligan, G. (1990). *In a different voice: Psychological theory and women's development* (2nd ed.). Cambridge, MA: Harvard University.

Girard, K., & Koch, S. J. (1996). *Conflict resolution in the schools.* San Francisco: Jossey-Bass.

Girdner, L. K. (1989). Custody mediation in the United States: Empowerment or social control? *Canadian Journal of Women and the Law, 3,* 134–154.

Girdner, L. K. (Ed.) (1990). Mediation and spouse abuse [Special issue]. *Mediation Quarterly, 7*(4).

Goldberg, S. B., Green, E. D., & Sander, F. E. A. (1989). Litigation, arbitration or mediation. *American Bar Association Journal, 75,* 70–72.

Goldberg-Wood, G., & Middleman, R. (1991). Advocacy and social action: Key elements in the structural approach to direct practice in social work. *Social Work with Groups, 14*(3/4), 53–63.

Goldstein, W. M., & Hogarth, R. M. (Eds.) (1997). *Research on judgment and decision making: Currents, connections, and controversies.* Cambridge: Cambridge University Press.

Gould, K. H. (1987). Life Model versus Conflict Model: A feminist perspective. *Social Work, July–August,* 346–351.

Gould, P., & Gould, G. (1988). *From no to yes: The route to constructive agreement* (Videotape). Toronto: International Telefilm (with John Cleese).

Green, R. G. (1998). *Justice in aboriginal communities: Sentencing alternatives.* Saskatoon, SK: Purich.

Greey, M. (1994). *Honouring diversity: A cross-cultural approach to infant development for babies with special needs.* Toronto: Centennial Infant and Childcare Centre.

Grellert, E. A. (1991). The self of the therapist: Attending to countertransference. *Treating Abuse Today, 1*(4), 22–25.

Halabi, R. (1998). *Working with conflict groups: The educational approach of The School for Peace* (Unpublished paper), Neveh Shalom—Wahat Al-salam, Nahshon, Israel.

Hart, B. C. (1987). Alternative dispute resolution: Negotiation, mediation and minitrial. *Federation of Insurance & Corporate Counsel Quarterly, 37,* 113–131.

Hepworth, D. H., & Larson, J. A. (1993). *Direct social work practice: Theory and skills* (4th ed.). Pacific Grove, CA: Brooks/Cole.

Hessler, R. M., Hollis, S., & Crowe, C. (1998). Peer mediation: A qualitative study of youthful frames of power and influence. *Mediation Quarterly, 15*, 187–198.

Holton, S. A. (Ed.) (1998). *Mending the cracks in the ivory tower: Strategies for conflict management in higher education.* Bolton, MA: Anker.

Hopkins, B. R. (1994). *Charity, advocacy, and the law.* New York: Wiley.

Hudson, J., Morris, A., Maxwell, G., & Galaway, B. (Eds.). (1996). *Family group conferences: Perspectives on policy and practice.* Monsey, NY: Willow Tree.

Hunt, D. E. (1987). *Beginning with ourselves: In practice, theory, and human affairs.* Cambridge, MA: Brookline Books.

Irving, H., & Benjamin, M. (1987). *Family mediation — Theory & practice of dispute resolution.* Toronto: Carswell.

Irving, H., & Benjamin, M. (1995). *Family mediation: Contemporary issues.* Thousand Oaks, CA: Sage.

Ivey, A. E., & Ivey, M. B. (1999). *Intentional interviewing and counseling: Facilitating client development in a multicultural society* (4th ed.). Pacific Grove, CA: Brooks/Cole.

Jabbour, E. J. (1996). *Sulha: Palestinian traditional peacemaking process.* House of Hope. Palestinian Authority: Wi'am Palestinian Conflict Resolution Center.

Kadushin, A. (1992). *Supervision in social work* (3rd ed.). New York: Columbia University Press.

Kaminski, L., & Walmsley, C. (1995). The advocacy brief: A guide for social workers. *The Social Worker, 63*(2), 53–58.

Kaminsky, H., & Yellot, A. (1997). Community mediation: The grassroots of alternative dispute resolution. In E. Kruk (Ed.). *Mediation and conflict resolution in social work and the human services.* Chicago: Nelson-Hall.

Kaner, S. (1996). *Facilitator's guide to participatory decision-making.* Philadelphia: New Society.

Kaplan, N. M. (1997). Mediation in the school system: Facilitating the development of peer mediation programs. In E. Kruk (Ed.). *Mediation and conflict resolution in social work and the human services.* Chicago: Nelson-Hall.

Kauffman, N. (1991). The idea of expedited arbitration two decades later. *Arbitration Journal, 46*(3), 34–38.

Kavanaugh, K. H., & Kennedy, P. H. (1992). *Promoting cultural diversity.* Newbury Park, CA: Sage.

Kelly, J. B. (1996). A decade of divorce mediation research: Some questions and answers. *Family and Conciliation Courts Review, 34*, 373–385,

Kirst-Ashman, K., & Hull, G. (1993). *Understanding generalist practice* (Advocacy, pp. 464–492). Chicago: Nelson-Hall.

Knowles, M. S., Holton, E. F., & Swanson, R. A. (1998). *The adult learner: The definitive classic on adult education and training.* Houston, TX: Gulf.

Kolb, D. A. (1974). Management and learning processes. In D. A. Kolb, I. M. Rubin, & J. McIntyre (Eds.). *Organizational psychology: A book of readings.* Upper Saddle City, NJ: Prentice-Hall.

Kolb, D. M. (1992). Women's work: Peacemaking in organizations. In D. M. Kolb & J. M. Bartunek (Eds.). *Hidden conflict in organizations* (pp 63–91). London: Sage.

Kraybill, R. (1985). Teaching children how to fight. *MCS Conciliation Quarterly, 4*(1), 8–9.

Kraybill, R. (1987). Ten commandments of meeting facilitation. *MCS Conciliation Quarterly, Fall Issue,* 4–5.

Kressel, K., & Pruitt, D. G. (1985). Themes in mediation of social conflict. *Journal of Social Issues, 41,* 179–198.

Kressel, K., & Pruitt, D. G. (1989). *Mediation research.* Newbury Park, CA: Sage.

Kruk, E. (Ed.) (1997). *Mediation and conflict resolution in social work and the human services.* Chicago: Nelson-Hall.

Kruk, E. (1998). Family mediation in Canada: The state of the art. *Interaction, 10*(2), 12–16.

Kübler-Ross, E. (1997). *On death and dying.* New York: Macmillan.

Landau, B., Bartoletti, M., & Mesbur, R. (1997). *Family mediation handbook* (2nd ed.). Toronto: Butterworths.

Lang, M. (Ed.). (1996). Transformative approaches to mediation (Special Issue). *Mediation Quarterly, 13*(4).

Lax, D. A., & Sebenius, J. K. (1987). The negotiator's dilemma: Creating and claiming value. In *The manager as negotiator: Bargaining for cooperation and competitive gain.* New York: Free Press.

LeBaron, M. (1997). Mediation, conflict resolution and multicultural reality: Culturally competent practice. In E. Kruk (Ed.). *Mediation and conflict resolution in social work and the human services* (pp. 315–335). Chicago: Nelson-Hall.

LeBaron Duryea, M. (1994). *Conflict analysis and resolution as education* (Training Materials and Trainer Reference Manual). Victoria, BC: UVic Institute for Dispute Resolution.

LeBaron Duryea, M., & Grundison, J. B. (1992). *Conflict and culture: A literature review and bibliography.* Victoria, BC: UVic Institute for Dispute Resolution.

Lederach, J. P. (1986). Mediation in North America: An examination of the profession's cultural premises. Unpublished Comprehensive Examination Paper. University of Colorado, Denver.

Lederach, J. P. (1995). *Preparing for peace: Conflict transformation across cultures.* Syracuse, NY: Syracuse University Press.

Leitch, M. L. (1987). The politics of compromise: A feminist perspective of mediation. *Mediation Quarterly, 14/15,* 163–175.

Levinger, G., & Rubin, J. Z. (1994). Bridges and barriers to a more general theory of conflict. *Negotiation Journal, 10,* 201–215.

Lewicki, R. J. (1997). Teaching negotiation and dispute resolution in colleges of business: The state of the practice. *Negotiation Journal, 13,* 253–269.

Lewicki, R. J., Litterer, J., Minton, J., & Saunders, D. (1998). *Negotiation* (3rd ed.). Burr Ridge, IL: Richard D. Irwin.

Lewin, K. (1948). Action research and minority problems. In G. W. Lewin (Ed.). *Resolving social conflicts.* New York: Harper & Row, pp. 56–70.

Linzer, N. (1999). *Resolving ethical dilemmas in social work practice.* Boston: Allyn & Bacon.

Loewenberg, F., & Dolgoff, R. (1996). *Ethical decisions for social work practice.* Itasca, IL: F. E. Peacock.

Lurie, A., Pinsky, S., Rock, B., & Tuzman, L. (1989). The training and supervision of social work students for effective advocacy practice. *The Clinical Supervisor, 7*(2/3), 149–158.

MacFarlane, J. (1999). *Dispute resolution: Readings and cases.* Toronto: Emond Montgomery.

MacKearcher, D. (1997). *Making sense of adult learning.* Toronto: Culture Concepts.

Maida, P. (1986). Components of Bowen's family therapy and divorce mediation. *Mediation Quarterly, 12,* 51–63.

Mandell, D. (1991). Interpersonal processes in the social work interview: A Comparison of Feminist Counseling and the Life Model (Unpublished paper), University of Toronto, Faculty of Social Work, Toronto, ON.

Marlow, L. (1987). Styles of conducting mediation. *Mediation Quarterly, 18,* 85–90.

Marlow, L. (1997). *Divorce mediation: A practice in search of a theory.* Syracuse, NY: Syracuse University Press.

Marx, K. (1964). *Selected writings in sociology and social psychology,* T. B. Biltmore (Trans.). New York: McGraw-Hill.

Maryama, G. (1992). Lewin's impact on education: Instilling cooperation and conflict management skills in school children. *Journal of Social Issues, 48*(2), 155–166.

Maslow, A. H. (1987). *Motivation and personality* (3rd ed.). New York: Harper & Row.

Mathis, R. D., & Yingling, L. C. (1998). Family Modes: A measure of family interaction and organization. *Family and Conciliation Courts Review, 36,* 246–257.

Mayer, B. (1987). The dynamics of power in mediation and negotiation. *Mediation Quarterly, 16,* 57–86.

Mayer, B. (1997). Mediation and dispute resolution in the field of social policy. In E. Kruk (Ed.). *Mediation and conflict resolution in social work and the human services.* Chicago: Nelson-Hall.

McCormick, M. A. (1997). Confronting social injustice as a mediator. *Mediation Quarterly, 14,* 293–307.

McMan Youth Services (1996). Parent-Youth mediation manual. Calgary, AB: Author.

Menkel-Meadow, C. (1984). Toward another view of legal negotiation: The structure of problem-solving. *U.C.L.A. Law Review, 31,* 754–842.

Miller, B. (1997). *Great powers and regional peacemaking: Patterns in the Middle East and Beyond. Journal of Strategic Studies, 30*(1), 103–172.

Mnookin, R. H., & Kornhauser, L. (1979). Bargaining in the shadow of the law: The case of divorce. *Yale Law Journal, 88,* 960–997.

Mnookin, R. H., Susskind, L. E., & Foster, P. C. (Eds.) (1999). *Negotiating on behalf of others: Advice to lawyers, business executives, diplomats, politicians, and everyone else.* Thousand Oaks, CA: Sage.

Montville, J. V. (1993). The healing function in political conflict resolution: In D. J. D. Sandole & H. van der Merwe (Eds.), *Conflict management.* Manchester, UK: Manchester University Press.

Morse, P. S., & Andrea, R. (1994). Peer mediation in the schools: Teaching conflict resolution techniques to students. *NAASP Bulletin, 78*(560), 75–82.

Murdach, A. D. (1980, November). Bargaining and persuasion with non-voluntary clients. *Social Work*, 458–461.

Murray, H., Gillese, E., Lennon, M., Mercer, P., & Robinson, M. (1996). *Ethical principles in university teaching.* Toronto: Society for Teaching and Learning in Higher Education, University of Toronto, OISE.

Mustill, L. (1996). Judicial processes and alternative dispute resolution. *Israel Law Review, 30,* 350–372.

Myers, I. M. (1987). *Introduction to type in organizations.* Palo Alto, CA: Consulting Psychologists Press.

Nader, L. (1992, Winter). Trading justice for harmony. *Forum,* 12–14.

National Association of Social Workers (NASW) (1991). *Standards of Practice for Social Work Mediators.* Silver Spring, MD: Author.

National Institute for Dispute Resolution (1987). Dispute resolution and higher education: A brief introduction. *MCS Conciliation Quarterly, Spring Issue,* 2.

Nichols, M. P. (1995). *The lost art of listening.* New York: Guilford.

Nicol, A. (1997). *Advocacy* (unpublished paper). Alberta Child Advocates, Edmonton, AB.

Nicoterra, A. M. (1995). *Conflict and organizations: Communicative processes.* Albany, NY: State University of New York Press.

Noble, C., Dizgun, L. L., & Emond, D. P. (1998). *Mediation advocacy: Effective client presentation in mediation proceedings.* Toronto: Emond Montgomery.

Noonan, M. (1998). Understanding the "difficult" patient from a dual person perspective. *Clinical Social Work Journal,* 129–140.

Noone, M. (1996). *Mediation* [Essential legal skills series]. London, UK: Cavendish.

Palczewski, C. H. (1996). Argumentation and feminisms. *Argumentation and Advocacy (Special issue), 32*(1).

Palmer, S. E. (1983, *March–April*). Authority: An essential part of practice. *Social Work,* 120–125.

Panitch, A. (1974). Advocacy in practice. *Social Work, 19,* 326–332.

Parsons, R. J., & Cox, E. N. (1997). Mediation in the aging field. In E. Kruk (Ed.). *Mediation and conflict resolution in social work and the human services.* Chicago: Nelson-Hall, p. 163–178.

Pastorino, R. (1997). A mediation approach designed by adolescent disputants. *Mediation Quarterly, 14,* 251–266.

Pearson, J. (1997). Mediating when domestic violence is a factor: Policies and practices in court-based divorce mediation programs. *Mediation Quarterly, 14,* 319–335.

Pennell, J., & Ristock, J. R. (1997). Feminist links, post-modern interruptions toward a critical social work education. *Social Work Discussion Papers: Trends in social work education.* St. John's, NF: Memorial University.

Picard, C. A. (1998). *Mediating interpersonal and small group conflict.* Ottawa, ON: Golden Dog Press.

Picard, C. A., & Melchin, K. R. (1988). *Conflict management in a church context.* Ottawa, ON: Picard and Associates.

Pinderhughes, E. (1983, June). Empowerment for our clients and for ourselves. *Social Casework,* 331–338.

Pratt, D. D. (1989). Three stages of teacher competence: A developmental perspective. In E. R. Hayes (Ed.). *New directions for continuing education, No. 43: Effective teaching styles.* San Francisco: Jossey-Bass.

Pruitt, D. G., & Carnevale, P. C. (1993). *Negotiation in social conflict.* Pacific Grove, CA: Brooks/Cole.

Putnam, L. L., & Sondak, H. (1991). Integrating communication and negotiation research. In Bazerman, M. H., Lewicki, R. J., & Sheppard, B. H. (Eds.), *Research on negotiation in organizations (Volume 3),* Greenwich, CT: JAI Press, 139–164.

Rabie, M. (1994). *Conflict resolution and ethnicity.* Westport, CT: Praeger.

Rapoport, A. (1974). *Fights, games and debates.* Ann Arbor, MI: University of Michigan Press.

Rahim, M. A., & Blum, A. A. (Eds.) (1994). *Global perspectives on organizational conflict.* Westport, CN: Praeger.

Rave, E., & Larson, C. (1995). *Ethical decision making in therapy: Feminist perspectives.* New York: Guilford.

Rawls, J. A. (1971). *Theory of justice.* Cambridge, MA: Harvard University Press.

Reisch, M. (1990, January). Organizational structure and client advocacy: Lessons from the 1980s. *Social Work,* 73–74.

Rich, P. (1993). The form, function, and content of clinical supervision: An integrated model. *Clinical Supervisor, 11*(1), 137–178.

Rifkin, J., Millen, J., & Cobb, S. (1991). Toward a new discourse for mediation: A critique of neutrality. *Mediation Quarterly, 9,* 151–164.

Rikhye, I. J. (1984). *The theory and practice of peacekeeping.* New York: St. Martin's.

Robbins, S. P. (1998). *Organizational behavior: Concepts, controversies, applications* (8th ed.). Upper Saddle City, NJ: Prentice Hall.

Roderick, T. (1987–88). Johnny can learn to negotiate. *Educational Leadership, 45,* 87–89.

Rogers, C. (1957). The necessary and sufficient conditions of therapeutic personality change. *Journal of Counseling Psychology, 21,* 95–103.

Rogers, G., Benson, C., Clark, B., Sawa, R., Bouey, E., Mamchur, C., & Langevin, P. (1998). *A multidisciplinary investigation of conflict in field-based education.* Calgary, AB: University of Calgary.

Rossides, D. W. (1998). *Professions and disciplines: Functional and conflict perspectives.* Upper Saddle City, NJ: Prentice Hall.

Roth, B. J., Wulff, R. W., & Cooper, C. A. (1993). *The alternative dispute resolution practice guide.* Rochester, NY: Lawyers Cooperative Publishing (binder with updates).

Rothman, J. (1997). *Resolving identity-based conflict — In nations, organizations and communities.* San Francisco: Jossey-Bass.

Sandole, D. J. D., & van der Merwe, H. (Eds.) (1993). *Conflict resolution theory and practice: Integration and application.* Manchester, UK: Manchester University Press.

Schittekatte, M. (1996). Facilitating information exchange in small decision-making groups. *European Journal of Psychology, 26,* 537–556.

Schön, D. A. (1990). *Educating the reflective practitioner* (2nd ed.). San Francisco: Jossey-Bass.

Schrumpf, F., Crawford, D., & Usadel, H. (1997). *Peer mediation: Conflict resolution in schools*. Champaign, IL: Research Press.

Schwebel, A. I., & Clement, J. A. (1996). Mediation as a mental health service: Consumers' and family members' perceptions. *Psychiatric Rehabilitation Journal, 20*(1), 55–58.

Severson, M. (1998). Teaching mediation theory and skills in an interdisciplinary classroom. *Journal of Social Work Education, 34*, 185–194.

Shulman, L. (1992). Helping clients to negotiate the system. In *The skills of helping: Individuals, families, and groups* (3rd ed.) (597–629). Itasca, IL: Peacock.

Slaikeu, K. A., Pearson, J., Luckett, J., & Myers, F. C. (1985). Process and outcome in divorce mediation. *Mediation Quarterly, 19*, 55–74.

Sosin, M., & Caulum, S. (1983). Advocacy: A conceptualization for social work practice. *Social Work, 28*(1), 12–17.

State Justice Institute (1998). *An interim report of the mediator skills project: Assessing and supporting effective mediation*. Atlanta, GA: Author.

Stewart, D. D., & Stasser, G. (1998). The sampling of critical unshared information in decision-making groups: The role of an uninformed minority. *European Journal of Social Psychology, 28*, 95–113.

Strunk, W., & White, E. B. (1995). *The elements of style* (5th ed.). New York: Macmillan.

Stuart, B. (1997). *Building community justice partnerships: Community peacemaking circles*. Ottawa: Aboriginal Justice Section, Canadian Department of Justice.

Stulberg, J. B. (1981). The theory and practice of mediation: A reply to Prof. Susskind. *Vermont Law Review, 6*, 49–116.

Stulberg, J. B., & Keating, J. M. (1983). *An introduction to mediation: A manual for beginning mediators*. New York: Conflict Management Resources.

Susskind, L. E., McKearney, S., & Thomas-Larmer, J. (Eds.) (1999). *The consensus building handbook: A comprehensive guide to reaching agreement*. Thousand Oaks, CA: Sage.

Tannen, D. (1998). *The argument culture: Moving from debate to dialogue*. New York: Random House.

Taylor, A. (1997). Concepts of neutrality in family mediation: Contexts, ethics, influence and transformative process. *Mediation Quarterly, 14*, 215–236.

Thoennes, N. (1991). Mediation and the dependency court: The controversy and three courts' experiences. *Family and Conciliation Courts Review, 29*, 246–258.

Thomas, K. W., & Kilmann, R. H. (1974). *Thomas-Kilmann Conflict Mode Instrument*. Tuxedo, NY: Xiacom.

Tjaden, P. G. (1994). Dispute resolution in child protection cases. *Negotiation Journal, 10*, 373–390.

Torré, D. A. (1986). *Empowerment: Structural conceptualization and instrument development* (Unpublished doctoral dissertation). Cornell University, Itasca, NY.

Umbreit, M. (1995). *Mediating interpersonal conflicts: A pathway to peace*. Concord, MN: CPI Publishing.

Umbreit, M. (1997a). Humanistic mediation: A transformative journey of peacemaking. *Mediation Quarterly, 14*, 201–213.

Umbreit, M. (1997b). Victim-offender mediation in criminal conflict: Toward restorative justice. In E. Kruk (Ed.). *Mediation and conflict resolution in social work and the human services*. Chicago: Nelson-Hall.

Van Es, R. (1996). *Negotiating ethics: On ethics in negotiation and negotiating ethics*. Delft, The Netherlands: Eburon.

Vayda, E. J., & Satterfield, M. T. (1997). *Law for social workers—A Canadian guide* (3rd ed.). Toronto: Carswell.

Wall, J. A., & Callister, R. R. (1995). Ho'opononopono: Some lessons from Hawaiian mediation. *Negotiation Journal, 11*, 45–54.

Wallerstein, J. S. (1990). Transference and countertransference in clinical intervention with divorcing families. *American Journal of Orthopsychiatry, 60*, 337–345.

Walls, R. T., & Fullmer, S. L. (1995). Decision support services: Determining eligibility for human services. *Rehabilitation Counseling Bulletin, 38*(3), 248–261.

Warfield, W. (1993). Public policy conflict resolution: The nexus between culture and process. In D. J. D. Sandole & H. van der Merwe (Eds.). *Conflict management*. Manchester, UK: Manchester University Press.

Weinbach, R. W., & Grinnell, R. M. (1996). *Applying research knowledge: A workbook for social work students*. Needham Heights, MA: Allyn & Bacon.

Whitten, C. T. (1992). Making mediation services work: A market perspective. *Mediation Quarterly, 9*, 253–266.

Wilhelmus, M. (1998). Mediation in kinship care: Another step in the provision of culturally relevant child welfare services. *Social Work, 43*(2), 117–126.

Williams, J. M. (1996). *Styles: Ten lessons for clarity and grace* (3rd ed.). Glenview, IL: Scott, Foresman.

Wilmot, W. W., & Hocker, J. L. (1998). *Interpersonal conflict resolution*. Boston: McGraw-Hill.

Winslade, J., Monk, G., & Cotter, A. (1998). A narrative approach to the practice of mediation. *Negotiation Journal, 14*, 21–39.

Wood, G. G., & Middleman, R. R. (1991). Advocacy and social action: Key elements in the structural approach to direct practice in social work. *Social Action in Group Work, 14*(3/4), 53–63.

Wood, J., Sept, R., & Duncan, J. (1998). Managing conflict in relationships. In *Everyday encounters: An introduction to interpersonal communication* (pp. 207–235) (Expanded 1st Canadian edition). Toronto: ITP Nelson (Wadsworth).

Yilmaz, M. R. (1997). In defense of a constructive, information-based approach to decision theory. *Theory and Decision, 43*, 21–44.

Young, P. T. (1961). *Motivation and emotion: A survey of the determinants of human and animal activity*. New York: Wiley.

Zartman, I. W., & Touval, S. (1985). International mediation: Conflict resolution and power politics. *Journal of Social Issues, 41*, 27–46.

Zastrow, C. (1999). *The practice of social work* (5th ed.). Belmont, CA: Wadsworth.

Zey, M. (Ed.) (1992). *Decision making: Alternatives to rational choice models*. Newbury Park, CA: Sage.

Index

TO THE OWNER OF THIS BOOK:

I hope that you have found *Conflict Resolution for the Helping Professions* useful. So that this book can be improved in a future edition, would you take the time to complete this sheet and return it? Thank you.

School and address: _____

_____

Department: _____

Instructor's name: _____

1. What I like most about this book is: _____

_____

_____

2. What I like least about this book is: _____

_____

_____

3. My general reaction to this book is: _____

_____

_____

4. The name of the course in which I used this book is: _____

_____

5. Were all of the chapters of the book assigned for you to read? _____

   If not, which ones weren't? _____

6. In the space below, or on a separate sheet of paper, please write specific suggestions for improving this book and anything else you'd care to share about your experience in using this book.

_____

_____

_____

_____

OPTIONAL:

Your name: _____ Date: _____

May we quote you, either in promotion for *Conflict Resolution for the Helping Professions,* or in future publishing ventures?

    Yes: _____ No: _____

    Sincerely yours,

    Allan Edward Barsky

FOLD HERE

BUSINESS REPLY MAIL

FIRST CLASS   PERMIT NO. 358   PACIFIC GROVE, CA

POSTAGE WILL BE PAID BY ADDRESSEE

ATTN: Helping Professions, Lisa Gebo

BROOKS/COLE/THOMSON LEARNING
511 FOREST LODGE ROAD
PACIFIC GROVE, CA   93950-9968

FOLD HERE